ERRATA

Page 82, line 10: Mrs. *Fouse* should be Mrs. *Grove.*

Page 111, third line from bottom: Mr. *Miller* should be Mr. *Rapp.*

Page 215, tenth line from bottom: Mr. *Kanel* should be Mr. *Bishop.*

"NICHOLAUS FAUSS SEIN TAGBUCH" [2].

GENEALOGY

OF THE DESCENDANTS OF

THEOBALD FOUSE (FAUSS)

INCLUDING

MANY OTHER CONNECTED FAMILIES

BY

GAIUS MARCUS BRUMBAUGH, M.S., M.D.

Member Pennsylvania German Society, National Genealogical Society, American Association for the Advancement of Science, American Medical Association, Medical Society of the District of Columbia, etc., Washington, D. C.

AND

JOHN GARNER FOUSE [No. 80]

Member Grand Army of the Republic, Pittsburgh, Pa.

WAVERLY PRESS
WILLIAMS & WILKINS COMPANY
BALTIMORE
1914

Notice

In many older books, foxing (or discoloration) occurs and, in some instances, print lightens with wear and age. Reprinted books, such as this, often duplicate these flaws, notwithstanding efforts to reduce or eliminate them. The pages of this reprint have been digitally enhanced and, where possible, the flaws eliminated in order to provide clarity of content and a pleasant reading experience.

Originally published
Baltimore
1914

Reprinted by:

Janaway Publishing, Inc.
732 Kelsey Ct.
Santa Maria, California 93454
(805) 925-1038
www.janawaygenealogy.com

2014

ISBN: 978-1-59641-331-3

Made in the United States of America

This Publication

is

Affectionately Dedicated

to the

Memory of the Mothers and Fathers

of the

Within Named Descendants

Preface.

"Every man is a bundle of his ancestors"—EMERSON.

The existing disastrous war in Europe terminated all present effort to further investigate the origin of the "Fauss," "Faass" name (see page 1). In a recent letter to the undersigned, Dr. A. B. Faust, author of the admirable *German Element in the United States*, etc., and dean of the Department of German, Cornell University, wrote:

"I at once thought of the possibility of some connection of the Fauss family with the name Faust, though I believe the name Faust is more frequent in middle Germany, especially in Hessen. My own family came over in 1849, and had been located in the region of Fulda, Hessen, since 1712, or longer. I am not sure about their location before that."

The late Andrew Brumbaugh, born July 5, 1830, in Blair County, Pennsylvania, and died September 3, 1901, in Stark County, Ohio, patiently gathered much original material bearing upon the Fouse families. Every scrap of that material has been carefully compared and incorporated into the later data secured. He was visited, assisted, and encouraged by Mr. John Garner[4] Fouse [80], and Mr. Adam Garner[4] Fouse [82], at a time when his letters bear pathetic testimony to the general indifference and lack of coöperation meeting his efforts to gather family information. That active interest and assistance by these gentlemen, and by Mr. Ephraim Brumbaugh, historian of the Descendants of Conrad Brumbaugh, Hartville, Ohio, has been continued to the writer.

This volume is the outgrowth of the extensive research required to produce *Geneaology of the Brumbach Families*, issued in April, 1913, and is a companion volume to it. The author especially acknowledges the active and persistent coöperation of his associate, Mr. John Garner[4] Fouse [80], in furthering all portions of the undertaking, and especially in the most important financing of the publication of the results attained. It remains to be seen how prompt, and extensive will be the assistance rendered by the other numerous members of the generally prosperous Fouse families, in subscribing for the volume.

Considerable space has been given to certain families intermarrying with members of the strictly Fouse families, and this is especially true of the Miller families. Any later family history of that large connection (and of others) will necessarily use data herein contained, and the unpublished material gathered in this research. It has not been noted in the text that the late Mr. Lewis Miller, Akron, Ohio, was the originator of the "Chautauqua Idea."

It is hoped that this volume may be a tie more closely uniting the Fouse, Brumbaugh, Miller, and other similar families; that it may be actually worth the large expenditure of time, labor, strength, and money spent upon its preparation; that it may prove a lasting monument to the departed, and a lively incentive to greater undertaking and success by the living. It is also hoped that the many kind friends who have so actively assisted in furnishing personal biographic, and family material may feel repaid through possession of the completed volume.

ABBREVIATIONS AND EXPLANATIONS.

The reader will find preceding, or following, each proper name of Fouse descendants a number in a bracket, thus: [2] + Nicholas^2 Fouse. The cross following the bracket, and preceding the individual name, indicates that at its numerical place further along in the volume will be found additional details concerning the said person; omission of the cross means that details have not been secured, for various reasons. The superior figure over the given, or Christian, name indicates the generation in America.

The numbering system is especially simple, and by means of the numbers lines of descent can be quickly traced backward and forward. The number in bracket always indicates the same individual, except that it is applied to the husband and wife, where referring to either of these in the text.

The biographies have been made as complete as possible. Modesty in some cases, and in others absolute failure to reply to important and repeated inquiries, is responsible for the omission of some facts, and even of some children whose names could not therefore, be included in the work.

Miss Clara Frank^5 Fouse [439], and the writer's wife, Catherin Elliott (Brown) Brumbaugh, materially assisted in the proofreading. The Joyce Engraving Company, Washington, D. C., and Messrs. Gatchell & Manning, Philadelphia, Pennsylvania, made the excellent half-tones. The publishers, Messrs. Williams & Wilkins Company, The Waverly

Press, Baltimore, Maryland, are deserving of special commendation for their prompt, careful, and satisfactory completion of the work intrusted to them. Throughout the text acknowledgment has been made for individual assistance. To all co-laborers, including custodians of public records, and the working force of the Library of Congress, sincere and cordial thanks are herewith returned.

This volume goes forth with warm Christmas greetings to all concerned.

Gaius Marcus Brumbaugh (M.D.)

Washington, D. C., December 11, 1914.

ILLUSTRATIONS

PLATE NUMBER

"Nicholaus[2] Fauss Sein Tagbuch" [2] 1
Fouse Homestead, Owned by Adam Garner[4] Fouse [82] 2
Deed of "Nicholaus Fauss" [2] and Margaret (Brumbaugh) Fouse to William[3] Fouse [14], January 8, 1825 3
Autographic Family Record of Nicholas Fauss [2] 4
Elizabeth[3] (Fouse) Miller [10], and Christina (Miller) Fouse [13] 5
Bible Record of Abraham Miller, Born May, 1749 6
Bible of Abraham Miller (2 views), and Elias Miller (Born December 14, 1836), and Joseph Miller (Born December 12, 1822) 7
Elizabeth (Miller) Fouse [12] 8
Land Patent to John[3] Fouse [13], October 8, 1818 9
William[3] Fouse [14] 10
Frederick[3] Fouse [15] 11
Rev. Theobald[3] ("Dewalt") Fouse—1861 [16] 12
Adam[3] Fouse [17], and Susanna (Garner) Fouse 13
Agreement for Building the Clover Creek (Pennsylvania) German Reformed Church, January 2, 1832—I and II 14, 15
Jonathan[4] Miller [21], and Lydia (Cassler) Miller 16
Children of Jonathan[4] Miller [21], and Lydia (Cassler) Miller 17
Christena[4] (Miller) Snyder [26], and Henry Snyder 18
Sarah[4] (Garner) Peightel [32], Henry Peightel, and Family 19
Danial[4] Garner [33], Elizabeth (Sorrick) Garner, and Angeline Alveretta[5] Garner [170] 20
Benjamin[4] Garner [36], and Catharine (Sorrick) Garner 21
Philip[4] Garner [37], and Susanna (Acker) Garner 22
William[4] Garner [38] 23
Mary[4] (Fouse) Heimbaugh [41], and Elizabeth[5] (Heimbaugh) Bowser [234] 24
Abraham[4] Fouse—Age 83, [43] 25
Jonathan Hoover [44], and Catharine[4] (Fouse) Hoover 26
Samuel Cramer and Christena[4] (Fouse) Cramer [45] 27
Frederick[4] Fouse [49], and Elizabeth (Gearty) Fouse 28
Theobald A.[4] ("Dewalt") Fouse [51] 29
Margaret[4] (Fouse) Nicodemus [52], and Jacob A. Nicodemus 30
William Acker[4] Fouse [54], and Catherine (Greaser) Fouse 31
Catharine[4] (Fouse) Greaser [55], and George Greaser 32

PLATE NUMBER

Elizabeth[4] (Fouse) Boyd [56], Albert G. Boyd, and Mary Catherine (Boyd) [337] 33
Jacob Acker[4] Fouse [57] 34
Christian[4] Fouse [61], and Eliza (Frank-Shontz) Fouse 35
Benjamin[4] Fouse [65], and Anna (Greaser) Fouse 36
Mary[4] (Fouse) Hoover [68], and Benjamin Hoover 37
Dewalt Shontz[4] Fouse, D.D. [71] 38
David[4] Fouse [75], and Margaret Ann [Summers) Fouse 39
Margaret[4] (Fouse) Nicodemus [76], and George Nicodemus 40
Elizabeth[4] (Fouse) Greaser [77] 41
George Greaser 42
Barbara[4] (Fouse) Rhodes [79], John McGraw Rhodes, and Family 43
John Garner[4] Fouse [80], and Mary Ellen (Shoemaker) Fouse 44
John Garner[4] Fouse [80], and Family 45
Sarah Ann[4] (Fouse) Hoover [81], Benjamin Franklin Hoover, and Children 46
Adam Garner[4] Fouse [82], and Family 47
Henry Smith[4] Fouse [83], and Family 48
Levi Garner[4] Fouse [84] 49
Fidelity Mutual Life Insurance Company Building 50
Rev. Abraham[5] Miller [85] 51
Adam Lewis[5] Miller [86], and Family 52
Elizabeth[5] (Bair) Miller [96], Elmer Ellsworth[6] Miller [534], and Others 53
Rev. La Fayette[5] Cassler [106] and Melvina Amelia (Weaver) Cassler 54
Samuel Dean Heffner, Mary Jane[5] (Peightel) Heffner [159] and Children 55
Rev. Henry Summers[5] Garner [181] 56
Benjamin F.[5] Garner [186], Emma (Keister) Garner 57
Lucinda[5] (Garner) Roth [192], and John Roth 58
David[5] Heimbaugh [236], and Amanda [Bair) Heimbaugh—1883, and Recently 59
Mary[5] (Heimbaugh) Brumbaugh [237], and Samuel Brumbaugh 60
Daniel[5] Fouse [249], and Family 61
Standing: Edwin P.[5] Fouse [281], Fernando F.[5] [284], Manodes W.[5] [283], Wm. Frederick[5] Fouse [285]
Sitting: Reuben E.[5] Fouse [279], John M.[5] [278] and Jacob J.[5] Fouse [280]—Sons of Frederick[4] Fouse [49] 62
William Duncan[5] Fouse Group [288] 63
Jacob Fouse[5] Greaser [331], and Family, and Jacob Bassler 64
Benjamin Simonton[5] Fouse [343] 65
Ella Grace[5] (Fouse) Jackson [361], Theodore C. Jackson and Children 66
Rev. Reuben Fouse[5] Shultz [367] 67

PLATE NUMBER

Catherine Fouse[5] (Hoover) Fink [391], Frank Harold[6] Fink [1556], and Benjamin Franklin Fink 68
Rev. David Henry[6] Fouse [395] 69
Rev. Charles Frederick[6] Brouse [638] 70
Robert Patton Habgood, Daisy May[6] (Heffner) Habgood [764], and Children 71
Rev. Ernest Newton[6] Evans [767] 72
Group at Wedding of Margaret Acker[6] Greaser [1296], and George W. Garner, February 24, 1904, Clover Creek, Pennsylvania 73

Genealogy of the Fouse Families

[1] **THEOBALD[1] FAUSS (FOUSE)** was born in "1725" (?) and lived in Rheinville, Rheinfelz, Bavaria. The name "Fauss," "Faass," became "Fouse" in the United States. About 1746 Theobald Fauss married *Margaret* ———, and moved to Deux Ponts, or Zweibrücken,[a] where he died in 1765, at age 40.

Efforts have thus far failed to trace the ancestry in Germany, and this volume is confined to "Fouse Families in America." Pages 383–404 in *Brumbach Families* are devoted to details concerning the Fouse families (Nicholas Fauss [No. 2] married Margaret Brumbaugh [E 8]). The researches connected with that volume, and the subsequent extensive investigations of Mr. John Garner Fouse [80] and of the compiler, have combined to make this volume possible.

The following pages are recollections, and early investigations of Mr. John Garner Fouse:

"Grandfather (Nicholas Fouse) wrote the name 'Fauss.' A few words in reference to the Anglicizing of the name may not be amiss. The three older boys were taught to write German, and followed their father in the orthography of the name. The revised spelling originated through Mr. Henry Beaver (Blair County, Pennsylvania) who was the first to teach English in the schools of the hitherto German community. He seems to have followed the sound rather than the letters. After the English form was introduced, the German was practically abandoned, and the revised form of the name came into general use. Theobald was a native of Rhenish Bavaria, and, we understand, a direct descendant of a prominent family of the Reformation period. We know of nothing beyond our great-grandfather, Theobald Fauss, who was born in 1725, and we do not know the date of his marriage; it must however, have occurred about 1746. The Christian name of his espoused was Margaret. To this union were born four sons and one daughter. The eldest, our grandfather, Nicholas, was born May 7, 1748.

[a] Zweibrücken, Deux Ponts, a town of Rhenish Bavaria—on the Erbach, near its confluence with the Serre, 50 miles west of Speyer. The French name "Deux Ponts," and the German "Zweibrücken" both signifying "two bridges,"—its old castle being situated between two bridges (*Lippincott's Gazetteer*).

Those were troublous times, immediately preceding the Seven Years' War, which began in 1756, and ended in 1763. The many conflicts for territorial aggression and the religious persecutions of the war-ridden provinces along the Rhine, left the citizens in destitute circumstances. At the time of our great-grandfather's death, 1765, he left a widow and five children to eke out an existence as best they could. The four younger children, Jacob, Valentine, Theobald, Jr., and Margaret were undoubtedly a care upon their mother. Nicholas[3], the oldest, was born May 7, 1748, and confirmed 1762 in one of the Reformed churches in Zweibrücken—the record has not yet been located. There is no record of the ages of the other children.

"Aunt Margaret[3] [9] who was the first child, third generation, said on certain occasions that the daughter, her aunt Margaret[2] [6], was quite small at the time of her grandfather's death—so she was informed by her father. All however seem to have been accorded careful training and grew up industrious, rendering obedience to a kind and faithful mother. By tradition we learn that they stood by her faithfully until death, which occurred in the early part of 1784. We need not wonder that the youths of this war-stricken country were anxious to emigrate to America where they might enjoy the freedom inculcated through the forefathers, who had struggled nobly for religious liberty. It is to them that we may give the credit for the stability of character, now recognized in many of the Fouse kindred.

"When the Revolutionary War ended, a number of the German mercenaries employed by King George, returned to their native land with glowing accounts of the new world. These accounts inspired the eldest son [2], Nicholas[2], our grandfather, with the idea of coming to America. He was a lock and edge toolsmith by trade. The youngest son, Theobald[2] [5], was a shoemaker, and resolved to accompany his brother. It was not an easy matter for subjects in those petty kingdoms, who were able to bear arms, to leave their country. The rulers were in constant fear of outbreaks on the frontiers, and, these being well guarded, it taxed the ingenuity of the young men to get away. Accordingly they resolved to start out as journeymen, and in May, 1784, left their quiet home in the town of Zweibrücken in the quiet of the night.

"Concerning the dear ones left behind, we can only recall a conversation between father, Uncle William and Aunt Margaret, a short time before the latter's death. It was then stated that Jacob and Valentine were married; the former kept a hostelry, and the latter was a baker.

There was no correspondence of any moment for a long time, and the only letter received informed grandfather that his brothers Jacob and Valentine were well and were prospering in business. This was sometime prior to 1811. That immediate locality was then all in confusion, on account of the encroachments of the French army, which led to the overthrow of Napoleon in 1815. To the best of their recollection there was no information after that from those remaining in the fatherland.

"In taking up the thread of the story of the two adventurers we must depend entirely upon what we gathered from our parents, uncles, and Aunt Margaret, more particularly the latter. It seems that grandfather's experience in the army fitted him for the effort to get away, without disclosing his real purpose. He, with a kit of tools for smithing, and Theobald, with tools and materials for shoemaking, found it an easy matter to make the ordinary guard believe that they were journeymen prosecuting their trades. But the critical moment came when they reached the boundary where a written form was essential. Taking their departure so stealthily prevented the local authorities from learning of their intentions. The edict had gone forth that no one subject to military duty should leave the country; but with little or no baggage, and their tools on their backs, they succeeded. While on their way to Frankfort on the Main, they were challenged by the officer in command of the forces on the boundary of their own kingdom; and, after relating their story, he directed a clerk to fill out a passport. The latter hesitated, and suggested that these men might be on their way to leave the country. The officer replied 'Ach, Schreibnur' (Write what I tell you), which he did, and the two men went on their way rejoicing.

"There is no data as to the date they sailed, nor of the vessel on which they took passage, but subsequent events indicate that they landed at Baltimore in October, 1784, after being on the Altantic ocean fully five months. The Fouse brothers had a companion in the person of Conrad Nicodemus[a], who settled in the same locality as grandfather. Their friend-

[a] The following persons took the Patriots' Oath of Fidelity March, 1778:

Conrad Nicodemus appeared in open court, No. 4, Lower Antietam Hundred, Washington County, Maryland.

Conrad Nicodemus, No. 107, on Henry Schnebley's Return, Washington County, Maryland, p. 61.

Frederick Nicodemus, No. 20, before Andrew Rentch, March 7, 1778, Washington County, Maryland, p. 70.

All above references are from *Unpublished Manuscripts, Hodges*, in Library of D. A. R., Washington, D. C.

ship continued until death. Mention has been made of Nicolas being a locksmith. After landing at Baltimore, it did not require much time for him to decide that for his occupation it would be better for him to go to the frontier. Theobald, in the shoemaking trade, concluded to remain in Baltimore, where he had obtained a position prior to the elder brother's departure. He soon established a good trade, and concluded to remain there."

Children of [1] *Theobald*[1] *and Margaret Fauss:*

[2] + Nicholas[2], *b* May 7, 1748; *d* August 9, 1825; *m Margaret*[3] *Brumbaugh.*
[3] Jacob[2].
[4] Valentine[2].
[5] + Theobald Jr.[2]; *d* 1828; *m Catharine* ———.
[6] Margaret[2].

[2] **NICHOLAS**[2] **FOUSE,** son of [1] Theobald[1] and Margaret (———) Fouse, was born May 7, 1748 at Zweibrücken, Bavaria, Germany; was confirmed, when 14 years old, a member of the German Reformed Church. His father died in 1765, and Nicholas became the main support of the family. After the death of his mother, he sailed for the United States, landing at Baltimore, Maryland, in October, 1784. He soon went to Sharpsburgh, Maryland, and there became the village blacksmith. He there also met and married *Margaret*[3] *Brumbaugh,*[a] born May 5, 1766; daughter of *Jacob*[2] *Brumbaugh*, son of Johannes Henrich[1] Brumbach. When 14 years old Margaret was confirmed a member of the German Reformed Church at Funkstown, Maryland, near what was later called Hagerstown. Soon after their marriage in November, 1785, they began housekeeping at or near Funkstown, Washington County, Maryland.

"Here grandfather worked at the anvil, and found an excellent helper in his recently acquired helpmate. Several of our uncles, as well as father, spoke of her as an expert in handling the hammer, when necessity called for her services. When grandfather started smithing at Funkstown he had no apprentice, and thus at times needed grandmother's help." (J. G. F.)

"October 12, 1786, [9] Margaret[3], their eldest child, was born. They lived at Funkstown until 1789. By their united efforts and economy they saved some money, and then considered the feasibility of purchasing land

[a] See pp. 383–404, *Brumbach Families*, 1913.

where they might make a permanent home. Great grandfather Jacob Brumbaugh had previously taken a trip into central Pennsylvania, and found a beautiful spot east of the Alleghanies, later called 'Morrison Cove,' where in 1788 he preempted a large tract of land and settled in the same year. It was also stated that Mr. Nicodemus who had accompanied them across the ocean, located in the Cove, and preempted a large tract of land, which was at that time in Bedford County. The favorable report of this beautiful country was an inducement for them to go there and locate permanently. Preparations were made to emigrate there early in the spring of 1789. It was essential to procure a covered wagon and a yoke of oxen for the undertaking. Into that vehicle were packed the smithing tools, necessary wearing apparel, bedding, food, etc. It afforded shelter for the family, which consisted of the parents and two children, [9] Margaret[3] and [10] Elizabeth.[3] It was not then the custom to keep a diary of daily occurrences, as we are willing to do in the present age. There is nothing to indicate any serious difficulties encountered on the way, a distance of about 150 miles, except the very rough, ungraded roads through the forest. It is stated the route was over the old Baltimore, Chambersburg and Bedford road, later turnpike, turning to the north at Bloody Run, later Everett, Pennsylvania; and then passing up Yellow Creek, through the gap to where Loysburg, or Pattonville, afterwards was established. They entered the Cove at the south end, then proceeded north about 16 miles, a short distance from where Rebecca Furnace was later erected. There they settled temporarily on land preempted by Margaret's father, Jacob Brumbaugh, where they lived nearly four years, and where [11] Catharine[3] and [12] Jacob[2] were born."

The Census of 1790[a] enumerates "Nicholas Fouss" in Huntingdon County (Blair County was established in 1846), Pennsylvania, as having "2 Free white males under 16 years" and a wife. The interesting photographic reproduction of the family record as kept by Nicholas in this *Tagbuch*,[b] establishes the fact that the enumerator should have recorded two *females* rather than two males. However, that Census is a mine of genealogical wealth. It also gives Anthony Bever, Jacob Brumbough, John Brumbough, Michle Garnur, Abraham Miller, etc., as amongst their neighbors.

"During that time they selected a place about five miles north of where they first pitched tents. Here Nicholas bought a tract of 135 acres

[a] *Heads of Families—Pa.*—1790, p. 123.
[b] Owned by *John Garner[5] Fouse.* See Plates 1 and 4.

from Benjamin Tudor, January 3, 1793, as per deed recorded in Huntingdon County, Pennsylvania, Book B, No. 1, page 490. He paid for this tract of land £56 in gold and silver. Benjamin Tudor preempted this unimproved tract September 27, 1791; Patent book 18, page 230. In 1793 they built a small log house of four rooms with a crude chimney in the center, with a fireplace on either side for cooking and to keep them comfortable in cold weather. This was the homestead house, and was near where Beavertown was later located. Ere many days the indispensable blacksmith shop was erected. Aunt Margaret told us that grandfather frequently referred to this experience as an important period in his life. Here among the tall oaks, with no part of the land under cultivation, it was necessary to eke out an existence for the small family. The greater part of his time was occupied in manufacturing, sharpening and repairing tools, so much needed in clearing the land. Here was where grandfather's mechanical ingenuity could be utilized. The country was rapidly filling up with emigrants who had to be supplied with tools such as axes, mattocks, and shovels for the wooden plough. Carpenter tools were in great demand, such as the broad axe, adz, chisels, plane-bits, etc. All these were manufactured in the original blacksmith shop. The parents delighted to speak to their children of their experiences during the pioneer days, how they labored and toiled in order to make a comfortable home for all. After the house work was done and the children had been put to bed, the mother often repaired to the shop and there assisted grandfather in doing important work. Her assistance could then be rendered without molestation. There were no railroads nor means of transportation, other than by wagons, for their crude iron and steel, from which all kinds of wares could be produced. Nails, hinges, locks and bolts were in great demand, and all these were made by hand, mostly at night. The greater part of the day had to be utilized in subduing the forest, and bringing the land under cultivation. It was said that when grandfather was engaged in the clearings and some of the neighbors came with an axe, or some other tool to be repaired, they would work in grandfather's stead while he went to the shop and put the tool in order. Thus by perseverance and continued labor, he succeeded in gradually clearing the land he bought for a home. These pioneer fathers laboring together, soon reduced the forests of sturdy oak and pine to cultivated fields, dotted over with homes of industrious husbandmen, and made the valley blossom as the rose. The house hastily constructed from the roughly hewn logs, roof of clapboards, and mother earth for floor until boards could be procured, proved quite sufficient to bring contentment to the hearts of our pious grandparents. Here they lived and reared a large family of healthy children. To the four children already named were added six sons, in the following order: [13] John[3], [14] William[3], [15] Frederick[3], [16] Theobald[3], [17] Adam[3] and [18] Johnathan[3]. June 24, 1805, grandfather bought 42 acres from Levi Roberts, to be added to the homestead (Book K, No. 1, page 318 recorded in Huntingdon County, Pennsylvania).

"With the increasing members of the family, the need for space multiplied, and this need was met by building an addition to the house. The children in due course of time were trained to work and help, which increased the income and helped to support the family. Modern improvements were then unknown, and the important matches were invented after the pioneer days here described. 'I remember,' said Aunt, 'of making hasty visits to neighbors' houses for fire when our fire died out. Rather than to kindle by friction we would run to the neighbors to borrow fire and had sometimes to go to several houses in succession.' The practice was to cover embers or coals in the huge fire places with ashes and preserve the fire, which was not always a success, and often caused much trouble. In those days cook stoves were untirely unknown, all cooking had to be done on the hearth.

"Margaret said that at the age of thirteen years, she was out in the field raking hay, and got very much heated. Not having knowledge of the danger she might incur, she waded the creek on her way home in order that she might get cooled off. She took a cold which produced swelling of the limbs, causing her untold suffering. There was no doctor nearer than Huntingdon, a distance of twenty miles, so they were obliged to use home remedies. The disease, however, did not yield to their applications, and became a severe case of 'white swelling,' which 'confined her to bed for a period of eighteen months before her limbs opened.' She said during this time her suffering was so great that she lost nearly all her hair. Her mother could not undress to sleep and rest a single night in comfort, until after her limbs opened. She was obliged to sit and lie in bed for eleven years more before her limbs were healed so that she was again able to sit upon a chair, and begin to move around. The disease stiffened her limbs, and stunted her growth. With difficulty she learned to walk on crutches, which were used throughout her remaining life. She was then very grateful for the tender care given her by her dear parents, whose nursing through all those years saved her life. She was the tender branch of the family, but she was never wanting for care or sympathy from the family. She spoke of the trials to which they were subjected, yet always referred to her parents in the most endearing terms. She also referred to the Christian training. It was the father's custom on Sabbath evening to turn the home into a place of worship, as they had no church until 1810, all services previous thereto were held in the homes of different members of the church. The missionary circuit was very large, so they could not have preaching oftener than once in ten or twelve weeks, and then the people had to go over rough roads ten to fifteen miles to get to each other's houses, where preaching was appointed.

"The houses were small and poorly furnished, yet the settlers were glad to be there, for they went to learn and to hear the Gospel preached to them. The people were poor, and all had bare floors in their dwellings. On a certain occasion about the year 1809, Conrad Nicodemus and his wife, who came across the ocean with grandfather, made a carpet and put it on their floor. When it came their turn again to have preaching at their house, the people were astounded to see the floor covered and did not know what to name the covering. They thought Nicodemus was getting very proud and extravagant, since they had their floor covered with ,coverlids.'

"The evening services at their home were especially precious to them, and their father's prayers always made a lasting impression upon all. They also had prayer meetings at the homes of the different members of the church every few weeks, where a chapter in the Bible was read and a short exhortation made by one of the members, or by the leader. This was quite an enjoyment to our pious grandparents, and later it taught their children to love the services. Many of these German fathers and mothers were good singers. They had been taught that art in Germany from text or music books, but sang in this country mostly from memory. Grandfather Nicholas Fouse, was noted for his talent in music. He was able to teach his children from memory all the old melodies in their Hymnal, and had an effective way of imparting this knowledge.

"The Sunday evenings at grandfather's home were passed in devotion, by reading the scripture, studying the catechism, and singing songs and hymns. Father and Uncle Theobald were especially mindful of this training. It was no doubt an incentive to make the latter, later on, a minister of the Gospel. They especially delighted to sing the old hymns which used to be sung under the parental roof. To some of these they were quite partial, such as the Forty-second Psalm; Es ist gewiszlich an der zeit; Wachet auf ruft uns die Stimme; Wie Schon leuchtet uns die Morgenstern; and many others.

"Nicholas[2] [2] was never so busy but that he could find time to 'say grace' at meals. His children were obliged to study the catechism and read the Bible, and grandfather would explain passages to them. He was sincere in the observation of the Sabbath, and on that day allowed no labor about the place except what was absolutely necessary for the comfort of the family and the proper care of the livestock. He did not believe in social visiting on Sunday, but was ever ready to look after sick neighbors, to speak words of cheer and comfort, as well as to offer his sympathy. He was devoutly Reformed in his theology, for such was his training in the Palatinate, and he labored to perpetuate this doctrine through the members of his family by personal instruction."

"Defections in the ranks of the church of the Reformation in that community were, unfortunately, quite frequent at this particular period; largely due to the ana-Baptist element that came from the old world to enjoy religious freedom. Aunt Margaret said that it required very little effort to pass as a preacher, in those early days, among these people; and the stronger the denunciation of the orthodox churches, the greater was their success amongst the skeptical. As a rule these ministers were illiterate, and without any theological training. In that peculiar period, when church facilities were inadequate to meet the wants of the people, Nicholas[2] [2] more earnestly labored to supply the spiritual and intellectual needs of his household. His religious interest was not confined to his own household. In December 1809 he took part in the purchase of a lot of 82 perches from Tobias Hainley, on which to erect a house of worship, deeded to Nicholas Fouse and Abraham Miller, trustees for the German Reformed church and Christian Acker and Adam Sorrick for the Lutheran church (See Book P, No. 1, page 561, Huntingdon County, Pennsylvania), who as elders of the respective organizations were charter members of the Union church in which they worshipped as long as they remained in the community, or until they passed into the realms above. Their remains rest in the adjacent graveyard, part of the original plot. Grandfather Fouse was one of the pillars of the congregation and church, though he lived three miles distant. This church was built in 1810, and was the first church of these denominations built in the Cove.

"Margaret said 'There were no schools, but father took special care to have the children learn to read and write, while yet quite young. The Heidelberg catechism had to be studied and served as one of the text-books. Father did not think it so essential for the girls to learn to write, but he thought differently for the boys. The three elder lads took their first lessons in German penmanship from father and also improved any opportunity that came to them to attend private schools. These were the only kind then in existence. Only a few had been established, the nearest one being two and one-half miles from their home. The four younger boys had advantages over the older ones as they had school nearer, and could take up English as well as German. At best, however, the schools were only of ordinary character and lasted but two or three months, in midwinter and they were mostly taught by persons who should have gone to school rather than have undertaken to instruct.' Every year brought additional advantages; and in this year, 1854, when looking back over the past, she was filled with wonder at what had been accomplished through improvements in her time. (In the above named year Aunt Margaret moved to our house and lived with us to the time of her death." J. G. F.)

"After the yoke of foreign oppression was thrown off, forests were turned into fertile fields, mineral deposits were developed, wheels of industry were put in motion and means of transportation established. We, whose ancestors participated either directly or indirectly in these achievements, may justly be proud of what they did. To their memory we gratefully offer reminiscences and chronologies which we trust may tend to perpetuate family ties which meant so much to our forefathers. May these serve to stimulate the spirit of kinship in the hearts and minds of the present and future Fouse and Brumbaugh generations."

"About the beginning of the nineteenth century they built an addition to their log house. With this annex, they thought themselves comfortably fixed. Their home seemed to have acquired additional charms. The worst of Aunt Margaret's suffering was over. Her limbs were healing, and she could begin to do various chores about the house, such as required no walking. She became the seamstress of the family. The goods for clothing were all home spun. She could take no part in the preparation of the raw material. The flax was raised on the farm. The men cared for it until it reached the switch stand, then her mother and her two sisters took charge of it until it was ready for the loom. The same was necessary with the wool from the sheep's back. It had to be prepared for their winter clothes. Nearly all her brothers learned to weave, and employed their evenings alternately in that way. They had a weaver's shop at the south end of their house where the weaving was done by the hand loom, by either daughters or sons. Some of them were not so apt at it. Hard work through the day was frequently offered as an excuse to their mother to get out of it, but mother always managed to have them weave during the winter evenings."

"There were a number of little happenings of which this dear Aunt [9] spoke as opportunity offered, but only those which made special impression on us are recalled, as we talked with her in the early 50's. For us children to sit in her room and learn from her was then a pleasure, and now quite a benefit in writing these recollections. In stature, Aunt was the smallest in the family. She had a strong face with fixed purposes, and was noble hearted and true. She loved to speak of the things that were elevating. Though most of us were young, yet her talks had a marked influence upon us. Her little white cap with ruffled lace, was fittingly in keeping with her neat and tidy appearance. She moved about with difficulty, but everything was in its place. Her room was always invitingly cozy. It was a pleasure to be with Aunt and do her errands. She laid special stress on grandfather's appreciation of the liberty vouchsafed to his posterity under the comparatively new government. He was an earnest advocate of free schools, wanted church separated from state; though he never took an active interest in politics, he supported Washington, Federalism and the national Republican party. He was an advocate of a strong central government. When the war of 1812 broke out, the two eldest boys belonged to the local militia. Aunt said, 'Father was very anxious on the day the drafting took place, fearing it might require his boys to go. He had them prepare for it, telling them that if it fell to their lot, they could not do otherwise than go. Luckily, they escaped. He had such a horror of the scalping and butchering practice by the allies of the English army. He was loyal and advocated vigorous prosecution of the war. He had no use for anyone sympathizing with the enemy, and advised them to go where they belonged.' Some of the neighbors, descendants of the Germans and Hessians whom King George had brought over to fight our patriot fathers, were subject to adverse criticism, and nicknamed 'hirelings.' Grandfather thought these criticisms unjust; and denounced it as wrong, that they were forced, through their petty rulers, to go and fight for the English. When they laid down their arms, many of them became good citizens, and he thought they justly deserved to be respected by their neighbors, because their sympathies were with the American patriots. It fell to the lot of the son of one of these Hessian families, to go to the frontier with the others who took their departure at the muster of the militia on the Fouse premises. He bravely took up arms in defense of his adopted country. The prayers and benedictions of these German fathers being pronounced, they took their departure. It is true grandfather's love for the right enabled him to frown upon the apparent injustice to these people, by casting reflections on the descendants of the Hessians, who were forced to serve in the English army against their better judgment."

"Aunt often spoke of the good health enjoyed by the family, aside from herself being crippled. No serious illness invaded the home until the summer of 1814, when Jonathan [18], the youngest of the family, a bright healthy boy of six years, was taken with fever and spasms, and for a time was seriously ill. Aunt Margaret said they always looked upon him as especially bright until that time. After a time he was restored to good general health, but his mind was impaired. At first they thought he would outgrow it, but he never could memorize, or learn to know one letter from another. All efforts to teach him were futile. It was a source of deep distress to the mother. Aunt Margaret was the eldest, but helpless on account of her limbs, and her brother, Jonathan, was helpless because he could not care for himself. She said, 'My parents felt that we would, eventually become a charge upon others, though time proved that we were never considered such by any of them, for which I am very grateful.'

"The forests had been subdued; cultivated fields, with abundant crops, were the results of the united efforts of her father, mother and the family. Economy and care had brought us to a point when we considered ourselves in comfortable circumstances. The daughters were well satisfied with calico dresses for Sunday wear, and the boys wore linsey pantaloons, and thought it quite an improvement over the coarse linen weekday clothes. Coffee was used once a week, and that always on Sunday morning. Being a rare thing, it was much relished by the younger members of the family, and they always looked forward to this weekly treat with delight."

"As already stated, grandfather was very attentive to the work in the shop. He looked upon this as the important factor in maintaining the family. Indeed, it was the only source of ready cash. Internal improvements had not yet reached this part of the country. There was no outlet for the products of the farms as all were producers. The nearest markets were Pittsburgh and Baltimore. The former was reached by teams, and the latter by rafting over the Frankstown and Raystown branches of the Juniata River (all feeders of the Susquehanna); and then only once or twice a year, during the time of freshets or floods, in the spring and fall. Notwithstanding this, there was progress, and at the close of the war with Great Britain, grandfather purchased an additional property, adjoining the homestead, of 34 acres and allowances from Patrick

FOUSE HOMESTEAD OWNED BY ADAM GARNER[4] FOUSE [82]

Dimond (Book P, No. 1, page 98, August 11, 1815). This tract was also added to the homestead which now contained 211 acres and allowances, or 226 acres. (See Plate 2). Large possessions, however, were no aspiration to a man of grandfather's disposition. He prized true Christian contentment above all else. Father, as well as our uncles, frequently referred to the satisfaction, expressed by their father in regard to his financial condition. He did not believe that great wealth contributed to real happiness. He believed in making good use of what was his own. This conclusion was largely due to his training in the fatherland, where every foot of land was made to produce. His trade confined him to the shop, to a circumscribed space, all of which contributed to his remarks in later years: that while there were many chances to buy land cheap, he cared not to purchase, as he could not convince himself that there was any advantage in having more land than he could keep in order. Personally he gave little or no attention to farm work after his boys had grown up; and he could scarcely adapt himself to the strides the young Americans were making, being strongly inclined to follow the methods of the old country. I remember a conversation between Uncle William and father, relative to this particular feature, which evinced the fact that while he did not approve of the American methods, he gradually gave way to the wishes of the boys. Uncle William spoke in particular about the difference of opinion as to how the crops should be thrashed. To flay it out was a wearisome pastime for the winter months. Many of the neighbors had adopted what they considered an improved plan, treading the grain with the horses. This the father thought was wasteful, because it broke so many grains, and he thought injured the straw for feeding purposes, especially as far as rye was concerned. At this time they spoke of him as exacting, yet kind and indulgent. There were no threshing machines invented wherewith to thresh out the crops in those early days."

FURNACES AND THE IRON INDUSTRY

"About 1812 John Royer built Springfield Furnace, in Woodberry Township, about five miles northwest of the Fouse home. He preempted a large tract of land, some of which was rich in hematite iron ore, and most of it was well covered with forest trees from which he made charcoal. Soon afterward Dr. Peter Schoenberger, proprietor of the iron works at Marietta, Lancaster County, Pennsylvania, preempted large tracts of mountain land, also a large tract known as 'The Barrens' containing considerable hematite ore. About 1817 he built Rebecca Furnace, later in Huston Township, four miles south of the original Fouse farm. All this activity gave the pioneers a ready market for produce, stock, etc. Extensive hauling was necessary, as the pig iron had to be conveyed from the furnaces ten miles to Maria Forges and twenty miles to Petersburg. In common with many others in the 'Cove,' the Fouse sons earned money by chopping wood at thirty-five cents per cord in the winter, and, during the summer, the farm was further cleared and cultivated. The success of the iron works soon led to the establishment of other similar furnaces and forges, and Morrison's Cove became a veritable hive of industry offering a good home market for everything the farmers could produce, as well as for their labor by team, etc."[a]

"Prior to the completion of the canal and Portage Railroad, in 1833, there were a large number of charcoal-furnaces and forges in this portion of Huntingdon County and their product was hauled to Pittsburgh at a cost of from twenty to thirty dollars per ton."[a]

March 13, 1819, Nicholas bought another tract containing 134 acres from John Paulis,[b] and he soon transferred the same to his cousin, *Jacob Brumbaugh.* March 20, 1819, he bought a tract of 138 acres from *Henry Acker,*[c] known as the "mountain farm," and this was deeded to his son, William[3] [14] on January 8, 1825.[b] This deed is reproduced because of the signatures, and also because of the provisions made in the same whereby the son, William[3] [14], was to annually deliver certain supplies to the parents—the same clause appeared in the several deeds made at this time, through which the father turned over to his sons all his real estate.

January 1, 1825, he sold to Frederick[3] [15] 112 acres,[b] and on the same date to Theobald[3] [16] 113 acres[b]—the home farm consisted of 226 acres. Frederick[4] and Theobald[4] were also to deliver ample firewood.

DEED OF NICHOLAS FOUSE AND MARGARETH TO WILLIAM FOUSE, JANUARY 8, 1825

"This Indenture made this Eighth day of January in the year of our Lord one thousand eight hundred and twenty-five Between Nicholas Fouse of the township of Woodberry in the County of Huntingdon and State of Pennsylvania and Margareth his wife of the One part and William

[a] *Brumbach Families—Brumbaugh*, p. 389.

[b] Recorded in Book Q, No. 1, p. 264, Huntingdon County, Pennsylvania.

[c] Recorded in Book M, No. 1, p. 154–155, 156, Huntingdon County, Pennsylvania.

against themselves and their heirs & against
all person or persons whomsoever Claiming or to
Claim the same from or under any of
them shall and will warrant and forever defend
by these presents, In witness whereof they have
hereunto set their hands and seals the day
and year first above Written —

Witness present —

Henry Brauer — Nicholaus Fauss (Seal)

John Miers — Margaret [her mark] Fouse (Seal)

Rec'd on the day of the date of the above indenture of and
from William Fouse the Consideration money therein
mentioned

Witness — Nicholaus Fauss

Henry Brauer —

DEED OF "NICHOLAUS FAUSS" [1] AND MARGARET (BRUMBAUGH) FOUSE, JANUARY 8, 18[illegible]

Fouse of the township, county, &c., aforesaid of the other part, Witnesseth . . . consideration . . . Eighteen hundred dollars . . . Thence by Tusseys mountain . . . thence by lands of Christian Acker," &c.—see photographic copy of said deed. The signature of Nicholas, it should be remembered, was made shortly before his death. (See Plate 3.)

After an illness of almost a week, Nicholas died August 9, 1825, aged 77 years, 3 months 2 days, and was buried in the Union Cemetery, now Lutheran, on the Clover Creek Road, four miles south of Williamsburg, Pennsylvania. Thus ended a life to which the stalwart sons and the neighbors always referred with pride.

"But few of the grandchildren ever saw either of the grandparents, Nicholas and Margaret Fouse. We have no picture of them, as the art of taking pictures was not in use in that age. Grandfather (as we were told) was about 5 feet, 8 inches in height; heavy set with strong muscles, broad shoulders, ruddy face, medium fleshy; weight 180 pounds. He was kind and indulgent to his children, yet stern, and had them understand that his word was law and must be obeyed. Grandmother was a large sized woman of strong build, strong bones and muscles, was round faced and more inclined to be fleshy than grandfather; about his weight. She had a kind and true heart and was very fond of her children, and loved them very dearly; and in return they loved her and were faithful and true to her, and tried to reward her for her kindness towards them."

"Grandfather died intestate. No letters of administration were required, as he disposed of his real estate before his death. The family agreed to adjust the matter of personal property among themselves. At the time of marriage of each of his children, grandfather did what he could to give them a start. They were all impressed with the idea that their father sought to deal justly with each of them, and jealously guarded against partiality. They were truly imbued with the idea that justice and equity must prevail in the division of all the effects. Since Theobald occupied the original house (which was not commodious at best) for two families, it was concluded to erect a small house for the mother and the crippled sister. Such a house was built in 1826. Father did the carpenter work, while the brothers Frederick and Theobald, delivered the timber on the ground, etc. The building was located about midway between the houses occupied by the brothers. Here father and Jonathan, the youngest brother, found rest and repose, and called it their home, because 'Mother was there.' This, however continued but a few years."

"Mother frequently spoke of it having been her desire to emigrate to Ohio, where the others had gone a number of years before. Father's reply was 'I cannot leave mother.' Whereupon these arrangements were entered upon with a view that as soon as he located on the premises, he would build a house for his mother. But grim death called her hence, August 8, 1829, aged 63 years, 8 months and 4 days. As already stated, she was a strong robust woman. The cause of her death was strangulated hernia, resultant, as the family believed from over exertion in her early days. She was revered and respected by all who knew her. Father could never refer to her without feelings of emotion, out of gratitude for the love she manifested for all her offspring. The agony endured in her closing days must have been almost beyond human comprehension. Medical science had not then made it possible to alleviate such suffering. But amidst all she remembered the dependents, Margaret and Jonathan. She remained conscious until within a few moments of her death. She turned to the eldest and said, 'Peggy, such de zuflucht bei den Friedrich' (You seek a home with Frederick) and then turning to father said, 'Adam, gebst du acht auf den Jonathan.' (Adam, you take care of Jonathan.) They both assured her that her wishes would be respected. Father and the other children told her that Margaret and Jonathan would never be in want, if it were in their power to avert it. Upon this assurance her spirit took its flight, and she was laid to rest beside grandfather's grave in the old church yard adjoining the Lutheran and Reformed Union Church, where they worshiped and where their children were further instructed in the Heidelberg Catechism, and were baptized and confirmed, by the Reformed missionary preacher, the Rev. John Dietrich Aurandt, their pastor for many years in that country. He also gave Rev. Theobald Fouse, his first lesson in theology. Plain marble tombstones mark their resting places in the grave-yard, then attached to where the present Lutheran church now stands, three miles north of where the old Fouse mansion stood."

"The death of the mother closed the earthly career of one whose influence for good was a decided power, and an important element in the community. These devoted parents had nobly fulfilled their parts in life, as was clearly testified in the lives of those whom they left behind. They were highly respected in the community in which they resided, and by honesty and industry, with singleness of purpose, each member of the family built a record which reflected the excellent training given by their parents." (J. G. F.)[a]

[a] See p. 21 for a continuation of personal recollections.

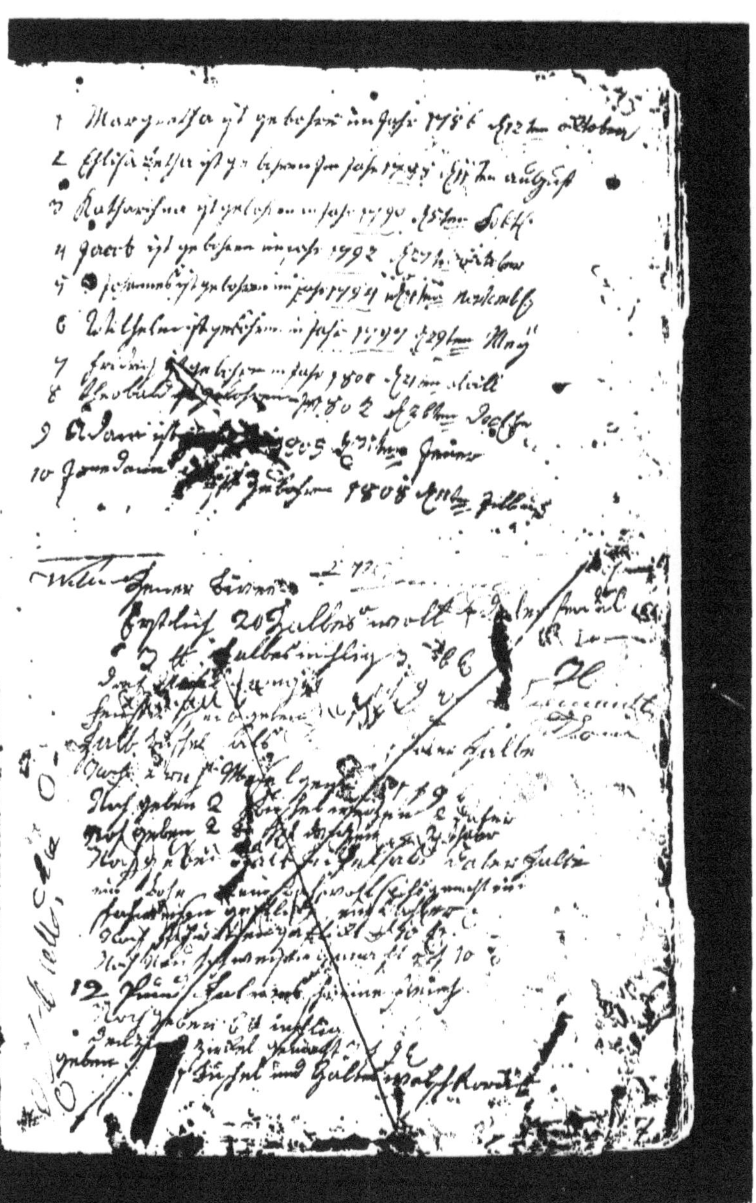

AUTOGRAPHIC FAMILY RECORD OF NICHOLAS FAUS[illegible] FOUS[illegible] IN THE [illegible]

Children (10) *of* [2] *Nicholas*[2] *and Margaret* (*Brumbaugh*) *Fouse:*

[9] + Margaret[3], *b* October 12, 1786; *d* May 9, 1855; *unm.*
[10] + Elizabeth[3], *b* August 11, 1788; *d* July, 1869; *m Abraham Miller.*
[11] + Catharine[3], *b* September 5, 1790; *d* December, 1870; *m John Philip Garner.*
[12] + Jacob[3], *b* November 7, 1792; *d* May 2, 1845; *m Elizabeth Miller.*
[13] + John[3], *b* November 11, 1794; *d* July 20, 1825; *m Christina Miller.*
[14] + William[3], *b* May 29, 1797; *d* January 1, 1874; *m* (1) *Susan Bowers; m* (2) *Susan Keely; m* (3) *Elizabeth Longenecker.*
[15] + Frederick[3], *b* April 27, 1800; *d* September 9, 1873; *m Catharine Acker.*
[16] + Theobald[3], *b* December 26, 1802; *d* August 23, 1873; *m Nancy Shontz.*
[17] + Adam[3], *b* January 31, 1805; *d* May 5, 1887; *m Susanna Garner.*
[18] + Jonathan[3], *b* July 11, 1808; *d* April 4, 1879; *unm.*

[5] **THEOBALD[2] FOUSE**, the youngest son of [1] Theobald[1], accompanied his oldest brother Nicholas[2] [2] to this country, landing in Baltimore, October, 1784, and he remained there during his life. He was a shoemaker of no mean pretentions, prospered, and married within two years after landing. The records of this marriage have been lost or destroyed.

Their children were: Jacob[3], Catharine[3], Caroline[3], Mary[3] and Harry[3].

All passed away without leaving a record of the mother's maiden name, or date of death; the latter is said to have been due to pulmonary trouble, at 37 years of age. About three years later, he married (2) *Mrs. Catharine Wakeman Schuman.* This union was blessed with two children: Elizabeth[3] and Magdalena[3].

The *Heads of Families, First Census of the U. S. 1790*, page 18, enumerates him as at "Baltimore Town, Md." with a son over 16, another under 16, and 3 females.

His will (Book 13, page 101), dated March 10, 1828, was executed before the witnesses Geo. Valiant, G. Schleict and David Pugh and bequeaths his house and lot in South Liberty Street, and furniture, to his wife *Catharine.* After her decease the same to to go "to my son-in-law James Larew, my son-in-law Frederick Browen, my daughter Mary Eddy, the two children of my daughter Elizabeth Adams to wit Mary and Joshua to be divided among them share and share alike, and likewise my son-in-law David Pugh to have his lawful share; to the heirs of my son Jacob," etc. Theobald[2] [5] died prior to August 6, 1828, and September 8, 1848 Jacob M. Fouse was appointed executor.

JACOB[3] FOUSE (3–1) married *Harriet Evans*. Children to this union were two:

Jacob[4] and Henry[4].

CATHARINE[3] (3–2) married a *Mr. Browen*, and they had three children:

Mary[4], married *John Michael Craft.*
Caroline[4], married *John George Craft.*
Catharine[4], married *John Mathias Craft.*

These sisters married brothers and, as far as traceable, left no posterity. Further inquiry is being made in Washington City, where the Crafts were last located.

CAROLINE[3] (3–3) married *Jacob Larue*, to whom were born:

Elizabeth[4], married *James Mitchell.*
Caroline[4], married *James Mitchell* (second wife).
Margaret[4], never married.

It appears from the information gathered that Elizabeth[4] died within a year after marriage and her sister—Caroline[4] became Mrs. Mitchell. All died young, having a tendency to lung disease.

MARY FOUSE[3] (3–4) married *Thomas Nicholson.* There were two children:

Henry[4], married *Mary Adams.*
William[4], never married.

Mrs. Nicholson, upon her husband's death, married a *Mr. Eddy.* To this union was born one child, George. We have not been successful in procuring subsequent records of this family.

HARRY FOUSE[3] (3–5) died under 21 years of age, without issue—buried in the graveyard by the Second Reformed Church of Baltimore, Maryland.

ELIZABETH[3] FOUSE (3–6, first born, second wife) married *Thos. Adams.* Two children born to this marriage:

Joshua[4], married *Mary Manners.*
Mary[4], married *Henry Nicholson*, her cousin.

It seems impossible to get further definite information in the foregoing families. The source of the information published is William and Mary Pugh, the surviving children of the seventh generation of the Theobald Fouse family.

MAGDALENA[3] FOUSE (3-7) married *David Pugh.*

"DIED, in Baltimore, January 30th, 1876, Mrs. Magdalene Pugh, greatly beloved by all that knew her.

"Mrs. Pugh had been for many years a member of the Reformed church on Second Street, while Rev. Dr. Heiner was yet the active pastor, of whom she often spoke in words of affectionate regard. Some time after his death, she, with her family, became connected with the Third Reformed church on corner of Paca and Saratoga Streets, to which she gave her heart and active service. She loved to be in the sanctuary and to join in its solemn services of prayer and praise, and while her health permitted she was always and promptly in her place. Her religious character was inward and solid. She was a lady of clear mind, tender feelings, constitutionally opposed to all forms of ostentation and really devoted to what she regarded as duty. Though her death was preceded by a long siege of sickness, which was at times specially distressing, she was graciously sustained through it all. No murmur ever escaped her lips. Her final experience of God's gracious nearness was especially gratifying to her friends. In view of her uniform calmness of feeling, she scarcely expected such vivid tokens of divine favor in her last moments. She labored to the last to express her gratitude to God for this distinguished favor. Though dead, she nevertheless speaks to us. Let her children and friends listen to this silent voice, and be lured by it onward and still onward on the same 'Highway' on which she was conducted to the great 'Building of God' in Heaven.

G."

There were five children:

- John H.[4], single. Died February, 1901.
- Elizabeth A.,[4] single. Died February 8, 1903.
- Joseph[4], died at age 17.
- William G.[4]
- Mary F.[4], unmarried.

JOHN H.[4] PUGH.

"Mr. John H. Pugh, for many years well-known in commercial and financial circles in this city, died at about 3 o'clock yesterday morning at his residence, 1020 West Lanvale street, of paralysis. He was identified with the old Baltimore Gas Light Company and its successors for about 25 years, and after retiring from its service was prominently connected with the stockholding interests in the company. He was a native of Baltimore and a son of the late David Pugh, of Wales, who came to this country in the early part of the last century and built the gasworks here, the first in America, of which he was the chief engineer. Mr. Pugh never married. He leaves a brother, Mr. William G. Pugh, who is connected with the Consolidated Gas Company, and one sister, Miss Mary F. Pugh, with whom he resided.

"The funeral of Mr. John H. Pugh, who died last Tuesday, took place yesterday from his late home, 1020 West Lanvale Street. Services were conducted by Rev.

Conrad Clever, D.D., pastor of the Third Reformed Church. The pallbearers were members of Oriental Lodge, I. O. O. F. Interment was at Greenmount Cemetery. Stewart & Mowen had charge of the funeral."

ELIZABETH A.[4] PUGH.

"PUGH.—Died, in Baltimore, on the 8th day of February, Miss Elizabeth A. Pugh, a valued member of the Third Reformed church.

"The deceased illustrated, in her life and character, those graces which should be found in the conduct of those who are followers of Jesus. Her hand was always open to the cause of the Gospel. She was always ready to listen to the numerous appeals that have to be made. She always gave as the Lord had blessed her. Through long years of suffering, which only acted as the trimming of the vine, she grew in grace and in the love of her Saviour. Her loyalty to the Reformed Church never wavered. She firmly believed that it had a mission. Every sign that this was being apprehended and executed by others brought joy to her heart. Though she was prevented from doing much, she was ever ready to encourage others. She fell asleep in Jesus, and testified that His love did not fail, when the feet were chilling in the cold waters of the river of death. Her church has lost a valuable member, her family a life that was an inspiration, and her circle of friends one who leaves a large space vacant. May God bless this bereavement of His hand to the glory of His name and to the good of His people. One of His chosen has fallen, but the work still goes on."

WILLIAM G. PUGH (4-4) married *Julia Morrow*. To them was born a son William Morrow[5]. The mother dying, left the child to the care of the father, grandmother and aunts and Wm. G. later married *Mary Stevenson* and to this union were born the following children:

John David[5], James G.[5] and Margaret Stevenson[5].

WILLIAM MORROW[5] PUGH (5-1) married *Eleanor Myers*. To them were born the following children:

Joseph[6], Julian[6], and Eleanor[6].

JOHN DAVID[5] PUGH (5-2) married *Addie Austin* and they live at Harrisburg, Pennsylvania. To them were born:

Mary[6], Margaret[6], Hale[6], and Eliza[6].

JAMES G.[5] PUGH (5-3) married *Helen Nussear*, residing near Lutherville, Maryland. There is one child, William Nussear[6] Pugh.

MARGARET STEVENSON[5] PUGH, (5-4) married *Alexander Johnson*. They live at Govans, Baltimore County, Maryland. There are two children:

Mary Stevenson[6], and Nannie Gardner[6].

Families of the Third Generation

"The continued narrative here given is my own recollection of reminiscences as obtained from time to time. I place it at the disposal of those who wish to make it a permanent record.

"The Fouses partook of the nature of their parents. They had a strong physique; were hale, hearty, and naturally industrious, and willing to earn their living by the sweat of the brow. They were frugal and economical; they dealt honestly; they were charitable and willing to help their neighbors in time of need; and their integrity has never been doubted. They loved character and a good name more than money, as shown by the lives they lived in the several communities. They esteemed each other as members of a large family, and were glad to meet and visit each other frequently, learning of each other's welfare, and trying to contribute to each other's happiness. They generally made useful citizens in their communities, and were willing to assist in supporting churches and missions in their neighborhood. They were particular to pay their honest obligations. Each one sought by integrity, industry and frugality to secure a good position of usefulness, and to procure a home for himself or herself, in which laudable amibitions all succeeded."

"Father and aunt also spoke of the marriages of the older children in grandfather's family: Catherine[3] [11], the third daughter, was the first to leave the parental roof of this pioneer family. On April 14, 1811, she married *John Philip Garner*, at the old Fouse homestead in Huntingdon County, Pennsylvania."

"April 3, 1828, father [17] Adam[3], married *Susanna*, daughter of *John Michael Garner, Jr.* They soon afterward took up housekeeping in the little stone spring house, a few rods west of Uncle Frederick's home. Here they resided until the fall of the following year. The early part of that year father purchased the interest of the heirs in the farm of Samuel Hoover, two miles south of where he was then residing. He made this purchase with the view of making it his permanent home. Grandmother told father at that time, that if they moved away, she and Margaret, nicknamed 'Peggy,' would go with them." (J. G. F.)

The next to leave the parental roof was the second daughter *Elizabeth*[3] [10]. She married *Abraham Miller*, also of Huntingdon County, Pennsylvania, on March 10, 1814. Soon after their marriage they emigrated to Ohio, and settled in the forest where they opened a farm in Plain Township, Stark County, and there resided during their lives. Their residence was six miles north of Canton.

"On June 21, 1814, the same year, Jacob[3] [12], the fourth child, married *Elizabeth Miller* at the Fouse homestead in Huntingdon County, Pennsylvania. The following year they also emigrated to Ohio, and settled on the west side of Congress Lake, Lake Township, Stark County, where they opened a farm and resided there during their lives, fourteen miles north of Canton.

"A few years later, John[3] [13], the fifth child, married *Christina Miller*, a sister of Elizabeth. They were married on March 12, 1817, and soon thereafter emigrated to Ohio. At first they lived nearly one year in the original log house, erected by Abraham Miller on the Miller homestead. During this time Mr. Fouse selected a quarter section of land, twelve miles north of Canton, in Lake Township, Stark County. He entered his claim, and letters of patent were granted him on October 8, 1818, for 160 acres. He then erected a small house on his claim and moved there the same fall, and commenced to improve the property. Mr. Fouse's career was short. He died in July 1825. They had four children, but the oldest, Nicholas, died in infancy. The mother left the farm after Mr. Fouse's death and moved down to her brother's, Abraham Miller, where they had lived the first year. Their farm and effects were appraised, and Abraham Miller was appointed guardian for the three children. The farm was rented, and out of the proceeds, the widow got her one-third, and the guardian the remainder for the benefit of the children. In 1848, on the fourth of May, Frederick, their son married *Elizabeth Gearty*, and shortly after that, went to farming on their old homestead. Priscilla died at age 16, and Savilla had married *Isaac Madlem*. The mother Christina, remained with her brother for a few years longer and then the remainder of her days she lived with her children, Savilla and Frederick.

"William Fouse[3] [14] married Susan, daughter of *Peter Bowers*, on August 6, 1818. After their marriage, they moved to the mountain tract, in the spring of 1819, of which we have already spoken, where he devoted his time and energy in reducing the forest and cultivating the soil, besides conducting a small country store for the accommodation of the farmers of the neighborhood. The younger brothers continued their labors on the old farm under the direction of grandfather, performing that which was necessary for the comfort of those dependent upon support at his hands until March 1823."

The father had passed the allotted span of life, being 75; and willingly quit his activities in the shop. He thus gave Frederick, Theobald and Adam a better chance to practice smithing under his supervision.

"July 4, 1821, *Frederick* married *Catherine Acker*, daughter of *Leonard Acker*. Soon after a house was erected on the eastern side of Clover Creek, on the homestead which later on became the farm house. Frederick continued working under grandfather's management until the spring of 1823, when he (Nicholas Fouse) sold his farming implements and live stock to Frederick and Theobald and had them farm on shares until 1825."

"March 25, 1823, *Theobald* married *Nancy*, daughter of *Christian Shontz*. They then started housekeeping in part of the old Fouse mansion house. It was the purpose to have these two brothers, Frederick and Theobald, farm jointly, and, if needs be, eventually divide the farm, which was done January 1, 1825. Under the new order of things Adam was thrown upon his own resources. We remember hearing him say (referring to the time that his brothers, Frederick and Theobald, took up farming) that his father told him he could not give him any land to make a start. That he was now free and at liberty to adopt any vocation that he might desire, though he was only 18 years of age. He continued as in the past to chop cordwood in the winter, unless very inclement and cold, and then he worked at the loom. In the summer he followed the carpenter trade which consisted mostly of hewing logs, as nearly all the buildings, both houses and barns, were simply plain log structures. Shingles, however, took the place of clap boards and thatched roofs. These were all hand made and required much labor. The two brothers, Frederick and Theobald, each farmed the land which they bought from their father January 1, 1825, until the fall of 1832, when Theobald was offered a farm by Thomas Jackson in Woodcock Valley, and joining that of his father-in-law Christian Shontz, containing 216 acres for $3000. He then talked the matter over with Frederick, who agreed to buy Theobald's part of the homestead farm, then Theobald bought the Jackson farm that fall and moved there in the spring of 1833. This gives the reason for Theobald moving to Woodcock Valley, Huntingdon County, Pennsylvania."

[9] **MARGARET**[3] **FOUSE**, daughter of [2] Nicholas[2] and Margaret (Brumbaugh) Fouse, was born October 12, 1786. Notwithstanding her

sickness and suffering, as heretofore detailed, and being a cripple all her life, she was a very useful woman in her community. She was the sewer and dressmaker not only for the family, but also for the community. She also did the knitting of the stockings, mittens, and gloves. She could not go to school, and her parents were her instructors. She was proficient in the German language, and it was a comfort to her to read the Holy Scriptures daily, and to have that Book of Books as a teacher and comforter all her days. She was always in her place in church, when she was well, and when the weather was not too inclement.

"Uncle Frederick, soon after grandmother's death (August 8, 1829), built two rooms to the north end of his house, where Aunt Margaret could live in comfort. He also kept a safe horse (named 'Nelly') for her to ride to church and elsewhere. She could not go alone however, someone had to go with her to help her on and off the horse, as well as open gates or let down bars. There were no buggies or carriages in that neighborhood in those early days. She was also a lover of prayer meeting, and was always present at the appointments unless the weather was too inclement. She always took an active part in the meetings. She was greatly gifted in prayer and her supplications to the Lord for mercy upon the people of this sinful world would touch every heart within hearing. To serve the Lord was her chief concern."

"Mention has been made of Aunt Margaret having moved to our house in 1854. She felt age creeping over her. Though she had a healthy heart and a strong constitution, she felt that she was getting frail because of her sufferings and age. She was nearing three score and ten years. She began to be much afflicted with rheumatism, and since Uncle Frederick's wife had died ten years prior, and had but one daughter (Elizabeth) at home, Aunt felt that since our parents were living and had three daughters at home, that if she took sick, there would be more help with us to wait on her. Aunt was very thoughtful through her life, and prepared for temporal as well as spiritual life; long years before her death she prepared her burial clothes, and when the hour of demise came all was ready. She many times spoke of being ready and willing to die whenever the summons came. In the spring of 1855, she became very much afflicted with a complication of diseases which were fast weakening her, and someone had to be with her all the time. Sister Elizabeth mostly attended to her wants and was her nurse. She had a bed in aunt's room and cared for her at night. Aunt's suffering in her last sickness did not last long. She breathed her last on May 9, 1855, aged 68 years, 6 months and 27 days.

ELIZABETH[3] (FOUSE) MILLER [10], AND CHRISTINA (MILLER) FOUSE [13].

Thus all her sufferings were over and she was laid to rest in the faith of her Savior, whom she loved and served all her days."

[10] **ELIZABETH[3] FOUSE**, daughter of [2] Nicholas[2] and Margaret (Brumbaugh) Fouse, was born August 11, 1788; March 10, 1814, she married *Abraham[2] Miller, Jr.*, born January 31, 1787; son of *Abraham[1]* and *Elizabeth (Clapper) Miller.* Soon after their marriage in Pennsylvania they moved to Ohio, settling on a farm purchased June 24, 1813, part of Southeast Quarter, Section 4, Plain Township 11, Range 8, six miles north of Canton, Stark County, Ohio, where they continued to reside during their lives. They were among the pioneer settlers of the state and were members of the Reformed Church at Cairo, Ohio (see Plate 5).

ABRAHAM MILLER, SR., father of *Abraham Miller, Jr.* [10] came from the province of Bavaria, Germany, about 1776. He landed at Baltimore, Maryland, but unfortunately the early records of that port of entry were not preserved. Soon after landing he went to the neighborhood of Funkstown, Frederick County (now Washington), Maryland. These were stirring times, and after considering the situation of the Revolutionary patriots he enlisted as a private in a company then recruiting near Funkstown. See *Records of Maryland Troops in the Continental Service during the War of American Revolution 1775-1783*,—"Capt. Henry Hardman's Return, made July 19, 1776. Passed by Henry Shryock, July 19, 1776; page 51, *Abraham Miller.*" "A List of Recruits belonging to the German Regiment Commanded by Lieut.-Col. Weltner, White Plains, September 5, 1778;" page 267, *Abraham Miller*, 9 months. The same reference, page 324, "A List of Substitutes Furnished by the Different Battalions after their being Classed in Order for the Draught, Frederick County,—Passed June 3, 1778 *Abraham Miller, Jr.*, 9 months, German Regiment." We thus have records of Revolutionary service apparently for both father and son at the same time, with terms of service coinciding.[a]

To serve as a soldier was nothing new to the patriarch, Abraham Miller, Sr., as from tradition we learn, he had served in the Seven Years War in the army of the German Kingdom before coming to this country, and, by having such experience at soldiering in the fatherland, he was an excellent soldier for this country. We have no record of the full number of engagements in which he participated, but we know that he served

[a] Rev. Abraham Miller [85], Kent, Ohio, was a member of Sons of American Revolution. He died April 24, 1911. Abraham Miller, Jr. [10] was born January 31, 1787, and the junior Revolutionary soldier may have belonged to another family.

with his company and regiment in the following battles: Stony Point, Brandywine, Germantown, Trenton, Monmouth, at the siege of Yorktown, and was with Washington's army at Valley Forge. He fought with credit to the close of the war, and then was honorably discharged. After their discharge, these soldiers returned to Funkstown, the place of their enlistment.

Soon after Abraham Miller, Sr., returned from the Revolutionary War, he married *Elizabeth Clapper* and engaged in farming. Pages 118-123, Maryland Census of 1790, for Washington County, Maryland, give Abraham Miller as having one male over 16, one under, and two females, which corresponds with his family record, as his oldest son Abraham, Jr., was born January 31, 1787. We do not find him making any purchase of land until October 27, 1796 (Book E, No. 1, Huntingdon County, Pennsylvania, page 428), 170 acres, for which he paid £200 to William Phillips. He also bought 50 acres from Phillip Hartman (Book G, No. 1, do., page 511) October 3, 1799. This was part of the tract for which warrant was granted to William Phillips, March 28, 1774, and patented to him September 25, 1791, all of record in Huntingdon County, Pennsylvania. The patent covered 220 acres. Abraham Miller secured the whole of it. The farm he purchased was four miles north of Grandfather Nicholas Fouse's [2] home on the same stream (Clover Creek). We find Mr. Miller sold a parcel of land from this tract to Adam Sorrick, on June 27, 1798, containing four acres. The consideration was £8, 17 shillings and 6 pence. This deed is recorded in Huntingdon County, Pennsylvania. Here we notice by the record that at that time Mr. Miller was a widower, as the deed has only his signature. The whole farm then laid in Huntingdon County, Pennsylvania, in the township of Woodberry, lying on both sides of Clover Creek. It is one of the best farms in Morrison's Cove, and has a splendid spring of water on it. The Clover Creek public road, leading to Williamsburg, passes near the spring and the buildings, which are three miles south from said town, and one mile north from the Union Church and graveyard, where Mrs. Abraham Miller, and Grandfather and Grandmother Fouse are buried. We find that this Union Church is where the Millers and Fouses worshipped at that time. Here we conclude that Grandfather Miller and Grandfather Fouse knew each other for many years. While, Mr. Miller came to this country first, they no doubt kept up a correspondence between them. As already stated, when Mr. Miller landed at Baltimore, Maryland, he speedily went to Funkstown, etc. Grandfather Fouse apparently followed him. After the close of the Revolutionary War they must have met each other, and renewed their acquaintance. They were both married in the neighborhood of Funkstown, Maryland. Mr. Miller soon after his marriage must have taken up the occupation of farming and remained in the state of Maryland until 1795—see land purchased. Grandfather Fouse had come to Pennsylvania in 1789, and Abraham Miller in 1796, and then purchased a home from William Phillips, four miles from the Fouse home and adjacent to where Grandfather Fouse and Grandfather Miller as elders were charter members and trustees in buying a lot of land (82 perches) to establish a German Reformed and Lutheran Union Church (Book P, No. 1, page 561). Christian Acker and Adam Sorrick were the Lutheran trustees. The church was then built in 1810 and was the first church in the Cove of these denominations. Mr. Miller was also one of the pillars of this congregation and church while in the community. His residence was within one mile of the church. They had the same faith and worshipped at the same church for many years. Abraham [10] and Elizabeth Miller [12], son and daughter of the patriarch, married into the Fouse family and were children of the patriarch's first wife, Elizabeth (Clapper) Miller who died in 1796. Christina, who later married John Fouse [13], was a daughter of his second wife, and was a noble and kind hearted woman, as well as the other children in the patriarch's family.

Two years later Mr. Miller married for his second wife, *Sibilla Lower* of the neighborhood where he then lived. She also was noble hearted and true, and was a good wife to him and a kind mother to his children. She was frugal and helped him in every way she could, and reared their children in the nurture and admonition of the Lord. Mr. Abraham Miller and his wife, Sibilla, sold the remainder of their farm, containing 216 acres, to Michael Bosler, on the eighteenth day of April, 1812, for a consideration of five thousand, eight hundred and fifty ($5850) dollars. We notice here that United States money came into use in payment of this tract. This deed was also recorded in Huntingdon County, Pennsylvania, April 19, 1814. In 1846 Blair County, was established in Pennsylvania, and all is now in that county. We know not whether Grandfather Miller left the farm immediately after its sale, but it appears he remained in that neighborhood nearly two years after the sale, as he and his son Abraham, made several trips to Ohio, where they selected and purchased a farm June 24, 1813, containing 168.6 acres, in the virgin forest, from Abraham Croft. The consideration was $1344.48, which is a part of the Southeast Quarter, Section 4, Plain Township 11, Range 8, six miles north of Canton.

They prepared to emigrate the next spring to their new farm. His son Abraham, then married Elizabeth Fouse [10], March 10, 1814. A few days later the father and son and their wives, with the family, started on their trip to Ohio. For their transportation they used a Conestoga wagon, and a good team of horses. After they landed in Ohio for a time they had no shelter, as their property was unimproved. They camped under a large maple tree. For shelter from the sun, they tied the tops of bushes and corner of sheets stretched from one bush to another for a covering under which to cook and eat. At night for refuge from large brown wolves, and other wild animals, they slept in their covered wagon until a house could be logged up. They soon erected a small log house, put on a roof of clap boards; and when chunked and daubed, and dried, it was ready for use, and was occupied by them for some years, until a better one could be built. This house was built near a good spring, which furnished water for all purposes. The place where the original house stood is marked, but the house is razed. These grandparents and their children were truly amongst the pioneer settlers of that part of the state. The farm mostly had large and heavy timber on it, but there was no market for the same. The land was of the best quality. At first it was hard for them to eke out a living. There were no railroads in those days, all transportation had to be done by teaming or hauling. Goods for the supply of merchants at Canton had to be hauled by teams from Pittsburgh, a distance of one hundred miles. Through this hauling farmers could earn a little extra money. When in need of salt and sole leather, which they were obliged to have, they would take a load of wheat to Cleveland, a distance of fifty miles, and often were thankful when the wheat would sell for enough money, wherewith to buy a barrel of salt and a side of sole leather, and pay the expenses. Those pioneer days gave the husbandmen and their families many hardships which later generations do not comprehend. At first many tears were shed by the women, until they became accustomed to the country and climate. As there were then many swamps in Ohio, early settlers suffered much from fever and ague, which increased their hardships. In those days all were producers and but few consumers, since there were no manufacturing establishments nearer than Cleveland and Pittsburgh, and even there the population was small, and the produce markets overstocked. Land was then cheap and persons living in towns, had large lots and raised for themselves nearly all they needed. Money was very scarce and hard to earn, so every person was obliged to economize. But the Millers had considered all this and

Anno 1749 den [illegible] May ist der
Abraham Müller auf diese
Jammer volle Welt gebohren

Susanna Müllerin ist gebohren
6 Augus 1784

Anno 1785 den 15 August ist [illegible]
Tochter Catharina Müllerin auf diese
Jammer volle Welt gebohren
worden

Abraham Müller [illegible]
[illegible] Anno Domini Christi
[illegible]
[illegible] 1785

BIBLE RECORD OF ABRAHAM MILLER BORN MAY 1749

went energetically to work to open the new country, as they believed they could better their situation. They were men of intelligence and determination, and through their integrity, industry and frugality, they and their descendants usually made their mark. They were, in general, men of good habits and of high moral character, and were much esteemed in their communities. The children of the Patriarch Abraham Miller were noble hearted, naturally industrious and charitable. They were natural mechanics, some were inventors, and all carried business to successful issues.

TRANSLATION OF PLATE 6 (SEE ALSO PLATE 7)

Abraham Miller was born May, 1749.

Susana Miller is born June 1784.

Year 1785 the 15th August is my daughter Catherina born.

Abraham Miller bought this book in the year of our Lord 1785.

Another record, not shown, reads: "Henry Miller son of Abraham Miller was married to Magdalena Weaver, daughter of Valentine Weaver Dec. 18, 1816."

Children of ABRAHAM MILLER (born May, 1749, died August, 19, 1824) *and* ELIZABETH CLAPPER MILLER:[a]

Susanna, *b* June 5, 1784; *d* July 28, 1856; *m Abraham Lantzer (Lancer).*

Catharina, *b* August 15, 1785; *d* November 28, 1862; *m Philip Henney.*

John, *b* 1786; *d* March 18, 1875; *m* (1) *Elizabeth York; m* (2) *Elizabeth Tawney Aultman.*

Abraham, *b* January 31, 1787; *d* May 4, 1852; *m Elizabeth Fouse* [10].

Elizabeth, *b* May 31, 1789; *d* April 8, 1866; *m* Jacob Fouse [12].

Mary, *b* December, 1790; *d* December 15, 1834; *m Christopher Henney* (brother of Philip Henney).

Henry, *m Magdalena Weaver.*

Lewis, *b* March 17, 1794; *d* October 12, 1864; *m Elizabeth Henney* (—— *Sorrick* (?) or —— *Weaver* (?) also reported).

Daughter by (2) *Sibilla Lower.*

Christina, *b* March 17, 1801; *d* September 18, 1880; *m John Fouse* [13].

[a] Data furnished by William M. Miller, New Berlin, Ohio; Miss Rose L. Miller, Canal Fulton, Ohio; and Adam Lewis Miller, Easton, Missouri.

LAST WILL AND TESTAMENT OF ABRAHAM MILLER

"In the name of God, Amen, I, Abraham Miller of Plain township in the County of Stark and State of Ohio, being in good health of body and of sound and disposing mind and memory (praised be God for the same) and being desirous to settle my worldly affairs whilst I have strength and capacity so to do—do make and publish this my last will and testament, hereby revoking and making void all wills by me at anytime heretofore made;

"And first and principally I commit my soul into the hands of Almighty God who gave it and my body to the earth to be buried in a decent manner at the discretion of my Executors hereinafter mentioned; and as to such wordly Estate wherewith it has pleased God to intrust me in life, I dispose of the same as follows:

"I will that all my just debts as shall be by me owing at my death, together with my funeral expenses and all charges touching the proving of or otherwise concerning this my will, shall in the first place out of my personal Estate and effects be fully paid and satisfied. I give and bequeath unto my son *Abraham Miller* the plantation on which he now dwells, being the South East quarter of Section four, township eleven and Range eight, subject however to the payment of one hundred and fifty dollars, which he shall pay to my Executors hereinafter mentioned, in the following manner, fifty dollars thereof to be paid three years after my decease and then fifty dollars annually until the whole is paid,—and also subject to the maintainance of his mother as is herein after mentioned, and on the payment as aforesaid and on the faithful maintainance of his mother he shall hold the said quarter Section to him and heirs and assigns forever; I also give and bequeath unto him one horse and mare, one wagon, plow, harrow, the iron of the old carriage wheels,— and all the horse gears belonging to me, my two hackles, a large splitting axe, two iron wedges, a frow, a drawing knife, all which is now in his possession, as also my windmill,—I also give and bequeath unto my three sons *John Miller*, *Henry Miller* and *Lewis Miller* all the fractional Section of land which I hold, being Section fifteen in the first township and tenth range—containing four hundred and seventy seven acres and Sixty five hundredths to be divided as they have already agreed between them, subject also to the payment to my Executors the respective sums of One hundred and fifty dollars each, to be paid as follows—three years after my decease, each of them shall pay fifty dollars and then fifty dollars annually until

BIBLE OF ABRAHAM MILLER (2 VEIWS); AND ELIAS MILLER (BORN DECEMBER 14, 1836) AND JOSEPH MILLER (BORN DECEMBER 12, 1822).

the whole shall be paid, and on the payment of the whole they shall hold the same to them, their heirs and assigns forever,—I also give to my son *Henry* the bay horse which he took from home—and unto my son *Lewis* I give the gray mare which he took from home and the wagon and all other articles which I gave them from home they shall hold in partnership—I give unto my son *John* the sum of fifty dollars which is to be considered in lieu of the horse and other articles which I have given unto my other sons which said fifty dollars shall be allowed him in the first payment which shall come due on his land.

I give unto my daughter *Susanna* who is intermarried with *Abraham Lancer* the South West quarter of Section number four in the Eleventh township and Eighth range, which she shall have and hold to herself, her heirs and assigns forever. Although it is my wish and desire that the said Lancer do the shoemaking for myself and wife during our natural life, if we find him the leather.

"I give and bequeath unto my four daughters viz: *Catherine* who is intermarried with *Philip Henney*, *Elizabeth*, who is intermarried with *Jacob Fouse* [12], *Mary* who is intermarried with *Christopher Henny*, and *Christina* who is intermarried with *John Fouse* [13]—each of them four hundred dollars which shall be paid them by my Executors out of my estate so soon as it can be collected, which shall be paid equally, that is to say every dollar collected at one time, shall be equally divided between them, until each of them shall have received the sum of four hundred dollars.

"It is my will and desire that my loving wife *Sibilla* shall have, during her natural life, the dwelling house in which I now dwell, the springhouse, stable, garden and all other improvements and the inclosed land from my southerly fence to run northward to the crossing of the second run or rivulet and contain about three acres,—It is also my will that after my decease my son Abraham give unto my loving wife her maintainance in the following manner, to wit, to give her annually fifteen bushels of good wheat, five bushels of rye, twenty bushels of corn, ten bushels of oats, twenty five pounds of good scutched flax, ten bushels of potatoes, one hundred pounds of good pork, fifty pounds of good beef, twenty pounds of sugar,—hay for one cow, to be delivered on her stable, all the above articles to be delivered at her house,—he is also to furnish her with a good sufficiency of firewood ready cut to be laid on the fire or in the stove, and to be delivered at her house and to be continued so to do during her natural life.

"It is also my will that three hundred dollars of money be left outstanding during her life and that my Executors pay her annually the interest thereof and if the said interest is not sufficient for her, the Executors shall be bound to collect and pay her of the principal;—I also give and bequeath unto her all my household goods and moveable effects of which I may be possessed at my decease, all my cattle, sheep and hogs and the live stock belonging to me,—I also give her a small debt which is now owing to me by *John Fouse* [13],—my son *Abraham* has my stock of bees on the shares—now it is my will that he give her annually the third of the honey and wax during her life—I have two large Bibles and two other large books which it is my will that she have them during her life and at her decease they are to revert to my children, and all other (of) my household and kitchen furniture, beds and bedding, which shall be left at the decease and is not otherwise disposed of, shall be equally divided among her children or their legal representatives by my Executors and the house and land shall thenceforth belong to my son Abraham, his heirs or assigns.

"Further it is my will, that after all and singular the legacies and bequeaths before mentioned are distributed and divided so as aforesaid and anything should remain that, in that case such residue shall be equally divided among all my sons and daughters aforesaid or their lawful heirs.

"And lastly, I appoint my son *Abraham* and *John Fouse* my Executors of this my last will and testament, hereby revoking all wills, legacies and bequeaths by me heretofore made, allowing this and no other to be my last will and testament. In witness whereof—I the said Abraham Miller have to this will, set my hand and seal, dated the sixteenth day of August in the year of our Lord, Eighteen hundred and twenty three.

ABRAHAM MILLER (Seal).

Signed, sealed, published and declared by the said Testator as his last Will and Testament in the presence of us who in his presence and at his request have subscribed as witnesses.

JOHN KRYDER
ABRAHAM HALM

Stark County, Ohio, S. S.

"I, John Myers, Clerk of the Court of Common Pleas of Stark County, Ohio, do hereby certify that the foregoing is a true copy from the last will and testament of Abraham Miller deceased as the same remaining on file in the office of said Court, and which was duly proved and ordered to be recorded in said Court on the second day of November A. D. 1824.

[Seal] JOHN MYERS, clk. pro. Tempore.
Common pleas, Stark Co., Ohio."

Children of Elizabeth (Fouse) and Abraham Miller Jr. (10):

[19] + Margaret[4], *b* May 13, 1815; *d* September 13, 1834. (No children.)
[20] + John[4], *b* April 4, 1817; *d* April 4, 1839; *m Catharine Clay.*
[21] + Jonathan[4], *b* September 15, 1818; *d* October 21, 1875; *m Lydia Cassler.*
[22] + Catharine[4], *b* August 19, 1820; *d* March 30, 1863; *m Jacob H. Bair.*
[23] + Elizabeth[4], *b* March 22, 1822; *d* May 2, 1890; *m William Cassler.*
[24] + Solomon[4], *b* September 21, 1823; *d* May 21, 1890; *m* (1) *Eliza Bishop*; *m* (2) *Mrs. Hettie A. Gibble.*
[25] + Susannah[4], *b* October 10, 1825; *d* November 10, 1839.
[26] + Christena[4], *b* July 13, 1827; *m Henry Snyder.*
[27] + Mary Ann[4], *b* March 23, 1830; *d* April 17, 1876; *m Samuel J. Miller.*
[28] + Priscilla[4], *b* May 30, 1832; *m William L. Miller.*

[11] **CATHARINE[3] FOUSE**, daughter of [2] Nicholas[2] and Margaret (Brumbaugh) Fouse, was born September 5, 1790. April 14, 1811, at the Fouse homestead in Huntingdon County, Pennsylvania, she married *John Philip Garner* of Woodcock Valley, same county, born September 1, 1790; son of *John Michael* and *Catharine (Seiss) Garner*, and brother of John Matthew Garner, who married Mary Brumbaugh ([E 18] *Brumbach Families*, pages 424-430, in which is a summary of "The Garner Family"). Soon after their marriage they moved into Woodcock Valley, same county, upon a farm which her husband bought from his brother John Michael Garner for $494.50, being about one mile north of where the village of Marklesburg (James Creek Post Office) was later established. Here they prospered and there seemed to be a bright future before them; but, alas, the storm of life overtook them on Christmas eve, 1824, when their buildings were destroyed by fire. Mr. Garner was a powerful worker, being a model of physical strength and endurance, as well as a good manager; but the fright, together with the loss of property, caused him to loose his natural energy and manliness of purpose. He withdrew from business interests, and Mrs. Garner naturally and modestly assumed the control and management of the family and farm. She admirably succeeded in

training the children to correct habits of life. Mr. Garner did many chores on the premises, and for a number of years made his own shoes. After the infirmities of age came upon the parents, all their children being married, they disposed of the homestead to their son-in-law John Acker [30], in 1868, and made their home with their son William [38] in Morrison's Cove. When they vacated the farm it was well equipped with buildings. The red stone dwelling house, frame barn, wagon shed, weave house, wash house, two story stone spring house, wood house, blacksmith shop, pig pen and cave constituted the improvements at the eastern end of the farm; and at the central part of the farm stood the red house erected in 1854. The frame barn was built in 1848, the sons Frederick [34] and Adam [35] did the carpenter work.

These aged parents were not permitted to remain very long at their latest home. Grim death took Mrs. Garner in December 1870, aged 80 years, and Mr. Garner followed her to the Great Beyond in July of the next year, aged 81 years. They were both laid to rest in the old church grave-yard on the Fouse premises already named. They were members of the German Reformed Church, and lived and died in that faith.

John Philip Garner, above mentioned, was a son of John Michael Garner, Sr., who was born at Wurtemberg, Germany, in 1728. He came to America with his parents at the age of 10 years, according to tradition. The parents must have emigrated to America in 1739 and landed at Baltimore, Maryland, in the fall of the same year, and it took them six months to cross the ocean. In those early days there were no records kept at Baltimore of the date of landing, name of the ship, nor of the captain, nor the number of passengers carried; at least none have been preserved.

After the landing at Baltimore, they emigrated to Sharpsburg, then Frederick County, Maryland, and settled in that neighborhood, engaging in farming. We have not yet been able to learn the given names of the parents of John Michael Garner, Sr.

John Michael Garner, Sr., resided in the neighborhood of Sharpsburg Maryland, where he met Catharine Seiss, a native of Switzerland, and the acquaintance naturally ripened into marriage September 24, 1769. Soon after their marriage they went to housekeeping, and started at farming in the Maryland community. We learn by tradition that their home was near Antietam Creek, and close to where the Battle of Antietam was fought during the Civil War in 1862. Mr. Garner followed farming until the latter part of the War of the American Revolution, when the patriots were much in need of more men. He then felt it a duty to cast his lot with the patriots and accordingly enlisted in a company then recruiting near Funkstown, Maryland, by Capt. Henry Hardman. This company was to replenish a regiment of volunteer infantry recruited some time previous at Hagerstown, Maryland. Mr. Garner enlisted as a private, with other German citizens and patriots, to fight for liberty. They served with their company and regiment, and participated in several engagements and fought with distinction to the close of the war. After the victory was won and freedom proclaimed, they were honorably discharged and mustered out. After Mr. Garner's return home, he again continued to farm until the fall of 1785. He concluded he could better his condition by leaving Maryland, and by going to the wilds of Huntingdon County, Pennsylvania, where he could buy land much cheaper. Accordingly, they started that fall by the old Chambersburg and Bedford Road, now Turnpike, as far as Bloody Run, now Everett, where they turned north following Tussey's Mountain on the east side until they reached Hopewell Township (now Penn), Huntingdon County, Pennsylvania, in Woodcock Valley, where they settled on a farm one and one-fourth miles north of where the village of Marklesburg and James Creek Post Office afterward were situated. Later he purchased the pre-emption and improvement right to the tract of land on which they lived; pre-empted by Robert Whitner, containing 279 acres and 59 perches and allowances. On the twentieth of June, 1794, he paid to John Penn, Sr., and John Penn, Jr., £112 and 5 shillings for the deed of patent for this tract of land which was recorded August 19, 1794, in the County of Huntingdon, Pennsylvania, in Deed Book "D", page 248, in the name of "Michael Galding" in the place of John Michael Garner.

On this property they labored and reared their family of seven children, five sons and two daughters. The town of Huntingdon was their principal market, twelve miles distant, where everything they wished to market had to be hauled by teams. It was their principal place of transacting business. They improved and enjoyed this homestead as a home to the times of their death. Their remains rest in what is now known as "The Frank Graveyard," about one and one-fourth miles north of the village of Marklesburg, Pennsylvania, on the public road leading to Huntingdon, Pennsylvania.

George Garner died March 18, 1911, aged 89 years, 4 months and 22 days, and rests in the Lutheran Cemetary, near the village of Marklesburg, Huntingdon County, Pennsylvania. The farm is occupied by his son Winfield Scott Garner [292]. Many of the descendants continue to live in that community, while the majority of them are widely scattered over the United States. The Garner, Brumbaugh and Fouse connections are of much interest to many of the relatives. While the marriages appear much intermingled, yet there is not a single couple in consanguinity, or closely allied blood.

John Michael Garner, Sr., and *Catharine (Seiss) Garner*, had five sons and two daughters; all married and had families; viz., *John Garner*, the oldest son, married *Mary Fread* about 1796. They were blessed with nine children; Catherine, John, Michael, Matthew, Jacob, Philip, Susan, Mary and Henry Garner. The second son, *John Michael, Jr.*, on the sixteenth day of December, 1800, married *Catherine Acker*. They had fourteen children: Elizabeth, Mary, Susanna, (who married Adam[3] Fouse [17], April 3, 1828), Catherine, Barbara, Margaret, Magdalene, George, John, Michael, Philip (and a twin not named), Henry and Jacob Garner. *John Matthew Garner*, third child, on August 12, 1810, married *Mary Brumbaugh* (a sister to Grandmother Fouse). They had six children: Catherine, Susan, Elizabeth, John, George and Samuel Brumbaugh Garner. *Susan Garner*, fourth child, married *Daniel Stouffer*. They had nine children: Elizabeth, Catherine, Jonathan, Martha, Mary, Daniel, Nancy, Jacob and Frances Garner. *Anna Mary Garner*, fifth child, married *Jacob Grubb*, and they had ten children: Elizabeth, Abraham, Andrew, Catherine, Susan, Mary, Jacob, Samuel and John, (twins) and Sarah Garner. *George Garner*, the sixth child, married *Catherine Smith*, and had seven children: Elizabeth, Henry S., Hannah, Solomon, David S., Catherine and Andrew Garner. *John Philip Garner*, the seventh child, on April 14, 1811, married *Catharine[3] Fouse* [11] (third daughter of Nicholas[2] [2] and Margaret Brumbaugh Fouse). They had twelve children: Jonathan, Elizabeth, Margaret, Sarah Daniel, Frederick, Adam, Benjamin, Philip, William, Michael F. and Catherine Garner. John Michael Garner, had sixty-seven grandchildren.

The descendants of these families in general are upright, faithful and God-fearing people; and, as far as we know, were loyal to our government when the South rebelled, and when President Abraham Lincoln called for volunteers to put down the rebellion. About forty-two of these descendants volunteered, and bore arms in defense of their country. They were faithful and true soldiers, and did their duty. Some were left dead on the battlefields, some died in hospitals, some were captured and died in Southern prisons, while others had the privilege of returning to their homes to enjoy the freedom and liberty of this country for which they fought.

ELIZABETH (MILLER) FOUSE [12]

Children (12), surname Garner:

[29] Jonathan[4], *b* February 20, 1812; *d. y.*
[30] + Elizabeth[4], *b* November 19, 1814; *d* January 21, 1874; *m John Acker.*
[31] + Margaret[4], *b* August 17, 1815; *d* March 14, 1885; *m Jacob C. Hoover.*
[32] + Sarah[4], *b* September 28, 1817; *d* October 1, 1911; *m Henry Peightel.*
[33] + Daniel[4], *b* November 13, 1819; *d* 1899; *m* (1) *Margaret Aupperley*; *m* (2) *Elizabeth Sorrick.*
[34] + Frederick[4], *b* March 7, 1822; *d* September 1907; *m* (1) *Margaret Sorrick*; *m* (2) *Fanny Shiffler.*
[35] + Adam[4], *b* March 17, 1824; *d* March, 1851; *m Catharine Summers.*
[36] + Benjamin[4], *b* May 11, 1826; *d* —— —, 1906; *m Catharine Sorrick.*
[37] + Philip[4], *b* September 1, 1828; *d* November 11, 1896; *m Susan Acker.*
[38] + William[4], *b* December 15, 1831; *m Eve Sorrick.*
[39] + Michael F.[4], *b* August 3, 1833; *d* March 4, 1900; *m* (1) *Elizabeth S. Showalter; m* (2) *Alice Fenstermaker.*
[40] + Catharine[4], *b* May 1, 1835; *m Abraham Myers.*

[12] **JACOB[3] FOUSE**, son of [2] Nicholas[2] and Margaret (Brumbaugh) Fouse, was born November 7, 1792. June 21, 1814 he married *Elizabeth Miller* in Huntingdon County, Pennsylvania, born May 31, 1789; daughter of *Abraham* and *Elizabeth (Clapper) Miller.* Soon after their marriage they moved to Ohio, and settled on the west side of Congress Lake, part of Southwest Quarter, Section 3, Lake Township 12, Range 8, Stark County, fourteen miles north of Canton. They were pioneers, cleared a farm in the forest, and lived there throughout their lives. Both parents were members of the Reformed Church at Uniontown, Ohio. Jacob died May 2, 1845, and Elizabeth died April 8, 1866 (Plate 8).

Children (5):

[41] + Mary[4], *b* May 7, 1816; *d* May 11, 1897; *m Jacob Heimbaugh.*
[42] + Margaret[4], *b* August 4, 1818; *d* September 16, 1848; *m Michael Heimbaugh.*
[43] + Abraham[4], *b* April 6, 1820; *m Mary Rhudy.*
[44] + Catharine[4], *b* November 7, 1823; *d* November 19, 1843; *m Jonathan Hoover.*
[45] + Christena[4], *b* October 12, 1827; *m Samuel Cramer.*

[13] **JOHN[3] FOUSE**, son of [2] Nicholas[2] and Margaret (Brumbaugh) Fouse, was born November 12, 1794. March 12, 1817, he married *Christina Miller*, a sister of [12] Jacob's[3] wife, *Elizabeth Miller*, and daughter of *Abraham* and (2) *Sibilla* (*Lowry*) *Miller*; born March 17, 1801. Soon after their marriage, they also emigrated to Ohio. They began housekeeping in the original log house, erected by her brother Abraham Miller on the Miller homestead, where they lived nearly one year. During this time, Mr. Fouse selected part of Southeast Quarter, Section 9, Lake Township 12, Range 8, Stark County, Ohio. He entered his claim, and a patent was granted to him on the eighth day of October, 1818, signed by President Monroe, and Josiah Meigs, Commissioner-General Land Office, for 160 acres (see Plate 9). He then erected a small log house and removed there that fall. They were among the pioneer settlers, and lived twelve miles north of Canton. They were members of the Reformed Church at Uniontown, Ohio (Plate 5).

Children (4):

[46] Nicholas[4], *b* January, 1818; *d.y.*
[47] Priscilla[4], *b* March, 1819; *d* 1827.
[48] + Savilla[4], *b* September, 1820; *m Isaac Madlem.*
[49] + Frederick[4], *b* March, 1825; *d* January 13, 1884; *m Elizabeth Gaerte.*

[14] **WILLIAM[3] FOUSE** [2] son of Nicholas Fouse[2] and Margaret (Brumbaugh) Fouse) was born May 29, 1797. August 6, 1818 he married (1) *Susan Bowers*,[a] born in Blair County, Pennsylvania, October 19, 1797; daughter of *Peter Bowers*. After marriage they moved to the "mountain tract," in the spring of 1819, and he there reduced the forest, cultivated the soil, and also kept a small general store for the farmers of the neighborhood. He resided on a farm five miles south of Williamsburg, Blair County Pennsylvania, and was the owner of several farms. He was prosperous, a man of ability, and was noted for his strength.

Susan died June 19, 1850.

March 7, 1852, William[3] married (2) *Susan Keely*, born February 20, 1798, and died June 27, 1858. August 28, 1859, he married (3) *Elizabeth Longenecker;* and the latter died January 6, 1878, aged 72 years (Plate 10).

[a] [See 37].

JAMES MONROE, President of the United States of America.

TO ALL TO WHOM THESE PRESENTS SHALL COME, GREETING:

Know ye, That *John Fouse Assignee of Isaac Johnson*

having deposited in the General Land Office a Certificate of the Register of the Land Office at *Steubenville*

whereby it appears that full payment has been made for *the South East quarter of Section*

Nine in township Twelve of range Eight

of the Lands directed to be sold at *Steubenville* by the Act of Congress, entitled "An Act providing for the sale of the Lands of the United States, in the Territory north west of the Ohio, and above the mouth of Kentucky River," and of the Acts amendatory of the same, There is granted, by the United States, unto the said *John Fouse the quarter* lot or section of Land above described: To have and to hold the said *quarter* lot or section of Land, with the Appurtenances unto the said *John Fouse* heirs and assigns forever.

IN TESTIMONY WHEREOF, *I have caused these Letters to be made* PATENT, *and the Seal of the* GENERAL LAND OFFICE *to be hereunto affixed.*

[Given under] my hand at the City of Washington, the *eighth* *day of* *October* *in the year of our Lord one thousand eight hundred and* *eighteen* *and of the Independence of the United States of America the forty* *third*

By the President, *James Monroe*

Recorded Volume *28*, Page *436* *Josiah Meigs*, Commissioner of the General Land Office.

LAND PATENT TO JOHN[3] FOUSE (13), OCTOBER 8, 1818.

WILLIAM[4] FOUSE [14].

(From daguerreotype loaned by Anna M. Garner [202].)

FREDERICK[1] FOUSE [15].

REV. THEOBALD[4] ("DEWALT") FOUSE, 1861 [16].

(From *Brumbach Families*, copyright 1913.)

Children by first marriage (2), surname Fouse:

[50] Frederick[4], *b* December 2, 1818; *d* August 28, 1825.
[51] + Theobald A.[4] ("Dewalt"), *b* May 9, 1820; *d* June 10, 1892. April 13, 1843 he *m* (1) *Margaret Duncan*, *b* September 18, 1819; *d* May 18, 1849. (4ch.) April 8, 1851, he *m* (2) *Elizabeth Duncan*, *b* October 18, 1825, sister of (1) *Margaret*; *d* August 19, 1852. March 5, 1854, he *m* (3) *Agnes Greaser*, *b* August 29, 1830.

[15] **FREDERICK[3] FOUSE**, son of [2] Nicholas[2] and Margaret (Brumbaugh) Fouse, was born April 27, 1800. He married *Catharine Acker* July 4, 1821, and she was born October 10, 1797; daughter of *Leonard Acker*. Frederick was a farmer and blacksmith, and prospered. In 1830 he built on his farm one of the first sawmills in that locality. In 1859 he also built a grist mill about 15 rods below the sawmill; both on Clover Creek, and both of decided convenience and benefit to the public.

Frederick and his wife lived on the old homestead farm throughout life. They and their family united with the Reformed Church (Plate 11).

Children (8):

[52] + Margaret[4], *b* September 22, 1822; *d* 1906; *m Jacob A. Nicodemus.*
[53] + Solomon B.[4], *b* May 30, 1824; *d* October, 1858; *m Matilda Enyeart.*
[54] + William Acker[4], *b* December 26, 1825; *d* July 28, 1912; *m Catharine Greaser.*
[55] + Catherine[4], *b* May 2, 1827; *d* January 6, 1875; *m Geo. Greaser.*
[56] + Elizabeth[4], *b* April 17, 1830; *m Albert G. Boyd.*
[57] + Jacob Acker[4], *b* January 17, 1832; *m* (1) *Sarah Rhodes*; *m* (2) *Margaret Shontz Grove.*
[58] John[4], *b* May 9, 1834; *d* 1835.
[59] Paul[4], *b* May 15, 1836; *d* 1870; no children.

[16] **THEOBALD[3] FOUSE**, son of [2] Nicholas[2] and Margaret (Brumbaugh) Fouse was born December 26, 1802, on the original Fouse homestead, elsewhere described and illustrated (Plate 4). He was strong, energetic and active in his discharge of the duties devolving upon a large family operating a farm in those early days.

Early in life he learned by precept and example the lessons of obedience, industry, helpfulness and uprightness. Moreover, the religious life of the home produced a moulding influence on his plastic soul. From childhood he was piously inclined. Consciousness of the higher and better life was awakened by the home life and teaching, together with the fervent preaching of the gospel. It is generally understood that at a very tender age he had ministerial proclivities.

Presumably he was about 14 years of age, when he was received into full communion with the Reformed Church through the rite of confirmation by the Rev. John Dietrich Aurandt. Under the earnest and efficient instruction of this servant of God, in addition to his being taught the catechism by his devout father, he was well rooted and grounded in the doctrines and duties of the Christian religion. He therefore seems to have had rather a clear conception of what was involved in becoming responsible for his own religious life. The knowledge of the sacred scriptures and of Christian duty which he thus acquired in his boyhood was of great practical benefit to him later in life. His school advantages were limited to about three months of instruction in the German schools, and possibly the same period was spent in the English schools. Not being satisfied with these school facilities, he assiduously applied himself to studies in his parental home. No doubt it was a good Providence that selected this particular locality as his habitation in early life. It is true he was not blessed with educational and social advantages, such as children in the city enjoy, but he had natural environments especially conducive to the development of true manhood. The material world, as a book, was open before him. Here he could drink in knowledge as he could not from the printed page, or in the recitation room. Here he had representations and demonstrations of God's wisdom and power. The parental home being at the base of Tussey Mountain afforded him the opportunity of witnessing enrapturing and inspiring phenomena, such as draperies of shifting clouds and fog which the great Creator hung around its summit, or the awe inspiring lightning and fury of the storms. Cultivated fields, tangled woods, the ceaselessly restless streams, the cheery songs of birds, and many other objects made their impress on the young, susceptible mind. All these combined facilities and natural advantages moulded a good Christian character.

When a young man he found remunerative employment throughout the year. General farm work was his occupation in summer, and cutting cord wood for charcoal furnaces in the vicinity, during the winter. His daily work did not so absorb his mental energies as to retard his growth in grace. Spiritual and intellectual progress was not only continued, but also stimulated and energized by taking an active part in Christian work.

His custom was to attend and participate in the midweek cottage prayer meetings, as well as those held on the Sabbath. Attendance at these services would occasionally necessitate miles of travel. He was not satisfied with reading a portion of the sacred scriptures at these meetings, but to the best of his ability he would explain God's word, and conclude with earnest exhortations to consecration to the service of the blessed Master. In this way his ability as a public speaker came to be recognized, and it was the heart-felt conviction of many people that Theobald should become a minister of the Gospel.

He was married March 25, 1823, to *Nancy Shontz*, born October 9, 1804; daughter of *Christian Shontz*, born in Lancaster County, Pennsylvania, and *Margaret (Huber) Shontz*. They commenced housekeeping on part of the old Fouse homestead. As before stated, Theobald[3] and Frederick[3] [15] jointly conducted the farm until it was divided in the purchase from their father January 1, 1825. These brothers continued in ownership of the several farms until the fall of 1832, when Frederick[4] bought his brother's portion of the original farm, and Theobald[4] purchased a farm of 216 acres in Woodcock Valley from Thomas Jackson for $3,000, adjoining the farm of his father-in-law, Christian Shontz. It was on the east side of Tussey Mountain, and in a direct line only about one and one-half miles from the place of his birth. In the spring of 1833 they moved to this farm which was situated on the east side of his father-in-law's farm, and one and a half miles south of his sister Catharine's home.

His marriage, although a memorable event in the history of his life, did not so modify his plans for the future as to cause him to turn a deaf ear to the earnest cry for his services in the holy ministry. It was convenient to enter upon housekeeping under his parental roof, where the studies so auspiciously begun were further prosecuted. Under the guidance of the Holy Spirit the desire to become a Gospel minister was intensified. Not only his friends, but also his pastor, the Rev. Mr. Aurandt, who furnished him with such suitable literature as was at his command, encouraged him to heed what seemed to be an irresistible call. Father Aurandt, however, entered into rest (April 24, 1831) before this earnest spiritual son was far enough advanced to become his immediate successor in the pastoral office. Here now was a shepherdless flock. Who should lead them into the green pastures and by the still waters of God's grace? To this beginner in theological studies this circumstance presented the call with tremendous force.

At this date it cannot be determined what the leading motive of this move into Woodcock Valley was, but it seemed providential. He entered an open door of usefulness in that community. He became an important factor, especially in the kingdom of the blessed Lord, as the subsequent pages will indicate. From the very beginning of his settlement in this locality his presence as a Christian worker was felt. Amidst the cares and labors on his farm he managed to devote some time to the preparation of work in the Lord's vineyard. Occasional trips were made on horseback to Alexandria, fifteen miles distant, to receive instruction from the Rev. Moses Kieffer, the young and efficient pastor of the Water Street charge. Being an apt and diligent student in both the college and the seminary from which he graduated, Mr. Kieffer was evidently qualified to map out a course of study as well as to impart knowledge.

Mr. Fouse through the valuable assistance thus obtained, could study to advantage, and he made progress in the studies assigned. Accordingly at the annual meeting of Mercersburg Classis at Bedford, Pennsylvania, in July, 1842, he made application for license to preach the Gospel. Having sustained a satisfactory examination by the committee his request for license was granted. It is said at the time the Rev. B. S. Schneck congratulated the Reverend Kieffer, saying, "Your pupil gave a good account of himself."

The ordination and installation was held the first Sunday in October, 1842, in the Old Stone Lutheran Church about two miles north of Mr. Fouse's house and near the site of the village of Marklesburg, laid out a few years later. The committee conducting this impressive service consisted of the following brethren: Reverends Moses Kieffer, Jacob Ziegler, and Christian Winebrenner.

This servant of the Lord had almost reached the fortieth milestone in life's journey before entering upon what he conceived to be his real mission in the world. Many a one, being for years handicapped as he was in the course of preparation, would have abandoned all aspirations in that direction, and permanently adopted a pursuit requiring less mental preparation. But was not this delay of a disciplinary character? It certainly helped to develop patience, determination, faith and a steadfastness of purpose. During this period of qualification in theological studies, he engaged in practical work, such as visiting and praying for the sick and conducting prayer meetings. Hence in some particulars he entered upon his ministerial work better equipped in actual experience than many who have both a collegiate and a seminary training. At the outset he could appear before an audience to officiate at pulpit and altar with remarkable composure. This preacher of the Gospel had the distinction of entering upon his pastoral duties without a change of residence. Immediately after his installation he took up the work incident to the ministerial office, with a deep sense of its magnitude, on the one hand, and of his inefficiency on the other. But there was a firm reliance on Divine strength and guidance. His pastoral field was composed of four preaching points: Russell's and Grove's in Woodcock Valley, on the east side of Tussey Mountain, and Beavertown and Woodberry, in Morrison's Cove, on the west side. To this charge he soon added four more regular congregations: Marklesburg, or his home congregation, the Ridge congregation in Woodcock Valley, and two in Morrison's Cove, viz.—Mt. Pleasant and Sharpsburg. Beside serving the above named congregations regularly he often preached at Entriken's school-house, where he gathered a number of members. Soon after his death a regular congregation was established in the latter place, and a church was built to care for the members of that section. He also preached at stated times at Little Illinois, and Paradise Furnace, and Trough Creek Valley. During his pastorate he built four new churches and rebuilt two.

Tussey's Mountain, in 1846, became the dividing line between Huntingdon and Blair Counties. Woodbury, however, is in Bedford County. In the performance of ministerial duties on the west side of the mountain it required considerable traveling. The routes were somewhat circuitous, and some of the roads were decidedly rough, particularly the mountain roads. He crossed this mountain regardless of weather conditions, not only during the day but also at nearly all hours of the night, not fearing the wild animals, such as bears, panthers and wild cats which roamed thereon.

In the early part of his ministry he traveled exclusively on horseback, but toward the close the buggy was oftener used, the road conditions being somewhat improved. In making the circuit from his home to the remote congregations it necessitated about forty miles of travel. In extent of territory it was a laborious field. Nine or ten horses and eight saddles were worn out in the service. At that period of the country's settlement, there was no concentration of population within his pastoral bounds. The people constituting the members of his flock, and adherents of the Reformed faith, were widely scattered. Some of the members were already organized into congregations and had their houses of worship. There was an urgent demand for his services here and there. A prominent feature of his early labors was from time to time to gather together the shepherdless at convenient places and preach the Gospel to them, and, where circumstances warranted it, effect an organization. His home community afforded such a strategic point. A number of families of the Reformed household resided within a reasonable distance of his residence. To them and to all others interested a cordial invitation was extended to assemble on his premises for divine service, which was held either in the dwelling-house or in the barn. These meetings proved to be the humble beginning of an energetic and influential congregation.

An encouraging number became charter members of the organization. Among them there were thrifty people. On the pastor's farm a frame church was erected in 1847, being situated on a little eminence near Marklesburg. The pastor cheerfully donated a plot of ground for this edifice, and for burial purposes, besides generously contributing from his own purse toward the enterprise. His family took pleasure in furnishing the fuel (wood for two ten plate stoves), and performed the duties of janitor without compensation to the end of his ministry.

As here, so elsewhere congregations were organized and churches erected, until the great majority of the members of this charge were provided with houses of worship within a reasonable distance from their homes. At first he held services in dwelling-houses, barns or school-houses, for the spiritual edification of families desiring his comforting and instructive ministrations. In this way a nucleus of a congregation would be formed and later on an organization effected. Thus he lengthened the cords and strengthened the stakes of Zion, and proved himself to be a great organizer.

Jacob's Church near Grafton was built some years before the congregation was organized. For a while a congregation existed in the Little Valley, Huntingdon County. After a very influential family withdrew from this locality and settled in another part of the charge, this congregation became extinct. This pastoral charge, known as the Woodcock Valley charge, in the latter years of the Reverend Fouse's ministry consisted of Beavertown, East Sharpsburg, and Millerstown congregations in Blair County; and Hickory Bottom, near Woodberry, in Bedford County on the west side of the Tussey Mountain; and Grove's, Marklesburg, Russell's and Jacob's congregations in Huntingdon County, on the east side of the mountain.

In 1864 he reported to Mercersburg Classis five congregations and 519 members. At this date the Russell congregation was not a part of the Woodcock Valley charge. It was detached from this charge and added to an adjoining charge to strengthen it. But this arrangement not proving satisfactory to the members of the Russell church they were restored to their former charge, as they preferred Reverend Fouse to minister to them in holy things.

By the time he submitted the last annual statistical report of his charge to Mercersburg Classis (1873) there were eight congregations and a few over 700 members.

In some communities it was the custom for two or three denominations to unite in the erection of a church, but Mr. Fouse managed to build houses of worship without joining with other congregations.

The only union church in the charge was Grove's, and that was built prior to his ministry. The Menonites had a small interest in it, and a few members, but soon quit preaching there, after Mr. Fouse became the regular pastor. Scores and scores of people have wondered how this servant of the Lord who had no education, such as is acquired at the higher institutions of learning, and who had not even a good common school training, could maintain his position as pastor of the same field for a period of thirty-one years, and so acceptably officiate in two languages; for ofttimes the occasion required him to speak both in English and German at the same service, the transition from the one to the other being made without a pause. The only satisfactory explanation is, it was the gift of God. He fully relied on the ever present God who gave him wisdom, knowledge, and language when preaching his sermons, as he never used any prepared notes, but spoke as the Holy Spirit guided him.

The redeeming grace of God was his standard theme. The person, life, work, death, resurrection and ascension of the Christ formed his central subject. Hence in the selection of texts he confined himself almost exclusively to the New Testament. His discourses were practical, and were delivered with great fervor. Frequently he became so earnest and solemn in his presentation of Gospel truths that many in the audience would be moved to tears.

In one respect this eminently useful servant of the Lord had a peculiar position to fill as he had a large circle of his own kith and kin to whom to minister. Amongst his members were his brothers and sisters, father-in-law and his family, nephews and nieces. But he had the profound respect, confidence, and hearty support of all. Being a relative seemed to be much in his favor. His brothers and sisters, together with their children, apparently sought opportunities to be helpful to their pastor in building up the Kingdom.

His throne of power was the pulpit. On account of the territorial largeness of his field, he could not devote time and energy to pastoral visitations, as is the case where there is a concentration of membership. Catechising the young, visiting the sick, and burying the dead made heavy demands on his time and strength. It occurred now and then that his services were required at two different places at the same hour to conduct funeral services. In circumstances such as these, arrangements were usually made for him to officiate at one of the funerals at the appointed hour, and in the case of the other the interment would be made at the time selected, and the funeral service would be held subsequently on a Lord's Day instead of the regular service.

On funeral occasions his services were often desired outside of his own communion. He was well acquainted with the people. He knew them in the common ways of life; and, being of a deep sympathetic nature, he was peculiarly fitted for comforting the distressed. How often he had to traverse the vast territory over which his charge extended in addition to his regular Sunday services, we have no way of determining.

During the fierce struggle for the preservation of the Union this loyal and patriotic citizen urged his members publicly as well as privately to stand by the government. He deprecated war, but at the same time he felt that the Gospel of Jesus Christ is the gospel of freedom and loyalty to the civil authorities. It implies liberty. To be true to the principles enunciated in the sacred Scriptures, he could not do otherwise than encourage his members to defend the Federal government. This involved the consecration of some noble sons on the altar of this country. As a father he divested himself of all feelings of selfishness in the matter of surrendering sons for military duty. No effort was made to spare his own sons. Seven of his sons and two sons-in-law enlisted. Four sons and one son-in-law were in one company. Every section of his charge was represented in the army. The enlistment of so many of his kindred and others under his pastoral oversight multiplied his cares, and gave him additional duties and responsibilities. Two daughters and daughters-in-law with small dependent children were unable properly to operate the farms while their husbands were in the army. They naturally depended on Father Fouse for counsel. His presence and advice in these homes were much desired.

During this civil strife he had many sad duties to perform. A brave son or a valiant husband would fall on the battle-field, another would pass away in a hospital, another in a Confederate prison. The consequence was homes of sadness, and broken hearts were in need of the Balm of Gilead. This venerable pastor's tender and sympathetic nature was often deeply affected. He officiated at a large number of funerals of soldiers, speaking pathetic words of comfort and consolation. On two similar occasions he had need of other ministers coming to his home, and his home church, to dispense the consolations of the Gospel to him, as two of his noble soldier sons had entered into rest, and in the midst of these sorrows his beloved and faithful companion was called from her sphere of helpfulness to her eternal reward. Her congenial and consoling presence in the home and vicinity was greatly missed.

In making appointments for evening service no hour was mentioned. It was simply "At early candle light." Candles were then used to illuminate the churches. In the early part of his ministry there were no railroads, hence there was no uniformity of time in some of the rural districts. The people were in the habit of going to evening service at dark.

Two communion services were held annually at each church, one in the spring, the other in the autumn. They were commonly called "Big meetings." These were seasons of spiritual refreshing, and were largely attended. At times late comers could not gain admittance to the churches.

Prayer-meetings were frequently held before the regular services. The pastor was not expected to be present. This season of prayer and song deepened the spirituality of the people and prepared them to be devout worshippers at the service conducted by the pastor. This feature of the laymen's work tangibly aided the pastor. The families residing in close proximity to the church gladly entertained the visiting members. The pastor's home church was especially well attended by members of the other congregations. The injunction of St. Paul, "Use hospitality," was practiced in his home. Their thirteen beds were frequently occupied. It made no difference whether there were few or many to be provided with bed and board, all were welcome. Not only on such occasions were people well cared for at this hospitable home, but also at any time duty or interest made it necessary for people to be there. Jew and Gentile, rich and poor, friends and strangers there found an open door.

He became, in a certain sense, a benefactor when he purchased about 900 acres of land in one tract, the greater portion of which was covered with timber. It was within two miles of his home farm. No one in the neighborhood seemed to be able or willing to handle this proposition when the land was for sale. After he became the purchaser, he had the tract cut into 6 or 7 lots which were disposed of to accommodate people who desired to provide a home for themselves.

Mr. Fouse was beloved by his ministerial brethren and could affiliate with brethren of other households of faith. He was careful to avoid everything which would wound the feelings of others. The long continuance of his pastoral relation is evidence of the strong hold he had on the affections of his people. He was one of them. They helped to develop him, and he in turn helped to develop them into strong Christian characters. He was the right man in the right place, hence his success.

It was his delight to have ministerial brethren of neighboring charges and professors of literary institutions assist him in his work, which indicates that he was of a generous disposition and wished to have his people enjoy the presence and services of other clergymen.

As he left neither diary nor journal of his labors, it is impossible to give an exact summary of the sermons preached or of the thousands of miles traveled from the time he began his labors until his decease.

The leading statistics are approximately as follows: His ministry extended over thirty-one years; he baptized 900 adults and children; he confirmed 800, besides the reception of members in other ways; funerals, 580; marriages, 350.

He was not largely remunerated for his services, but did the work for the sake of precious souls. His benevolent contributions some years were large, but the more he gave the more he seemed to have.

This remarkably successful worker in the vineyard, after a brief illness, fell asleep in Jesus on Friday, August 22, 1873, aged 70 years, 8 months and 27 days. On the following Lord's Day his lifeless form was conveyed from his late residence to the church erected on his own premises, and in which he often preached the Gospel of consolation to sorrowful hearts. Not half the people could enter the church. Each of the eight congregations of the charge was largely represented. The deceased was so widely and so favorably known that people regardless of denominational affiliations felt that they had lost a friend, and manifested their respect for and appreciation of the departed by attending the funeral services. The services were in charge of the neighboring ministers of Mercersburg Classis, all of whom participated therein. The principal discourse was delivered by the Rev. Dr. Moses Kieffer of the same Classis. He said he regarded the deceased as his first student in theology. He was chairman of the committee to ordain the departed brother and friend. In his discourse he took occasion to encourage the shepherdless flock to remain steadfast in the faith, and he assured them that the chief Shepherd would in due time, send them an under shepherd to lead, guard and feed them. A deep solemnity pervaded the audience throughout the services. The mortal remains were then gently laid to rest close by the church, in the hope of the general resurrection in the last day. The interest manifested at the grave was likewise deep and impressive.

Within a reasonable time, after this beloved pastor was called from the church militant to the church triumphant, the members of the charge erected a suitable monument to mark the resting place of his body, as a feeble expression of their love for him who so faithfully and zealously ministered to them.

Almost forty years have elapsed since Father Theobald Fouse departed to receive his crown. One by one his family of fifteen children have crossed the narrow stream dividing time from eternity, until only one is left.

As will be observed elsewhere in this volume, one of his sons and two of his grandsons entered the Gospel ministry. The aged, weary father rests from his labors, yet his works follow him. Others are in possession of some of the fruit of his labors, and many precious souls were made happier and better for his having lived and labored (Plate 12).

Children (15):

[60] + Adam[4], *b* March 6, 1824; *d* September 29, 1885; *m Elizabeth Jane Simonton.*

[61] + Christian[4], *b* February 27, 1825; *d* July 18, 1882; *m* (1) *Barbara Summers*; *m* (2) *Eliza (Frank) Shontz.*

[62] + John[4], *b* June 26, 1826; *d* August 24, 1891; *m Rebecca Summers.*

[63] + Margaret[4], *b* September 10, 1827; *d* November 15, 1844.

[64] + Elizabeth[4], *b* December 12, 1828; *d* June 7, 1893; *m Anthony Beaver Shultz.*

[65] + Benjamin[4], *b* March 5, 1830; *d* August 22, 1865; *m Anna Greaser.*

[66] + Catharine[4], *b* January 11, 1832; *m Samuel H. Grove.*

[67] William[4], *b* June 8, 1833; *d* July 31, 1834.

[68] + Mary[4], *b* March 10, 1835; *d* March 24, 1885; *m Benjamin Hoover.*

[69] David[4], *b* December 20, 1836; *d* June 26, 1838.

[70] Henry[4], *b* July 2, 1838; *d* August 3, 1840.

[71] + Dewalt Shontz[4], *b* November 15, 1840; *d* March 13, 1912; *m Sarah Ann Geissinger.*

[72] + Reuben Shontz[4], *b* July 17, 1844; *d* June 28, 1862; *unm.*

[73] + Frederick Shontz, *b* April 9, 1846; *d* October 1, 1902; *m Hattie E. Long.*

[74] + Samuel Shontz[4], *b* May 6, 1848; *m* (1) *Margaret Byers; m* (2) *Maria Stouffer.*

[17] **ADAM[3] FOUSE,** son of [2] Nicholas[2] and Margaret (Brumbaugh) Fouse, was born January 31, 1805. April 3, 1828, he married *Susanna Garner*, born December 20, 1804, daughter of *John Michael* and *Catharine (Acker) Garner*, and brother of *John Mathew Garner*, who married *Mary Brumbaugh* ([E 18] of *Brumbach Families*).

In the spring of 1829, Adam Fouse purchased the farm of the Samuel Hoover heirs, on the banks of Clover Creek, Huntingdon (now Blair) County, Pennsylvania, two miles south of the farm on which he was reared. "He and his mother were planning that after father and mother moved to their new home grandmother and Aunt Margaret [9] were soon to follow. But on August 8, 1829, by the sudden death of grandmother, all these plans were changed. Father moved the same fall, as had been planned, and took Jonathan with him, and gave him a home and cared for him. Uncle Frederick[3] [15] took Margaret[3] [9] to his home, thus the two brothers fulfilled their dying mother's request."

Adam[3] Fouse and his wife continued living on this farm to the time of their death. By occupation he was a farmer and carpenter, and did his own smithing. He was a man of much ability and a prosperous farmer. Mr. and Mrs. Fouse were consistent members of the Reformed Church, and reared their children in that faith (Plate 13).

CLOVER CREEK GERMAN REFORMED CHURCH

January 2, 1832, the Fouse children and some neighbors met and entered into an agreement to build a German Reformed Church on the old homestead in honor of Nicholas[2] Fouse [2] and Margaret[3] (Brumbaugh) Fouse. Frederick[3] [15] and Theobald[3] [16] agreed to give the ground for the church and graveyard site, besides paying their pledges—the agreement is reproduced, showing the signatures, terms, etc. (see Plates 14 and 15).

"The contract was then given and the church built the same year, 1832. Frederick Fouse then having a sawmill, agreed to furnish the lumber, which was sawed early in the spring and a dry kiln built to dry and season the lumber such as had to be dry. The church was built in the fall as shown in the contract elsewhere. But twenty years later this

ADAM[6] FOUSE (17), AND SUSANNA (GARNER) FOUSE.

(From *Brumbach Families*, copyright 1913.)

AGREEMENT FOR BUILDING THE CLOVER CREEK (PA.) GERMAN REFORMED CHURCH JANUARY 2, 1832. I.

(From *Brumbach Families*, copyright 1913.)

AGREEMENT FOR BUILDING THE CLOVER CREEK, PA., GERMAN REFORMED CHURCH, JANUARY 2, 1832. II.

(From *Brumbach Family*, copyright 1913.)

church became inadequate for the community, and was rebuilt (named Salem's Reformed Church) in 1853, when all the original Fouse promoters were yet living. The building committee for the new church to be built was Frederick[3] [15] and Adam[3] [17] Fouse. The new church was built of brick, 40 by 60 feet in size. The building committee then gave a contract to make the brick on the Fouse premises and sold the old church to D. L. Martin for a storeroom and dwelling at Fredericksburg, Pennsylvania, but excepted the floor, joist and pews to put in the basement of the new church. The building committee did its work well. They gave their energy and time, besides each paid $1,000 to help pay for the new church. This church was dedicated in October, 1853. The sermon was preached by the Rev. Henry Harbaugh, D.D. assisted by the pastor, Rev. Theobald[3] Fouse [16], and Rev. F. A. Rupley, D.D."

"This was a fine country church and large enough to accommodate the people of that growing community. But unfortunately some years later, the stone foundation under one corner gave way and caused a large crack at the north end of the church, which made it unsafe. A congregational meeting was called and the members voted to rebuild the church. The consistory then bought a lot adjoining the old lot but separated from it by the public road, and built the new church on it in 1884. This church was erected during the pastorate of Rev. J. David Miller. The dedication sermon was preached by Rev. I. N. Peightel, assisted by Rev. F. A. Rupley, D.D. and the pastor. This was the third church erected mostly by the Fouse kin inside of fifty-two years. Then all the Fouse promoters were dead except Adam[3] [17], who saw the new church completed, and worshipped there three years, when his days were ended. He rests in peace in the old churchyard, and lived to the ripe age of 82 years, 3 months and 4 days."

"The new church was also built of brick, two stories high, and is a fine structure for a country church. In the construction of this church they used most of the material from the old church such as was found to be in good condition, which saved them a lot of money. The building committee for this church was Adam Garner Fouse [82], Geo. B. Greaser [see No. 55], S. B. Isenberg and John M. Rhodes. In this congregation and six others, comprising the Woodcock Valley charge, Uncle Theobald Fouse, preached from 1843 to 1873; or from his installation until his death, August 23, 1873, aged 70 years, 6 months and 27 days."

"The children in father's family were all instructed in the Heidelberg catechism and confirmed by Uncle Theobald Fouse [16] during his ministry.

Father was a consistent member of this congregation and was elected an elder at its organization, and held that office until his death, May 5, 1887, the last survivor of this pioneer family to be called to rest. He served as elder in this congregation fifty-five years, and took a great interest in this church and was one among its most cheerful and liberal givers. He was also much interested in home and foreign mission work, and gave assistance to both. We never knew father to be away from church service unless he was away from home, or on account of sickness. He was the leader at prayer meetings (after uncle Theobald moved to Woodcock Valley). He was also Sunday school superintendent for many years. He reared his children in the nurture and admonition of the Lord. He required all his children to attend church, prayer meeting, and also Sunday school, while under the parental roof. He never omitted to say grace before meals. He always required the Bible to be read by the children, and had family worship in the evening before retiring. We shall always respect our parents for such Christian training."

"While father could read fairly well in the English language, his prayers were always in German. He was a great lover of his mother tongue. He was kind and indulgent to his children, and was kind and charitable to the helpless and poor. He always took great pleasure in visiting the sick, praying with them, and speaking words of cheer and comfort to them, as well as showing his sympathy."

"Nicholas[3] Fouse [2] and his wife Margaret rest in the lot purchased by the former in 1809. Four of our uncles and aunts are laid to rest in the old churchyard on the Fouse premises, now in Blair County, viz:—Margaret[3] [9], Catharine[3] [11], William[3] [14], and Frederick[3] [15]; Father is also buried there; Theobald[3] [16], and Jonathan [18] in the Reformed Churchyard near Marklesburg, Huntingdon County, Pennsylvania; Jacob[3] [12] and John[3] [13] in the Union Churchyard, Uniontown, Stark County, Ohio; and Elizabeth[3] [10] in the Union Churchyard (Snyder's) near Cairo, Stark County, Ohio.

In most cases husbands and their wives are laid side by side. All graves are marked with marble monuments or tombstones, where they may be seen by future generations." (J. G. F.)

Susanna (Garner) Fouse died April 6, 1870, aged 65 years, 3 months, 16 days (Plate 13).

Children (10):

[75] + David[4], *b* April 1, 1830; *d* March 1, 1909; *m Margaret Ann Summers.*
[76] + Margaret[4], *b* May 28, 1831; *d* September 12, 1902; *m George Nicodemus.*
[77] + Elizabeth[4], *b* October 12, 1832; *m George Greaser.*
[78] Daniel[4], *b* February 1, 1834; *d* ——, 1838.
[79] + Barbara[4], *b* November 11, 1835; *m John McGraw Rhodes.*
[80] + John Garner[4], *b* June 6, 1837; *m Mary Ellen Shoemaker.*
[81] + Sarah Ann[4], *b* August 22, 1840; *m Benjamin Franklin Hoover.*
[82] + Adam Garner[4], *b* December 13, 1842; *m* (1) *Sarah Frank; m* (2) *Eloise (Reese) Guthrie.*
[83] + Henry Smith[4], *b* August 25, 1845; *m Mary Jane Aurandt.*
[84] + Levi Garner[4], *b* October 21, 1850; *m Mary Bell Hause.*

[18] **JONATHAN[3] FOUSE**, son of [2] Nicholas[2] and Margaret (Brumbaugh) Fouse, was born July 11, 1808. A severe attack of brain fever weakened him mentally, and he could not count or read. Otherwise physically healthy he grew to be a strong man, industrious, and a fine laborer under the direction of others. He was helpful in the home, of a cheerful disposition and religiously inclined. He died April 4, 1879, aged 70 years, 8 months, 23 days.

Families of the Fourth Generation

[19] **MARGARET[4] MILLER**, daughter of [10] Elizabeth[3] (Fouse) Miller and Abraham Miller, was born May 13, 1815; died September 13, 1834; unmarried.

[20] **JOHN[4] MILLER**, son of [10] Elizabeth[3] (Fouse) Miller and Abraham Miller, was born April 4, 1817. He was married to *Catharine Clay*, with whom he resided during his short career, in Plain Township, Stark County, Ohio. To this union one child was born.
[85] + Abraham[5], *b* February 25, 1838.

[21] **JONATHAN[4] MILLER**, son of [10] Elizabeth[3] (Fouse) Miller and Abraham Miller, was born on the old Miller homestead near Canton, Ohio, September 15, 1818; and on September 19, 1839, married *Lydia Cassler*, daughter of *Lewis* and *Nancy* (*Wise*) *Cassler*.[a] Mr. Miller lived on the old homestead for several years after his marriage where his first child was born December 14, 1840. About 1841 or 1842, they moved to a farm which Mr. Miller owned and, about 1847, bought a water power sawmill adjoining his farm; about a year later he erected a more modern mill at this place. About 1850, he sold his farm, but retained the mill, and bought a farm which had belonged to his father-in-law, Lewis Cassler. Mr. Miller undertook various other enterprises, and lost all that he had gained up to that time. He was a born mechanic, and after his losses worked at various occupations with but indifferent success. In 1865, he bought 160 acres of unimproved land in Clinton County, Iowa, and in 1866, with his family, took up his residence there. In the spring of 1869, he sold this land and with his family again set out, this time for Missouri. After traveling by wagon for over 300 miles they arrived at Maryville, in the northwestern part of that state some time in the following June. He rented a farm for two seasons, and in 1871 moved to Easton, Buchanan County, where he opened a blacksmith and repair shop, which business he followed to the time of his death, October 21, 1875. Mrs. Miller lived with her children until her death June 20, 1907 (Plate 16).

[a] See [23]—Lydia Cassler and William are brother and sister.

JONATHAN[6] MILLER [21], AND LYDIA (CASSLER) MILLER.

CHILDREN OF JONATHAN[4] MILLER [21] AND LYDIA (CASSLER) MILLER.

Children (8) surname Miller (Plate 17):

[86] + Adam Lewis[5], *b* December 14, 1840; *m Sarah Etta Cocklin.*
[87] Nancy[5], *b* March 26, 1843; *d* January 14, 1860.
[88] + John Cassler[5], *b* May 29, 1845; *m Dora Emeline Anderson.*
[89] A son, *b* June 27, 1847; *d* September 5, 1847.
[90] + Elizabeth[5], *b* October 27, 1849; *m John F. Rapp.*
[91] + Mary[5], *b* May 23, 1853; *m Jacob Hoppel.*
[92] + Fyanna[5], *b* April 6, 1856; *m Sampson S. Whitmore.*
[93] + Lydia[5], *b* December 21, 1858; *unm.*

[22] **CATHARINE[4] MILLER,** daughter of [10] Elizabeth[3] (Fouse) Miller and Abraham Miller, was born August 19, 1820. She married *Jacob H. Bair,* with whom she resided on a farm near her parents' home in Plain Township, Stark County, Ohio, until her death which occurred on March, 1863.

To this union were born nine children, surname Bair:

[94] Abraham[5], *b* December 30, 1837; *d* November, 1860.
[95] Male child, *b* ——, 1839; *d. y.*
[96] + Elizabeth[5], *b* November 10, 1840; *m Jacob Solomon Miller.*
[97] Solomon[5], *b* June 10, 1843; *d* February 13, 1863.
[98] + Mary Ann[5], *b* August 14, 1845; *m George Snyder.*
[99] + Franklin[5], *b* September 14, 1847.
[100] Priscilla[5], *b* May 4, 1851; *d* June 27, 1854.
[101] Mandilla[5], *b* May 4, 1851; *d* March 8, 1880.
[102] + Jefferson[5], *b* August 5, 1855.

[23] **ELIZABETH[4] MILLER,** daughter of [10] Elizabeth[3] (Fouse) Miller and Abraham Miller, was born March 22, 1822, and on January 9, 1840, was married to *William Cassler,* born Lititz, Lancaster County, Pennsylvania, March 3, 1814; son of *Lewis* and *Nancy (Wise) Cassler,* and brother of Lydia (Cassler) Miller [21]. Elizabeth and William resided on a farm near Cairo, Stark County, Ohio, where she died May 2, 1890. Her husband died August 29, 1897, aged 83 years, 5 months and 26 days.

Children (7), surname Cassler:

[103] Male child[5], *b* and *d* November 21, 1840.
[104] + Nancy[5], *b* May 20, 1842; *d* March 22, 1881; *m John Corey.*
[105] + Lovina[5], *b* April 9, 1844; *m C. Polk Dallas Machamer.*

[106] + LaFayette[5], *b* December 15, 1846; *m Melvina Amelia Weaver.*
[107] + Margaret[5], *b* September 24, 1849; *m Solomon Wetzel.*
[108] + Lewis David[5], *b* August 5, 1852; *m Lucinda Henney.*
[109] + Elizabeth[5], *b* September 9, 1856; *d* August 27, 1880; *m Anthony Wayne Machamer.*

[24] **SOLOMON[4] MILLER**, son of [10] Elizabeth[3] (Fouse) Miller and Abraham Miller, was born September 21, 1820. February 2, 1847, he married (1) *Elizabeth Bishop*, and settled on a farm near the parental homestead where he continued to reside until the time of his death, which occurred May 1, 1890.

Children by first marriage (4):

[110] + Ottilla[5], *b* December 12, 1847; *m William Wise.*
[111] + Jemmima[5], *b* May 22, 1850; *m George Lamberson.*
[112] + Nathaniel[5], *b* September 22, 1851; *m* (1) *Lizzie Wetzel; m* (2) *Mrs. Emma Stambaugh.*
[113] Samuel C.[5], *b* March 3, 1855; *d* April 9, 1855.

Mrs. Elizabeth Miller died October 7, 1863, and on January 13, 1871, Mr. Miller married *Mrs. Hettie A. Gibble.*

Children by second marriage (3):

[114] Lyba[5], *b* January 20, 1874.
[115] Robert[5], *b* November 11, 1875.
[116] Vernon[5], *b* June 1, 1878.

[26] **CHRISTINA[4] MILLER**, daughter of [10] Elizabeth[3] (Fouse) Miller and Abraham Miller, was born July 12, 1827, and April 27, 1847, married *Henry Snyder*, born April 10, 1824; and with him resided on a farm near Cairo, Stark County, Ohio, until his death in 1898. She is living in the village of Cairo (Plate 18).

Children (11), surname Snyder:

[117] John A.[5], *b* September 21, 1848; *d* September 5, 1876.
[118] + Lucinda[5], *b* November 4, 1850; *m Christian Fulmer.*
[119] Priscilla[5], *b* June 21, 1852; *d* March 1, 1854.
[120] + Mary Elizabeth[5], *b* July 24, 1854; *m Henry Fulmer.*
[121] + Sarah[5], *b* June 9, 1856; *m Milton M. Guiley.*
[122] + Savilla[5], *b* May 2, 1859; *m Rufus Brouse.*
[123] + Cora[5], *b* March 23, 1861.

HENRY SNYDER AND CHRISTINA[4] (MILLER) SNYDER [26].

[124] + Catharine[5], *b* December 5, 1862; *m Harvey C. Bishop.*
[125] + Celesta[5], *b* July 24, 1865; *m George Ingold.*
[126] + Christina[5], *b* January 13, 1868; *m David Schumaker.*
[127] + Joshua H.[5], *b* October 15, 1872; *m Clara E. Bair.*

[27] **MARY ANN[4] MILLER,** daughter of [10] Elizabeth[3] (Fouse) Miller and Abraham Miller, was born March 23, 1830, and April 21, 1853, married *Samuel J. Miller,* with whom she resided on a farm adjoining the farm of her parents, until her death which occurred on April 17, 1876. Last reported address was Canton, Ohio.

Children (8), surname Miller:

[128] Theodore W.[5], *b* May 12, 1854; *d* September 3, 1854.
[129] Alice[5], *b* July 21, 1856; *d* December 7, 1862.
[130] + Alonzo Lee[5], *b* January 10, 1858; *m Ellen Essig.*
[131] + Mason E.[5], *b* April 17, 1861; *m Ada Aungst.*
[132] + Malez S.[5], *b* October 23, 1863; *d* September 21, 1893; *m Ellen Walters.*
[133] + Ira S.[5], *b* December 5, 1870.
[134] Ida M.[5], *b* December 5, 1870; *d* March 19, 1892; *m Albert Marker.*
[135] Charles Webster[5], *b* August 26, 1874; *d* February 11, 1896.

[28] **PRISCILLA[4] MILLER,** daughter of [10] Elizabeth[3] (Fouse) Miller and Abraham Miller, was born May 30, 1832, and on March 6, 1855, was married to *Wm. L. Miller,* with whom she resided on a farm near Cairo, Stark County, Ohio. She died January 28, 1911, and he died about a year later.

Children (9), surname Miller:

[136] + Mary M.[5], *b* August 13, 1855; *m* (1) *Ozias Bair; m* (2) *George Richie.*
[137] + Martha M.[5], *b* February 18, 1857; *m Charles F. Hill.*
[138] + Manodes[5], *b* January 24, 1859; *m Louisa Black.*
[139] + Mandana[5], *b* August 6, 1861; *m Zenas Fry.*
[140] Mahlon[5], *b* November 9, 1864; *d* October 4, 1865.
[141] + Marvin M.[5], *b* November 29, 1866; *m Ella Miller.*
[142] + Magnus M.[5], *b* September 6, 1869; *m Henry Reel.*
[143] + Martin C.[5], *b* November 9, 1872; *m Mildred Lanberance.*
[144] + William Murray[5], *b* April 1, 1875; *m Melvina Harter.*

[30] **ELIZABETH[4] GARNER,** daughter of [11] Catherine[3] (Fouse) Garner and John Philip Garner, was born November 19, 1814, in Huntingdon County, Pennsylvania. She spent her early life at the parental home, described elsewhere in this volume. About 1834 she married *John Acker*, son of *Henry* and *Susanna* (*Ditch*) *Acker*. They located on the latter's parental home farm close by the Nicholas Fouse homestead. Here they remained until they were removed by death.

They acquired some property in addition to Mr. Acker's homestead. When Mrs. Acker's parents were advanced in years, and too infirm to care for themselves, Mr. Acker purchased their farm. He had also other real estate holdings. Elizabeth died January 21, 1874, at the age of 59 years. Her husband died in 1885. They set their children a good example of piety; were devout members of the Beavertown Reformed Church. They were an unassuming couple; they led busy, useful and honorable lives, and were kind and hospitable.

Children (8), surname Acker:

[145] Catherine[5], *b* May 21, 1835; *d* March 3, 1839.
[146] Jacob[5], *b* September 27, 1836; *d* October 17, 1836.
[147] + Susan[5], *b* January 8, 1838; *m Daniel Myers.*
[148] Margaret,[5] *b* March 3, 1840; *d* August 27, 1842.
[149] + Sarah[5], *b* August 27, 1842; *m Jacob Lecrone.*
[150] + Nancy[5], *b* December 14, 1844; *m John Duerner.*
[151] + Adam[5], *b* March 19, 1847; *m Agnes Greaser.*
[152] + Dewalt[5], *b* October 16, 1849; *m Sadie Imler.*

[31] **MARGARET[4] GARNER,** daughter of [11] Catharine[3] (Fouse) Garner and John Philip Garner, was born August 17, 1815, in Woodcock Valley, Huntingdon County, Pennsylvania, north of where the village of Marklesburg was subsequently located. On March 26, 1835, she was married to *Jacob C. Hoover* of Morrison's Cove, born February 26, 1809; son of Samuel Hoover, who was son of Adam Hoover. They began housekeeping in the house at the sawmill near the residence of Mrs. Hoover's grandfather, Nicholas Fouse. It is quite a coincidence that the two sisters Elizabeth and Margaret should begin housekeeping so closely together. About 1842, Mr. Hoover, whose trade was carpentering, purchased and took possession of a farm four miles north of Martinsburg, on Piney Creek, Huston Township, Huntingdon (now Blair) County, Pennsylvania, and this proved to be their place of residence until their translation from earth

SARAH (GARNER) PEIGHTEL [32] HENRY PEIGHTEL, AND FAMILY.

to the spirit world. Here they faithfully worked, year after year, performing such duties as are incident to farm life. To some people it might seem to be a monotonous life, but to them it was not so; there was a thrill of joy in the thought that they were doing their duty. Mr. Hoover was born and reared on the banks of Clover Creek two miles south of the original Fouse homestead in Huntingdon (now Blair) County, Pennsylvania, on what was then known as the Samuel Hoover homestead farm, later purchased by Adam Fouse [17]. Mr. Hoover and Mr. John Acker, who married sisters and daughters of John Philip Garner, were the carpenters to build the Reformed Church on the Fouse premises in the year 1832. Mr. Hoover had a fair education and taught subscription school several terms. He took much interest in educating his only son Daniel to become teacher and surveyor.

In 1865, while Mr. Hoover was plowing, he discovered the barn on fire at the far end from the house. A strong wind prevailed, and both barn and house were destroyed. The origin of the fire was a mystery, and it was a heavy loss. Their only son was at the time doing military duty in the United States Army.

Bereft of their only daughter and feeling that they could, to a limited extent, have a daughter's place supplied, they adopted a girl and later another one. Mrs. Hoover proved herself to be a very kind and indulgent mother to these adopted girls. It was her delight to keep her house in a very tidy condition, and in this particular it would have been hard to find her peer.

Mr. and Mrs. Hoover were members of the Beavertown Reformed Church. Mrs. Hoover died March 14, 1885 (69-6-28) and Mr. Hoover died September 12, 1885 (76-6-14).

Their son Daniel, who never resided elsewhere and who had practically taken possession of the homestead while the parents were living, naturally inherited all the property, real and personal.

Children (2) surname Hoover:

[153] + Daniel[5], *b* July 28, 1836; *m Eliza Jane Rhodes.*

[154] Catherine[5], *b* July 28, 1842; *d* November 30, 1844.

[32] **SARAH[4] GARNER,** daughter of [11] Catharine[3] (Fouse) Garner and John Philip Garner, was born September 28, 1817, at the homestead, one mile north of the present site of Marklesburg, Huntingdon County, Pennsylvania. She was joined in holy wedlock with *Henry Peightel* of the vicinity of McConnellstown, Pennsylvania, in 1836. They settled a

mile south of the latter place and continued to reside there until after Mr. Peightel died.

Although the parents had limited school advantages, they took a deep interest in the education of their children and afforded them the best public school and social advantages obtainable in the neighborhood. The school house being situated within about two minutes' walk of the house, neither distance nor inclement weather was a hindrance to their attendance. Proximity to the school house was an inducement to the teachers to apply at the Henry Peightel home for boarding during the term, and their applications were favorably considered. Here the children were practically fitted for life's duties. The parents being devout members of the Reformed Church at McConnellstown, naturally had their children attend upon the services of God's house at that place and also go there to Sunday school, and all became members of the Reformed Church.

The Christian home life, together, with the preaching of the Gospel and the instruction imparted in the Sunday school, greatly helped to develop Christian character. It was in the home more particularly that the mother's influence was manifested. She was devoted to her family; she planned and toiled for them; and she had a sweet, gentle voice.

When, on account of the infirmities of age after her husband's death, she could not superintend the work on the farm, her only son occupying his own farm a few miles distant and all the daughters except one being established in their own homes, she with the youngest daughter Lydia vacated the farm and moved to McConnellstown, Pennsylvania. She resided there until she fell asleep in Jesus, October 1, 1911, at the ripe age of 94 years and 3 days.

During the last days of her earthly pilgrimage her memory was impaired and eyesight failed her. Notwithstanding this she was exceedingly patient. It is remarkable that a person could attain to such a great age with only a few gray hairs. Her daughter Lydia Ida[5] [163] faithfully ministered to her in the declining years of life (Plate 19.)

Children (9), surname Peightel:

[155] + John[6], *b* November 14, 1839; *d* April 14, 1894; *m* (1) *Margaret Hamer; m* (2) *Margaret B. Greaser.*
[156] Catharine[6], *b* ————; *d. y.*
[157] Elizabeth[6], *b* ————; *d. y.*
[158] Isaac[6], *b* ————; *d. y.*
[159] + Mary Jane[6], *b* February 18, 1848; *m Samuel Dean Heffner.*

DANIEL[4] GARNER [33], ELIZABETH (SORRICK) GARNER, AND ANGELINE ALVERETTA GARNER [170].

[160] + Margaret Ann[5], *b* June 6, 1850; *m George P. Booth.*
[161] + Sarah Alice[5], *b* June 8, 1852; *m Micaiah Reden Evans*, M.D.
[162] + Susanna[5], *b* May 19, 1854; *m William S. Hallman.*
[163] + Lydia Ida[5], *b* November 15, 1857; *unm.*

[33] **DANIEL[4] GARNER,** son of [11] Catharine[3] (Fouse) Garner and John Philip Garner, was born November 13, 1819. June 22, 1841, he married (1) *Margaret Aupperley*, who was of German parentage. They started housekeeping in the original Nicholas Fouse mansion, where they lived for several years. He then moved to Frederick Fouse's farm at Beavertown where he lived and farmed until 1851. He then sold his farming utensils and moved to the sawmill house that was built for Grandmother Fouse in 1826, where he lived one year, then emigrated to the state of Wisconsin, Grant County, and farmed there for several years. Then he bought a farm in Fennimore Township, twelve miles north, and farmed there until he became disabled, when he rented this farm and returned to South Lancaster where he lived to the time of his death.

"He was a man highly esteemed, his life honorable and upright; his life at home and abroad was always the same, ever ready to do good. His home was always open to all, whether rich or poor. His early religious training was a solace and a comfort. He was never so happy as when his children and grandchildren were gathered around his amply provided table, and never too tired to give thanks to his Creator for all of his manifold blessings."

"There was no German church near, and soon a few were gathered together and a Presbyterian Church was established. Father's house was the haven of rest for the ministers. Sometimes they held services in our house, but later built a small chapel west of us at what was called 'Hurricane'. It was built on Uncle Benjamin Garner's land, and a cemetery near by in which five of my uncles' small children were buried, three dying with cholera. Later father, mother, three sisters and two brothers united with the Congregational Church of Lancaster. Father, mother and sister Angeline [170] were buried from church within 3 years."

"When the Civil War broke out my brother Dawald [165], aged 19, enlisted; with father's consent and blessing left for the scene of war and bloodshed. Father was a staunch Republican." (Letter from Mariah J.[5] (Garner) Clifton [169]).

Mrs. Margaret Garner died May 6, 1852. Mr. Garner married (2) *Elizabeth Sorrick*, born April 3, 1828; daughter of *Peter* and *Catharine*

Sorrick. Elizabeth died April 16, 1896, and Daniel[4] Garner died April 11, 1899 (Plate 20).

Children by the first marriage (5):

[164] + Mary Ann[5], *b* October 24, 1841; *m Henry Smith.*
[165] + Dawald[5], *b* May 5, 1843; *m Mary A. Hedges.*
[166] + Margaret[5], *b* February 28, 1845; *m Edward Shaffer.*
[167] + Catharine[5], *b* October 19, 1847; *m Fred. Leibert.*
[168] + Elizabeth Ann[5], *b* March 8, 1850; *m William Warren Waddle.*

Children by the second marriage (7):

[169] + Mariah Jane[5], *b* May 25, 1854; *m Watson Elihugh Clifton.*
[170] Angeline Alveretta[5], *b* February 11, 1856; *d* August 14, 1897; *unm.*
[171] + Reuben Peter Philip[5], *b* April 21, 1858; *m Fannie Luella Starr.*
[172] + William Daniel[5], *b* May 2, 1860; *m Emma Jane Neuroth.*
[173] + Abigail Landa[5], *b* April 17, 1863; *m August Kohlenburg.*
[174] + Emma Luella[5], *b* February 3, 1866; *m Bernard Irwin Kerr.*
[175] + Ulysses Grant[5], *b* February 21, 1869; *m Caroline Hoeffner.*

[34] **FREDERICK[4] GARNER,** son of [11] Catharine[3] (Fouse) Garner and John Philip Garner, was born near Marklesburg, Huntingdon County, Pennsylvania, March 7, 1822. He spent his early life on the parental home farm. April 17, 1845, he married *Margaret Sorrick* of Blair County, daughter of George Sorrick. They began housekeeping at Marklesburg, their dwelling house being possibly the third house erected in that village, and on the lot adjoining the one belonging to Adam Garner. About 1853, they disposed of their property and moved to Williams County, Ohio. On account of climatic conditions they did not long remain there, but returned to Pennsylvania and settled in the vicinity of Mrs. Garner's parental home. Margaret died March 28, 1855.

January 11, 1857, Mr. Garner married (2) *Fanny Shiffler,* who lived near Sharpsburg, Blair County, Pennsylvania. In 1859 Mr. Garner moved with his family near Louisville, Ohio. After some years of residence there he sold his farm and purchased one close by Canton, Ohio, and in this locality he spent the remainder of his days.

After his second wife was called away by death, Mr. Garner married again, on September 14, 1886, (3) Miss *Caroline Shock,* born in Stark County, Ohio.

Frederick Garner was a carpenter in early manhood, but, after permanently locating in Ohio, his chief employment was tilling the soil. He was industrious, honest and kind hearted, and a life long member of the Reformed Church. He died at the ripe age of 85 years, in September 1907: His widow's address is Canton, Ohio.

Children by first marriage (3):

[176] + Alfred[5], *b* October 25, 1845; *m Celinda Schlodtt.*
[177] + Eli[5], *b* March 21, 1850; *m Maggie McCartney.*
[178] Catharine[5], *b* February 13, 1854; *d* April 29, 1855.
Son by second marriage:
[179] + Franklin[5], *b* November 9, 1858; *m Melissa Roath.*

[35] **ADAM[4] GARNER,** son of [11] Catharine[3] (Fouse) Garner and John Philip Garner, was born March 17, 1824, at the homestead near the site of Marklesburg in Hopewell, now Penn Township, Huntingdon County, Pennsylvania. He was baptized April 19, 1824 by Rev. J. D. Aurandt, the sponsors being his Uncle Adam Fouse and Susanna Garner his espoused wife. He spent his childhood and youth on the home farm. His educational advantages were very limited. At that period of our country's history, the school term was short and the branches taught were orthography, reading, writing and arithmetic. The lack of a knowledge of books was in some measure supplemented by home training. Home is the first and most important school of character. Here the young learn cheerfulness, patience, self-control and the spirit of service and duty. He learned to speak the German and English languages. This energetic young man made choice of the carpenter's trade. Environments had much to do in turning his mind to this occupation. The village of Marklesburg, laid out in 1844, one mile south of the parental home, became an inviting field for mechanical labor. Frederick and Adam Garner, two enterprising brothers were early on the ground as mechanics and purchasers of lots for dwelling houses. They selected adjoining lots, the latter's deed was dated March 28, 1845. Adam erected a substantial frame dwelling house which is now owned and occupied by Henry H. Summers.

September 11, 1845, Adam Garner was united in matrimony with *Catharine Summers*, born May 23, 1823, see [61], daughter of *Henry* and *Sarah (Boyer) Summers*, by Rev. Theobald Fouse. This young couple came from parental homes where industry, honesty, economy and the love of God were impressed on the mind by precept and example. Hence in making the transition from these homes to their own they had rather a clear conception of the obligations and responsibilities of home life. The housewife was diligent and faithful in her sphere, as was the mechanic in his.

One day in February, 1851, while shingling a roof a raw wind prevailed, his body became benumbed by cold. This exposure was followed by typhoid fever which ended the earthly career of a modest, industrious, and useful man, and a consistent Christian, March 9, 1851 (26 years, 11 months and 23 days). His body was laid to rest in the graveyard connected with the Marklesburg Reformed Church. Of this church he was an humble and faithful member. He and his brother Frederick were the contractors for the church edifice, built in 1847. The latter received as his share $57 and the former $50. The results of Adam's toil can be given approximately. He with his brother Frederick erected four houses and one barn besides the church above mentioned, and by his own labor or supervision six barns, three dwelling houses, several shops and stables —he also made furniture.

The desolate widow, having dependent children to care for, was under the necessity of adjusting domestic affairs in accordance with existing conditions. While the children were small it seemed expedient to change the place of residence several times, but not far from Marklesburg.

After twelve years of widowhood, September 24, 1863, she was joined in matrimony to *Jacob Garner* (a first cousin of her first husband and as his third wife), born November 7, 1821, son of *John Michael* and *Catharine (Acker) Garner*. This resulted in moving from Marklesburg to near Williamsburg, Blair County, Pennsylvania. In this home she performed her duties faithfully and satisfactorily for almost 18 years. She fell asleep June 11, 1881, aged 58 years and 19 days. Interment was made at the Lutheran Church four and one-half miles south of Williamsburg, Pennsylvania. She was a devout member of the Lutheran Church from her youth.

Children (3) of Adam and Catharine (Summers) Garner:

[180] + Harrison[5], *b* August 20, 1847; *m Lou Maclaskey.*
[181] + Henry Summers[5], *b* May 29, 1849; *m Anna Mary Kunkle.*
[182] Adam, Jr.[5], *b* August 2, 1851; *d* August 28, 1855.

[36] **BENJAMIN[4] GARNER**, son of [11] Catharine[3] (Fouse) Garner and John Philip Garner, was born May 11, 1826, in Huntingdon County, Pennsylvania. On March 2, 1848, he married *Catharine Sorrick*, born July 23, 1826, in Woodbury Township, Blair County, Pennsylvania; daugh-

BENJAMIN[4] GARNER [36], AND CATHARINE (SORRICK) GARNER.

PHILIP[4] GARNER [37], AND SUSANNA (ACKER) GARNER

ter of Peter Sorrick. Mr. Garner was a member of the German Reformed Church at Marklesburg, Pennsylvania, and his wife was a member of the Lutheran Church on Clover Creek, Pennsylvania. Mr. Garner was a carpenter and followed that trade until about 1854, when they moved to Lancaster, Grant County, Wisconsin, he having bought a farm there. He then followed farming for a number of years. They both united with the Presbyterian church at that place, no church of their persuasion being located there.

In the fall of 1864, Mr. Garner enlisted as a private in Company E, Twentieth Regiment of the Wisconsin Volunteer Infantry. He participated in several engagements, noticeably Franklin Creek, Mississippi, and Spanish Fort, Alabama. He was honorably discharged at Galveston, Texas, July 14, 1865.

Some years after his return home he purchased some land near Hickman, Nebraska. Here he farmed for a number of years. His wife died in 1895 of typhoid pneumonia. After his wife's death, he was afflicted with many infirmities, and was much affected by the loss of his eyesight. Mr. Garner was blessed with earthly goods, and he and his wife did much in the support of the church and charity. He died October 31, 1904. The bodies of himself and his wife rest side by side in the cemetery at Hickman, Nebraska (Plate 21).

Children (9):

[183] Solomon[5], *b* October 20, 1849; *d* August 24, 1854.
[184] Reuben[5], *b* November 27, 1851; *d* August 25, 1854.
[185] Mary Ann[5], *b* February 23, 1854; *d. y.*
[186] + Benjamin F.[5], *b* October 1, 1855; *m Emma Keister.*
[187] William[5], *b* February 27, 1858; *d* August 20, 1859.
[188] + Levi[5], *b* April 14, 1860; *m Sarah McMahan.*
[189] + Lizzie[5], *b* May 14, 1863; *m* (1) *Henry Deisel; m* (2) *Charles E. Lovett.*
[190] + Sarah Jane[5], *b* June 8, 1866; *m William Gammill.*
[191] Matilda[5], *b* October 22, 1871; *d* August 27, 1873.

[37] **PHILIP[4] GARNER,** son of [11] Catharine[3] (Fouse) Garner and John Philip Garner, was born September 1, 1828, and on October 24, 1852, he married *Susanna Acker,* born April 5, 1832; daughter of *John Acker, Jr.,* and *Elizabeth (Bowers[a]) Acker.* After his marriage, Mr.

[a] Sister of (1) Susan (Bowers) Fouse [See 14].

Garner turned his attention to tilling the soil. They started housekeeping on a farm belonging to Adam Fouse, Sr., one-half mile north of Rebecca Furnace on Clover Creek, Blair County, Pennsylvania. They continued on this farm until the spring of 1864, when they moved to Iowa, near Davenport, where they lived to the times of their death. Their farm is among the best in the state, in a beautiful plateau near the Mississippi River. Their children inherited the land and now cultivate it. They divided the land and built new buildings, and occupy them for their homes. Mrs. Garner died August 1, 1895, and Mr. Garner died November 11, 1896 (Plate 22).

Children (7):

[192] + Lucinda[5], *b* October 2, 1853; *m John Roth.*
[193] Martha Amanda[5], *b* August 2, 1856; *d* March 22, 1857.
[194] + Annetta[5], *b* May 23, 1858; *m John P. Jacobs.*
[195] + Isabel[5], *b* April 21, 1861; *m* [200] *Reuben[5] Garner.*
[196] + Harrison C.[5], *b* June 29, 1865; *m Minnie Minam.*
[197] Franklin[5], *b* December 25, 1868; *d* January 19, 1881.
[198] Rilla May[5], *b* July 14, 1871; *d* May 19, 1880.

[38] **WILLIAM[4] GARNER,** son of [11] Catharine[3] (Fouse) Garner and John Philip Garner, was born December 15, 1831, at the homestead in Woodcock Valley, Huntingdon County, Pennsylvania. He grew up on the farm engaging in such work as farmers' boys usually perform. On the twenty-ninth of December, 1853, he married *Eve Sorrick* of Morrison's Cove. The distance between the parental homes of this young couple in a bee line would be possibly two miles, but Tussey Mountain being between the said homes made the distance by public road about six miles. Their first experience at housekeeping and operating a farm was on Mr. Garner's parental home farm. Here they resided and labored for about eight years, when they crossed Tussey Mountain to take possession of the farm of Mr. Garner's Uncle William Fouse. Their next home was on his Uncle Adam Fouse's farm, joining the Rebecca Furnace farm, where he farmed until 1866, when he purchased a farm a mile and one-fourth south of the old Fouse homestead. During their residence there, arrangements were made for Mr. Garner's parents to spend the remainder of their days at his home, but they were not permitted to tarry long in this home. The mother was called to her reward in December, 1880, and the father in July, 1881. Wheat growing in Morrison's Cove not being so remunerative as some years pre-

WILLIAM GARNER [38]

viously, Mr. Garner decided to go west, and with his family moved to Nemaha County, Kansas, where they purchased a farm and lived there for a number of years. As it will appear on another page, their oldest daughter was the only child who married before the departure of the family for Kansas. They then sold the farm in Nemaha County, and bought another in Jackson County, four miles from Holton, where they have since lived. The farm contains 80 acres, and is of the best land in the state for the production of corn, etc.

William Garner died at his home in Jackson County, Kansas, May 14, 1914 (83 years, 4 months, 23 days) from the effects of old age. He united with the German Reformed Church when a boy, and was a member of that church at death. The body was interred in the cemetery at Holton, Kansas. The widow, three sons and five daughters survive him. Mrs. Garner's address is Holton, Kansas, R. R. No. 3 (Plate 23).

Children (13):

[199] + Julia Ann[5], *b* February 11, 1855; *m Emanuel B. Acker.*
[200] + Reuben[5], *b* December 24, 1856; *d* April 23, 1896; *m* [195] *Isabel[5] Garner.*
[201] + Catharine[5], *b* January 25, 1859; *m Charles H. Sanders.*
[202] + Mary Jane[5], *b* January 6, 1861; *m J. L. Saterfield.*
[203] Franklin[5], *b* March 18, 1863; *d. y.*
[204] Lizzie[5], *b* March 24, 1864.
[205] + Alice[5], *b* October 16, 1866; *m William Schermer.*
[206] + William, Jr.[5], *b* March 29, 1869; *m Martha Herde.*
[207] + Harrison[5], *b* November 22, 1871; *unm.*
[208] Clara E.[5], *b* April 22, 1875; *d. y.*
[209] + Elmer D.[5], *b* November 19, 1876; *m Daisy J. Booth.*
[210] Emma[5], twin, *d. y.*
[211] Ellen[5], twin, *d. y.*

[39] **MICHAEL F.[4] GARNER**, son of [11] Catharine[3] (Fouse) Garner and John Philip Garner, was born August 1, 1833, and on April 26, 1862, married (1) *Elizabeth S. Showalter.* By occupation Mr. Garner was a carpenter but a large part of his life he followed farming. He rented a farm from his Uncle Adam Fouse, north of Rebecca Furnace, where he lived for a number of years. His wife died February 10, 1877. He then abandoned farming and again followed the carpenter trade. March 20, 1880, Mr. Garner married (2) *Alice Fenstermaker* and then lived for sev-

eral years in Pleasant Valley in Blair County, Pennsylvania, where he followed his trade. Later he moved to Ohio, on a farm near Canton, where he followed farming to the time of his death, March 4, 1900. Mrs. Garner's address is Canton, Ohio.

To the first union six children were born, viz:

[212] + Adam[5], *b* February 15, 1863; *m Sarah Knepper.*
[213] Joseph Frank[5], *b* April 12, 1865; *d* February 14, 1866.
[214] + William S.[5], *b* March 11, 1867; *m Lydia May.*
[215] Mary Ann[5], *b* December 12, 1869; *d* January 22, 1878.
[216] + Margaret[5], *b* August 23, 1872; *m Eli Smith.*
[217] Abraham[5], *b* September 9, 1876.

To the second union three children were born, viz:

[218] + James Calvin[5], *b* April 20, 1882; *m Emma Miller.*
[219] + Henry Edward[5], *b* December 15, 1885; *m Mabel Grace Hershberger.*
[220] Harrison[5], *b* February 16, 1889; *d* August 26, 1892.

[40] **CATHARINE[4] GARNER,** daughter of [11] Catharine[3] (Fouse) Garner and John Philip Garner, was born May 1, 1835, at the homestead near where Marklesburg (Penn Township, Huntingdon County, Pennsylvania), was later located. In December, 1855, she was married to *Abraham Myers* of the same community, her uncle Rev. Theobald Fouse officiating. The ceremony was performed in the Red House which became the family dwelling house a year or more previous to this occasion. This young couple settled in Marklesburg. Mr. Myers being a carpenter, continued to work at his trade. After some years of residence in this village they moved to Catherine's parental home to take charge of the farm, as all her brothers were located elsewhere and the aged parents could not operate the farm. Here they remained until Mr. Myers by will became the owner of the undivided half of his maternal grandfather's farm. They took possession of this property and subsequently acquired the other half of the farm by purchase. This has been and is one of the most desirable farms in that locality.

Mr. Myers died July 6, 1885. The earning power of the family had begun auspiciously. His plans in the line of business were carried out. Mrs. Myers with the assistance of the family made farming a success. All the children were trained to be industrious, honest and upright.

MARY[1] (FOUSE) HEIMBAUGH, AND ELIZABETH (HEIMBAUGH) BOWSER [234].

The mother like her sisters is a tidy housekeeper. She has lived to see the day that nearly all her children have homes of their own. Mrs. Myers is a member of the Reformed Church at Marklesburg, and all her children in early life became members of the same Church.

The children received the usual education afforded by the public schools of the township in which they resided. They are now rather widely scattered, as will appear elsewhere in this volume.

Mrs. Myers with one daughter continues to occupy the home property. A farmer and his family have possession of part of the dwelling house.

Children (11), surname Myers.

[221] + Reuben[5], *b* September 5, 1856; *m Rachel Harnish.*
[222] + Elizabeth[5], *b* December 10, 1857; *m Daniel Grove.*
[223] + Milton[5], *b* November 14, 1859; *m* (1) *Mary Grace Beaver; m* (2) *Florence Summers.*
[224] + Mary Jane[5], *b* October 31, 1862; *m Daniel Shultz.*
[225] + Sarah Catharine[5], *b* March 20, 1864; *m Martin Grove.*
[226] + Laura Alice[5], *b* April 1, 1866; *m Nevin Peightel.*
[227] + William H.[5], *b* October 27, 1867; *m Lizzie A. Betrick.*
[228] Ida May[5], November 2, 1869; *d* January 21, 1901.
[229] + Margaret[5], *b* October 27, 1871; *unm.*
[230] + Benjamin[5], *b* November 5, 1873; *unm.*
[231] + Franklin[5], *b* April 17, 1876; *m Annie Agnes*[6] *Brumbaugh.*

[41] **MARY[4] FOUSE**, daughter of [12] Jacob[3] and Elizabeth (Miller) Fouse, was born May 7, 1816, and on April 20, 1837, married *Jacob Heimbaugh* [see 42]. They settled on a farm in Suffield Township, Portage County, Ohio, where they continued to reside to the end of their lives. Mrs. Heimbaugh died May 11, 1897, her husband dying several years previously (Plate 24).

Children (8), surname Heimbaugh:

[233] + Abraham[5], *b* March 25, 1838; *m Adaline Reed.*
[234] + Elizabeth[5], *b* January 13, 1839; *m Samuel Bowser.*
[235] + Christine[5], *b* April 16, 1842; *d* April 17, 1886; *m Lewis Pontius.*
[236] + David[5], *b* March 15, 1844; *m Amanda Bair.*
[237] + Mary[5], *b* September 28, 1846; *m Samuel Brumbaugh.*
[238] + Emanuel[5], *b* October 30, 1848; *m Amanda Snyder.*

[239] + Sevilla[5], *b* August 4, 1851; *d* December 29, 1897; *m David L. Foust.*
[240] + Pierce[5], *b* February 20, 1854; *m* (1) *Lovina Pero; m* (2) *Katie Limerick.*

[42] **MARGARET[4] FOUSE,** daughter of [12] Jacob[3] and Elizabeth (Miller) Fouse, was born August 4, 1818. July 11, 1840, she married *Michael Heimbaugh,* with whom she resided in Suffield Township, Portage County, Ohio, until her death which occurred September 16, 1848. Michael and Jacob [see 41] were brothers.

Children (3), surname Heimbaugh:

[241] William H.[5], *b* November 14, 1841; *d* October 14, 1850.
[242] Jacob[5], *b* January 26, 1844. He died in Kentucky while serving in the Union Army during the Civil War.
[243] Catherine[5], *b* October 21, 1845; *unm.*, and lived near South Bend, Indiana.

[43] **ABRAHAM[4] FOUSE,** son of [12] Jacob[3] and Elizabeth (Miller) Fouse, was born April 6, 1820, and married *Mary Rhudy.* During the greater part of his life, he lived on a farm in Lake Township, Stark County, Ohio. Later he resided at Hartville, in the same county. Abraham died in 1904, aged 84 years (Plate 25).

Children (6):

[244] Jacob[5], *b* April 25, 1851; *d* March 1864.
[245] + Barbara Ann[5], *b* August 8, 1852; *d* January 8, 1888; *m Daniel Wertenberger.*
[246] Elizabeth A.[5], *b* July 5, 1854.
[247] + Franklin[5], *b* March 14, 1856; *m Laura E. Bishop.*
[248] + Ellen[5], *b* March 19, 1860; *m Adam Miller.*
[249] + Daniel[5], *b* January 12, 1863; *m Minnie Jane Shanafelt.*

[44] **CATHARINE[4] FOUSE,** daughter of [12] Jacob[3] and Elizabeth (Miller) Fouse, was born November 7, 1823, and on November 19, 1843, was married to *Jonathan Hoover,* born February 8, 1818, son of *Samuel Hoover,* and brother of *Jacob C. Hoover;* and with him resided on her father's farm until March, 1867, when they moved to a farm near Myersville, Summit County, Ohio. Both died there recently.

Mrs. Catharine Hoover and her husband Jonathan Hoover were both consistent members of the Reformed Church at Uniontown, Ohio. For

ABRAHAM[4] FOUSE [4.] AT AGE 83.

JONATHAN HOOVER AND CATHARINE[4] (FOUSE) HOOVER [44].

SAMUEL CRAMER, AND CHRISTENA[4] (FOUSE) CRAMER [48]

many years he was an honored elder in the church. They attended the church regularly, as well as prayer meeting and Sunday school. They long attended Milheim Congregation in the Uniontown charge. Mr. Hoover died April 28, 1892, aged 74 years, 2 months and 2 days, and Mrs. Hoover died September 19, 1897, aged 70 years, 9 months and 15 days. They reared their family in the nurture and admonition of the Lord, and like their parents delight in doing good and serving the Lord (Plate 26).

Children (11), surname Hoover:

[250] + Franklin D.[5], *b* October 12, 1844; *m* (1) *Mollie Zentz; m* (2) *Kate Housel.*
[251] + William[5], *b* December 17, 1845; *m Emma C. Heimbaugh.*
[252] + Elizabeth[5], *b* August 27, 1847; *m John Strosacker.*
[253] Jonathan[5], *b* January 14, 1849; *d* September 29, 1850.
[254] + Priscilla[5], *b* October 3, 1850; *m Brison W. Myers.*
[255] Jacob C.[5], *b* October 26, 1853; *d* March 9, 1864.
[256] + Sarah A.[5], *b* January 22, 1856; *m Emanuel P. Sprigle.*
[257] + Ellen M.[5], *b* April 29, 1858; *m Frank A. Yarrick.*
[258] + Daniel C.[5], *b* September 24, 1860; *m Ada Bixler.*
[259] + Wilson[5], *b* December 8, 1862; *m Bertha M. Foust.*
[260] + Ida A.[5], *b* April 14, 1865; *m Albert Schick.*

[45] **CHRISTENA[4] FOUSE,** daughter of [12] Jacob[3] and Elizabeth (Miller) Fouse, was born October 12, 1827. June 26, 1846 she was married to *Samuel Cramer*, born April 7, 1817, with whom she resided on a farm near Uniontown, Stark County, Ohio, and in the decline of life they moved into the village where Mrs. Cramer still resides. Mr. Cramer died some years ago (Plate 27).

Children (6), surname Cramer:

[261] + Abraham[5], *b* December 22, 1847; *m Amanda Myers.*
[262] + Elizabeth[5], *b* July 10, 1849; *m William Miller.*
[263] + Isaac[5], *b* November 20, 1851; *m Alice Kreighbaum.*
[264] + Mary E.[5], *b* April 28, 1856; *m John Swope.*
[265] + William H.[5], *b* April 26, 1861; *m Laura Frederick.*
[266] + Catherine O.[5], *b* February 18, 1865; *m John Bridenstine.*

[48] **SAVILLA[4] FOUSE,** daughter of [13] John[3] and Christina (Miller) Fouse, was born in 1820, and in 1838 was married to *Isaac Madlem.* She

died December 25, 1875. During a portion of Mrs. Madlem's life they resided on a farm in Plain Township, Stark County, Ohio.

Children (9), surname Madlem:

[267] + Hiram B.[5], *b* October 7, 1839; *m Mary A. Zentz.*
[268] + Mary Ann[5], *b* July 1, 1841; *m Frank Ream.*
[269] + Franklin[5], *b* November 12, 1843; *m* ——— *Miller.*
[270] Adam[5], *b* March 12, 1845; *d. y.*
[271] + William,[5] *b* June 5, 1847; *m Ducetta Slabaugh.*
[272] Fyanna[5], *b* June 6, 1850; *d* ———, 1864.
[273] Savilla E.[5], *b* December 7, 1852; *d* ———, 1854.
[274] + Isaac D.[5], *b* October 18, 1856; *m Ann Edie.*
[275] Sarah[5], *b* September 22, 1859; *d* ———, 1863.

[49] **FREDERICK[4] FOUSE,** son of [13] John[3] and Christina (Miller) Fouse, was born March 17, 1825. In his early days, he went one session to college at Canton, Ohio, then taught school one winter, which was an assistance to him in training for business. He was a man of ability, had mechanical ingenuity, and was a good business man. He had been elected to fill several offices in his township; was a powerful worker and quick in thought and action. In politics he was a Democrat. On May 4, 1848, he married *Elizabeth Gaerte,* born November 25, 1827, daughter of Caspar Gaerte (see [86]), and with her occupied his parental homestead for many years. They then settled on a farm near Akron, Ohio, where he died January 13, 1884 (Plate 28).

Children (11):

[276] + Malinda[5], *b* January 8, 1849; *m Philip Fulmer.*
[277] Infant[5], *b* and *d* June 16, 1850.
[278] + John M.[5], *b* October 7, 1851; *m Susan Royer.*
[279] + Reuben[5], *b* May 4, 1853; *m Salina Royer.*
[280] + Jacob J.[5], *b* January 17, 1855; *m Emma J. Wise.*
[281] + Edwin P.[5], *b* May 1, 1857; *m Mary Rose.*
[282] Adam[5], *b* July 24, 1859; *d. y.*
[283] + Minodes[5], *b* February 12, 1861; *m Christina Rose.*
[284] + Fernando[5], *b* December 14, 1864; *m Lydia Rose.*
[285] + William F.[5], *b* February 2, 1867; *m Ada Keller.*
[286] + Ira[5], *b* May 20, 1870; *d* October 20, 1896; *m Bessie Greenland.*

ELIZABETH (GAERTE) FOUSE AND FREDERICK[1] FOUSE [40].

THEOBALD A. ("DEWALT") FOUSE [illegible]

(From *Brumbach Families*, copyright 1913.)

[51] **THEOBALD ("DEWALT") ADAM[4] FOUSE,** son of [14] William[3] and Susan (Bowers) Fouse, was born May 9, 1820, and on April 13, 1843, married (1) *Margaret Duncan,* who was born September 18, 1819, and died May 18, 1849. They resided on a farm on Clover Creek, Blair County, Pennsylvania. *There were four children born to this union:*

[287] + George W.[5], *b* June 29, 1844; *d* December 13, 1861.
[288] + William Duncan[5], *b* December 23, 1845; *m Linda B. Knode.*
[289] + Daniel Duncan[5], *b* May 23, 1847; *m Malinda Bossler.*
[290] Rozilla[5], *b* May 18, 1849; *d* August 19, 1849.

April 8, 1851, Mr. Fouse married his first wife's sister, (2) *Elizabeth Duncan,* born October 18, 1825, and died August 12, 1852. They were daughters of *Edward* and *Susanna Duncan. To this second union one son was born:*

[291] + Calvin Sylvester[5], *b* December 28, 1851; *m Rosanna Fisher.*

March 5, 1854, Mr. Fouse married (3) *Agnes Greaser,* born August 29, 1830, in Germany. *To this union were born eight (8) children:*

[292] + Anna Malinda[5], *b* January 3, 1855; *m Winfield Scott Garner.*
[293] + Mary Elizabeth[5], *b* June 26, 1856; *d* July 20, 1909; *m Charles Winfield Ferry.*
[294] + Susan[5], *b* August 26, 1857; *m William P. Erb.*
[295] Martin G.[5], *b* November 5, 1859; *d* August 27, 1901.
[296] Levi R.[5], *b* December 18, 1861; *d* June 28, 1873.
[297] + Mahlon L.[5], *b* November 29, 1864; *m* (1) *Anna M. Cooper; m* (2) *Ella Jane Bear.*
[298] + Dewalt H.[5], *b* March 6, 1868; *m Magdalene Lavina Weisgerer.*
[299] + Laura A.[5], *b* December 9, 1872.

Mr. Fouse and his wives were members of the Reformed Church, and all are buried at Salem's Reformed Church at Drab. Their children were all brought up in the faith of the Reformed Church and are all members thereof (Plate 29).

[52] **MARGARET[4] FOUSE,** daughter of [15] Frederick[3] and Catherine (Acker) Fouse, was born September 22, 1822, and on March 2, 1843, was married to *Jacob A. Nicodemus* who was born December 4, 1819, and died at Foreston, Ogle County, Illinois, May 3, 1887; son of *Jacob* and ——— *(Aerlenbaugh) Nicodemus.* After her husband's death, Mrs. Nicodemus continued her residence at Foreston until her death, which occurred in 1906. Both Mr. and Mrs. Nicodemus, as well as their children, were

all members of the Reformed Church. The parents are interred at Foreston, Illinois (Plate 30).

Children (13), surname Nicodemus:

[300], [301] Twins and not named.
[302] + Wesley Fouse[5], *b* April 26, 1846; *m Lucinda Acker.*
[303] + Susanna Fouse[5], *b* December 25, 1847; *m* (1) *Daniel Acker, m* (2) *George Bowers.*
[304] + Reuben Fouse[5], *b* May 16, 1850; *m Mary H. Boydston.*
[305] + Mary Agnes[5], *b* June 14, 1852; *m Levi Diehl.*
[306] + Frederick Fouse[5], *b* September 1, 1854; *m Rebecca Bowman.*
[307] + Theobald Fouse[5], *b* May 12, 1856; *m Clara Masse.*
[308] + Esther Fouse[5], *b* April 24, 1858; *m David M. Diehl.*
[309] + William Fouse[5], *b* February 27, 1860; *m Anna Mary Myers.*
[310] + Jacob Fouse[5], *b* February 6, 1862; *m Mary Clarissa Lantz.*
[311] + Catherine Fouse[5], *b* February 26, 1864; *m John O. Fager.*
[312] + Margaret Elizabeth Fouse[5], *b* June 22, 1866; *m Joseph M. Faber.*

[53] **SOLOMON B.[4] FOUSE,** son of [15] Frederick[3] and Catherine (Acker) Fouse, was born at the original Fouse homestead, May 30, 1824. March 7, 1854, he married *Matilda Enyeart,* born near Marklesburg station, Huntingdon County, Pennsylvania, February 14, 1835. She was the daughter of *Thomas* and *Mary (Wilson) Enyeart* who lived on the Raystown branch of the Juniata River near Marklesburg. Thomas Enyeart was born December 11, 1808, and died June 28, 1854—he was son of William and Elizabeth (Wilson) Enyeart. Mary (Wilson) Enyeart was born November 30, 1814, and died September 3, 1875—she was daughter of Samuel and Mary (Wilson) Glasgow.

Mr. Fouse was reared on the farm, but upon becoming of age he learned the carpenter trade and followed the latter until 1855. During this time he erected many houses and barns in Blair County, and some in Ohio. In 1856, he turned his attention to farming, which he continued until his death, October 6, 1858. His remains lie in the cemetery at Salem's Church, on the Nicholas Fouse premises. Mr. and Mrs. Fouse were members of the Reformed Church.

Children (2):

[313] + Annma[5], *b* August 5, 1855; *m George B. Daugherty.*
[314] Ruth[5], *b* March 13, 1859; *d* August 8, 1863.

JACOB A. NICODEMUS AND MARGARET[1] (FOUSE) NICODEMUS.

September 26, 1861, at Beavertown, Blair County, Pennsylvania, Mrs. Matilda (Enyeart) Fouse married (2) *John Eberly*, of Waterside, Bedford County, Pennsylvania, born December 20, 1822, and died October 16, 1890, aged 67 years, 9 months, 26 days—buried at Waterside. Matilda Fouse Eberly died February 15, 1907 (72 years, 1 day) and was buried in Rose Hill Cemetery, Altoona, Pennsylvania.

[54] **WILLIAM ACKER[4] FOUSE,** son of [15] Frederick[3] and Catherine (Acker) Fouse, was born December 26, 1825, and on June 1, 1848, married *Catherine Greaser*, born February 14, 1827; daughter of *Geo.* and *Agnes Greaser.* They resided on a farm on Clover Creek, near Drab, Blair County, Pennsylvania. Mr. Fouse died July 28, 1912, aged 86 years, 7 months and 3 days (Plate 31).

Children (11):

[315] + Susan[5], *b* February 28, 1849; *m Henry C. Rhodes.*
[316]   Mary Agnes[5], *b* June 28, 1850; *d* May —, 1854.
[317] + Reuben[5], *b* April 5, 1852; *m Anna Collins.*
[318]   George[5], *b* February 11, 1854; *d* September 13, 1863.
[319]   Calvin[5], *b* December 23, 1855, *d unm.* February 2, 1898.
[320] + Margaret[5], *b* December 23, 1857; *m Joseph Detweiler.*
[321] + Samuel[5], *b* April 7, 859; *m Martha Detweiler.*
[322] + Elizabeth[5], *b* September 16, 1860; *m Martin L. Acker.*
[323] + Jane[5], *b* August 20, 1863; *m Jacob Detweiler.*
[324]   Ellen[5], *b* March 27, 1867; *d.*
[325] + William[5], *b* September 23, 1869; *m Jane Reiley.*

[55] **CATHARINE[4] FOUSE,** daughter of [15] Frederick[3] and Catharine (Acker) Fouse, was born May 2, 1827. She married *George Greaser*, born March 8, 1825, in Ellerbach, Hessen Darmstadt, Germany; son of *George* and *Agnes (Katzelmoyer) Greaser.* Catharine and her husband lived on a farm near Beavertown, Blair County, Pennsylvania. About 1862 they moved to the Greaser homestead, about 3 miles south, where Mrs. Greaser died January 6, 1874. Mr. Greaser died July 4, 1879. Both were interred at Salem Reformed Church, Clover Creek, Pennsylvania. George Greaser had married (2) *Elizabeth Fouse* [77][a] (Plate 32).

[a] See p. 91.

Children (10), surname Greaser:

[327] + Frederick[5], *b* February 25, 1851; *d* November 15, 1889; *m Elizabeth Acker.*
[328] + Lucinda[5], *b* November 11, 1852; *m John Daughinbaugh.*
[329] Philip[5], *b* June 30, 1854; *d* May 8, 1902.
[330] + Daniel Fouse[5], *b* April 27, 1856; *m Sarah Acker.*
[331] + Jacob Fouse[5], *b* August 1, 1858; *m Susan Ellen Bassler.*
[332] + Paul G.[5], *b* July 4, 1860; *m Eleanore Mehrwein.*
[333] Levi[5], *b* May 20, 1862; *d* May 12, 1884.
[334] + Rosan[5], *b* April 14, 1866; *m William H. Kemberlin.*
[335] + Susan F.[5], *b* April 16, 1868; *m Jacob Obenour.*
[336] + Mary Elizabeth[5], *b* September 15, 1871; *m William S. Wagner.*

[56] **ELIZABETH[4] FOUSE,** daughter of [15] Frederick[3] and Catharine (Acker) Fouse, was born April 17, 1830. January 3, 1865 she was married to *Albert G. Boyd*, born July 14, 1805. Mr. Boyd died November 25, 1886. His wife died October 29, 1913, and was buried in the Salem Reformed Church cemetery, close to where she was born.

The family lived for a time at Iola, Allen County, Kansas; later near Foreston, Ogle County, Illinois; and last their address is Hackettstown, N. J., R. R. No. 1 (Plate 33).

One daughter, surname Boyd:

[337] + Mary Catherine[5], born October 15, 1870; *m* (1) *Harry C. Boerner*; *m* (2) *Thomas F. Miller.*

[illegible]] **JACOB ACKER[4] FOUSE,** son of [15] Frederick[3] and Catharine (A[illegible]) Fouse, was born January 17, 1832. January 2, 1855 he married (1) *Sarah Rhodes*, born August 27, 1834, daughter of *Abram* and *Eliza* (*McGraw*) *Rhodes* (see [79]). Mrs. Fouse died January 19, 1858, and was buried in Salem Reformed Church cemetery.

September 1, 1859, Mr. Fouse married (2) *Margaret Shontz Grove*, born December 16, 1838; daughter of *John* and *Catharine* (*Shontz*) *Grove*, also a sister of *Nancy Grove*, who married *Henry[6] Brumbaugh* ([E224] in *Brumbaugh Families*). The ceremony was performed by Mr. Fouse's uncle, Rev. Dewalt[4] Fouse [16].

Jacob Fouse was reared on the old Fouse homestead farm which he purchased. After his second marriage he sold it and purchased one near McConnellstown, Huntingdon County, Pennsylvania, and moved upon it.

ELIZABETH (FOUSE) BOYD [56], ALBERT G. BOYD AND MARY CATHERINE BOYD [337].

JACOB ACKER[4] FOUSE [57].

His farming always produced successful results, but in 1904 the family moved to Huntingdon, where he leads a retired life. He is a Republican, member of the Reformed Church, and an active man, as can be seen by reference to Plate No. 34. Residence, 714 Warm Spring Avenue, Huntingdon, Pennsylvania.

Son by first marriage:

[338] + Jacob R.[5], *b* January 7, 1858; *m Mrs. Lavenia (Blackburn) Good.*

Children by second marriage (3):

[339] + Mary Alice[5], *b* August 16, 1860; *m Samuel Grubb Lininger.*
[340] + Harry Brumbaugh[5], *b* May 22, 1864; *m Mary Louise Wicke.*
[341] + Anna Grace[5], *b* May 30, 1870; *m Lemuel Lawrence Vanorman.*

[60] **ADAM[4] FOUSE,** son of [16] Theobald[3] and Nancy (Shontz) Fouse, was born March 6, 1824, in the original Nicholas Fouse homestead mansion erected in 1793, on the banks of Clover Creek, Huntingdon (now Blair) County, Pennsylvania, the birthplace of not only his father (Theobald[3] Fouse [16]) but five brothers, children of Nicholas[2] and Margaret (Brumbaugh) Fouse [2] were born, viz: John, William, Frederick, Adam and Jonathan—also six more of the older brothers and sisters, children of Theobald and Nancy Shontz Fouse, viz: Christian, John, Margaret, Elizabeth, Benjamin and Catherine. Adam, the first of fifteen children in his parents' family, shared in the privileges of a good Christian home. In his boyhood days, subscription schools afforded the only opportunity to secure education, and were kept open only several months during midwinter; besides the teachers were required to teach both the German and the English languages, and often did not succeed very well in either. However Adam, being studiously inclined, made good progress in the branches taught. In the spring of 1833, he, with his parents, moved to Woodcock Valley, in the same county. A year later the public school law of Pennsylvania was passed, but was yet in its formative state. While he attended public school in connection with the duties of the oldest son on the farm, it gave him many advantages for self improvement, and he thereby acquired a fair business education.

In 1849, Mr. Fouse married *Elizabeth Jane Simonton,* at the home of her father, *Jefferson Simonton,* near Marklesburg, Huntingdon County, Pennsylvania. Miss Simonton was born June 18, 1832. After marriage, they resided near Marklesburg until his death. Early in life Mr. Fouse was a carpenter and had also learned the trade of tanning and followed the latter business for many years; later he purchased a farm adjoining that of his father. He then abandoned the tanning trade and took up farming, which business he followed until his death September 28, 1884. Mrs. Fouse survives and with her youngest daughter (unmarried) lives on the farm. They are members of the Reformed Church. The remains of Mr. Fouse rest in the Reformed Church cemetery near Marklesburg, Pennsylvania. The farm is owned by their son Benjamin Simonton[5] Fouse [343], of Huntingdon, Pennsylvania.

Owing to physical disability, Mr. Fouse was denied the privilege of emphasizing his loyalty to the government, by bearing arms in the field in defence of our country's flag. He was, however, a great comfort and blessing to his aged father, while his seven brothers were at the front.

About 1868, Adam was elected county commissioner for Huntingdon County, Pennsylvania, on the Republican ticket—he always was a member of that political party.

"Adam Fouse was a lifelong member of the Reformed Church; was for many years in the eldership; he was a worker, as teacher and superintendent, in the Sunday school. He was a man of exemplary life; never entered a liquor saloon, never used tobacco in any form; he was held in respect and in the kind regards of his neighbors and associates."[a]

Children (5):

[342] Mary Ann[5], *b* May 24, 1849; *d* at age 40; *unm.*
[343] + Benjamin Simonton[5], *b* October 10, 1851; *m Mary M. Knode.*
[344] + William Simonton[5], *b* June 6, 1853; *m Martha J. Shell.*
[345] + Nancy Simonton[5], *b* July 18, 1855; *m John C. Greaser.*
[346] Naomi[5], *b* November 27, 1872; *unm.*

[61] **CHRISTIAN[4] FOUSE**, son of [16] Theobald[3] and Nancy (Shontz) Fouse, was born February 27, 1825. December 4, 1845 he married (1) *Barbara Summers*, born February 6, 1825; daughter of *Henry* and *Sarah (Boyer) Summers.* Barbara died February 8, 1864.

Owing to the close ties between the Summers, Boyer, and Fouse family lines further details are here given, largely furnished from the records of Rev. Henry Summers Garner [181]: Henry Summers, Sr., married Barbara ———, and they lived to the north of Hagerstown, Maryland, from which locality came so many of the early settlers in the Woodcock Valley, Hunt-

[a] *Biographical Encyclopaedia of Juniata Valley;* Runk and Company, p. 247.

CHRISTIAN[4] FOUSE [61] AND ELIZA (FRANK-SHONTZ) FOUSE.

ingdon County, Pennsylvania. About 1780 (?)[a] they moved into that valley, and he there died in 1809 and his wife died in 1827. They had children: Daniel; Jacob; *Henry*, born February 25, 1793, and died March 23, 1845; Mary; Catharine; Margaret; Susan; Henry Summers, Jr., married Sarah Boyer, born May 15, 1799, and died February 21, 1872. Sarah Boyer was daughter of Henry Boyer, born May 15, 1799.

Henry and Sarah (Boyer) Summers had children: Jacob, born February 2, 1822, and married Elizabeth Enyeart, April 2, 1863; Catharine, who married Adam Garner [35]; Barbara, born February 6, 1825, and married Christian Fouse [61]; David, born September 17, 1826, unmarried; Sarah, born September 21, 1830, married Daniel Harris; Henry, born June 2, 1834, married Elizabeth Beaver.

After the death of his wife, Barbara, Christian[4] Fouse enlisted as a private in Co. K, 78th Reg. Pa. Vol. Inf. to serve during the war. At its close he was honorably discharged, and mustered out of the service. He returned home and resumed farming.

May 22, 1866, Christian married (2) *Eliza (Frank) Shontz*, widow of *William D. Shontz*,[b] and sister of *Sarah (Frank) Fouse*, the first wife of *Adam Garner*[4] *Fouse* [82], and sister of *Maria (Frank) Brumbaugh*, widow of the late *Andrew Boelus Brumbaugh, M.D.* ([226] in *Brumbach Families*).

Christian Fouse and Eliza, with part of the latter's children by her first marriage, actively farmed near Alexandria, Huntingdon County, Pennsylvania, until shortly after Christian's death July 18, 1882. Mrs. Fouse lived at Huntingdon, Pennsylvania with her daughter Mrs. Ella Grace[5] Jackson [361] until her death November 6, 1914 (Plate 35).

Children by first marriage (11):

[347] + Sarah Ann[5], *b* October 20, 1846; *d* March 3, 1894; *m James Stone.*
[348] Nancy[5], *b* December 21, 1847; *d* September 25, 1848.
[349] + Joseph[5], *b* June 18, 1849; *m Anna B. Fisher.*
[350] + Henry Summers[5], *b* November 12, 1850; *d* July 10, 1905; *m Emma May Grove.*
[351] Andrew[5], *b* March 28, 1852; *d.*
[352] + Dewalt[5], *b* July 17, 1853; *m Eliza Jane Lininger.*

[a] The name of Henry Summers does not appear in the First Census of the United States; 1790, for Pennsylvania or Maryland—G. M. B.

[b] William D. Shontz was killed in the battle of the "Wilderness," Virginia, May 10, 1864. His funeral sermon was preached June 26, 1864, by Rev. "Dewalt"[3] Fouse [16].

[353] + Catherine[5], *b* December 22, 1854; *m Lewis Schoch.*
[354] Isaac[5], *b* March 25, 1856; *d* October 6, 1899.
[355] David S.[5], *b* March 21, 1858; *d* March 6, 1862.
[356] Milton[5], *b* December 10, 1859; *d* January 23, 1862.
[357] + Margaret[5], *b* June 28, 1862; *m Samuel Gilliland Rudy.*

Children by second marriage (4):

[358] + Frank[5], *b* March 27, 1868; *m Ida May Aultman.*
[359] Clara[5], *b* March 5, 1869; *d* May 18, 1881.
[360] + Mary Elizabeth[5], *b* June 27, 1873; *m Henry Musser Hosterman.*
[361] + Ella Grace[5], *b* July 31, 1877; *m Theodore Cunningham Jackson.*

[62] **JOHN[4] FOUSE,** son of [16] Theobald[3] and Nancy (Shontz) Fouse, was born June 26, 1826. November 22, 1854, he married *Rebecca Summers,* daughter of *Jacob* and *Elizabeth (Boyer) Summers* and a sister of Margaret Ann Summers, who married David[4] Fouse [75]. After John's marriage, he resided for several years on the John Plummer farm, in Woodcock Valley, in Huntingdon County, Pennsylvania. He next moved near his father's home, on a part of the old Entriken farm, which had been purchased by his father from the Entriken estate. Here he continued to reside until about 1866, when he moved into the house formerly occupied by his Grandfather Shontz, and subsequently purchased a part of the old home farm, which has since belonged to his descendants. In the early part of 1865, he enlisted and served as a private in Co. K, 78th Pa. Vol. Inf. At the close of the war, after being honorably discharged, he returned home and resumed farming, in which he was always successful. He died August 24, 1891, and is buried in the churchyard belonging to the Reformed Church near Marklesburg, Pennsylvania, of which church he was a lifelong member. His wife was also buried in the same churchyard (1906). She also was a life long member of the Reformed Church. John was small of stature, but a hard worker, and for several years before his death did not enjoy good bodily health.

One son:

[362] + Jacob Summers[5] Fouse, *b* ———, 1855; *m Martha Ellen Donnelson.*

[64] **ELIZABETH[4] FOUSE,** daughter of [16] Theobald[3] and Nancy (Shontz) Fouse, was born December 12, 1828; died June 7, 1893. She was united in marriage to *Anthony Beaver Shultz;* son of *David* and *Eliza-*

BENJAMIN FOUSE [65], AND ANNA (GREASER) FOUSE.

beth (*Beaver*) *Shultz*. They resided during all their married life on farms near Entriken, Huntingdon County, Pennsylvania; first, for a few years, on a rented farm, and then on a farm of their own. In the early part of 1865, Mr. Shultz entered the United States Army for one year, or during the war. He served as a private in Co. H, 78th Pa. Vol. Inf. At the close of the war, being honorably discharged, he returned to his farm. Mr. Fouse and his wife were members of the Reformed Church near Marklesburg, and they lie buried in the cemetery belonging to that church.

Children (*13*), *surname Shultz:*

[363] + Dewalt Fouse[5], *b* August 26, 1848; *m Margaret Greaser.*
[364] + Nancy[5], *b* September 11, 1851; *m John Russell Lynn.*
[365] + Elizabeth[5], *b* February 5, 1853; *m Andrew Russell Lynn.*
[366] + David Fouse[5], *b* August 5, 1854; *m Sarah Catharine*[5] *Brumbaugh.*
[367] + Reuben Fouse[5], *b* October 31, 1855; *m Erminie Cook.*
[368] + Mary Ann[5], *b* April 24, 1857; *m John Shirley Beaver.*
[369] Christina[5], *b* September 28, 1858; *d* March 11, 1859.
[370] + Catharine[5], *b* December 17, 1859; *m Jacob Russell.*
[371] + William Henry[5], *b* September 17, 1861; *m* (1) *Margaret Summers;* *m* (2) *Minnie Simpson; m* (3) *Malinda Detweiler.*
[372] Anna Maria[5], *b* February 9, 1863; *d* September 16, 1865.
[373] Sarah[5], *b* February 26, 1865.
[374] + Margaret[5], *b* February 26, 1865; *m Albert Criswell.*
[375] + Anthony Howard[5], *b* May 23, 1870; *d* May 2, 1893; *unm.*

[65] **BENJAMIN[4] FOUSE,** son of [16] Theobald[3] and Nancy (Shontz) Fouse, was born March 5, 1830. After his marriage with *Anna Greaser*, (daughter of George Greaser, Sr.) on February 2, 1860, he lived at the old home near Marklesburg until enlistment in the Union Army, in Co. K, 78th Pa. Vol. Inf., in 1865. He died in the Crittenden General Hospital at Louisville, Kentucky, August 22, 1865. His remains were brought home, and buried in the graveyard of the Reformed Church near Marklesburg, Pennsylvania. Mrs. Fouse lives with her daughter near Drab, Pennsylvania, which is her postoffice address (Plate 36).

Children (*3*):

[376] + Mary Agnes[5], *b* November 17, 1860; *m Levi Lininger.*
[377] + Martha Jane[5], *b* November 3, 1863; *m Edward Elwood Haffley.*
[378] + Benjamin G.[5], *b* August 29, 1865; *m Annie Rachel Schell.*

[66] **CATHARINE[4] FOUSE,** daughter of [16] Theobald[3] and Nancy (Shontz) Fouse, was born January 11, 1832. February 10, 1853, she married *Samuel H. Grove*, born January 31, 1826; son of *Benjamin Grove*. For a year or two after their marriage, they resided at the old Benjamin Grove home in Woodcock Valley. Later they moved to a farm near Entriken, where their children were born and where they resided until her death in the spring of 1868. Mr. Grove enlisted in Co. D, 205th Pa. Vol. Inf., in which he served from 1864 until the close of the war. After being honorably discharged, he returned to his home and engaged in farming, which was his main occupation during life. Mrs. Fouse died suddenly a few days after their youngest child, Samuel T.[5], was born.

Children (10), surname Grove:

[379] Anna E.[5], *b* March 31, 1854; *d* September 30, 1854.
[380] + John F.[5], *b* August 12, 1855; *m Mary E. Summers.*
[381] + Martha J.[5], *b* April 14, 1857; *m Henry Irwin Harris.*
[382] + Margaret E.[5], *b* August 24, 1858; *m Anthony W. Beaver.*
[383] + Benjamin F.[5], *b* January 7, 1860; *m C. A. Reed.*
[384] + Rachel[5], *b* April 29, 1861; *m Blair S. Summers.*
[385] + Dewalt F.[5], *b* August 15, 1862; *m Edith Blanche Sheckler.*
[386] + George S.[5], *b* March 5, 1864; *m Emma R. Stover.*
[387] William R.[5], *b* May 21, 1866; *d* August 2, 1866.
[388] Samuel T.[5], *b* March 17, 1868; *d* September 17, 1868.

[68] **MARY[4] FOUSE,** daughter of [16] Theobald[3] and Nancy (Shontz) Fouse, was the first child born to these parents in Woodcock Valley, Huntingdon County, Pennsylvania, that lived to adult life. She was born March 10, 1835, and died March 21, 1885.

Mary Fouse, on January 8, 1857, married *Benjamin Hoover*, born October 31, 1828; son of *Ludwig* and *Susannah (Grove) Hoover*. The Hoover family is of German origin, early settling in Maryland, later in Pennsylvania. Benjamin Hoover successfully cultivated the homestead farm near Grafton, Huntingdon County, Pennsylvania, giving especial attention to fruit and stock raising. He was highly esteemed in his community; was a Democrat in politics; and an active member in the Reformed Church, serving as deacon or elder therein until his death December 15, 1893 (Plate 37).

Children (6), surname Hoover:

[389] Sarah Jane[5], *b* November 14, 1857; *d* January 6, 1862.
[390] + Reuben Fouse[5], *b* September 6, 1859; *m Anna M. Fenstermaker.*

BENJAMIN HOOVER AND MARY[4] (FOUSE) HOOVER [68].

DEWALT SHONTZ[4] FOUSE, D.D. [71].

[391] + Catherine Fouse[5], *b* July 26, 1861; *m Benjamin Franklin Fink.*
[392] + Nancy F.[5], *b* October 10, 1863; *m William Heffner.*
[393] + Elizabeth F.[5], *b* July 1, 1866; *m John Keith Brumbaugh.*
[394] + Benjamin Franklin[5], *b* July 18, 1873; *m Lucy Hellyer.*

[71] **DEWALT SHONTZ[4] FOUSE, D.D.,** son of [16] Theobald[3] and Nancy (Shontz) Fouse, was born November 15, 1840, in the house now owned by Samuel Shontz Fouse [74], in Woodcock Valley, Huntingdon County, Pennsylvania. During his youth, he helped his father on the farm and attended the public schools of the neighborhood. In the summer of 1858, he attended a select school at Marklesburg, Pennsylvania, taught by William A. Houck. In the winter of 1858-59, he taught school at what was called "High Germany." In the summer of 1859, he again attended the select school at Marklesburg, but taught this year by Andrew B. Brumbaugh, afterward Dr. Brumbaugh, of Huntingdon, Pennsylvania. In the fall of 1859, he entered Franklin and Marshall College at Lancaster, Pennsylvania, and continued there until the fall of 1861, when on September 16, he enlisted in Co. C, 53rd Reg. Pa. Vol. Inf.—Capt. John H. Wintrode, of Marklesburg, Pennsylvania. This regiment was attached to 4th Brigade, 1st Division, 2nd Army Corp., commanded most of the time by Gen. William Scott Hancock. He participated in the opening campaigns about Washington during the winter and spring of 1862; then in the Peninsula campaigns from Yorktown to Richmond; was actually engaged in the battles of Fair Oaks, Allen's Farm, Savage Station, White Oak Swamp, and Malvern Hill. When the army was moved back to Washington, he took part in the battles of Chantilla, South Mountain and Antietam—then in the battle of Fredericksburg, December 13, 1862; Chancellorsville, May 3-4, 1863; Gettysburg July 1-3, 1863; Bristow Station and Auburn in the fall of 1863, and at Mine Run, November 1863. During the winter of 1863 and 1864, his command lay along the Rapidan River in Virginia, and participated in all the great battles of 1864, from the Rapidan to Petersburg—known as the "Wilderness campaign." When Mr. Fouse enlisted, he was made Third Sergeant of the Company, and later First Sergeant; and December 1, 1862, was commissioned First Lieutenant of Co. C, 53rd Pa. Vols., in which capacity he commanded the Company most of the time, frequently acted as Adjutant of the Regiment, and in the fall of 1864, acted as Assistant Adjutant General of the 4th Brigade, 1st Division, 2nd Army Corps. His time having expired, and being afflicted with malarial troubles, he resigned and was mustered out

of service October 9, 1864. He returned home and voted for Abraham Lincoln in November of the same year.

He then entered the Theological Seminary at Mercersburg from which he graduated in May, 1867. Thus, while his seminary course was complete, his college course was cut short by the war. He was ordained to the ministry in May, 1867, at Pattonsville, Bedford County, Pennsylvania. In June, 1867, Mr. Fouse went to Iowa and took as his first field the Boulden charge which he served seven years. On leaving the Boulden charge, he took the Lisbon charge which he served until October 1, 1889, when he accepted the office of "General Superintendent of Home Missions." This position he held until July, 1905, when the Board by direction of General Synod elected a general superintendent and three district superintendents. Mr. Fouse became a district superintendent for the Interior Synod, which office he held until October 1, 1910. The most of his ministry has been among the missions of the West. On June 16, 1892, the honorary degree of Doctor of Divinity was conferred on him by the Heidelberg University, Tiffin, Ohio.

January 30, 1868, Mr. Fouse married *Sarah Ann Geissinger* of Huntingdon County, Pennsylvania; born February 24, 1836; daughter of *John* and *Jane (Barrack) Geissinger*. Mrs. Fouse died October 1, 1904, in Denver, Colorado, while visiting her son Rev. David Henry[5] Fouse [395]. Mr. Fouse then made his home with his only daughter, Mrs. Mary Naomi[5] Kinsley [398], at Lisbon, Iowa, until his death March 13, 1912 (Plate 38).

A MINUTE FROM THE RECORDS OF THE BOARD OF HOME MISSIONS[a]

"Report adopted by the Board of Home Missions at its meeting in July, 1909, with regard to the long and self-sacrificing service of Superintendent Dewalt S. Fouse:

"The Board of Home Missions of the Reformed Church in the United States here places on record, its appreciation of the long and faithful services of Rev. D. S. Fouse, D.D. Forty-two years ago to-day he preached his first sermon as a missionary in the West. Fresh from the Seminary, he had caught a vision of opportunity to which he could not be disobedient and which still abides in his heart. His earnest, self-sacrificing and successful labors as a missionary for 22 years made him the natural and eligible candidate for the important office of General Superintendent of Home Missions when all the Home Missionary interests and activities of the Church were consolidated under the General Synod twenty years ago. Here he found a wide field of usefulness and he gave himself to his work with all his characteristic earnestness and zeal. He held this position until four years ago, when he was assigned the specific oversight of the Mis-

[a] *Reformed Church Messenger*, vol. lxxxi, no. 12, March 21, 1912.

sions in the Interior Synod. Dr. Fouse has lived to see the work in the West grow from a few struggling missions to a mighty Synod, while at the same time the whole Church has been awakened and developed in missionary interest and liberality. He was a pioneer. He helped to lay the foundation for the years to come. While such noble service always brings its own sufficient reward, it is eminently fitting in view of his retirement from office that the Board should here place on record this testimonial of its appreciation of the important work which this worthy servant of the Church has accomplished.

(Signed) Charles E. Miller,
Paul S. Leinbach, *Committee.*"

Pittsburgh, Pa., July 7th, 1909.

AN APPRECIATION BY DR. CHARLES E. SCHAEFFER.

"The death of Rev. Dr. Dewalt S. Fouse removes from the ranks of our ministry one of its leading members. For many years he occupied such a prominent position and figured so conspicuously in our church councils, and particularly in the missionary work in this country, that it will seem strange not to see him in our midst. His earthly life began in a quiet and peaceful country home in Central Pennsylvania. He sprung from strong and sturdy stock. His early life was spent on the farm where he not only developed a strong physique, but also acquired those habits of industry and perseverance, of thrift and economy which stood him so well in his subsequent career. Upon the completion of his theological studies he responded to a call in the then far West. Our Church at that time had but a few congregations west of the Mississippi River. A few of the pioneers of our faith had established several outposts in that large open field, but the territory lay almost an unbroken wilderness before them. The great and influential cities that now characterize our civilization in the West were then but small towns, and some had no existence at all. Dr. Fouse was not the only minister who heard and heeded the call of the wild, but most of the others who went West stayed a while and then returned to the East and stayed here. Dr. Fouse became indigenous to Western soil. He stayed out there during all his future days. He had caught the vision, he recognized the opportunity and thus be became early in his ministry a force for his Church and the Kingdom which perhaps he could not have exerted elsewhere. After serving in the pastorate for a number of years he was on March 29, 1889, elected by the Board of Home Missions as its General Superintendent. He entered upon the duties of his office October 1, 1889. Our Home Missionary work was at that time in a critical situation. It was a time of reorganization. For a number of years prior to this the District Synods had been carrying forward the home mission work of our Church. General Synod's Board was practically inactive. But now there was to be a reconstruction. The District Synods were asked to hand their home mission work over to the General Synod's Board, and conditions required that there should be a strong and efficient leader at the head of this work, one who could inspire confidence and rally the different sections of the Church. He was charged with a grave responsibility. The transfer of the work of the District Synods was not unanimously approved by the Church. There was considerable feeling in the matter, prejudice was aroused. The situation demanded an exceptional man to head this work. The unanimous choice of the Board fell upon Dr. Fouse. He had been a member of the Board for some time and was at least partially acquainted with its methods and work. He was then in the very prime of his life. His strong physical presence, his broad, manly shoulders were suggestive of native and acquired ability to carry heavy and responsible burdens. He gave himself wholly to his work. He rallied the divided forces of the Church. He brought into line the various elements and gave the Church a vision of its task as it never had before. Living as he did, on the western border of our Church, he was far from the base of supplies and was removed from the inspiration which association with his brethren and representatives of other denominations in this work could bring. Frequently his duties took him away from his home and family for months at a time. It was the time when the apportionment system came into full vogue. In the Ohio Synod he collected for a time much of the apportionment by a house-to-house canvass. This gave him valued experience and a knowledge of actual conditions among the people which he highly prized.

With the reorganization of the Board in 1905, when headquarters were established in Philadelphia, he became the Western superintendent, with special oversight of the missions in the Interior Synod. To this special work he devoted his last years. Many of the missions in the Interior Synod owe their origin to Dr. Fouse's initiative. The brethren eagerly sought his counsel in the matter of organization, location and building of churches. For years he was a leader on the floor of the Interior Synod, and his ripe judgment was generally followed. The Interior Synod at Freeport, Illinois, 1909, upon the completion of his twenty years' service with the Board of Home Missions, established a Church-building Fund and named it in his honor, the "Dr. D. S. Fouse Church-building Fund." He took a deep interest in Iowa Classis, of which he was the treasurer for many years. It was his zeal and energy that brought Iowa Classis always into the front line in the payment of the apportionment. He would never allow any of its congregations to be delinquent in its apportionment. He likewise was warmly attached to his church at Lisbon, where he and his family worshipped for many years.

His large physical frame sheltered a heart as tender and true as that of a woman. "It is the heart that makes the theologian." In life's struggle heart counts for more than head. He was of a peculiarly cheerful, hopeful, optimistic nature. His sense of humor saved him from many times of despair. He could put life and spirit into a brother who found himself in the depths. One can scarcely realize that the work with which he was identified and which is of such vast significance, is but a little more than a generation old. He is one of the last of those early pioneers. He lived his life into his work, and being dead he yet speaketh. His career is a testimony as to what true devotion and zeal may accomplish for the Kingdom.

In October, 1909, after serving the Church for twenty years, he resigned his position as district superintendent."

Children (4):

[395] + David Henry[5], *b* July 1, 1869; *m Margaret Owen.*
[396] + Samuel G.[5], *b* February 27, 1871; *m Helen Chambers.*
[397] + John Dewalt[5], *b* June 1, 1873; *m Bertha May Gauby.*
[398] + Mary Naomi[5], *b* April 18, 1879; *m Jason Daul Kinsley.*

[72] **REUBEN[4] SHONTZ FOUSE,** son of [16] Theobald[3] and Nancy (Shontz) Fouse, was born July 17, 1844. He enlisted in Co. C, 53rd Pa. Vols. on September 16, 1861, when he was but a little over 17 years old. He seemed to be robust in body, but, in fact, was not as strong as the appearances seemed to indicate. While camped on the north side of the Chickahominy River, Virginia, he was taken down with a low form of typhoid fever, as the physician termed it. He did not seem to suffer because of this indisposition; and, therefore, when the battle of Fair Oaks began on May 31, and the troops were ordered to march, he was determined to fall into ranks and go with his Company, although entreated to remain in camp. The river was very much swollen because of the recent heavy rains, and the soldiers were compelled to wade in the water to their arm-pits in order to reach the bridge. The Regiment with the rest of the Brigade arrived on the battlefield of Fair Oaks during the night, and early on June 1, became engaged with the enemy. The subject of this notice was in this, his first and last battle, and nobly did his duty. But a seemingly deep seated disease had seized him, and during the month of June, as the troops were camped in front of Richmond, he declined in health, until on the morning of June 28, he died in the little shelter tent with his messmates about him. At this time, and a few days previous, there was terrific fighting on the right of our army, as General Porter endeavored to stem the onslaught of Stonewall Jackson. That night the whole army began to retreat for the James River. A rough box was procured, the body embalmed, and given into the care of Corporal H. B. Geissinger for burial. By him it was taken home, and lies buried in the churchyard near his native home, the church in which he was baptized and confirmed.

[73] **FREDERICK SHONTZ[4] FOUSE,** son of [16] Theobald[3] and Nancy (Shontz) Fouse, was born April 9, 1846. He enlisted on July 21, 1861, for three years, or during the war. He became a member of Co. G, 5th

Reg. Pa. Reserves. He was only 15 years old when he enlisted. He served in his Regiment until the end of his enlistment, in 1864. In the summer of that year, he reënlisted and became a member of Co. D, 205th Pa. Vols., in which he served until the end of the war.

December 13, 1862, at the battle of Fredericksburg, Virginia, he was severely wounded. Let us quote his own words: "Few of us who were rushed across the pontoon bridges, and ordered to scale 'Marie Heights,' expected to survive. In the midst of the fray, I was severely wounded by a minnie ball—my right arm was shattered below the shoulder. As best I could, I scurried to the rear, reported at the field hospital, and was put in line for amputation. I was unwilling to submit to amputation, and prevailed upon a nurse to staunch the blood and bandage the wound. I then went across the bridge to the general hospital five miles distant, where after no little persuasion the surgeon put the arm in splints and recommended that a 2 months' furlough be granted to me. After some delay I was allowed to go home, and in May returned to my Company." In 1901 an abscess formed causing intense suffering until some foreign matter was removed. The arm began to heal, but an abscess formed in the right ear. This required an operation under which he died October 1, 1902, almost 40 years after he received his original wound. He was buried in West Laurel Hill Cemetery, Philadelphia, Pennsylvania, in which city he lived for many years.

April 8, 1866, he married *Harriet Emma Long*, born January 20, 1849; daughter of *George* and *Caroline Emma (Craig) Long*. After marriage they lived for some years in Huntingdon, Pennsylvania, where he served for a time as deputy sheriff. He was present at the execution of Boner and Van Bodenburg, the two murderers of the Peightels. He resided for thirty years in Philadelphia where he was engaged most of the time in the insurance business for different companies. Mrs. Fouse yet resides in Philadelphia.

Children (7):

[399] Claud Long[5], *b* July 22, 1867; *d* August 1, 1868.
[400] Ralph Wiestling[5], *b* August 8, 1869; *d* November 14, 1872.
[401] + Clyde Everett[5], *b* May 1, 1871; *m Elsie Irene Deike.*
[402] George Barton[5], *b* January 4, 1874; *d* June 24, 1880.
[403] Frederick Lowman[5], *b* February 17, 1876; *d* August 12, 1880.
[404] + Caroline Edith[5], *b* January 19, 1881; *m A. Bailey Megrew.*
[405] Hattie May[5], *b* October 8, 1884; *d* April 12, 1887.

DAVID[6] FOUSE [75], AND MARGARET ANN (SUMMERS) FOUSE.

[74] **SAMUEL[4] SHONTZ FOUSE,** son of [16] Theobald[3] and Nancy (Shontz) Fouse, was born May 6, 1848. He enlisted in Co. K, 78th Pa. Vols., as a recruit early in 1865. His extreme youth precluded his entrance into the army at an earlier date, although he desired very much to enlist prior to this time. He served to the end of the war, his discharge dating September, 1865. He returned home, and engaged in farming for his father. After being at home several years, he married (1) *Margaret Beyers,* who bore him one child ([406] Carrie J.[5]) which died in infancy. Mrs. Fouse also died soon after the death of her child.

A few years later, he married (2) *Maria Stouffer.* They have no children of their own, but adopted a little girl, who has become as near to them as one of their own could possibly be. She is married to Bruce Summers, and resides on the old Fouse homestead, which is now owned by the subject of this notice. Samuel S. has purchased a property in Marklesburg and resides there, while his farm is in the care of Bruce Summers. The world has dealt kindly with him, excepting that his army life gave him a recurrence of rheumatism, which some years ago made it necessary to remove the right eye—a very great loss. He is a useful citizen, and a strong support of the Reformed Church congregation, whose building stands on his farm, and for which he gave the church a deed.

[75] **DAVID[4] FOUSE,** son of [17] Adam[3] and Susanna (Garner) Fouse, was born April 1, 1830, at the homestead on the banks of Clover Creek, about five miles northeast of Martinsburg, Huston Township, Huntingdon (now Blair) County, Pennsylvania. He was the first of ten children in his father's family, all with one exception growing to manhood and womanhood, the one son Daniel dying in his youth. Prior to David's birth, his father had purchased a large farm on which he reared his family in a well regulated Christian home, where they were taught to work. The father being a successful farmer, purchased other farms, and had much building to do. David, being the oldest, had a large responsibility resting on him, as is the case with most older children in assisting their parents. When David was four years of age, the law was passed creating the public school system in Pennsylvania. It was many years after this before the system was understood and appreciated; hence when David reached school age the system was only in a formative state, and the farmer's boy at that time had small chances for learning. However, with these disadvantages, and the short terms of school in the winter, added to his anxiety to assist in the work at home, he managed to acquire a fair proficiency in

reading, writing, arithmetic, spelling and geography. Mr. Fouse was a robust farmer, 6 feet 1½ inches tall, and possessed much mechanical ability. Being skilled in the use of blacksmith's and carpenter's tools, he did all his own smithing and carpentering, as well as much in that line for his neighbors.

January 20, 1853, Mr. Fouse married *Margaret Ann Summers*, born April 15, 1827; daughter of *Jacob* and *Elizabeth* (*Boyer*) *Summers* and sister of Rebecca who married John Fouse [62]. Mr. Fouse owned a farm one and one-fourth miles to the south of Marklesburg, in Huntingdon County, Pennsylvania, which was their homestead where his children were born, reared and taught the art of farming. This farm is owned by his son John S.[5] Fouse [411].

Mr. and Mrs. Fouse were members of the Reformed Church and reared their six children in the same faith. Mrs. Fouse died December 9, 1896, and Mr. Fouse died March 1, 1909; both are resting in the cemetery of the Reformed Church, near Marklesburg, Huntingdon County, Pennsylvania (Plate 39).

Children (6):

[407] + Adam S.[5], *b* November 20, 1856; *m Anna Huff.*
[408] Mary E.[5], *b* October 29, 1858; *d* April 18, 1859.
[409] + Alfred S.[5], *b* April 12, 1861; *m Margaret Hood.*
[410] + Franklin S.[5], *b* June 15, 1862; *m Alice Shultz.*
[411] + John S.[5], *b* December 2, 1864; *m Catherine Horni.*
[412] + Susan[5], *b* July 13, 1866; *unm.*

[76] **MARGARET[4] FOUSE,** daughter of [17] Adam[3] and Susanna (Garner) Fouse, was born May 28, 1831. October 5, 1851, she married *George Nicodemus;* son of *Jacob* and ——— (*Aerlenbaugh*) *Nicodemus.* They moved to Ohio, where they lived about eight years; they then settled on a farm in Illinois, where they resided during the Civil War. Mr. Nicodemus joined the Union Army and served in Co. R, 15th Reg. Ill. Vol. Inf. At the close of the war he was honorably discharged and returned to his home and family to again pursue his occupation of farming. After some years they left Illinois and moved to Hartley, O'Brien County, Iowa. Mr. Nicodemus died July, 1900, and Margaret, his wife, died September 12, 1902. They both rest in the cemetery at Hartley (Plate 40).

Children (9), surname Nicodemus:

[413] + Susan[5], *b* February 15, 1853; *m Daniel Hoffa.*
[414] + Mary E.[5], *b* October 4, 1854; *m August Marr.*

MARGARET[6] (FOUSE) NICODEMUS [76], AND GEORGE NICODEMUS.

ELIZABETH[4] (FOUSE) GREASER [77].

GEORGE GREASER [55 AND 77].

JOHN McGRAW RHODES (794), BARBARA[4] (FOUSE) RHODES, AND FAMILY

[415] + Sarah[5], *b* November 21, 1856; *m Philip Schadt.*
[416] + Adam F.[5], *b* May 6, 1858; *m Lizzie Lambly.*
[417] Barbara S.[5], *b* February 26, 1861; *d* November 19, 1861.
[418] + Edwin[5], *b* August 22, 1863; *m Kate Lambly.*
[419] + John H.[5], *b* August 13, 1866; *m* (1) *Della Dart Walker; m* (2) *Mary Amanda Vinson.*
[420] + Isaac C.[5], *b* March 17, 1869; *m Myrtle L. Walt.*
[421] + Margaret Ida[5], *b* January 15, 1872; *m Edward Hugill.*

[77] **ELIZABETH[4] FOUSE,** daughter of [17] Adam[3] and Susanna (Garner) Fouse, was born October 12, 1832. November 18, 1877 she married *George Greaser*. son of *George Greaser*, but her husband was accidentally killed July 4, 1879. Mr. Greaser had married (1) *Catharine Fouse* [55],[a] who died January 6, 1874.

Mrs. Greaser has lived all her days on the old homestead farm on Clover Creek, four miles northeast of Martinsburg, and has an interest in the said farm. She was born two years before the present mansion house was built, and saw every building erected which now remains on the farm, excepting the smoke-house. The landscape view of this farm appears as Plate No. 2. Mrs. Greaser's address is Martinsburg, Blair County, Pennsylvania, R. R. No. 2 (Plates 41 and 42).

[79] **BARBARA[4] FOUSE,** daughter of [17] Adam[3] and Susanna (Garner) Fouse, was born November 11, 1835. November 3, 1859, she married *John McGraw Rhodes*; son of *Abraham* and *Eliza* (*McGraw*) *Rhodes* [see 57]. They live on a farm near Clappertown, Blair County, Pennsylvania. In connection with farming, they have also conducted a store for a number of years. Their postoffice address is Barbara, Pennsylvania, named after Mrs. Rhodes (Plate 43.)

Children (3), surname Rhodes:

[422] Adam[5], *b* December 4, 1860; *d* September 15, 1861.
[423] + Sarah Jane[5], *b* September 15, 1862; *m David Barchley Barnett.*
[424] + John F.[5], *b* April 15, 1868; *m Lemma Nenomia Hazzard.*

[80] **JOHN GARNER[4] FOUSE,** son of [17] Adam[3] and Susanna (Garner) Fouse, was born June 6, 1837. He was the sixth child in his father's family. He entered public school at the age of 7 years and made good

[a] See p. 75.

progress in the branches taught, notwithstanding the short terms and the limited training of teachers. At best the public schools in the rural districts were of poor quality, as the school system was yet in its formative state, the law establishing public schools in Pennsylvania having been passed in 1834.

At the age of 20 years he was requested by the secretary of the board of education of Huston township to teach school, and after due consideration responded to the request. He continued to teach for seven successive winters, two terms at Beavertown, one at home or Acker school, Huston township, two terms at Sharpsburg, and two terms at the Skyles school in Taylor township, all in Blair County, Pennsylvania. In the summer he worked on the farm and at his leisure endeavored to better qualify himself to teach the branches taught. He attended a normal institute at Martinsburg, Pennsylvania, under the superintendency of attorney John Dean, later judge of common pleas court of Blair County, and afterwards judge of the supreme court of Pennsylvania. The institute was in session five weeks in the spring of 1858, and in the fall of the same year he attended a select training school for the improvement of teachers, for two months, at Marklesburg, Huntingdon County, Pennsylvania. This school was taught by William A. Houck, later Reverend Houck. In the spring of 1859, he took another course of two months training at the same place, the school being conducted during that session by the late Dr. Andrew Boelus Brumbaugh, of Huntingdon, Pennsylvania.

After the Civil War was in progress he helped to recruit a company of soldiers and himself enlisted as a private in Co. E, 104th Pa. Vol. Inf. After being in the service some time he was appointed Third Sergeant of his Company and served in that capacity until the close of the war. His Regiment was under the command of Brigadier-General McKibben of the Provisional Division in front of Petersburg, Virginia, and under Major General Ferrero in the Third Brigade, Twenty-fourth Corps, Army of the Potomac. On August 25, 1865, he received an honorable discharge at Portsmouth, Virginia. His Regiment was then ordered to Camp Cadwalder (located at Philadelphia) and there mustered out of service. Upon his return home he engaged in farming and taught school that winter.

September 20, 1866, he married *Mary Ellen Shoemaker*, daughter of *Henry* and *Matilda (Snyder) Shoemaker* of Martinsburg, Pennsylvania, who was born May 15, 1840. She was educated in the public schools of Martinsburg and went several terms to the Juniata Collegiate Institute of her native town. She was accomplished in the necessary branches of

JOHN GARNER[5] FOUSE [80], AND MARY ELLEN (SHOEMAKER) FOUSE.

JOHN GARNER FOUSE [80] AND FAMILY (1897)

education to assist her to be a useful and a good helpmate and was well versed in the art of good housekeeping; always was agreeable, kind-hearted and a true companion. She always had an even disposition, and always met people with a smile and greeted everyone with kindness. She was an excellent wife, and a good, kind mother—a good, thoughtful adviser in her family. In her walk through life she showed herself to be a Christian. She loved her church, and her Saviour; and was in her place at church when her health permitted, taking an active part in all Christian work. She was guarded in her conversation, and never talked more than was necessary. She was very much loved by her family and everyone who had the pleasure of knowing her.

After their marriage, Mr. Fouse's father ceded a part of the homestead farm to them, and they bought forty acres in addition from the Peter Shoenberger estate in 1867. In the same year, with the assistance of his father, he built a house and barn on the property and moved there in the fall. Thereafter he devoted his time to farming, dealing in live stock and selling machinery. He continued these pursuits until March, 1888, when he sold all of his property and with his family moved to Pittsburgh, Pennsylvania, to assume the management of the Alta Friendly Society, which pursuit he now follows. Before moving to Pittsburgh, he bought a property at 300 Orchard Place, Knoxville (Mt. Oliver P. O.), Pittsburgh, Pennsylvania, where the family live. Mr. Fouse, wife and children are all members of the Reformed Church. Mrs. Fouse died January 14, 1912, after a lingering illness, and suffering for two years; aged 71 years and 8 months. Funeral services were held at her late residence, 300 Orchard Place, Knoxville, Pennsylvania, by her pastor J. H. Prugh and Rev. Lewis Robb, January 16, at 2 p.m. Her body rests in the family lot in the South Side Cemetery, Pittsburgh, Pennsylvania (Plates 44[a] and 45).

Children (9):

[425] + Emma Getty[5], *b* July 7, 1867; *m Isaac Kagarise Bechtel.*
[426] + Mary Matilda[5], *b* February 23, 1869; *unm.*
[427] + Ella Elizabeth[5], *b* September 6, 1871, *unm.*
[428] + Harvey Shoemaker[5], *b* September 21, 1873; *m Susan Gillmore Chambers.*

[a] Mrs. Fouse's picture, in the double plate, is enlarged from the last she had taken—a small tintype in her bathing suit at the seashore. The group photograph was taken some years ago.

[429] Ida Bell[5], *b* February 19, 1876; *d* March 8, 1897.
[430] + Orlando[5], *b* May 6, 1878; *m Laura Helen O'Conner.*
[431] + Ira Shoemaker[5], *b* September 22, 1880; *unm.*
[432] + John Marvin[5], *b* September 28, 1881; *unm.*
[433] + Edith Lillian[5], *b* August 1, 1885; *m Hagey H. Campbell.*

[81] **SARAH ANN[4] FOUSE,** daughter of [17] Adam[3] and Susanna (Garner) Fouse, was born August 22, 1840. October 1, 1868, she married *Benjamin Franklin Hoover* of Woodbury, Pennsylvania, son of *David Hoover.* They live on a farm near Martinsburg, Pennsylvania, and are members of the Reformed Church at that place (Plate 46).

Children (5), surname Hoover:

[434] + Flora Fouse[5], *b* September 3, 1869; *m Albert B. Miller.*
[435] + Minerva Fouse[5], *b* August 23, 1871; *unm.*
[436] + Janetta Fouse[5], *b* September 1, 1873; *unm.*
[437] + Adam Fouse[5], *b* September 5, 1877; *m Virginia Bowl.*
[438] David Mahlon[5], *b* August 25, 1880; *d* June 27, 1881.

[82] **ADAM GARNER[4] FOUSE,** son of [17] Adam[3] and Susanna (Garner) Fouse, was born December 13, 1842. With his brothers and sisters he shared the privileges and blessings of a well regulated Christian home. Educational facilities in his early life were limited. Though the public school system was established somewhat previous to his school age, yet when he entered, it was still in a poorly developed state. Not until in the early fifties was the value of having public schools fully appreciated. During this decade he attended the winter terms of three months' duration, and spent the remainder of the year helping on the farm. He was of a studious nature and employed a large portion of his leisure time with his books in order to advance himself in the branches then taught. In this way he prepared himself for teaching, which profession he afterward followed. He, however, attended a select training school for teachers for a term of nine weeks in the fall of 1859 at Marklesburg, Huntingdon County, Pennsylvania. This school was conducted by the late Dr. Andrew Boelus Brumbaugh. In the fall of the same year he passed a favorable examination under County Superintendent John Dean, later Judge Dean, and was appointed a teacher when he had not yet reached the age of 17 years. He taught for five terms, the first at Beavertown, the second at the Skyles school, and the remaining three terms at the home or Acker

SARAH ANN[4] (FOUSE) HOOVER [81], BENJAMIN FRANKLIN HOOVER AND THEIR CHILDREN.

ADAM GARNER[4] FOUSE [82], SARAH (FRANK) FOUSE, ADAM IRVING[5] FOUSE [441], AND CLARA FRANK[5] FOUSE [439].

(*From Brumbach Families*, copyright 191[illegible].)

school, all in Blair County, Pennsylvania. At the home school he had as pupils a number of his old fellow classmates. After having taught these five terms he enlisted in Co. E, 104th Pa. Vol. Inf., to serve one year, or during the Civil War. His Regiment was under the command of Lieut. Col. Theophilus Kephart of Norristown, Pennsylvania, in the Third Brigade, Provisional Division under Brigadier-General McKibbin, and Maj. Gen. E. H. Ferrero, 24th Corps, Army of the Potomac. He was honorably discharged at Portsmouth, Virginia, on August 25, 1865. At once returning home, he relieved his father at the plow, it being near the time for fall seeding of wheat. He had long desired to prepare for the Gospel ministry, rather intensified by the tendency in army life away from the Divine, and his father's consent was earnestly sought. The latter had planned to give to each member of his household a home, and he expected each member to do his part. He ultimately consecrated the youngest of the family to the Divine calling.

Ever obedient, Mr. Fouse accepted the plan in good faith, turning his best efforts toward making the changes to follow the division of properties and the erection of buildings, at the same time taking an active part in the affairs of the community. November 25, 1870, he was elected president of the Huston Township Coöperative Mutual Fire Insurance Company which he managed successfully until March, 1876. In the meantime he also filled the position of secretary to the board of school directors of the same township for three years.

October 19, 1871, Adam Garner Fouse married (1) *Sarah Frank*, born September 4, 1842, on the Frank homestead in Penn Township, Huntingdon County Pennsylvania (where married); daughter of *Jacob* and *Elizabeth* (*Baer*) *Frank;* and sister of *Elizabeth* (*Frank-Shontz*) *Fouse*, second wife of *Christian Fouse* [61]; and also sister of *Maria Baer* (*Frank*) *Brumbaugh*, widow of the late *Andrew Boelus Brumbaugh*, *M.D.*, of Huntingdon, Pennsylvania. Mrs. Fouse was educated in the public schools, was refined, kind-hearted and true. He brought his bride to the Fouse homestead farm (see Plate 2), now owned by himself and his sister Elizabeth Greaser, where he had been engaged in farming. This was nothing new to her since she was reared on the farm. She was an excellent and faithful wife, and a good, kind mother, doing all she could to make her family and others happy. She was amongst the best of housewives, doing everything neatly and with care. She was a Christian lady, loved her church and Saviour; took an active part in all Christian work, and was always in her place at church when her health permitted. She was of a quiet nature, amiable and very conservative in conversation about others. She was very much loved by her family, and all who had the pleasure of her acquaintance.

They continued on the farm until February, 1876, when Adam Garner Fouse went to Philadelphia to assume the management of a mercantile reporting agency, but the business did not appeal to him, and after two years he returned to farming. In 1888, a year after his father's death, he returned to Philadelphia to assume the management of the Alta Friendly Society. He continued at this until January 1, 1893, when he received the appointment of comptroller of the Fidelity Mutual Life Insurance Company of Philadelphia, in which position he continues.

The health of Mrs. Fouse began to fail in 1905 and she died September 3, 1906, in Philadelphia, after a lingering illness of over a year. She was buried in the Salem Reformed Church Cemetery, on the original Fouse premises at Beavertown. After the death of his wife he continued housekeeping with his two children, Clara and Adam Irving, until September 28, 1909, when he married (2) *Mrs. Eloise* (*Reese*) *Guthrie*, daughter of *Benjamin Thomas* and *Anna M. Reese*, born January 8, 1864, near Westchester, Chester County, Pennsylvania. She attended public school in the neighborhood, graduated from the Downingtown High School, and then taught school until her marriage to Mr. Guthrie, in 1884. Her parents are of Quaker lineage. Mrs. Fouse is an excellent housekeeper, and a refined, excellent lady. Mr. Fouse and his family attend the Presbyterian Church. Residence was 838 North Forty-first Street, Philadelphia, Pennsylvania[a] (Plate 47).

Children by the first marriage (*3*):

[439] + Clara Frank[5], *b* July 10, 1872; *unm.*
[440] Amy Elizabeth[5], *b* July 22, 1875; *d* September 19, 1876.
[441] + Adam Irving[5], *b* September 29, 1877, *m Xenia Arvilda Hampton.*

[83] **HENRY SMITH[4] FOUSE,** son of [17] Adam[3] and Susanna (Garner) Fouse, was born August 25, 1845. He is the ninth child of his father's family and shared the privileges and blessings of a Christian home. Educational facilities had improved and its importance was better understood than in the time of the older children who attended the public school in its earlier stages. He attended the school during the winter months. The term was then extended to four months and thereby gave him better opportunity. He was not interested in learning, as were his brothers and sisters, but more inclined to mechanical pursuits. He was strong, able-

[a] After December 15, 1914, Martinsburg, Pennsylvania.

HENRY SMITH FOUSE [83] AND FAMILY

bodied and a good workman; but disliked farming, preferring to work with machinery, and at the carpenter trade. He did some farming, but later followed carpenter contracting which is his present occupation. During the Civil War he enlisted as private, at 19 years of age, in Co. B, 208th Reg. Pa. Vol. Inf., of which Alexander Bobb, of Martinsburg, Pennsylvania was Major; First Brigade, 3rd Division commanded by Maj. Gen. John F. Hartranft (of Norristown, Pennsylvania); 9th Army Corps, in front of Petersburg, Virginia, Army of the Potomac. Mr. Fouse participated in several engagements and was wounded at the battle of Fort Steadman, March 25, 1865. His command wished him to enter the camp hospital, but he refused, preferring to remain with his Company and Regiment. During the final battle, in front of Petersburg and Richmond April 1-3, 1865, when the Confederate lines were broken, he marched with his command until word was received of the surrender of General Lee, at Appomattox Courthouse. He then returned via Petersburg to City Point on the James River, and via Chesapeake Bay and Potomac River to Washington, D. C., where he remained until June, 1865, when occurred the national parade and inspection, after which he was honorably discharged. After his discharge, he returned to his home and worked with his father on the farm until 1867. He then took up the carpenter trade, and in that year assisted in building several houses and barns on his father's properties, and on others. December 12, 1867, he married *Mary Jane Aurandt*, born January 20, 1848, daughter of *David* and *Elizabeth (Kemp) Aurandt*. Residence, 513 Fifth Avenue, Altoona, Pennsylvania (Plate 48).

Children (10):

[442] + David Milton[5], *b* September 23, 1868; *m* (1) *Nancy Bechtel; m* (2) *Lizzie Falkender.*
[443] + Adam Franklin[5], *b* March 27, 1870; *m* (1) *Bertha Kunes; m* (2) *Martha Johnson.*
[444] Flora[5], *b* February 12, 1872; *d.*
[445] Oliver[5], *b* March 9, 1873; *d* October 6, 1873.
[446] Eleanor[5], *b* March 19, 1874; *d* April 1, 1877.
[447] Elmer Aurandt[5], *b* September 9, 1876; *d* March 22, 1877.
[448] + Ora Elizabeth[5], *b* July 31, 1878; *m Samuel Nicodemus.*
[449] + Frederick Augustus[5], *b* October 12, 1880; *m Matilda Miller.*
[450] + Mary Endora[5], *b* March 20, 1884; *m Andrew C. Karns.*
[451] + Ella Melissa[5], *b* September 15, 1888; *unm.*
[452] Orville Fouse (adopted).

[84] **LEVI GARNER[4] FOUSE,** son of [17] Adam[3] and Susanna (Garner) Fouse was born October 21, 1850. He entered the public schools, and like the other children attended school only during the winter months, working on the farm in the summer. Being the youngest child, his father decided to give him a college education and fit him for some profession. His father desired him to study for the ministry. In March, 1868, he entered Heidelburg College, Tiffin, Ohio. After the term he returned home for the vacation and concluded to enter Mercersburg College for the fall term, which he did and remained until December, 1869. Against the wishes of his father he abandoned college and undertook to prepare himself for commercial life. He secured a position as clerk with Jones and Laughlin, Pittsburgh, in a store run in connection with their iron works, remaining until 1871. He then visited his father's home. At this time he assisted in organizing The Huston Township Mutual Fire Insurance Company, home office Fredericksburg, Blair County, Pennsylvania. He was made general agent and solicitor for the company. Soon thereafter he associated himself with Samuel Wineland Grabill in a mercantile business from April, 1871, to April, 1872, at which time he sold his interest in the business to his partner, and resigned his agency in the fire insurance company. He then engaged in the manufacture and sale of "The Dr. Wengert Family Medicine" with main office at York, Pennsylvania. The business prospered at first, but the panic in 1875 caused heavy losses, and, in 1874, Mr. Fouse turned his attention to the mercantile reporting business. In December, 1878, he founded the Fidelity Mutual Life Insurance Company of Philadelphia, and the Fidelity Mutual Aid Association (now known as the Alta Friendly Society). Both companies were successful from the start. Mr. Fouse has continuously been president and actuary of the former, and a director of the Alta Friendly Society. Prior to 1896, under the presidency and management of Mr. Fouse, the Fidelity Mutual Life Insurance Company erected an office building at Nos 112-116 North Broad Street, Philadelphia, at a cost of $1,000,000, for the accommodation of their steadily increasing business. "In the thirty-five years of his presidency, the Fidelity Mutual grew to be one of Philadelphia's largest financial institutions, operating in forty-one states, and with $135,000,000 in outstanding insurance" (Plate 50).

"Mr. Fouse was regarded as one of the best constructive minds in the life insurance business. He was the originator of the disability clause in life insurance, under which total and permanent disability relieves the policy holder of all further premium payments. When Ex-President Cleve-

LEVI GARNER[1] FOUSE [84].
Courtesy of Fidelity Mutual Life Ins. Co.

land became Chairman of the Association of Life Insurance Presidents one of his first official acts was to appoint Mr. Fouse a member of the Executive Committee, in which capacity he continued to serve until the time of his death."

"In the early days of his life insurance career he served the United States Army Officers' Association in the capacity of consulting actuary, computing valuable war-hazard tables from the government records, dating back to the inception of the War Department. These tables are recognized as authoritative. He also did important work for the Order of Foresters, the Ministerial Sustentation Fund of the Presbyterian Church, and for other organizations, but in recent years his duties in connection with his own company demanded practically all of his time."

In 1900 Mr. Fouse took an active part in the organization of the Philadelphia Casualty Company. "Mr. Fouse was a fluent writer and contributed largely to insurance literature. Articles written by him appeared in the 'Yale Readings in Insurance, 1909', published by the American Academy of Political and Social Science, and in numerous insurance journals, statistical, economic, and other publications. He lectured on life insurance before the Wharton School of Finance and Commerce of the University of Pennsylvania during the year 1904-05. His lectures were published in the *Annals of the American Academy of Political and Social Science*."

"At the time of his death, Mr. Fouse was a director of the Third National Bank, the Central Trust and Savings Company and prominently identified with a number of other Philadelphia institutions. For many years he had been an elder in Northminster Presbyterian Church and, until his health began to fail, he was also superintendent of Northminster Sunday School. He was prominently connected with Pocono Pines Assembly, a member of University Lodge No. 610, F. & A. M., a Knight Templar, a member of the American Academy of Political and Social Science, American Statistical Association, the Manufacturers' Club of Philadelphia, and numerous other organizations"[a]

January 19, 1870, Levi Garner Fouse married *Mary Bell Hause*, born February 11, 1851; daughter of *Harmon* and *Susan* (*Minnich*) *Hause*, of Mercersburg, Pennsylvania. He was partially paralyzed in 1900, but had been frequently at his office until several weeks before his death in Philadelphia, January 16, 1914 (Plates 49 and 50).

[a] *L. G. Fouse, Founder and President The Fidelity Mutual Life Insurance Company of Philadelphia—Dean of the Life Insurance Presidents of America*, 1914, pp. 7–8. Plates 49, 50 are also kindly loaned by the said Company, and appeared in the Memorial here mentioned.

RESOLUTIONS PASSED BY THE BOARD OF DIRECTORS OF THE FIDELITY MUTUAL LIFE INSURANCE COMPANY

"It becomes our sad duty to record upon the minutes of this Company the death on January 16, 1914, of L. G. Fouse, its President and Founder, whom God, in His all-wise providence, has removed from the field of life's labors.

While a sense of deep loss to this Company is heavy upon us; and while the grief of a personal bereavement almost too great for words is in our minds and hearts; nevertheless, we feel that it is a privilege, sorrowful yet proud, to inscribe here our debt of admiration and love to the leader whose ability, wisdom, and single-minded goodness were an inspiration to the institution which he directed, to the business of life insurance throughout the country, and to all those who came into contact with his work and personality.

The Fidelity Mutual Life Insurance Company was conceived by him thirty-five years ago, and under his continued Presidency has grown to the splendid position it now occupies in the insurance and financial world.

He brought to the work of this Company all the energies of a powerful mind, an unclouded vision, and a strong executive genius. A born organizer and builder, with that patient, unswerving devotion to a purpose and that capacity for infinite detail which marks constructive talent, he possessed also the clear-eyed imagination, the almost prophetic zeal of the explorer and discoverer who ever leads the way to new and greater fields.

He devoted this rare combination of gifts to the development of this Company, not as a passive leader and advisor, but as a worker of works, laboring unceasingly and untiringly with all the resources of a powerful mind in a strong man's body. Possessed of a remarkable ability to read character and determine fitness, he surrounded himself with associates who loved their work as men love only the work for which they are suited and able. Toiling as many hours—and as many minutes—as the last man under him, he had a kindliness and thoughtfulness for the interests of others which endeared him to his fellows from the topmost to the lowest. Yet his kindness was never without justice; and his justice never without kindness. Leading, he always himself worked; and working, he always lead.

Thirty-five years of such work and such leadership, inspiring and teaching all who worked with him, resulted in building this Company into a monument that stands enduringly in the respect of the insurance world and in the faith and security of thousands of American homes.

FIDELITY MUTUAL LIFE INSURANCE COMPANY'S BUILDING, AND ITS FIRST PRESIDENT.
Courtesy of F. M. L. I. Co.

Nor has the Company of which he was President for so many years alone benefited by his genius and labors. The life insurance business at large has gained in strength, in ideas, and in ideals, by his connection with it. The independence of thought, the imagination to conceive, and the courage to test conception, gave, not only to his own Company, but to all life insurance many of its best and most advanced features. The high purpose, the sincere belief in the dignity and public benefit of insurance as an institution which he carried into all his work made that business a better business for all who are engaged in it.

Society at large has lost in him a useful citizen and forceful member. The same strength of body, mind and character which made him a towering figure in the field of his work, exerted an influence beyond that field which is almost impossible to measure. This influence of strength was widened and deepened by the kindliness, the sincerity and goodness which won the love and loyalty of all those whose lives came into contact with his.

Thus, while it is with deep regret we here inscribe our sorrow for the loss of our President and our friend, we feel that there is much we cannot lose, and for which we and this Company must be ever thankful. For the work that he has done cannot die, the child of his creation is a living thing that must ever grow. All the work, the ideas, the improvements which grew under his guidance, remain. Beyond all, the spirit of labor, courage, and loyalty to the highest ideal of life insurance which his example fostered in this Company will continue to be the guiding light which will lead to greater heights untrod; while the memory of his strength and his kindness will ever be an inspiration to those who carry on the work.

Therefore, be it resolved that we, the Board of Directors of The Fidelity Mutual Life Insurance Company, lament the loss of our President and friend; and that the foregoing expression of our love and regard for his worth and goodness be spread upon the minutes of the Company; and that a copy thereof be sent to his family as a token and assurance of our sympathy for them in their great loss."[a]

[a] *L. G. Fouse, Founder and President*, etc., 1914, pp. 19–21.

MEMORIAL STATEMENT ADOPTED BY THE ASSOCIATION OF LIFE INSURANCE PRESIDENTS AT A MEETING HELD IN NEW YORK, FEBRUARY 6, 1914.

"It is with profound sorrow that the Association of Life Insurance Presidents records the death of Mr. Levi Garner Fouse. Always original, forceful and far-seeing, his services to the Association were peculiarly helpful at the time of its organization, and as a member of its Executive Committee his active interest continued to the time of his death. His loyalty and willingness to coöperate in all that was best for the interests of the Association were abundantly shown by the time he devoted willingly to its affairs. Even in the days when physical infirmity made it impossible for him to attend its meetings, by personal correspondence and through his fellow-officers whom he sent to represent him, he kept closely in touch with its activities and thus continued to lend a hand to its work.

As organizer and head of The Fidelity Mutual Life Insurance Company his ability as a business man and his clearness of vision as an underwriter were amply shown. The strength and success of his Company are enduring evidence of his integrity, persistency and capacity. Its prosperous condition is a great tribute to his faithfulness and energy.

In all movements looking toward bettering conditions for all life insurance companies he was a force. He served his own Company well but always in a way that served also the best interests of the life insurance business as a whole. In his death this Association and all life insurance companies must join in mourning a common loss."[a]

ADDRESS BY REV. W. COURTLAND ROBINSON, D.D., AT FUNERAL SERVICES OF LEVI GARNER FOUSE, JANUARY 19, 1914.

"Many of us who are here this afternoon have been witnessing with grave concern, the slow weakening of a great oak, and now the tree has fallen in the forest. Not indeed, as we sometimes feared, by a sudden stroke of the woodman, but rather slowly sinking by the insidious working of hidden enemies of health and life.

"The passing of such a man from our community brings to us a sense of crisis. So many interests are touched, when such a power hath been taken out, that we realize that there must be many radical adjustments,

[a] *L. G. Fouse, Founder and President,* etc., 1914, p. 21.

and we look forward, it may be with some solicitude. We can understand the spirit of the Psalmist when he cried,—'Help, Lord, for the Godly men grow few, and the righteous fail from the children of men.' And at such a time thoughtful people look again to the foundations; to those who are closest it seems as if the 'earth were removed and the mountains cast into the midst of the sea' and those of serious mind look to the rock on which they stand. They peer eagerly to see, if possible, the invisible and eternal.

"Memories come into the mind as it were a flood, and we pick out those things that we love and hang them upon the walls of our mind. And it may be that we view the future through windows that are clouded with anxiety and sorrow.

"We have gathered here this afternoon to do honor to the memory of a man whom we knew, and that we may extend our hands in loving sympathy to those who are most sorely bereaved. * * *

"When a man dies, there is an instinctive and inevitable summing up, the forming of a judgment. 'It is given unto man once to die and after that judgment.' Not only the righteous and perfect judgment of God, but the more imperfect judgment of men. We are as those who climb the mountain side, and look back upon the valley. We see its courses and beauties more clearly than when we were a part of it. As we walk side by side in this work-a-day world, our judgments are superficial and unjust. We see the incidents on the surface, and sometimes do not see the great current of the stream. We have our rival ambitions, our contrary opinions, and our diverse emotions; and thus we never see men or things as we should. A small thing close to the eye shuts out the greater thing beyond. Perhaps this is why the Master said, 'Judge not that ye be judged' and why the Apostle said 'Who art thou that judgest?' But when death intervenes we see the life in its entirety; then we catch its tendencies, and gather up its forces; then we see more clearly whither it was going, and the great purposes hidden within it. Even then indeed our judgment is not perfect, for who can know the heart of man save God, Who made the heart, and Whose all-seeing and loving eye penetrates its holiest sanctuary?

"I take it that if you and I were but to bring to our mind in a single adjective, the chief impression of Mr. Fouse, we would use the adjective 'strong.' He was a strong man. Nothing feeble about him. Strong physically, at least so it seemed. That was my impression of him a little more than six years ago when I first saw him. He gave me then the impression of a man of great physical strength, for then he was at the full flood of his manhood. He walked like a strong man, he looked like a strong man. No labor too hard, no burden too heavy, no problem or perplexity too exacting, but he would go forward to it with courage and confidence. He seemed to glory in physical strength. But even then I am told disease had begun its devastating work. Doubtless he overused this gift of God, and labored when he should have rested. He bore burdens that should have been put aside—persisted when nature cried out for respite.

"Strong intellectually. He was splendidly endowed of mind. He improved it by careful training. He investigated, and he was able to bring correct deductions from his investigations. He had a mind both analytic and synthetic, and surely when both are given unto one man, they make his mind strong. Again and again we would discover how carefully he thought out things. Even after his first sign of illness, I was surprised to learn how he studied into his own trouble, and how accurately he measured it all. I am told that, more than most men, he mastered the details of his business, and understood the methods and ways and the intricacies of the complicated insurance world.

"Out of this came the great strength of judgment. His conclusions were formed carefully. I do not believe that any of us, can remember what we might call a 'snap judgment.' When a conclusion was arrived at, it was based on reason. It was buttressed and protected—it was hard to find the weak place in the armor or a hole in the wall. He had a reason for the faith in him. Not that he was infallible, but he always knew why he decided thus or so. He was therefore strong in purpose. Having reached his conclusion, and brought it to the light of conscience, and viewed the whole affair, he had a strong purpose. Enemies could not frighten him, or yet good friends swerve him. A purpose once formed went on steadily to the end. This was his characteristic even after feebleness of flesh had crept upon him. A splendid fidelity of purpose. Of course possessing these qualities he was strong in execution, a masterful executive. We only have to look at the great company represented here, which he took as a little blade, and which has grown to be a great tree, for thirty-five years he has been executive head. It takes a master mind to do such things. We had the benefit of it in our own church. For twenty-two years he was the executive head of our Bible school, and he led it always with great care, with great attention to details, and yet with a splendid massing of forces. He gave to us and this school just as willingly of his strong nature as to his business.

"It is not disparaging to the many noble and willing workers to say that the school today, of which we are proud, owes a special and peculiar debt to him.

"Yes, strong in execution, and equally strong in sympathy; not a self-centered man. He loved to overflow the interests of his own company. He reached out to the larger things, always pressing on to the greater insurance world. The interest of his own Bible school did not confine his interest, he must reach to the Association. The interest of his own church, which he surely loved, did not confine him, he must think of his denomination. He had a peculiar feeling and sympathy for the ministers of our church; and it is doubtless due to his executive ability, more than to anyone, that we have the splendid plan of Ministerial Sustentation in the Presbyterian Church today. Not his idea originally, but in due time it fell to him to give it just that moulding that made it practical, and led to its adoption by the church. All the ministers who will receive this benefit will owe a debt to him. ' He showed a strength in sympathy for others. He had in his nature that which was touched by things and people, never demonstrative, it was often hidden; it might be shown in a very business like fashion,.and yet it was there. Again and again I have talked with him concerning men and things and I do not recall an utterance that did not have in it a sign of charity and sympathy for others. He loved to give young people a chance. There are those who would testify to this. Only this morning I was told how he did just the right thing in the right time to relieve a mother anxious for her daughter. He was strong in sympathy and affection. Strong in sympathy, strong in faith. He believed in God and in Jesus Christ His Son, and was never ashamed of his faith. Self confident among men there was notable in him great reverence and humility when he approached God, conscious of his own imperfections, he yet gloried in his Saviour. He loved the church and the congregation of God's people. He loved this church faithfully, and so long as health permitted he was always in it and at our mid-week services. For many years he was elder, the highest honor bestowed on laymen in the Presbyterian Church, and faithfully filled the duties. He watched every phase of the work more carefully than any other man I know, for most of us become more or less specialists.

"One of the pathetic things that we have witnessed these last few months is his insistent coming to this room in great feebleness, because he loved the house of his Father. Strong in faith. Yes I am sure I have chosen the right word, a strong man. Yet there is that which is stronger than the strongest man, there is that which causes the strongest to grow weak. The strong hath become weak and fallen in his place.

"Is that all? If it were all, I indeed would not be a comforter, but a messenger of despair. I go to this Book which he loved, and which he loved to have youth and children learn, and I find that it speaks another message, which tells me of 'joy at God's right hand.' 'That he has rested from his labors and his works follow.' It tells me that 'God will satisfy those who trust Him, with long life,' that means more than a few years; and it tells me that Jesus has gone 'to prepare a place for those who trust Him.' It tells me that 'eye hath not seen nor ear hath heard nor hath it entered the heart of man the glories that God hath prepared for them that love Him.' It tells me that we are saved not by our poor faulty righteousness, for no man is perfect, but it tells me that believers are clothed upon with the spotless righteousness of Jesus, if so be that they put their trust in Him and acknowledge His name. It tells me that he will take those who have thus trusted Him, and as an Advocate and Friend, lead them by the hand into the very presence of the Father and present them before Him, clothed in His own spotless radiant majestic righteousness. We sorrow dear friends, but we sorrow not as others who have no hope. If we believe that Jesus died and rose again, even so they that believe in Jesus will God bring with Him.' "

The above sermon is published by direct permission, and from notes furnished by Dr. Robinson. The same is also published, together with a large amount of exceedingly interesting "Resolutions," "Tributes from the Press," "Letters and Tributes," pictures, etc., in the 60 page Memorial recently issued by the Fidelity Mutual Life Insurance Company to which the reader is referred.

Children of Levi Garner[4] Fouse and Mary Bell (Hause) Fouse (3):

[453-454] Infants, died young.
[455] + Harry Hause[5], *b* May 12, 1874; *m Mary Ella Steese.*

CIVIL WAR RECORD OF THE FOUSES[a]

"We will now say a few words in reference to the loyalty of the Fouse relatives, during the Civil War, when the South rebelled, and when war was declared by the President (Abraham Lincoln) of the United States. While the Fouse families regretted the necessity for the President's call

[a] Placed in this portion of the book because most of the volunteers were of the fourth generation.

to arms, yet sympathized with the North, all the Fouses then living and their kin, were true to the North; and when the call came from the President for men to defend the Union, many of them volunteered (encouraged by their parents) to take up arms to assist in crushing the rebellion. Like all good and true soldiers they were brave and did their duty. Some were left dead and lost on the battlefields; some died in the hospitals; some were wounded and recovered; and fortunately most of them were permitted to return home to enjoy the freedom and liberty of the Union, vouchsafed to them by the Constitution of the United States, after a bloody war of four years.

"The reader not acquainted with the characters and spirit of the Fouse clan might infer from an examination of the military records of the participants in the Civil War of the sixties, that they spring from a warlike tribe, and that they foster a passion for war. But those who are familiar with their history know them to be law abiding and peace loving citizens. They deprecate and deplore war more on account of the dire consequences, but they seem also to realize that God now and then carries forward His work through the terrible agency of war.

"The idea of militarism is ingrained in human life and character. The nation that has none of it has never held much of a position in the world and has never accomplished much of anything for the welfare of mankind. The Bible teaches that through the instrumentality of war the Canaanites were dispossessed of the land promised to Abraham's posterity and Israel was made a nation. In the historical account of many wars is not the hand of God discernible? War and conquest, have built up Kingdoms and Republics like Greece and Rome, England and the United States."

"War in the hands of the great King saved England from the blighting invasion of Paganism, and the religion of Mohammed, and prepared her for the higher destiny that awaited her.

"It became necessary to resort to the sword to make the American Colonies free and independent states.

"In these heroic and bloody conflicts for freedom, the love of God and love of country were the noble and controlling passions of the human heart. Taking into consideration the great sacrifices that were made by the Revolutionary fathers to establish this American Republic so favorable for the development for a higher civilization and Christianity of a higher type than had been realized in any other part of the world, it is no wonder that when the call came for men to help defend the Union so many of the Fouse relationship promptly responded. They felt it was their duty to their Great King of Kings, and to their sweet land of liberty.

"The majority of them came safely through the military conflict and lived to see the nation stronger than it was before the bloody strife, and a portion of that strength is due to the development of certain elements in militarism in the people at large.

"A good percentage of the relationship doing military duty to preserve the Union had before their enlistment entered the services of King Emanuel, hence they were Christian soldiers before shouldering the United States musket. We hope that future generations of this noble and free country may never be called upon to take up arms in a similar conflict.

"After the soldiers' return from the army to their respective vocations, they took up the work of the Lord's valiant soldiers of the Cross.

"The records in the War Department at Washington, D. C., tell the number of the Fouse Kin who volunteered. Twenty-six took part in the Civil War and helped to subdue the rebellion, and are also noted in this history, giving the families to which they belonged. Rev. Theobald Fouse had seven sons in the Civil War, viz: Christian, John, Benjamin, Dewalt S., Reuben, Frederick, and Samuel, and two sons-in-law, Anthony Shultz and Samuel Grove. Adam Fouse had three sons in it, viz: John G., Adam G., and Henry S., and one son-in-law, George Nicodemus. Theobald A. Fouse had two sons, viz: George W. and William D. Jonathan Hoover, one son, William. Jacob C. Hoover, one son, Daniel. Jacob Heimbaugh, one son, David. Michael Heimbaugh, one son, Jacob. John Miller, one son, Abraham. Jacob Hopple, son-in-law of Jonathan Miller. Frederick Garner, one son, Alfred. Daniel Garner, one son, Dewalt, and two sons-in-law, William Warren Waddle, and Frederick Leibert. Sarah Peightel, one son, John. All these were in active service in the defense of their country.

"We believe that the present and future generations of the Fouse families will be thankful that so many of the 'Fouse Kin' were willing to enter the arena of the conflict (1861-1865)—if needs be to lay down their lives to save the Union for which their forefathers so nobly struggled and fought in 1776-1783" (Jno. Garner Fouse).

REV. ABRAHAM MILLER [85].

Families of the Fifth Generation

[85] **ABRAHAM[5] MILLER**, son of [20] John[4] and Catherine (Clay) Miller, was born February 25, 1838. His father died in 1839, and his mother in 1842, leaving him an orphan at the age of 4 years. After his mother's death, he was cared for by his grandmother, Mrs. Abraham Fouse Miller, who was kind and true to him as most good grandmothers are. He was early taught to work and practice economy. At school he was an apt student, loved his books and made good use of his time. He advanced rapidly in all the branches taught and passed a satisfactory examination. At 17 years of age, he began teaching and taught for several sessions, at the same time continuing to study for his own improvement. He had saved money and entered Heidelburg College, Tiffin, Ohio, to prepare himself for the ministry. While at college the Civil War broke out; and, under President Lincoln's first call for troops, he enlisted April 22, 1861, and was assigned to Co. H, 8th Reg. Ohio Vol. Inf. On account of illness he was honorably discharged August 1, 1861. He then returned to college, finished his course of studies and, at the General Synod of the Reformed Church at Dayton, Ohio, May 26, 1862, was licensd to preach the Gospel. He organized his first congregation in Louisville, Ohio, November 21, 1863, and in 1868-69, built a new church of brick. He organized a second congregation (St. Peters) near Marlboro, Ohio, during the same year. Both these churches have been replaced by larger and better structures. He built a third new church at North Georgetown, Ohio, in 1883. He organized a congregation at Salem, Ohio, 1892; built a new church at Alliance, Ohio, in 1896; also one at North Jackson, Ohio, in 1905. The last one he built at Kent, Ohio, in 1908. It seems Mr. Miller performed his share in the organizing of congregations, and in the building of churches. In 1900, Mr. Miller was elected chaplain of the Department of Ohio G. A. R. He was elected president of the East Ohio Synod at Canton, Ohio, in 1904, and rëelected at Akron, Ohio, 1905. He received the degree of Doctor of Divinity from Wurtemburg College, Springfield, Ohio. Mr. Miller was an able preacher and did a good work wherever he was located. He did missionary work exclusively throughout his life.

December 5, 1858, he married (1) *Mary Dipple*, who was born April

10, 1840. She died January 20, 1860, without issue. Mr. Miller then married (2) *Mary Smith*. This union did not prove congenial, and a separation followed. Mr. Miller again married, May 10, 1871, (3) *Mary Miller* (but no kin). She was born December 21, 1844, and died November, 1882, without issue. December 5, 1883, he again married (4) *Mary E. Stiber*, who was born May 1, 1859. This marriage proved a blessing to each of them, and they lived a happy and congenial life. But alas, the reaper death claimed Mr. Miller at his home, 200 Williams Street, Kent, Ohio, April 24, 1911. Thus the town of Kent lost a very able and good preacher, and a good citizen, beloved by all who knew him; and his wife, a kind, devoted and loving husband. They were childless. Mrs. Miller retains their home and her address remains the same (see [10], p. 25, and Plate 51).

[86] **ADAM LEWIS[5] MILLER,** son of [21] Jonathan[4] and Lydia (Cassler) Miller, was born December 14, 1840, on the old Miller homestead, near Canton, Ohio. In March, 1863, he went to Whitely County, Indiana, where on February 9, 1888, he married *Sarah Etta Cocklin*, born October 29, 1844; daughter of *Adam* and *Barbara* (*Gaerte*[a]) *Cocklin*. They moved to Clinton County, Iowa, where their first child was born March 18, 1869. In the spring of 1874, they moved to Buchanan County, Missouri. Mr. Miller followed farming until 1884. In 1876, he was elected Justice of the Peace for Marion Township, Buchanan County, Missouri, and has since held the office continuously. In 1895, Mr. Miller located at Stockbridge, Missouri, where he is engaged in carpet and rug weaving. Mr. and Mrs. Miller are members of the German Reformed Church, and he is an independent Democrat. Address, Easton, Missouri, R. F. D. No. 3, Box 58 (Plates 17 and 52).

Children (8):

[500] + Minerva Maud[6], *b* March 18, 1869; *m Abner Kreamer Hamm.*
[501] + Walter Scott[6], *b* May 26, 1871; *m Mary Ann Johnson.*
[502] + Rawlins Adam[6], *b* December 24, 1872; *m Luemma Estella Donaldson.*

[a] Mr. Adam Lewis[5] Miller says the name is "Gaerte," and that Caspar Gaerte, native of Alsace, or Lorain, was father of Elizabeth who married Frederick[3] Fouse [49] and of Barbara, mother of his own wife (see *Brumbach Families*, page 398).

Mr. Miller has greatly assisted in gathering Miller-Fouse facts for this portion of this volume, and cordial thanks are herewith extended to him.

ADAM LEWIS[6] MILLER [36] AND FAMILY.

[503] + Francis Preston^{6}, *b* November 15, 1875; *m Laura May Williams.*
[504] + Olive May^{6}, *b* September 29, 1877; *m Stephen Edgar De Vore.*
[505] + Irene Stella^{6}, *b* October 1, 1879; *m Christian Henry Zysset.*
[506] + Stanley Cocklin^{6}, *b* December 22, 1882; *m Lola Richter.*
[507] Sarah Alfareta^{6}, *b* April 18, 1887; at home.

[88] **JOHN CASSLER^{5} MILLER,** son of [21] Jonathan^{4} and Lydia (Cassler) Miller, was born May 29, 1845, on his father's farm near Canton, Ohio. In 1866, he with his father and family moved to Iowa, and in 1869 to Missouri, in 1871 to Easton, Missouri. In March, 1875, he moved to California, remaining there until 1879, then returned to Buchanan County, Missouri, and bought a farm near Easton. His mother and one unmarried sister kept house for him. In 1881 he entered mercantile business at San Antonio, Missouri. October 15, 1882, he married *Dora Emeline Anderson,* who was born March 8, 1859, daughter of *Robert G.* and *Elizabeth* (*Lyons*) *Anderson.* He served several years as postmaster at San Antonio, Missouri. In 1900, he moved to Montana. Mr. Miller's postoffice address is Kalispell, Montana, R. D. No. 3, Box 31 (Plate 17).

Children (*9*):

[509] Charles Augustus^{6}, *b* July 25, 1883; *unm.*
[510] Orin Albert^{6}, *b* June 27, 1886; *unm.*
[511] Ira Clyde^{6}, *b* March 30, 1887; *unm.*
[512] + Florence Mabel^{6}, *b* September 7, 1888; *m Charles William Driscoll.*
[513] Alva Edison^{6}, *b* December 25, 1891; *unm.*
[514] Homer Adam^{6}, *b* December 12, 1893; *unm.*
[515] Perry Anderson^{6}, *b* December 6, 1895; *unm.*
[516] Twin Brother^{6}, *b* December 6, 1895; *d* December 6, 1895.
[517] Clifford Omega^{6}, *b* January 29, 1902; *unm.*

[90] **ELIZABETH^{5} MILLER,** daughter of [21] Jonathan^{4} and Lydia (Cassler) Miller, was born October 27, 1849; March 19, 1874, she married *John Franklin Rapp*, born June 3, 1848; son of *George* and *Elizabeth* (*Schneider*) *Rapp*. Elizabeth was educated in the public schools of Stark County, Ohio, and John in those of Buchanan County, Missouri; both are members of the Cumberland Presbyterian Church, and they own and live upon a fine farm three miles southeast of Easton, Missouri. Mr. Miller is Republican. Address is Saxton, Buchanan County, Missouri, R. R. No. 1 (no children—Plate 17).

[91] **MARY[5] MILLER,** daughter of [21] Jonathan[4] and Lydia (Cassler) Miller, was born May 23, 1853. November 23, 1874, she married *Jacob Hoppel* of Easton, Missouri; son of *Jacob* and *Sarah* (*Leveringhouse*) *Hoppel.* Mr. Hoppel was educated in the public schools of Pennsylvania, and Mary in those of Ohio.

Jacob Hoppel enlisted in Co. C, 44th Mo. Vol. Inf., and participated in a number of engagements during the Civil War. He was honorably discharged at St. Louis in 1865, and returned to Easton, Missouri, where he engaged in farming. In 1903 he sold his property and moved to Spokane County, Washington, where they yet reside. Address, Deer Park, Washington, R. F. D. No. 2, Box 8 (Plate 17).

Children (5), surname Hoppel:

[520] Edwin M.[6], *b* May 1, 1876; *d* August 2, 1876.
[521] + Cora Lydia[6], *b* August 18, 1877; *m James Richard Heffley.*
[522] + Elmer Lee[6], *b* May 5, 1880; *m Bertha Grace Roberts.*
[523] Raymond Jacob[6] *b* September 23, 1882.
[524] Mary Elvira[6], *b* December 9, 1889.

[92] **FYANNA[5] MILLER,** daughter of [21] Jonathan[4] and Lydia (Cassler) Miller, was born April 6, 1856; June 2, 1881, married *Sampson Sollers Whitmore*, born March 23, 1841; son of *Benjamin* and *Annie* (*Zollars*) *Whitmore.* Mrs. Whitmore was educated in the public schools of Ohio, and her husband in those of Iowa; they are members of the Methodist Episcopal Church South.

After marriage, they moved to San Antonio, Missouri, and Mr. Whitmore, with his wife's brother John Cassler[5] Miller [88], engaged in mercantile business. In 1888 he was appointed deputy sheriff of Buchanan County, Missouri. Some time in the nineties they moved to Stewartsville, DeKalb County, Missouri, where they have since lived. He is a Democrat, a a notary public, conveyancer, etc. (Plate 17).

Children (6), surname Whitmore:

[526] + Lydia May[6], *b* November 23, 1881; *m Francis Sigel Atterberry.*
[527] Curtis Cleveland[6], *b* August 31, 1883; *d* November 26, 1900.
[528] + Octavia Dell[6], *b* March 23, 1886; *m Edward Joseph Hinderks.*
[529] + Olive Goldie[6], *b* November 19, 1888; *m Walter Leroy Hall.*
[530] Edna Elinor[6], *b* October 14, 1891.
[531] Fyanna Elizabeth[6], *b* September 18, 1894.

ELIZABETH (BAIR) MILLER [[illegible]], PEARL BELL (MILLER) ROBINSON [177[illegible]], ELMER ELLSWORTH MILLER [[illegible]], AND CHARLES ELMER[8] ROBINSON [2647].

[93] **LYDIA[5] MILLER,** eighth child of [21] Jonathan[4] and Lydia (Cassler) Miller, was born December 21, 1858. She has remained unmarried and resides with her sister Mrs. John F. Rapp Her postoffice address is Saxon, Missouri, R. F. D. No. 1 (Plate 17).

[96] **ELIZABETH[5] BAIR,** daughter of [22] Catharine[4] (Miller) Bair and Jacob H. Bair, was born November 10, 1840. December 27, 1860, she married *Jacob Solomon Miller*, who died July 14, 1893. Mrs. Miller resides at Etna Green, Kosciusko County, Indiana (Plate 53).

Children (11), surname Miller:

[534] + Elmer E.[6], *b* December 9, 1861; *m Florence C. Henry.*
[535] + Morris Monroe[6], *b* August 22, 1863; *m Amanda Byerly.*
[536] + Mary Mintie[6], *b* April 16, 1865; *m John Ellsworth Steffe.*
[537] + Amelia Mandilla[6], *b* September 9, 1867; *m William McCoy .*
[538] + Thomas Jefferson[6], *b* December 14, 1869; *m Ida May Larne.*
[539] + Orpha Alice[6], *b* July 3, 1872; *d* March 28, 1893; *m William Bowman.*
[540] + Frank Jay[6], *b* August 3, 1874; *m Nora Boone.*
[541] + Corwin J.[6], *b* October 12, 1876; *m Ada Youtzy.*
[542] + Orin Enew[6], *b* December 28, 1878; *m Nancy Jane Yazel.*
[543] + Minnie Estella[6], *b* October 19, 1880; *m Charles N. Jordan.*
[544] + Grover Lee[6], *b* November 18, 1884; *m Laoma E. Bliss.*

[98] **MARY ANN[5], BAIR,** daughter of [22] Catharine[4] (Miller) Bair and Jacob H. Bair, was born August 14, 1845. February 25, 1866, she married *George Snyder*, and with him is pleasantly located on a farm near Columbia City, Indiana. Address, Columbia City, Indiana.

Children (3), surname Snyder:

[546] A son, *b* January 13, 1867; *d* next day.
[547] + Minerva[6], *b* March 17, 1868; *m Simon Nolt.*
[548] + Jefferson Jay[6], *b* July 18, 1876; *m Dora C. Guster.*

[99] **FRANKLIN[5] BAIR,** son of [22] Catharine[4] (Miller) Bair and Jacob H. Bair, was born September 14, 1847, and on January 14, 1869, married *Sarah Lesher.* Mrs. Bair died April 20, 1895. Mr. Bair resides at Middle Branch, Stark County, Ohio.

Children (5):

[550] + Martha Jane[6], *b* December 1, 1869; *m Monroe C. Weaver.*
[551] + Otto Lee[6], *b* June 4, 1875; *m Alice Brown.*

[552] + Mary Mandilla^{6}, *b* May 20, 1877; *m John B. Bloomfield.*
[553] Edward F.^{6}, *b* June 18, 1881.
[554] Maud Alice^{6}, *b* June 15, 1883; *m Homer Stokes.*

[102] **JEFFERSON^{5} BAIR,** son of [22] Catharine^{4} (Miller) Bair and Jacob H. Bair, was born August 5, 1855, and April 2, 1882, married *Anna Fry.* Mrs. Bair died October 10, 1895. Mr. Bair resides on a farm in Plain Township, Stark County, Ohio. Address, Middle Branch, Ohio.

Children (6):

[557] Hubert J.^{6}, *b* November 22, 1882; address, Mesa, Washington.
[558] Paul^{6}, *b* January 8, 1885; address, Mesa, Washington.
[559] Roy L.^{6}, *b* December 10, 1887; address, Middle Branch, Ohio.
[560] Carl C.^{6}, *b* June 20, 1890; address, Middle Branch, Ohio.
[561] William J.^{6}, *b* July 14, 1892; address, Middle Branch, Ohio.
[562] Mary Elizabeth^{6}, *b* September 20, 1895; address, Middle Branch, Ohio.

[104] **NANCY^{5} CASSLER,** daughter of [23] Elizabeth^{4} (Miller) Cassler and William Cassler, was born May 20, 1842. July 10, 1873, she married *John C. Corey.* Mrs. Corey died March 22, 1881. The family lived at Massilon, Ohio, until Mr. Corey's death July 5, 1893.

Children (6), surname Cassler:

[565] William Edwin^{6}, *b* February 22, 1874; *d* at Akron, Ohio, March 5, 1913.
[566] Mary Elizabeth^{6}, *b* June 17, 1875; *m Thomas Smith.*
[567] + John Charles^{6}, *b* December 29, 1876; *m Inez Everetta Adams.*
[568] James Arthur^{6}, *b* August 13, 1878.
[569] Lewis Franklin^{6}, *b* September 25, 1879.
[570] Infant son^{6}, *b* March 16, 1881; *d* March 22, 1881.

[105] **LOVINA^{5} CASSLER,** daughter of [23] Elizabeth^{4} (Miller) Cassler, was born April 9, 1844. October 25, 1868, she married *Polk Dallas Machamer,* son of *John* and *Rachel (Miller) Machamer.* They lived at Cairo, Stark County, Ohio. Mr. Machamer died March, 1901, and Mrs. Machamer lives on a farm near Hartville, Stark County, Ohio.

Children (5), surname Machamer:

[573] Margaret^{6}, *b* May 30, 1869; *d* January 25, 1888.
[574] + Edward Lee^{6}, *b* September 25, 1870; *m Fanny Wetzel.*

REV. LA FAYETTE CASSLER [illegible] AND MELVINA AMELIA (WEAVER) CASSLER.

[575] + John S.[6], *b* April 4, 1874; *m Pearl Lantzer.*
[576] + Gerty[6], *b* July 1, 1880; *m Edward Wilamam.*
[577] Kirby[6], *b* August 4, 1881; *d* October 15, 1881.

[106] **LAFAYETTE[5] CASSLER,** son of [23] Elizabeth[4] (Miller) Cassler and William Cassler, was born December 15, 1846, near Cairo, Stark County, Ohio.

The subject of this biographical sketch was reared on the farm and spent his childhood and youth at the parental home. He obtained the rudiments of an education at the public school of the neighborhood in which the family resided, and made fair progress in the branches taught. He no doubt had to do his part of the work on the farm, and this did not give him so much time for self improvement as he desired. He later made excellent use of opportunities. In March, 1859, he made a public profession of his faith in Christ as his personal Saviour, and early in life he had the love for Gospel effort but was not prompt in yielding to the Divine call to the holy ministry. He, however, served the Master for about 27 years in the line of Sunday school work and prayer meetings, etc.

September 21, 1869, he married *Melvina Amelia Weaver,* born August 21, 1844; daughter of *George* and *Charlotte* (*Ginther*) *Weaver.* After living a number of years in Ohio, on account of Mrs. Cassler's physical condition, change of residence became a necessity. Therefore, on September, 1886, he removed to Cook County, Texas. Soon after his settlement in Texas he was induced to preach occasionally, but then refused to be known as a preacher. In August, 1893, he received a marvelous baptism with the Holy Ghost, and was at once commissioned to preach the Gospel. In 1895 he located in Custer County, Oklahoma, and immediately became a pioneer preacher with an unlimited field before him. He was ordained by Bishop Joseph Key, in November, 1899, at Ardmore, Oklahoma. He became a pioneer worker and evangelist in the propagation of Holiness in Oklahoma; also a member of the Oklahoma Holiness Association, and an incorporator of the Holiness Commission; and for a short time he was editor of the first publication of the said society. In the state road campaign of 1907, he took the platform for state wide prohibition and helped to make Oklahoma "dry." His labors are chiefly amongst the poor and neglected. He receives no stipulated salary in compensation for his services, and accepts only free-will offerings. For forty-two years he has been able to pay the Lord's tenth, and even more, and provide for his family and other necessaries that are incumbent on him to pay. He was pastor of the

Pentecostal Church of the Nazarene at Mangum, Greer County, Oklahoma, but recently took charge of the church of the same name at Castle, Oklahoma[a] (Plate 54).

Children (5):

[580] + Charlotte Elizabeth[6], *b* April 7, 1871; *m Harvey Augustus Geer.*
[581] + Bertha Millicent, *b* November 4, 1873; *m William Arley Gardner.*
[582] + Celesta Grace[6], *b* October 6, 1877; *m Hiram Weeks Newcomb.*
[583] + Philip Bliss[6], *b* July 10, 1883; *m Melvina Goins.*
[584] + Ruth Irene[6], *b* March 17, 1887; *m Clarence Dryden Girton.*

[107] **MARGARET[5] CASSLER,** daughter of [23] Elizabeth[4] (Miller) Cassler and William Cassler, was born September 24, 1849. December 28, 1873, she married *Solomon Wetzel*, born October 5, 1844; son of *Nathan* and *Elizabeth (Worstler) Wetzel.* Mr. Wetzel died December 28, 1910. They lived at South Whitley, Whitley County, Indiana, where Mrs. Wetzel continues to reside.

Children (3), surname Wetzel:

[586] Owen E.[6], *b* July 5, 1875, *unm.*
[587] Lizzie Irene[6], *b* April 14, 1878.
[588] Hubert Leroy[6], *b* April 3, 1890.

[108] **LEWIS DAVID[5] CASSLER,** son of [23] Elizabeth[4] (Miller) Cassler and William Cassler, was born August 5, 1852. September 20, 1874, he married *Lucinda Allis Henney*, born July 20, 1855; daughter of *Abraham* and *Margaret (Smith) Henney.* They live at Canton, McPherson County, Kansas, of which town Mr. Cassler has been mayor, and is postmaster. He also deals in lumber. Both himself and his wife were educated in the common school at Cairo, Ohio, and were together members of the Methodist Episcopal Church until her death February 22, 1914.

Children (4):

[590] + William Frederick[6], *b* November 17, 1875; *m Zetta Cole.*
[591] James Abraham[6], *b* November 5, 1881; *unm.*; attorney; McPherson, Kansas.
[592] + Chester Devain[6], *b* March 2, 1885; *m Anna Sinclair.*
[593] Ivan Margrett[6], *b* February 10, 1898.

[a] Owing to frequent changes of location, it was difficult to locate Rev. La Fayette Cassler. Once located, he was prompt to assist with facts, sent his photograph with check to pay for the illustration, and an order for four volumes of the history—one for each daughter.

[109] **ELIZABETH**[5] **CASSLER,** daughter of [23] Elizabeth[4] (Miller) Cassler and William Cassler, was born September 9, 1856. February 3, 1876, she married *Anthony Wayne Machamer*, son of *David Todd* and *Hannah (Wertenberger) Machamer.* Mrs. Machamer died August 27, 1880, and Mr. Machamer lives on a farm near Cairo, Stark County, Ohio.

Children (2), surname Machamer:

[596] + Minerva Celesta[6], *b* August 25, 1876; *m Elmer E. Markley.*
[597] + Erma Lucille[6], *b* May 15, 1878; *m Arthur E. Wise.*

[110] **OTTILLA**[5] **MILLER,** daughter of [24] Solomon[4] and Elizabeth (Bishop) Miller, was born December 12, 1847, and on April 18, 1869, married *William Wise,* who is a successful farmer near Inland, Summit County, Ohio.

Children (2), surname Wise:

[600] + Walter A.[6], *b* January 21, 1870; *m Jessie Thursby.*
[601] + Byron P.[6], *b* November 3, 1873; *m Lela Smith.*

[111] **JEMMIMA**[5] **MILLER,** daughter of [24] Solomon[4] and Elizabeth (Bishop) Miller, was born May 22, 1850. She married *George Lamberson.* They reside near Aultman, Stark County, Ohio.

One daughter (1), surname Lamberson:

[603] + Bertha Estell[6], *b* March 8, 1881.

[112] **NATHANIEL**[5] **MILLER,** son of [24] Solomon[4] and Elizabeth (Bishop) Miller, was born September 22, 1851, and on July 16, 1876, married (1) *Lizzie Wetzel.* The latter died October 1, 1889.

Mr. Miller married (2) *Mrs. Emma Stambaugh,* and the family live near Cairo, Stark County, Ohio.

Children by first marriage (6):

[605] Rolley S.[6], *b* February 3, 1877; *unm.*
[606] Daisy D.[6], *b* June 15, 1879.
[607] Son[6], *b* and *d* December 18, 1881.
[608] Charlotte[6], *b* September 11, 1883; *m John Tritt* December 20, 1906.
[609] Ina[6], *b* November 23, 1886.
[610] Etta Irene[6], *b* August 14, 1889.

[118] **LUCINDA⁶ SNYDER**, daughter of [26] Christina[4] (Miller) Snyder and Henry Snyder, was born November 4, 1850, and on October 11, 1868, married *Christian Fulmer*, born September 22, 1848. They resided at Cairo, Stark County, Ohio, but now live at 1213 West Lake Street, Canton, Ohio.

Children (9), surname Fulmer:

[613] + Clara E.[6], *b* August 17, 1872; address, 1213 West Lake Street.
[614] + Arlington C.[6], *b* January 25, 1874; *m Artie Hess.*
[615] A son[6], *b* April 16, 1875; *d. y.*
[616] A son[6], *b* and *d* April 12, 1876.
[617] + Carrie S.[6], *b* October 9, 1877; *m Henry Brown.*
[618] + Omah Alice[6], *b* September 23, 1880; *m Ezra Hubley.*
[619] Mary L.[6], *b* April 27, 1883.
[620] Sarah S.[6], *b* April 27, 1883.
[621] + Winnifred C.[6], *b* October 14, 1886; *m Calvin A. Grove.*

[120] **MARY ELIZABETH[5] SNYDER**, daughter of [26] Christina[4] (Miller) Snyder and Henry Snyder, was born July 24, 1854, and on February 17, 1870, married *Henry Fulmer.* They live on a farm near Cairo, Stark County, Ohio, R. D. No. 1.

Children (4), surname Fulmer:

[624] Calvin[6], *b* May 29, 1871; address Middle Branch, Ohio.
[625] + Marvin F.[6], *b* June 27, 1873; *m Emma Bell Rettig.*
[626] + Dora Celesta[6], *b* March 21, 1877; *m Sherman Hildebrand.*
[627] + Artie May[6], *b* April 1, 1880; *m Albert Allison.*

[121] **SARAH[6] SNYDER**, daughter of [26] Christina[4] (Miller) Snyder and Henry Snyder, was born June 9, 1856. She married *Milton M. Guiley*, at Midway; residence near Hartville, Stark County, Ohio, R. D. No. 1.

Children (5), surname Guiley:

[630] + John Albert[6], *b* August 15, 1877; *m Rateura L. Wolf.*
[631] + Robert Peter[6], *b* March 25, 1879; *m Winona Jane Banks.*
[632] + Arthur J.[6], *b* April 22, 1881; *m Hannah M. Strickler.*
[633] + Waldo Lee[6], *b* July 7, 1883; *m Edna F. Haverstack.*
[634] Milton Roy[6], *b* November 2, 1897.

[122] **SAVILLA^{5} SNYDER,** daughter of [26] Christina^{4} (Miller) Snyder and Henry Snyder, was born May 2, 1859. December 30, 1875, she married *Rufus Brouse*, born October 11, 1852; son of *Adam* and *Mary* (*Bair*) *Brouse*. Mr. Brouse is a farmer, member of Reformed Church, and the address is Middlebranch, Stark County, Ohio, R. R. No. 1.

Children (2), *surname Brouse:*

[637] + Corwin John^{6}, *b* March 31, 1876; *m Laura B. Bair.*
[638] + Charles Frederick^{6}, *b* June 27, 1884; *m Mary Helen Pease.*

[123] **CORA^{6} SNYDER,** daughter of [26] Christina^{4} (Miller) Snyder and Henry Snyder, was born March 23, 1861.

She was reared with the rest of her sisters and brothers and experienced the life work and duties on the farm. After her father's death in 1898, she with her mother moved to Cairo near the Reformed Church where they worship. Cora generally takes much interest in church work and at services is always in her place. She also takes an active part in the Sunday school and its workings, as well as the music for all the services held in the church. Their home is quite a rendezvous for the mother's children and grandchildren "because mother is there;" and all visitors are most welcome. Address New Berlin, Ohio, R. R. No. 1.

[124] **CATHARINE^{6} SNYDER,** daughter of [26] Christina^{4} (Miller) Snyder and Henry Snyder, was born December 5, 1862, and December 18, 1879, married *Harvey Clinton Bishop*. They reside upon a farm near Greentown, Stark County, Ohio, address Lake, Ohio.

Children (10), *surname Bishop:*

[640] + Ora Hadassa^{6}, *b* July 31, 1880; *m Ira Jacob Werstler.*
[641] + Henry Adam^{6}, *b* November 8, 1882; *m Bertha Kanel.*
[642] + Lawrence Leroy^{6}, *b* November 1, 1884; *m Martha Ellen Suffecool.*
[643] Hubert Carl^{6}, *b* December 18, 1888; *d* September 21, 1906.
[644] Edith Grace^{6}, *b* August 21, 1892.
[645] Paul Ester^{6}, *b* July 28, 1893.
[646] Lela Byril^{6}, *b* July 28, 1896.
[647] Martin Glenn^{6}, *b* November 12, 1898.
[648] Kermit Jay^{6}, *b* February 7, 1900.
[649] Mildred Catharine^{6}, *b* February 25, 1904.

[125] **CELESTA[5] SNYDER**, daughter of [26] Christina[4] (Miller) Snyder and Henry Snyder, was born July 24, 1865, and September 20, 1883, married *George Ingold*. Residence near Cairo, Stark County, Ohio; address Hartville, Ohio, R. D. No. 1.

Children (6), surname Ingold:

[652] Maud[6], *b* April 6, 1884; *d* August 12, 1885.
[653] Gilbert R.[6], *b* August 23, 1885.
[654] + Orin Sage[6], *b* March 16, 1887; *m Elizabeth Emma Cordin.*
[655] + Mary E.[6], *b* April 11, 1889; *m Russell Leroy[6] Fouse* [1023].
[656] Ralph Henry[6], *b* January 16, 1895.
[657] Williard Jason[6], *b* May 20, 1897.

[126] **CHRISTINA[5] SNYDER,** daughter of [26] Christina[4] (Miller) Snyder and Henry Snyder, was born January 13, 1868, and December 16, 1890, married *David Schumaker*, and with him resides on her parental home farm near Cairo, Stark County, Ohio; address is New Berlin, Ohio, R. D. No. 1. (No issue.)

[127] **JOSHUA H.[5] SNYDER**, son of [26] Christina[4] (Miller) Snyder and Henry Snyder, was born October 15, 1872, and November 28, 1894, married *Clara E. Bair*, born June 24, 1874. Residence near Cairo, Stark County, Ohio; address Middlebranch, Ohio, R. D. No. 1.

One son (1):

[660] John Ellsworth[6], *b* June 23, 1897.

[130] **ALONZO LEE[5] MILLER**, son of [27] Mary Ann[4] Miller and Samuel J. Miller, was born January 10, 1858; and on June 7, 1891, married *Ellen Essig*. Address is Greentown, Stark County, Ohio.

One son:

[662] Elmer Lee[6], *b* July 7, 1906.

[131] **MASON E.[5] MILLER**, son of [27] Mary Ann[4] Miller and Samuel J. Miller, was born April 17, 1861, and December 25, 1889, married *Ada* ("*Eada*") *Aungst*, residence Chicago, Illinois.

Children (2):

[664] Zella E.[6], *b* April 5, 1891.
[665] Zora J.[6], *b* April 5, 1891; *d* April 29, 1891.

[132] **MALEZ S.[5] MILLER,** son of [27] Mary Ann[4] Miller and Samuel J. Miller, was born October 23, 1863; April 9, 1883, married *Ellen Walters,* who resides in Canton, Ohio. Mr. Miller died September 21, 1893.

Children (3):

[667] + Harvey Webster[6], *b* April 20, 1884; *m Evelyn M. Germget.*
[668] Maude Grace[6], *b* October 8, 1885.
[669] + Bertha May[6], *b* September 15, 1887; *m Erwin Faber.*

[133] **IRA S.[5] MILLER,** son of [27] Mary Ann[4] Miller and Samuel J. Miller, was born December 5, 1870. His address is New Berlin, Ohio, R. D. No. 1.

[136] **MARY M.[5] MILLER,** daughter of [28] Priscilla[4] Miller and William L. Miller, was born August 13, 1855, and April 30, 1876, married (1) *Ozias Bair.* They resided at Middlebranch, Stark County, Ohio, until his death, January 7, 1884. January 15, 1888, she married (2) *George Richie,* and resides with him in Canton, Ohio.

Children by first marriage (2), surname Bair:

[672] + Rufus[6], *b* July 23, 1879; *m Emma Indermuehle.*
[673] Manodes[6], *b* October 4, 1880.

Children by second marriage (2), surname Richie:

[674] Catharine[6], *b* June 29, 1889; *unm.*
[675] Laura May[6], *b* May 31, 1897.

[137] **MARTHA M.[5] MILLER,** daughter of [28] Priscilla[4] Miller and William L. Miller, was born February 18, 1857, and April 7 1873, married *Charles F. Hill,* who resides with his family at Middle Branch, Stark County, Ohio.

Children (2), surname Hill:

[678] + Chester Arthur[6], *b* March 28, 1881; *m Eva S. Meekes.*
[679] Irene Effie[6], *b* August 29, 1889.

[138] **MANODES[5] MILLER,** son of [28] Priscilla[4] Miller and William L. Miller, was born January 24, 1859, and July 6, 1884, married *Louisa Black;* resides in Cleveland, Ohio.

Children (2):

[681] Claud Wilbert[6], *b* April 25, 1887.
[682] Gertrude B.[6], *b* July 26, 1889.

[139] **MANDANA[6] MILLER**, daughter of [28] Priscilla[4] Miller and William L. Miller, was born August 6, 1861, and February 3, 1884, married *Zenas Fry*. They reside in Plain Township, Stark County, Ohio; address is Berlin, Ohio, R. D. No. 1.

Children (10), *surname Fry:*

[684] + Mina P. Stormfelt[6], *b* December 1, 1880; *m Charles Heiser.*
[685] + Mary P.[6], *b* December 8, 1884; *m Lloyd Ream.*
[686] + Bertha[6], *b* November 23, 1886; *m Elmer Haverstock.*
[687] William E.[6], *b* September 5, 1888; *unm.*
[688] + Eva M.[6], *b* February 13, 1890; *m Albert Moore.*
[689] Emma M.[6], *b* January 9, 1892.
[690] Martha[6], *b* September 26, 1894.
[691] Lucy[6], *b* October 9, 1896.
[692] Zenas[6], *b* August 13, 1898.
[693] Hilda[6], *b* September 6, 1900.
[694] Edna[6], *b* April 20, 1904.

[141] **MARVIN M.[6] MILLER**, son of [28] Priscilla[4] Miller and William L. Miller, was born November 29, 1866, and June 9, 1895, married *Ella Miller*. Residence at Greentown, Stark County, Ohio.

Children (7):

[697] Ralph[6], *b* November 21, 1895; *d y.*
[698] Hubert Clair[6], *b* February 27, 1897.
[699] Hilda May[6], *b* May 10, 1900.
[700] Marie Dorothy[6], *b* December 15, 1901.
[701] Blanche Ethel[6], *b* August 20, 1903.
[702] Lester Lee[6], *b* February 23, 1905.
[703] Mildred[6], *b* April 19, 1908.

[142] **MAGNUS M.[5] MILLER**, daughter of [28] Priscilla[4] Miller and William L. Miller, was born September 6, 1869, and May 10, 1891, married *Henry Reel*. The address is Canton, Ohio, near which city the family live.

Children (3), surname Reel:

[706] Roy Martin[6], *b* September 20, 1891.
[707] Lottie May[6], *b* June 22, 1894; *unm.*
[708] Priscilla Catharine[6], *b* August 23, 1899.

[143] **MARTIN C.[5] MILLER,** son of [28] Priscilla[4] Miller and William L. Miller, was born November 9, 1872, and December 29, 1901, married *Mildred Lanberance,* who was born December 12, 1864. His address is Cleveland, Ohio. (No issue reported).

[144] **WILLIAM MURRAY[5] MILLER,** son of [28] Priscilla[4] Miller and William L. Miller, was born April 1, 1875. April 1, 1901, he married *Melvina Harter,* born April 19, 1878.

Mr. Miller has been much interested, and has assisted considerably in securing information in his family lines. His address is New Berlin, Stark County, Ohio, R. R. No. 1.

Children (2):

[711] Minerva May[6], *b* December 22, 1901.
[712] Clifford Alton[6], *b* June 26, 1904.

[147] **SUSAN[5] ACKER,** daughter of [30] Elizabeth[4] (Garner) Acker and John Acker, was born January 8, 1838, and May 13, 1856, married *Daniel Myers* of Huntingdon County, Pennsylvania, where they resided until the year 1865. They then moved to Johnson County, Iowa, and later moved to Spokane, Washington; address 1832 College Avenue, that city.

Children (15) surname Myers:

[714] + John A.[6], *b* February 25, 1857; *m Sarah A. Markel.*
[715] Adam[6], *b* December 3, 1858; *d* July 17, 1885.
[716] + Elizabeth[6], *b* April 6, 1860; *m Edwin W. Curtis.*
[717] Daniel[6], *b* February 16, 1862; *d* October 20, 1870.
[718] Jacob[6], *b* May 14, 1864.
[719] + Dewalt[6], *b* November 20, 1866; *m Minnie B. Southern.*
[720] Abraham[6], *b* December 4, 1868; *d* January 24, 1885.
[721] Henry[6], *b* December 4, 1868; *d* December 8, 1870.
[722] + Sarah[6], *b* December 21, 1870; *m Robert E. Hall.*
[723] William C.[6], *b* October 21, 1872; *d* August 24, 1874.

[724] Robert[6], *b* March 21, 1874; *d* August 21, 1874.
[725] Martin Luther[6], *b* March 25, 1875; *d* April 24, 1877.
[726] Edward[6], *b* April 15, 1876; *d* August 4, 1876.
[727] + Susanna E.[6], *b* April 15, 1878; *m Robert Kennedy.*
[728] David Sylvester[6], *b* November 25, 1881; *d.*

[149] **SARAH[5] ACKER,** daughter of [30] Elizabeth[4] (Garner) Acker and John Acker, was born August 27, 1842, and February 26, 1874, married *Jacob Lecrone.* They reside at Drab, Blair County, Pennsylvania.

Children (3), surname Lecrone:

[731] Alice[6], *b* September 20, 1875.
[732] + Anna[6], *b* September 20, 1878; *m Homer B.[6] Fouse* [1150].
[733] + Dora Jane[6], *b* April 7, 1881; *m Charles O. Acker.*

[150] **NANCY[5] ACKER,** daughter of [30] Elizabeth[4] (Garner) Acker and John Acker, was born December 14, 1844. She married *John Duerner* with whom she resides at Martinsburg, Blair County, Pennsylvania. They own and operate a nice farm about one mile southeast of the town. They bought a nice home in the town of Martinsburg, and now rent their farm and oversee it. (No issue.)

[151] **ADAM[6] ACKER,** son of [30] Elizabeth[4] (Garner) Acker and John Acker, was born March 19, 1847. In the fall of 1869, he married *Agnes Greaser,* born July 9, 1848. His address is Roaring Spring, Blair County, Pennsylvania.

Children (7):

[735] + Elizabeth[6], *b* February 18, 1871; *m George F. Swartz.*
[736] + Catharine[6], *b* August 27, 1873; *m Charles L. Metzgar.*
[737] + Nettie[6], *b* November 28, 1877; *m William C. Fagle.*
[738] John E.[6], *b* April 10, 1880; *unm.*
[739] + Margaret[6], *b* January 13, 1882; *m Daniel B. Noel.*
[740] + Harriet M.[6], *b* October 3, 1885; *m Calvin Prough.*
[741] + Elsie Mae[6], *b* February 2, 1888; *m Ernest Brindle.*

[152] **DEWALT[6] ACKER,** son of [30] Elizabeth[4] (Garner) Acker and John Acker, was born October 16, 1849, and February 24, 1887, married *Sadie Imler,* born July 28, 1845. He is the owner of the Acker homestead,

on which he was born near Drab postoffice, Blair County, Pennsylvania. He bought a property near Fredericksburg for a residence, and his address is Martinsburg, Pennsylvania, R. F. D. No. 2. They have no children, and live a retired life.

[153] **DANIEL[5] HOOVER,** son of [31] Margaret[4] (Garner) Hoover and Jacob C. Hoover, was born on Clover Creek, near Drab postoffice, July 28, 1836. About 1842, his father purchased a farm four miles north of Martinsburg on Piney Creek, Huston Township, Huntingdon (now Blair) County, Pennsylvania. He was the only son reared in his father's family (his sister died at the age of two years). He entered school at the proper age, when the public school system was in its formative period. He was an apt and industrious student and made rapid progress in the branches then taught. In addition he studied surveying under Professor Miller and the Scranton Correspondence School. He also attended a Normal Institute five weeks at Martinsburg, Blair County, Pennsylvania, in the spring of 1858. In the spring of 1859, he attended for two months a select training school for teachers at Marklesburg, Huntingdon County, Pennsylvania, taught by the late Dr. Andrew Boelus Brumbaugh of Huntingdon, Pennsylvania. He taught school for a number of winter sessions, worked on his father's farm in the summer and in addition did surveying. In later years he made surveying a business, in connection with his farm work. He was known as an expert in calculating surveys.

During the Civil War, he enlisted in the service of the United States as a private in Co. E, 104th Reg. Pa. Vol. Inf. A short time after entering the service he was appointed Third Corporal of his Company. Mr. Hoover was an excellent penman. He was detailed as clerk for several months by the government while in service. He served to the end of the war with distinction, was honorably discharged at Portsmouth, Virginia, on the 25th day of August, 1865, and was mustered out at Camp Cadwalader, Philadelphia, Pennsylvania. After returning home he resumed farm work and also did surveying.

April 1, 1871, upon the resignation of Jacob Higgins, he was elected secretary and treasurer of the Huston Township Cooperative Mutual Fire Insurance Company, Fredericksburg, Blair County, Pennsylvania, and rendered efficient service. December 2, 1867, he married *Eliza Jane Rhodes*, of Piney Creek, daughter of *A. D.* and *Eliza Ann Rhodes*. Mr. Hoover died November 23, 1910, and was buried in Fairview Cemetery, Martinsburg, Blair County, Pennsylvania.

Children (10):

[744] + Essington R.[6], *b* April 14, 1869; *m Della Shoenfelt.*
[745] + Jacob Newton[6], *b* December 8, 1870; *m Jennie Quarry.*
[746] + John Edwin[6], *b* June 6, 1872; *m Lola Vanallman.*
[747] + Lilly Edith[6], *b* August 15, 1875; *m George W. Mock.*
[748] Raymond L[6], *b* August 20, 1878.
[749] Homer G.[6], *b* November 14, 1881.
[750] Francis A.[6], *b* August 14, 1884; *d* August 13, 1885.
[751] Daniel H.[6], *b* October 7, 1887.
[752] Josephine[6], *b* April 3, 1890.
[753] B. Paul[6], *b* February 19, 1895.

[155] **JOHN[5] PEIGHTEL,** son of [32] Sarah[4] (Garner) Peightel and Henry Peightel, was born November 14, 1839. This was the only son who grew to manhood. He was reared on the parental home farm near McConnellstown, Huntingdon County, Pennsylvania. He was a young man of sterling qualities, and became quite a help to his father in operating the farm. In the winter season he attended the public school after the free school system became operative. The school term at that period was limited to three months. It was difficult to secure good teachers. Notwithstanding the many disadvantages the pupils had in those days, the subject of this sketch made satisfactory progress, and at the termination of his school days he had a fair business education.

December 4, 1862, Mr. Peightel married (1) *Margaret Hamer,* born August 27, 1840, of the same county. After marriage he continued to work on his home farm until in the early spring of 1865, when he enlisted to serve in the United States army. He was assigned to Co. K, 78th Reg. Pa. Vol. Inf. In September the same year, he was honorably mustered out of service. Returning home to his family he again engaged in farming. His wife died May 2, 1875, aged 34 years, 8 months and 5 days. September 20, 1877, married (2) *Margaret Bauer Greaser,* born August 30, 1846; daughter of *Jacob* and *Catharine (Bauer) Greaser,* who also died January 13, 1883, aged 36 years, 4 months and 13 days.

When the oldest children were grown up Mr. Peightel purchased and took possession of a farm in Hartslog Valley, about two miles north of his parental home. Here he spent the remainder of his life, passing away April 14, 1894, aged 54 years, 5 months. His son Thomas for some time before the termination of his earthly career was an invalid, the result of an accident.

SAMUEL DEAN HEFFNER, MARY JANE[5] (PEIGHTEL) HEFFNER [159], AND CHILDREN

Children by first marriage (5):

[756] + Nevin[6], *b* August 25, 1863; *m Laura Alice*[6] *Myers* [226].
[757] Thomas H.[6], *b* June 26, 1866; *d* 1896.
[758] Mary E.[6], *b* November 1, 1869.
[759] + William E.[6], *b* November 18, 1872; *m Margaret T. Lincoln.*
[760] Harry[6], *b* April 10, 1875; *d* August 17, 1875.

Daughter by second marriage (1):

[761] Margaret[6], *b* January 3, 1883; *d* August 11, 1883.

[159] **MARY JANE[6] PEIGHTEL,** daughter of [32] Sarah[4] (Garner) Peightel and Henry Peightel, was born at the homestead a mile south of of McConnellstown, Huntingdon County, Pennsylvania, February 16, 1848. She attended the public school from early childhood until she was in her teens. She was married to *Samuel Dean Heffner*, of McConnellstown, Pennsylvania, May 6, 1869. They resided in Huntingdon, Pennsylvania, a short time. The oil industry encouraged them to locate at Parker's Landing, Armstrong County, Pennsylvania, then at Petrolia, Butler County, Pennsylvania, and later at Bradford, Pennsylvania, where they still reside. Mr. Heffner is superintendent of the water departmentof Bradford. They attend the Presbyterian Church.

Mrs. Heffner is of a jovial disposition and consequently carries sunshine with her wherever she goes. Relations, friends and nephews are always welcome at her home (Plate 55).

Children (2), surname Heffner:

[764] + Daisy May[6], *b* February 17, 1873; *m Hon. Robert Patton Habgood.*
[765] + Henry Clay[6], *b* August 8, 1874; *m Minnie Hane.*

[160] **MARGARET ANN[6] PEIGHTEL,** daughter of [32] Sarah[4] (Garner) Peightel and Henry Peightel, was born June 6, 1850, at the homestead near McConnellstown, Pennsylvania. December 24, 1873, she was married to *George P. Booth* of Pittsburgh, Pennsylvania. She attends the Presbyterian Church. For a number of years they have resided at Bradford, Pennsylvania. (No children.)

[161] **SARAH ALICE[6] PEIGHTEL,** daughter of [32] Sarah[4] (Garner) Peightel and Henry Peightel was born near McConnellstown, Huntingdon County, Pennsylvania, June 8, 1852. All the daughters in the mother's

home were taught to be good housekeepers. Sarah attended the local public schools, and also was much interested in instrumental music.

In 1876 Sarah Alice Peightel married *Micaiah Reden Evans, M.D.*, born April 5, 1843, in Huntingdon County, Pennsylvania; son of *Abraham* and *Mary Ann (Corbin) Evans—Abraham* was son of *Roland* and *Mary Evans*. Dr. Evans attended the common schools, Saltillo Academy, and graduated (M.D. 1876) from Jefferson Medical College. He served three years in the army, (Co. C, 49th Reg. Pa. Vol., Co. A., 22d Reg. Pa. Vol. Cav., Co. G, 205th Reg. Pa. Vol. Inf.); taught ten terms in the public schools and has served as school director in Saxton, Bedford County and in Huntingdon, Pennsylvania; practiced medicine at Donation, and at Saxton, Bedford County, and at Huntingdon, where he continues in the active practice of his profession. He has served as president and secretary of Huntingdon County Medical Society and is deacon in Reformed Church, at Huntingdon.[a]

Children (3), surname Evans:

[767] + Ernest Newton[6], *b* December 16, 1876; *m Elizabeth Helen Vincent.*
[768] Mary Bertha[6], *b* ——.
[769] Lillian May[6], *b* ——.

[162] **SUSANNA[5] PEIGHTEL,** daughter of [32] Sarah[4] (Garner) Peightel and Henry Peightel, was born near McConnellstown, May 19, 1854. She attended public school. She was married December 23, 1880, to *William S. Hallman* of Huntingdon, Pennsylvania. For several years Mr. Hallman was proprietor of a temperance hotel in Huntingdon, but for a number of years they have been living a retired life in the same town. Mrs. Hallman, like her mother, delights in keeping her house in a tidy condition. They are members of the Reformed Church at Huntingdon Pennsylvania. (No issue).

[163] **LYDIA IDA[5] PEIGHTEL,** daughter of [32] Sarah[4] (Garner) Peightel and Henry Peightel, was born at the homestead a mile south of McConnellstown, Pennsylvania, November 15, 1857. Her school advantages were such as were obtainable in the public school within a few minutes walk of the Peightel residence. Their home being provided with an organ in her childhood, she took an interest in music, both instrumental and vocal. Early in life it was her pleasure occasionally to entertain com-

[a] Rev. Ernest Newton Evans [767] kindly furnished the material published herewith.

pany with her performances on the organ and singing. Her sisters being established in their own homes, it fell to her lot to remain with her mother in the dec ine of life. To be free from the cares and responsibilities of managing the farm and to be convenient to church and to enjoy other advantages, she and her mother moved to McConnellstown, Pennsylvania.

Lydia Ida patiently and faithfully performed the duties which devolved upon her in caring for her mother until the latter's earthly pilgrimage came to an end. She is a member of the Reformed Church at McConnellstown, where she resides.

[164] **MARY ANN**[5] **GARNER**, daughter of [33] Daniel[4] and Margaret (Auperly) Garner, was born in Huntingdon County, Pennsylvania, October 24, 1841. November 29, 1860, in Grant County, Wisconsin she married *Henry Smith*, who was born in Hessen Darmstadt, Germany, August 10, 1837, and is a son of *Adam* and *Elizabeth* (*Henkel*) *Smith*. Mr. and Mrs. Smith are members of the Evangelical Church and live on a farm near Stitzer, Grant County, Wisconsin.[a]

Children (*11*), *surname Smith:*

[771] + Daniel Adam[6], *b* March 8, 1862; *m Anna G. Schmidt.*
[772] Adolph Donald,[6] *b* November 25, 1863; *d* June 5, 1879.
[773] + Charles Henry[6], *b* December 23, 1865; *m Mary Sweeney.*
[774] + Margaret Angelina[6], *b* December 12, 1867; *m Louis W. Schuppner.*
[775] + Henrietta May[6], *b* December 12, 1869; *m Frederick Kirk.*
[776] + Louis Alvin[6], *b* October 24, 1871; *m Gertie Smith.*
[777] Abigail Lusinda[6], *b* March 13, 1874; *d* August 24, 1875.
[778] + Ida Matilda[6], *b* May 26, 1876; *m Converse Winson.*
[779] + Oscar Martin[6], *b* May 3, 1878; *m Anna Pittenger.*
[780] + Tressie Laura[6], *b* April 12, 1881; *m Benjamin W. Kirk.*
[781] Elizabeth Elsie[6], *b* September 29, 1883; address, Stitzer, Wisconsin.

[165] **DAWALD**[5] **GARNER**, son of [33] Daniel[4] and Margaret (Auperly) Garner, was born May 5, 1843. He united in marriage with *Mary A. Hedges*, and resides on a farm at Lancaster, Grant County, Wisconsin. Mrs. Garner died July 28, 1909.

Mr. Garner was a soldier in the United States Army during the Civil War. He enlisted at Lancaster, Wisconsin, August 11, 1862, and was with Captain Sefa Swan in Co. H, 25th Reg. Wis. Vol. Inf., under Colonel

[a] Mrs. Smith furnished considerable information.

Montgomery. Later he was assigned to the 14th Wis. Cavalry under Major Bush, and Smith's Division. He participated in a number of battles during his three years' service. He was mustered out of service on July 3, 1865, received an honorable discharge, and then returned home to Lancaster, Wisconsin, the place of his enlistment. Address is Cobb, Iowa County, Wisconsin.

Children (5):

[784] Frank W.[6], *b* September 22, 1870; *d* age one year.
[785] + George D.[6], *b* September 20, 1871; *m Matilda C. E. Schmidt.*
[786] + Florence Elenora[6], *b* August 4, 1873; *m Edward W. Schmidt.*
[787] + Nellie S.[6], *b* March 27, 1875; *m Harry C. Craig.*
[788] An infant[6], *d.*

[166] **MARGARET[5] GARNER**, daughter of [33] Daniel[4] and Margaret (Auperly) Garner, was born February 28, 1845. She married *Edward Shaffer*, born January 28, 1845; son of *William Shaffer* (born in Pennsylvania) and *Eliza Connor* (born in Louisianna). Mr. and Mrs. Shaffer are Congregationalists, and he is a wagon maker. Residence, Platteville, Grant County, Wisconsin.

Children (2), surname Shaffer:

[790] + Flora Etta[6], *b* June 28, 1878; *unm.*
[791] + Charles Melvin[6], *b* August 13 1881; *m Maria Shatka.*

[167] **CATHARINE[5] GARNER**, daughter of [33] Daniel[4] and Margaret (Auperly) Garner, was born October 19, 1847. April 8, 1866, she married *Fred Leibert*, born in Germany, June 7, 1840; son of *Cosman* and *Margaret (Winters) Leibert* (both parents born in Bavaria, Germany).

Mr. Leibert was a soldier in the United States Army during the war, 1861-65. He enlisted at Platteville, Wisconsin, August 11, 1862, and served to the close of the war. He was assigned to Co. E, 25th Reg. Vol. Inf. His company commander was Captain Shaw, and regimental officers were Major Rush and Colonel Montgomery. He participated in many of the important battles and was an excellent soldier. He was mustered out of service and received an honorable discharge June 1, 1865.

Mr. Leibert is proprietor of a blacksmith shop in Platteville, Grant County, Wisconsin.

Children (6), surname Leibert:

[793] + Maggie Etta[6], *b* June 30, 1867; *m William Frederick Dawley.*
794] Frederick E.[6], *b* April 19, 1869; *d* in infancy.

[795] + Nellie Retta[6], *b* September 6, 1871; *m Adolph Spink.*
[792] Clara Luella[6], *b* October 18, 1873; *d* in infancy.
[797] + Elsie Belle[6], *b* December 13, 1875; *m John William Akins.*
[798] + Sadie Mae[6], *b* September 16, 1881; *m Dennis Albert Roselip.*

[168] **ELIZABETH ANN[5] GARNER,** daughter of [33] Daniel[4] and (1) Margaret (Auperly) Garner, was born March 8, 1850, in Huntingdon County, Pennsylvania; married in Grant County, Wisconsin, December 17, 1866, *William Warren Waddle,* born in Grant County, Wisconsin, April 19, 1843. Mr. Waddle served two terms of enlistment in the Civil War, and was once wounded in battle. He settled in Iowa in 1874, lived at Merrill, that state. He was a carpenter, and later a farmer, and died in 1912. Mrs. Waddle lives at Webster, South Dakota.

Children (9), surname Waddle:

[801] Hattie[6], *b* October 30, 1867; *d* October 9, 1878.
[802] + William Garner[6], *b* June 29, 1870; *m Eliza Mae Otis.*
[803] + Thomas Warren[6], *b* December 3, 1871; *m Tillie Mathwig.*
[804] + Arthur[6], *b* June 1, 1874; *m Sylvia Pearl Crow.*
[805] + Nellie Mae[6], *b* July 16, 1877; *m Myron Elmer Kanago.*
[806] + Reuben[6], *b* September 15, 1879; *m Maude Myrtle Ramsbotham.*
[807] + Frederick[6], *b* May 27, 1881; *m Mattie Brown.*
[808] + Edward Dawalt[6], *b* February 22, 1883; *m Alburta Mae Baldwin.*
[809] + Laura E.[6], *b* June 7, 1885; *m John William Grebner.*

[169] **MARIAH JANE[5] GARNER,** daughter of [33] Daniel[4] and Elizabeth (Sorrick) Garner, was born May 25, 1854. She married *Watson Elihugh Clifton,* December 13, 1871. He was born in Platteville, Wisconsin, August 16, 1841; son of *William* and *Frances Clifton.* Mr. Clifton is a carpenter, Progressive Republican, and both he and his wife are members of the Congregational Church.

Mrs. Clifton has shown especial interest concerning her general portion of this family history, and cordial thanks are hereby returned to her for that assistance. Residence, Lancaster, Grant County, Wisconsin.

Children (2), surname Clifton:

[812] + Archie Roy[6], *b* July 17, 1874; *m Sarah Winnifred Goodnough.*
[813] + Lester Eugene[6], *b* April 12, 1879.

[171] **REUBEN PETER PHILIP[5] GARNER,** son of [33] Daniel[4] and Elizabeth (Sorrick) Garner, was born April 21, 1858. He married *Fannie Luella Starr,* born July 22, 1861; daughter of *William* and *Mary Starr.* Mr. Garner is a Congregationalist, Prohibitionist, and resides on his father's farm at Lancaster, Grant County, Wisconsin.

Children (2):

[815] + Laura Marie[6] *b* December 11, 1881; *m Clarence Hinch.*
[816] Edward Melvin[6], *b* May 16, 1884; *d* May 31, 1913.

[172] **WILLIAM DANIEL[5] GARNER,** son of [33] Daniel[4] and Elizabeth (Sorrick) Garner, was born May 2, 1860. April 10, 1901, he married *Emma Jane Neuroth,* daughter of *Christopher* and *Anna (Samuel) Neuroth.* Mr. Garner is a Progressive Republican, Congregationalist, and resides at Lancaster, Grant County, Wisconsin. (No children.)

[173] **ABIGAIL LANDA[5] GARNER,** daughter of [33] Daniel[4] and Elizabeth (Sorrick) Garner, was born April 17, 1863. She married *August Kohlenburg,* born April 11, 1863; son of *Gotlieb* and *Bertha (Storms) Kohlenburg.* Mr Kohlenburg is a farmer, Republican, and address is Drexel, Cass County, Missouri.

Children (4), surname Kohlenburg:

[818] Ethel May[6], *b* January 6, 1888.
[819] Ruben Hugo[6], *b* January 31, 1890.
[820] Allen Gotlieb[6], *b* August 9, 1893.
[821] Kail Kohlen[6], *b* January 18, 1899.

[174] **EMMA LUELLA[5] GARNER,** daughter of [33] Daniel[4] and Elizabeth (Sorrick) Garner, was born February 3, 1866, and on October 26, 1887, married *Barnard Irwin Kerr,* born May 5, 1865; son of *William* and *Martha Kerr.* Mr. Kerr was educated in the common schools; is a Democrat; and he and his wife are members of the Congregational Church. Address, Archie, Cass County, Missouri.

Children (3), surname Kerr:

[823] Gay Garner[6], *b* September 16, 1888.
[824] Irene Martha[6], *b* March 26, 1893.
[825] William Daniel[6], *b* September 7, 1897.

[175] **ULYSSES GRANT[5] GARNER,** son of [33] Daniel[4] and Elizabeth (Sorrick) Garner, was born February 21, 1869. February 11, 1902, he married *Caroline Hoeffner*, born December 2, 1880, daughter of *Leonard* and *Rosine* (*Vogel*) *Hoeffner*—latter both born in Germany. Mr. Garner is a contractor for concrete construction, and his address is Drexel, Cass County, Missouri.

Children (7):

[827] Elizabeth Caroline[6], *b* December 29, 1902.
[828] Paul Henry[6], *b* January 1, 1904.
[829] Lawrence Harold[6], *b* October 27, 1906.
[830] Virgil Ulysses[6], *b* August 21, 1908.
[831] Allen Norman[6], *b* May 16, 1909.
[832] Mabel Rosine[6], *b* January 13, 1911.
[833] Ruth Agnes[6], *b* January 31, 1913.

[176] **ALFRED[5] GARNER,** son of [34] Frederick[4] and Margaret (Sorrick) Garner, was born October 25, 1845, at Marklesburg, Huntingdon County, Pennsylvania. In 1859, for a brief period, he lived with his parents in William County, Ohio. After his father's second marriage, he spent several years with relatives in Morrison's Cove and in Woodcock Valley.

Before attaining 17 years of age, he enlisted in the service of the United States Government, Co. H, 107th Ohio Vol. Inf., and, after spending two years and nearly four months in the army, was honorably discharged. On his return home he worked at the carpenter trade and became a skilled mechanic. For a number of years he was in the employ of C. Aultman and Company, in their shops at Canton, Ohio. Frequently the said Company sent him out to carefully install machinery.

August 1, 1869, Mr. Garner married *Celinda Schlodtt*, born in Ohio, October 3, 1848. Since 1908 he has been prison chaplain in Canton, Ohio. Residence, 1427 Logan Avenue.

One son:

[836] Calvin L.[6], *b* August 23, 1870; *m Sallie E. Patterson.*

[177 **ELI[5] GARNER,** son of [34] Frederick[4] and Margaret (Sorrick) Garner was b rn March 21, 1850, at Marklesburg, Huntingdon County, Pennsylvania. At a very tender age he was deprived of a mother's care and sympathy. In his tenth year he went with his father and stepmother to Ohio to reside. As he grew up to manhood, he learned the carpenter's trade. For some years he worked for the C. Aultman Company in their shops at Canton.

March 13, 1873, he was married to *Maggie McCartney* of Blair County, Pennsylvania. They reside at Canton, Ohio.

Children (2):

[839] Wilbur L.[6], *b* May 28, 1876; *unm.*
[840] Paul[6], *b* May 18, 1884.

[179] **FRANKLIN[5] GARNER,** son of [34] Frederick[4] and Fanny (Shiffler) Garner, was born November 9, 1858, in Blair County, Pennsylvania. In very early childhood the family settled near Louisville, Ohio, and some years later close to Canton, Ohio.

He enjoyed good school advantages compared with those of his two brothers. Like his father and brothers, he became a carpenter. He worked for some time in the C. Aultman Company's shops at Canton but later followed agricultural pursuits.

January 27, 1881, he married *Melissa Roath,* born in Stark County, Ohio, April 10, 1862. They reside at Canton, Ohio.

One son:

[843] Howard[6], *b* June 7 1889.

[180] **HARRISON[5] GARNER,** son of [35] Adam[4] and Catharine (Summers) Garner, was born at Marklesburg, Huntingdon County, Pennsylvania, August 20, 1847. He was amongst the first children to begin life in this village. In his fourth year he was deprived of a father's fostering care. At the earnest solicitation of his paternal grandparents, in his seventh year he was transferred from his maternal home to the farm on which his fa her was born and reared. As he developed physically and mentally, he became more and more serviceable in the home and in the field. The farm was then operated by his uncle, William Garner. After entering his teens he spent a winter or two with his mother, and this afforded him better school advantages than he had while on the farm. In the fall of 1863, he began the study of telegraphy under W. C. Long at Marklesburg station. January 15, 1864, the teacher resigned, leaving the young pupil in charge of the office, depot agency, and a small store. The

REV. HENRY SUMMERS[3] GARNER [181].

inexperienced operator now realized the importance of an education to equip him for the performance of the duties of his office. He procured books and studied them, and in this way acquired knowledge fitting him more fully for his position, and at the same time adding to his fund of general information. In April, 1864, the railroad company transferred him to the Coffee Run office, now Entrekin, Pennsylvania, and June 27, 1864, he was promoted to the Huntingdon office, at $30 per month. In August, 1864, he went to Renovo, thence to Erie, Pennsylvania. He worked at various other offices for railroad companies, as at Galion, Dayton, and Cincinnati, in Ohio; and for the Western Union Telegraph Company, at Chicago, Illinois. In April, 1878, he withdrew from this line of work and became chief clerk in the store room of J. C. Tarrant's shoe factory at Cincinnati which position he filled until January, 1899. When his labors at the factory terminated, for the benefit of his health, he sought and found outdoor employment as a salesman which position he retained until his last illness, which was about ten days before his death, November 4, 1902, aged 55 years, 2 months, and 14 days. He was buried at Cincinnati, Ohio.

Mr. Garner united with the Lutheran Church at Marklesburg, Pennsylvania, in youth, and later united with the Methodist Episcopal Church in Cincinnati, Ohio. May 1, 1878, he married *Lou A. Maclaskey*, born March 5, 1853, in New England. They were married in Cincinnati, where they lived, and Mrs. Garner has recently made her home with her daughter in Chicago, Illinois.

Children (2):

[846] + Grace Tarrant[6], *b* April 11, 1880; *m Merle E. Robinson.*
[847] + Leslie Henry[6], *b* August 10, 1881; *m Ethel Weisbroett.*

[181] **HENRY SUMMERS[5] GARNER,** son of [35] Adam[4] and Catharine (Summers) Garner, was born May 29, 1849, at Marklesburg, Huntingdon County, Pennsylvania. Being under two years of age when his father was translated from this world to the one beyond, he never learned by actual experience what a priceless boon it is to be piloted through the formative and developing period of childhood and youth by a kind and wise father, but learned to know that a father's place was measurably supplied by others. It was his good fortune to be surrounded from childhood to early manhood by hallowed influences. In his boyhood days he was associated with men whose language was exceptionally chaste. Up to the time of

his seventh year, his home was wherever his mother was domiciled. At that time his mother was induced to forego, for a while at least, the comforts and cares of housekeeping to accommodate a relative in need of her services. This circumstance prepared the way for the son to enter the home of his maternal grandmother, Sarah (Boyer) Summers. The two dwelling houses being in close proximity on the same farm, the transition from the one home to the other was made without making much impression on his mind. As regards correct habits of life and domestic tranquillity this was a good home for a boy. Trained to habits of industry, economy and honest living, he was encouraged to attend public school regularly. On account of a siege of typhoid fever in the fall of 1863, the greater portion of a four months' school term was lost. But this sickness brought about a turning point in the history of this young man's life, in that it awakened a consciousness of his relationship to a kind Heavenly Father. At that time the Sunday school was in operation from spring until fall and closed in autumn. He was a regular attendant at the Sunday school services at the Marklesburg Reformed Church. It was his pleasure to read such books as the library contained. Many hours during the summer were devoted to reading this literature and committing to memory the answers to questions in a "Union Question Book." The knowledge of the Bible acquired at that period has been of service to him in riper years.

On his return from the Summers (now Fouse's) School in February, 1864, he was notified that arrangements were made to change his home—to go from his Uncle Jacob Summers to his Uncle Henry H. Summers, who then resided on the Daniel P. Brumbaugh farm. Early next morning he gathered together nearly all his belongings and tying them in a bundle journeyed on foot to the new home. He attended the Coffee Run public school the same day, and continued to the end of the term. A year later his uncle enlisted as a soldier in the Union army, and his family was then removed to his father-in-law's. Here there was employment for him in the summer of 1865. In the fall he concluded to accept a pressing invitation to enter his step-father's home near Williamsburg, in order to take advantage of school facilities superior to those heretofore enjoyed, with a view of preparing for teaching. A winter's term followed by a short session of subscription school and a quarter session at Martinsburg Collegiate Institute, in the fall of 1866, enabled him to pass the examination for teaching. He taught school that winter near Martinsburg, and saved sufficient funds so that he could spend the summer term of 1867 at Kishacoquillas Seminary, Mifflin County, Pennsylvania. This was followed by a second term of teaching, which was at the Acker schoolhouse, Morrison's Cove. He boarded at the hospitable home of Adam Fouse, a great uncle. In this home there was not only a religious, but a denominational atmosphere. Here he was "challenged" with the claims of the Christian ministry.

Having been confirmed at 16, after a course of catechetical instruction, by the Rev. Theobald Fouse, and wishing to do what he conceived to be his duty under the guidance of the Holy Spirit, he determined to prepare himself for the high and holy calling, and to go to school with that end in view. Mercersburg College was a young institution of much promise, and was attracting to her classic halls many young men, and some from the pastoral charge to which he belonged, and the conclusion was to go there. He passed through this college, ranked third in a class of nine, and began a seminary course at Mercersburg, but completed it at Lancaster, Pennsylvania, May, 1877. When Mercersburg College was changed to an Academy, the graduates of this college were enrolled as graduates of Franklin and Marshall College.

May 28, 1877, he was licensed to preach the Gospel by Mercersburg Classis in annual session at the Marklesburg Reformed Church. It was a singular coincidence that this occurred in the same church in which he had been confirmed. A period of patient waiting ensued. Discipline in it served to test and strengthen faith. Willing to work, a call came from the Schellsburg charge, Bedford County, Pennsylvania. For this charge there was earnest prayer made, but no one was written to in reference to the matter. With a due sense of the overwhelming solemnity of the sacred office and work, he entered upon the duties in said charge, being ordained and installed March 14, 1878. He labored in this charge over six years. Another field of usefulness presented itself and Juniata Classis decided he should go; hence Scottdale, Pennsylvania, was his next field. He was there from May 1, 1884, to September 30, 1888; at Fairview charge from October 1, 1888, to December 27, 1896; and at Harrold charge from January 1, 1896, to April 1, 1904. From that date to January, 1908, he served vacant charges, chiefly within the bounds of Westmoreland Classis and continued to reside at Greensburg, Pennsylvania. He spent four months in 1907, as principal of the schools at St. Paul's Orphan Home, Butler, Pennsylvania.

The years 1908 and 1909 were spent as pastor of Stoyestown charge, Somerset County, Pennsylvania. His present field is at Dayton, Armstrong County, Pennsylvania. His duties have been such as are incident to the office of a Gospel minister. The material part, or visible fruit of his labors is as follows: Organized three congregations; erected two churches for the newly organized congregations, one at Ruffsdale and one at Youngwood; repaired five churches and two parsonages; purchased three church bells; purchased six organs, four in one charge in eighteen months; freed three churches from debts of five to ten years standing, aggregating $3,600. His preference has been charges affording considerable out of door work, as his constitution required physical exercise. In 1909, he traveled about 3,100 miles chiefly in the buggy, and in the same year preached 161 times.

He has filled the following positions of trust and responsibility: treasurer of Classis, vice president of Synod, president of Classis, eight years a director of St. Paul's Orphan Home, president of public school board for three years. His life and labors as the servant of the Lord can be properly estimated by Him only who sees the end from the beginning.

October 17, 1888, Mr. Garner married *Anna Mary Kunkle*, born February 11, 1864, on the Kunkle homestead in Armstrong County, near Apollo, Westmoreland County, Pennsylvania; daughter of *Franklin* and *Leanna Catharine (Yockey) Kunkle*. Mrs. Garner attended district public schools, and several terms of select school elsewhere. She was organist for six years in the home church, and also after marriage, for about the same period in churches of which her husband was pastor. Her services as a singer are frequently desired. Address, Dayton, Armstrong County, Pennsylvania[a] (Plate 56).

Children (4):

[849] Mary Vida[6], *b* February 13, 1890; *d* May, 1895.
[850] Myron Elnathan[6], *b* March 13, 1894.
[851] John Nevin[6], *b* September 23, 1895.
[852] Leverne Franklin[6], *b* August 13, 1906.

[186] **BENJAMIN F.[6] GARNER**, son of [36] Benjamin[4] and Catharine (Sorrick) Garner, was born, October 1, 1855. March 12, 1879, he married *Emma Keister*. and resides on a farm near Hickman, Lancaster County, Nebraska (Plate 57).

Children (3):

[854] + Elmer[6], *b* January 24, 1880; *m Matilda Liesveld.*
[855] + Sarah[6], *b* December 15, 1884; *m Charles William Lafler.*
[856] Benjamin J.[6], *b* May 30, 1894.

[a] Mr. Garner has greatly assisted in gathering information, and in otherwise assisting in the preparation of this volume. Cordial thanks are hereby returned for that assistance.

BENJAMIN F. GARNER, JR. [186], EMMA (KEISTER) GARNER AND CHILDREN.

LUCINDA (GARNER) ROTH (192), AND JOHN ROTH.

[188] **LEVI[5] GARNER,** son of [36] Benjamin[4] and Catharine (Sorrick) Garner, was born, April 14, 1860, and January 31, 1883, married *Sarah McMahan.* Residence, Hickman, Nebraska.

Children (3):

[858] Harry[6], *b* September 20, 1883.
[859] Lillie[6], *b* July 5, 1888.
[860] Lloyd M.[6], *b* June 29, 1893.

[189] **LIZZIE[5] GARNER,** daughter of [36] Benjamin[4] and Catharine (Sorrick) Garner, was born May 14, 1863. She married (1) *Henry Deisel,* born September 11, 1861, and died in 1900. Mrs. Deisel, in 1904, married (2) *Charles E. Lovett,* of Kingman, Arizona. Residence is 134 East 35th Street, Los Angeles, California.

One son by first marriage, surname Deisel:

[862] Bennie Arthur[6], *b* June 28, 1884.

[190] **SARAH JANE[5] GARNER,** daughter of [36] Benjamin and Catharine (Sorrick) Garner, was born June 8, 1866, and February 15, 1888, married *William Gammill.* They reside in the vicinity of Hickman, Nebraska.

One daughter, surname Gammill:

[864] Elfa[6], *b* April 28, 1895.

[192] **LUCINDA[5] GARNER,** daughter of [37] Philip[4] and Susan (Acker) Garner, was born October 2, 1853, and February 21, 1888, married *John Roth.* They are actively farming a part of the homestead farm, and are comfortably situated in life. Address is 917 West Second Street, Davenport, Scott County, Iowa. (No issue reported. See Plate 58).

[194] **ANNETTA[5] GARNER,** daughter of [37] Phillip[4] and Susan Susan (Acker) Garner, was born, May 23, 1858. March 16, 1882, married *John P. Jacobs,* born April 23, 1855.

Annetta and her husband took the part of the farm with the old buildings, and therefore could start in farming without first building. They are comfortably and pleasantly situated, and successfully follow farming. Address, Davenport, Iowa.

Children (3), surname Jacobs:

[870] Harrison F.[6], *b* April 14, 1884.
[871] Edna[6], *b* ——.
[872] Lillie[6], *b* ——.

[195] **ISABEL[5] GARNER**, daughter of [37] Philip[4] and Susan (Acker) Garner, was born, April 21, 1861. January 28, 1890, she married *Reuben[5] Garner* [200], born December 24, 1856; son of *William[4]* [38] and *Eve (Sorrick) Garner.* Mr. Garner died April 23, 1896, and previous thereto they bought a farm, which Mrs. Garner continues to successfully manage. Address is Davenport, Iowa.

Children (2), surname Garner:

[875] Franklin[6], *b* July 16, 1891; *d* February 6, 1897.
[876] Cora May[6], *b* June 10, 1895.

[196] **HARRISON C.[5] GARNER,** son of [37] Phillip and Susan (Acker) Garner, was born June 29, 1865. September 26, 1888, he married *Minnie Minam,* born January, 1867.

Mrs. Garner died January 24, 1893. One daughter was born [878].

[199] **JULIA ANN[5] GARNER,** daughter of [38] William[4] and Eve (Sorrick) Garner, was born February 11, 1855, and August 24, 1873, married *Emanuel B. Acker,* born December 3, 1850. They resided in Blair County, Pennsylvania, until Mr. Acker's death, March 24, 1880. Several years thereafter, Mrs. Acker moved with her young family to Holton, Jackson County, Kansas, where she reared them to manhood and womanhood, and where they are now well situated. Her address is Holton, Kansas, R. D. No. 3.

Children (4), surname Acker:

[879] + Emma Ellen[6], *b* January 16, 1874; *m John Wolfgang Sommers.*
[880] + Harvey Mahlen[6] *b* September 7, 1875; *m Mary Margaret Linville.*
[881] + David Calvin[6], *b* June 3, 1877 *m Ruth Mueller.*
[882] + Lillie Elizabeth[6], *b* November 16, 1879; *m Oliver Francis Simmons.*

[200] **REUBEN[5] GARNER,** son of [38] William[4] and Eve (Sorrick) Garner, was born December 24, 1856. January 28, 1890, he married *Isabel[6] Garner* [195], born April 21, 1861; daughter of *Philip* [37] and *Susan (Acker) Garner*—see [195].

[201] **CATHARINE[5] GARNER,** daughter of [38] William[4] and Eve (Sorrick) Garner, was born January 25, 1859. February 26, 1882, she married *Charles H. Sanders*, born in Baltimore, Maryland, January 27, 1848. Mr. and Mrs. Sanders are members of the Presbyterian Church, and live upon an excellent farm near Holton, Jackson County, Kansas. (No children.)

[202] **MARY JANE[5] GARNER,** daughter of [38] William[4] and Eve (Sorrick) Garner, was born January 6, 1861, and November 1, 1885, married *J. L. Saterfield.* They reside on a farm near Havensville, Pottawatomie County, Kansas.

Mr. Saterfield died over eighteen years ago, and Mrs. Saterfield and her sons continued active farming. She has abandoned the farm, and moved to her parents' home to keep house and care for them in their declining years. Her address is Holton, Kansas, Route No. 3.

Children (4), surname Saterfield:

[886] Sevilla G.[6], *b* January 24 1887; *d* February 15, 1887.
[887] Murtie A.[6], *b* July 5, 1889; *d* young.
[888] + Harrison R.[6], *b* September 27, 1890; *m Alice Mae Bell Pointer.*
[889] Charles Henry[6], *b* January 26, 1894; address, Holton, Kansas.

[205] **ALICE[5] GARNER,** daughter of [38] William[4] and Eve (Sorrick) Garner, was born October 16, 1866. June 16, 1891, she married *William Schermer*, a native of Germany, born March 4, 1853. They lived on a farm near Holton, Jackson County, Kansas, but recently sold the same and moved into Holton. They are members of the Presbyterian Church.

Children (2), surname Schermer:

[892] Lawrence Frederick[6], *b* September 29, 1894.
[893] Myrtle Eve[6], *b* March 1, 1897.

[206] **WILLIAM[5] GARNER, JR.,** son of [38] William[4] and Eve (Sorrick) Garner, was born March 29, 1869, and was married March 17, 1897 to *Martha Herde*, who was born July 12, 1873. Mr. Garner sold his farm in Jackson County, Kansas, and moved to Greenwood County, Kansas. His address is Eureka, Kansas, Route No. 4.

Children (3):

[896] Walter F.[6], *b* February 18, 1899.
[897] Elmer Harris[6], *b* March 21, 1902.
[898] Earl W.[6], *b* July 2, 1906.

[207] **HARRISON[5] GARNER,** son of [38] William[4] and Eve (Sorrick) Garner, was born November 22, 1871. So far as known Mr. Garner lives near Davenport, Iowa, and is single. His reported address is Davenport, Iowa, Route No. 6.

[209] **ELMER D.[5] GARNER,** son of [38] William[4] and Eve (Sorrick) Garner, was born November 19, 1876, and was married February 16, 1898, to *Daisy J. Booth,* who was born May 13, 1879. Mr. Garner sold his farm in Jackson County, Kansas, and bought another in Greenwood County, Kansas. His address is Eureka, Kansas, Route No. 4.

Children (5):

[901] Lawrence Henry[6], *b* April 28, 1890.
[902] Agnes Leotia[6], *b* August 7, 1901.
[903] Percy Glenn[6], *b* February 15, 1904.
[904] Arthur Raymond[6], *b* July 18, 1907.
[905] Hazel Garnett[6], *b* August 17, 1908.

[212] **ADAM[5] GARNER,** son of [39] Michael F.[4] and Elizabeth (Showalter) Garner, was born February 15, 1863. He married *Sarah Knepper* on November 21, 1889, and resides near Canton, Ohio.

One son:

[908] Homer[6], *b* June 16, 1891.

[214] **WILLIAM S.[5] GARNER,** son of [39] Michael F.[4] and Elizabeth (Showalter) Garner, was born March 11, 1887, and was married to *Lydia May,* on February 16, 1905. His address is Canton, Ohio.

Children (3):

[911] Chalmer H.[6], *b* November 18, 1905.
[912 Elmer Ellsworth[6], *b* August 4, 1907.
[913] Grace May[6], *b* February 6, 1909.

[216] **MARGARET[5] GARNER,** daughter of [39] Michael F.[4] and Elizabeth (Showalter) Garner, was born August 23, 1872, and August 21, 1895, married *Eli Smith,* who was born August 23, 1871. Residence, Roaring Spring, Blair County, Pennsylvania.

Children (3), surname Smith:

[916] Ida May G.[6], *b* November 1, 1897.
[917] Homer T. G.[6], *b* November 5, 1902.
[918] Raymond G.[6], *b* May 29, 1904.

[218] **JAMES CALVIN[5] GARNER,** son of [39] Michael F.[4] and Alice (Fenstermaker) Garner, was born April 20, 1882, and was married to *Emma Miller*, February 19, 1908. His address is Canton, Ohio. (No issue reported.)

[219] **HENRY EDWARD[5] GARNER,** son of [39] Michael F.[4] and Alice (Fenstermaker) Garner, was born December 15, 1885. June 16, 1906, he married *Mabel Grace Hershberger*. Address, Canton, Ohio. (No issue reported.)

[221] **REUBEN[5] MYERS,** son of [40] Catharine[4] (Garner) Myers and Abraham Myers, was born September 4, 1856, and December 21, 1882, married *Rachel Harnish*, who was born September 12, 1858. He resides on a farm near Williamsburg, Blair County, Pennsylvania.

Children (9):

[926] Sarah Catharine[6], *b* November 7, 1883; *d* February 9, 1905.
[927] Anna May[6], *b* August 21, 1885.
[928] Daniel M.[6], *b* October 13, 1887.
[929] William N.[6], *b* October 12, 1889.
[930] Abraham[6], *b* July 26, 1891; *d*.
[931] Infant[6], *b* July 26, 1891; *d*.
[932] Bertha Pearl[6], *b* August 10, 1892.
[933] Reuben H.[6], *b* April 17, 1895.
[934] Earl McKinley[6], *b* August 26, 1898.

[222] **ELIZABETH[5] MYERS,** daughter of [40] Catharine[4] (Garner) Myers and Abraham Myers, was born December 10, 1857, and on December 27, 1883 married *Daniel Grove*, who resides at Grafton, Huntingdon County, Pennsylvania.

Children (3), surname Grove:

[939] Mary Alice[6], *b* May 1, 1891; address Pleasant Grove, Pennsylvania.
[940] Carrie Elizabeth[6], *b* August 6, 1893; address, Pleasant Grove, Pennsylvania.
[941] Charles Andrew[6], *b* February 2, 1897.

[223] **MILTON[5] MYERS,** son of [40] Catharine[4] (Garner) Myers and Abraham Myers, was born November 14, 1859, and November 10, 1892 married (1) *Mary Grace Beaver*, who died January 21, 1901.

After the death of his first wife, Mr. Myers married (2) *Florence Summers* March 8, 1908. Address is North Wales, Pennsylvania, R. F. D. care Wissahicken Farm.

Children by first marriage (3):

[944] Ora Blanche[6], *b* February 2, 1893; address, Manayunk, Pennsylvania.
[945] Royal Leonard[6], *b* June 9, 1987.
[946] Ada Ruth[6], *b* February 26, 1899.

Children by second marriage (3):

[947] Della May[6], *b* July 19, 1908.
[948] Elizabeth Catharine[6], *b* May 24, 1910.

[224] **MARY JANE[5] MYERS,** daughter of [40] Catharine[4] (Garner) Myers and Abraham Myers, was born October 31, 1862, and married *Daniel Shultz* of James Creek, Huntingdon County, Pennsylvania.

One son, surname Shultz:

[951] + Herman H.[6], *b* October 13, 1883; *m Clara Emigh.*

[225] **SARAH CATHARINE[5] MYERS,** daughter of [40] Catharine[4] (Garner) Myers and Abraham Myers, was born March 20, 1864, and December 30, 1886, married *Martin Grove*, who was born December 24, 1865. Postoffice address is Grafton, Huntingdon County, Pennsylvania.

Children (3), surname Grove:

[953] David H.[6], *b* March 4, 1888.
[954] Clara M.[6], *b* September 1, 1891.
[955] Lloyd M.[6], *b* August 24, 1894.

[226] **LAURA ALICE[5] MYERS,** daughter of [40] Catharine[4] (Garner) Myers and Abraham Myers, was born April 1, 1866. September 12, 1893 she married *Nevin[6] Peightel* [756], born August 25, 1863, son of *John* [155] and *Margaret (Hamer) Peightel.* Address, Huntingdon, Pennsylvania. (Children, etc are given under [756].)

[227] **WILLIAM[5] MYERS,** son of [40] Catharine[4] (Garner) Myers and Abraham Myers, was born October 27, 1867. September 8, 1901, he

married *Lizzie A. Betrick*, of Spokane, Washington, who was born June 27, 1867. They reside on the eastern side of Spokane, at 2607 Pacific Avenue, where they are comfortably situated. (No children.)

[229] **MARGARET[5] MYERS**, daughter of [40] Catharine[4] (Garner) Myers and Abraham Myers, was born October 27, 1871. She is unmarried, and is at home with her mother in Marklesburg (James Creek Postoffice), Huntingdon County, Pennsylvania.

[230] **BENJAMIN[5] MYERS**, son of [40] Catharine[4] (Garner) Myers and Abraham Myers, was born November 5, 1873. This young man spent most of his life on the farm with his mother, and was of much use to her in the management and working of the farm. He left his parental home in Huntingdon County, Pennsylvania, about seven years ago and went to the state of Washington; and, we understand, lives in the city of Spokane, where he has living a brother, an uncle, and a number of cousins. (Unmarried.)

[231] **FRANKLIN[5] MYERS**, son of [40] Catharine[4] (Garner) Myers and Abraham Myers, was born April 17, 1876. January 10, 1900 he married *Annie Agnes[6] Brumbaugh*,[a] born near Grafton, Huntingdon County, Pennsylvania, April 21, 1875; daughter of *David Boyer[5]* and *Susan Snowberger (Bechtel) Brumbaugh*. Mr. Myers is a farmer, and his address is Grafton, Pennsylvania, R. R. No. 1.

Children (5):

[960-961] Infants, *b* September, 1900; lived 10 days.
[962] Dorothy Mae[6], *b* December 30, 1902.
[963] Wilmer Brumbaugh[6], *b* May 27, 1905.
[964] Clara Eleanor[6], *b* June 19, 1909.

[233] **ABRAHAM[5] "HIMEBAUGH"[b] (HEIMBAUGH)**, son of [41] Mary[4] (Fouse) Heimbaugh and Jacob Heimbaugh, was born March 25, 1838. February 14, 1861 he married *Adaline Reed*, who was born April 27, 1842. Mr. Himebaugh followed thrashing for nearly forty years. He lives on a farm in Suffield Township, Portage County, Ohio. His address is Hartville, Ohio, R. F. D. No. 2.

[a] No. [E 866], *Brumbach Families*, page 623.
[b] Mr. Himebaugh thus writes his name.

Children (5):

[967] + Jacob Elias^{6}, *b* November 23, 1861; *m Amanda Catharine Schreiner,*
[968] + Samuel E.^{6}, *b* November 14, 1863.
[969] D. Franklin^{6}, *b* December 1, 1866; *d* March 4, 1885.
[970] + Mary^{6}, *b* December 25, 1874; *m Edwin Ambrose Wengert.*
[971] J. William^{6}, *b* February 18, 1881; moved west, address unknown.

[234] **ELIZABETH^{5} HEIMBAUGH,** daughter of [41] Mary^{4} (Fouse) Heimbaugh and Jacob Heimbaugh, was born January 13, 1839. January 30, 1859 she married *Samuel Bowser*, born 1836; son of *Daniel* and *Anna Bowser*. They resided in various places, but in November, 1869, settled on a farm near Weilersville, Wayne County, Ohio, where Mrs. Bowser continues to live. Mr. Bowser died July 18, 1877. The family are members of the Church of the Brethren (Plate 24).

Children (7), surname Bowser:

[974] Anna^{6}, *b* February 21, 1860; *d* September, 1863.
[975] + Mary^{6}, *b* November 6, 1862; *m Daniel Brubaker.*
[976] + Samuel^{6}, *b* March 28, 1864; *m Sarah E. Moore.*
[977] + Daniel^{6}, *b* March 28, 1864; *m Melvina Ober.*
[978] + Erastus^{6}, *b* December 12, 1869; *m Victoria Bowser.*
[979] + Lucinda^{6}, *b* February 4, 1875; *m Aaron Kurtz.*
[980] Lucetta^{6}, *b* February 4, 1875; *d* March 12, 1875.

[235] **CHRISTINA^{5} HEIMBAUGH,** daughter of [41] Mary^{4} (Fouse) Heimbaugh and Jacob Heimbaugh, was born April 16, 1842. August 5, 1860, at Uniontown, Stark County, Ohio, she married *Lewis Pontious*, and lived in Suffield, Portage County, Ohio. Mrs. Pontious was a member of the Church of the Brethren, and died April 17, 1886.

Children (7), surname Pontious:

[981] + Andrew Jackson^{6}, *b* April 2, 1861; *m Amelia E. Swartz.*
[982] + Sarah Elizabeth^{6}, *b* January 19, 1863; *m Jacob Scheefer.*
[983] William N.^{6}, *b* February 11, 1865.
[984] Daniel Otis^{6}, *b* April 7, 1867; *m Cecila Moore.*
[985] Mary Cora^{6}, *b* October 29, 1869; *m James H. Johnson.*
[986] Sevilla C.^{6}, *b* June 1, 1872; *m William Moore.*

[236] **DAVID^{5} HEIMBAUGH,** son of [41] Mary^{4} (Fouse) Heimbaugh and Jacob Heimbaugh, was born March 15, 1844. November 28, 1872

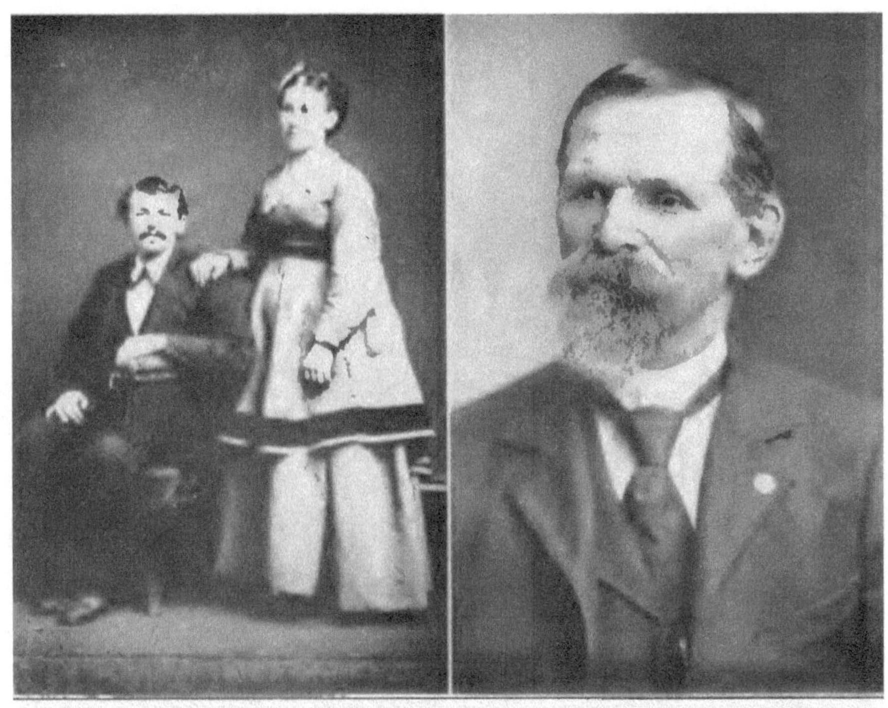

DAVID HEIMBAUGH (236) AND AMANDA (BAIR) HEIMBAUGH (1883 AND RECENTLY)

MARY (HELMBAUGH) BRUMBAUGH [illegible] AND SAMUEL BRUMBAUGH.

(From *Brumbach Families*, copyright [illegible])

he married *Amanda Bair*, daughter of *John* and *Mary Bair*. Mrs. Heimbaugh died about 1910. Soon thereafter Mr. Heimbaugh sold his home in Uniontown, Ohio, and has since made his home with his son on the farm at Fritches Lake. Address, Magadore, Ohio (Plate 59).

One son:

[987] John[6], *b* July 2, 1875.

[237] **MARY[5] HEIMBAUGH,** daughter of [41] Mary[4] (Fouse) Heimbaugh and Jacob Heimbaugh, was born September 28, 1846. January 31, 1869 she married *Samuel[5] Brumbaugh,* born March 24, 1844, at Randolph, Portage County, Ohio, son of *Henry[4]* and *Catharine* (*Stiffler*) *Brumbaugh.*

"They lived on a farm near New Baltimore, but live at Hartville, Stark County, Ohio, where he is a contractor, builder, and lumber dealer. He was educated in the public schools; served as constable and township assessor for several years, and also as a school director for over seventeen years; director of A. and A. Short Line Electric Railway; he and his wife are members of the Church of the Brethren" (Samuel Brumbaugh is No. [E 351] in *Brumbach Families*, see page 581-ch. appear also on pages 634 of said volume) (Plate 60).

Children (4), surname Brumbaugh:

[988] + Jennie Candas[6], *b* October 26, 1869; *m Cyrus Franklin Dulabahn.*
[989] + Alverna[6], *b* March 29, 1872; *m Israel Steffy.*
[990] + Ira Alvin[6], *b* September 28, 1875; *m Viola Austin.*
[991] + Howard[6], *b* March 5, 1882; *m Effie May Fall.*

[238] **EMANUEL[5] HEIMBAUGH,** son of [41] Mary[4] (Fouse) Heimbaugh and Jacob Heimbaugh, was born October 30, 1848, and December 24, 1876 married *Amanda Snyder*, who was born September 23, 1858; daughter of Jacob Henry and Margaret Snyder. They resided on a farm in Randolph Township, Portage County, Ohio. Emanuel died January 9, 1902. The family are members of the Lutheran Church. Address, Hartville, Ohio, R. R.

Children (5), surname Snyder:

[1000] Ida Luella[6], *b* March 6, 1879; *m Henry F. Schoner.*
[1001] Jacob Henry[6], *b* September 2, 1882; *m Maggie Newhouse.*

[1002] Maudie Savilla[6], *b* April 22, 1885; *d* February 21, 1894.
[1003] Charles Edward[6], *b* September 7, 1887.
[1004] Roscoe Franklin[6], *b* August 4, 1892.

[239] **SEVILLA[5] HEIMBAUGH,** daughter of [41] Mary[4] (Fouse) Heimbaugh and Jacob Heimbaugh, was born August 4, 1851. She was married to *David L. Foust*, with whom she settled at Glen Ullin, Morgan County, North Dakota, where she died December 29, 1897. (No issue.)

[240] **PIERCE[5] HEIMBAUGH,** son of [41] Mary[4] (Fouse) Heimbaugh and Jacob Heimbaugh, was born February 20, 1854. Mr. Heimbaugh married (1) *Lovina Pero*—they separated, and he married (2) *Katie Limerick.* He is reported to be employed in the White Sewing Machine Works, Cleveland, Ohio.

Son by first marriage:

[1006] Oscar[6].

[245] **BARBARA ANN[5] FOUSE,** daughter of [43] Abraham[4] and Mary (Rhudy) Fouse, was born August 8, 1852, and died June 10, 1888. She married *Daniel Wertenberger,* born September 30, 1847; son of *Jacob* and *Susanna* (*Cramer*) *Wertenberger.* Mr Wertenberger's address is Hartville, Stark County, Ohio.

Children (*3*), *surname Wertenberger:*

[1009] A son, *b* September 3, 1875; *d* in infancy.
[1010] Maggie Bell[6], *b* December 22, 1880, *d* April 18, 1887.
[1011] Linnie May[6], *b* April 23, 1886, *m Nelson Stambaugh,* address New Berlin, Ohio.

[247] **FRANKLIN[5] FOUSE,** son of [43] Abraham[4] and Mary (Rhudy) Fouse, was born March 14, 1856, and September 17, 1882 married *Laura E. Bishop,* born February 7, 1864. They reside on a farm near Sabetha, Nemaha County, Kansas. Address, Manchester, Kansas; R. R. No. 1, Box 35.

Children (*7*):

[1013] + Lydia Leota[6], *b* April, 5, 1885; *m Iran F. Coulson.*
[1014] Easton Leroy[6], *b* June, 19, 1888.

DANIEL[5] FOUSE [249] AND FAMILY

[1015] Lloyd Elbert[6], *b* May 15, 1890.
[1016] Mildred May[6], *b* July 11, 1893.
[1017] Leon Franklin[6], *b* November 11, 1896.
[1018] Vera Elizabeth[6], *b* November 7, 1906.
[1019] Etha Pearl[6], *b* March 7, 1909.

[248] **ELLEN[5] FOUSE,** daughter of [43] Abraham[4] and Mary (Rhudy) Fouse, was born March 19, 1860. May 28, 1901, she married *Adam Miller*, born February 21, 1851. Mr. Miller is a man of ability; is Justice of Peace at Greentown, Ohio; owns several farms in Stark County, Ohio, and a nice property in Greentown, Ohio, where they reside.

[249] **DANIEL[5] FOUSE,** son of [43] Abraham[4] and Mary (Rhudy) Fouse, was born January 12, 1863. October 16, 1887 he married *Minnie Jane Shanafelt*, born November 17, 1868; daughter of *John Shanafelt*. They reside on his parental homestead near Hartville, Stark County, Ohio; occupation farming. Address, Hartville, Ohio, R. R. No. 2, Box 134 (Plate 61).

Children (3):

[1023] + Russel Leroy[6], *b* January 18, 1889; *m Mary E.*[6] *Ingold* [655].
[1024] Freeman Burdett[6], *b* January 2, 1894.
[1025] Gilbert Eugene[6], *b* November 2, 1896.

[250] **FRANKLIN D.[5] HOOVER,** son of Catherine[4] (Fouse) Hoover and Jonathan Hoover, was born October 12, 1844, and May 27, 1870 married (1) *Mollie Zentz*.

Mrs. Hoover died April 26, 1873, and May 20, 1888, Mr. Hoover married (2) *Kate Housel*, who was born August 1, 1849. (No issue.) Residence, Lake, Stark County, Ohio.

Children (2), by first marriage:

[1028] + Verna[6], *b* July 29, 1871; *d* September 10, 1897; *m Charles Shoner*.
[1029] + Cleon[6], *b* April 18, 1873; *m Laura Schneider*.

[251] **WILLIAM[5] HOOVER,** son of [44] Catharine[4] (Fouse) Hoover and Jonathan Hoover, was born December 17, 1845, and August 18, 1867 married *Emma C. Heimbaugh*, who was born March, 1, 1848.

Mr. Hoover served in the Union army, in the war 1861-1865. He was assigned to Co. A, 19th Ohio Infantry, and served through the Atlantic

Campaign, participating in the battle of Jonesborough. After Lee's surrender, his regiment was ordered to San Antonio, Texas, where for some time they did guard duty. He was then mustered out of service; received an honorable discharge, and returned home in the autumn of 1865.

The family are members of the Methodist Episcopal Church; they live on a farm at Spring Lake, Stark County, Ohio. Address is East Akron, Ohio, R. R.

Children (2):

[1031] + Ella E.[6], *b* November 28, 1868; *m Walter Gillmore.*
[1032] + Clifford[6], *b* June 26, 1877; *m Mabel Cowan.*

[252] **ELIZABETH[5] HOOVER,** daughter of [44] Catharine[4] (Fouse) Hoover and Jonathan Hoover, was born August 27, 1847. November 27, 1872 she married *John Strosacker,* with whom she resides near Krumroy, Summit County, Ohio.

Children (2), surname Strosacker:

[1034] + Sadie[6], *b* May 18, 1875; *m Norman Weyrick.*
[1035] + Harry[6], *b* May 15, 1878; *m Birdie Greenhoe.*

[254] **PRISCILLA[5] HOOVER,** daughter of [44] Catharine[4] (Fouse) Hoover and Jonathan Hoover, was born October 3, 1850, and February 2, 1873 married *Brison W. Myers,* who was born April 4, 1849. Residence, North Springfield, Summit County, Ohio.

Children (4), surname Myers:

[1037] Jesse[6], *b* December 15, 1873; *unm.*
[1038] Ellen[6], *b* October 28, 1878.
[1039] Clinton[6], *b* May 12, 1884.
[1040] William[6], *b* May 29, 1887.

[256] **SARAH A.[5] HOOVER,** daughter of [44] Catharine[4] (Fouse) Hoover and Jonathan Hoover, was born January 22, 1856. March 10, 1881, she married *Emanuel P. Sprigle,* born May 23, 1856. They reside in Akron, Ohio, where Mr. Sprigle is engaged in business as contractor and builder.

Children (2), surname Sprigle:

[1042] Martin R.[6], *b* August 14, 1886.
[1043] Harold H.[6], *b* September 24, 1892.

[257] **ELLEN M.**[5] **HOOVER,** daughter of [44] Catharine[4] (Fouse) Hoover and Jonathan Hoover, was born April 29, 1858. December 30, 1884, she married *Frank A. Yarrick,* who was born March 16, 1858. They reside on a farm near Krumroy, Summit County, Ohio.

Children (2), surname Yarrick:

[1045] Beaulah M.[6], *b* October 23, 1886.
[1046] Warren[6], *b* November 30, 1898.

[258] **DANIEL C.**[5] **HOOVER,** son of [44] Catharine[4] (Fouse) Hoover and Jonathan Hoover, was born September 24, 1860. December 25, 1889 he married *Ada Bixler,* born June 4, 1870. Residence, Akron, Ohio.

One daughter:

[1048] Ethel E.[6], *b* November 12, 1892.

[259] **WILSON**[5] **HOOVER,** son of [44] Catharine[4] (Fouse) Hoover and Jonathan Hoover, was born December 8, 1862. He married *Bertha M. Foust.* They reside on a farm near Myersville, Summit County, Ohio. Mr. Hoover died September 5, 1902.

Children (2):

[1050] Floyd W.[6], *b* October 29, 1892.
[1051] Vera Loretta[6], *b* December 17, 1896.

[260] **IDA A.**[5] **HOOVER,** daughter of [44] Catharine[4] (Fouse) Hoover and Jonathan Hoover, was born April 14, 1865, and, in 1899, she married *Albert Schick.*

One daughter, surname Schick:

[1053] Esther[6], *d* at age 5.

[261] **ABRAHAM**[5] **CRAMER,** son of [45] Christena[4] (Fouse) Cramer and Samuel Cramer, was born December 22, 1847. March 5, 1872, he married *Amanda Myers,* who was born December 28, 1846. Occupation laborer. Their residence is Greentown, Ohio. Mr. Cramer died in April 1912. (No issue.)

[262] **ELIZABETH**[5] **CRAMER,** daughter of [45] Christena[4] (Fouse) Cramer and Samuel Cramer, was born July 10, 1849, and July, 1870 mar-

ried *William Miller*. Residence, Krumroy, Summit County, Ohio. The records of this family were unfortunately burned.

Children (6), surname Miller:

[1056] Charles E.[6], *b* 1871.
[1057] Perry L.[6].
[1058] Daniel C.[6].
[1059] Rosa B.[6].
[1060] Cora[6].
[1061] Christena.[6]

[263] **ISAAC[5] CRAMER,** son of [45] Christena[4] (Fouse) Cramer and Samuel Cramer, was born November 20, 1851. October 19, 1876 he married *Alice Kreighbaum*, who was born December 22, 1858. His address is Lake, Ohio.

Children (4):

[1064] Charles H.[6], *b* May 21, 1877.
[1065] Claud O.[6], *b* July 5, 1882.
[1066] Russel[6], *b* December 26, 1889.
[1067] Edna[6], *b* October 13, 1893.

[264] **MARY E.[5] CRAMER,** daughter of [45] Christena[4] (Fouse) Cramer and Samuel Cramer, was born April 26, 1856, and February 21, 1878, married *John Swope*. Late residence, Lake, Stark County, Ohio; present address, New Berlin, Ohio.

Children (5), surname Swope:

[1070] Arthur[6], *b* December 2, 1878.
[1071] Jennie[6], *b* May 20, 1880.
[1072] Charles[6], *b* October 29, 1881.
[1073] Archibald[6], *b* December 31, 1884.
[1074] Ford[6], *b* January 8, 1886.

[265] **WILLIAM H.[5] CRAMER,** son of [45] Christena[4] (Fouse) Cramer, and Samuel Cramer, was born April 26, 1861. February 21, 1884 he married *Laura Frederick*. His address is Lake, Ohio.

Children (3):

[1077] James Emil[6], *b* November 20, 1884.
[1078] Frankie[6], *b* June 1886; *d* August 1890.
[1079] Ollie[6], *b* September, 1889.

[266] **CATHERINE O.[5] CRAMER,** daughter of [45] Christena[4] (Fouse) Cramer and Samuel Cramer, was born February 18, 1865. September 14, 1884 she married *John Bridenstine,* born May 2, 1840. Mr. Bridenstine was a painter until his death December 15, 1902. Mrs. Bridenstine's address is Lake, Stark County, Ohio.

Children (6), surname Bridenstine:

[1082] Christina[6], *b* October 29, 1885.
[1083] Louisa[6], *b* April 19, 1888.
[1084] Irene[6], *b* December 20, 1890.
[1085] John Herman[6], *b* October 28, 1893.
[1086] Dawn Marie[6], *b* May 25, 1896; *d* April 4, 1898.
[1087] Mary Evelyn[6], *b* June 18, 1899.

[267] **HIRAM B.[5] MADLEM,** son of [48] Savilla[4] (Fouse) Madlem and Isaac Madlem, was born in Lake Township, Stark County, Ohio, October 7, 1839. November 28, 1860, he married *Mary A. Zentz* of the same county. Late residence, Petoskey, Emmet County, Michigan; present address is Clarion, Michigan, R. R. No. 1.

Children (2):

[1090] Ellen C.[6], *b* September 25, 1862.
[1091] + Dilla C.[6], *b* April 28, 1865; *m Isaac C. Kent.*

[268] **MARY ANN[5] MADLEM,** daughter of [48] Savilla[4] (Fouse) Madlem and Isaac Madlem, was born July 1, 1841. October 13, 1861 she married *Frank Ream.* They resided at Suffield, Portage County, Ohio, and both are reported to have died.

Children (3), surname Ream:

[1093] Isaac H.[6], *b* July 14, 1862.
[1094] Sarah E.[6], *b* April 8, 1865.
[1095] Irwin F.[6], *b* July 31, 1871.

[269 **FRANKLIN[5] MADLEM,** son of [48] Savilla[4] (Fouse) Madlem and Isaac Madlem, was born November 12, 1843. He married a *Miss ——— Miller.* Their address is given as New Berlin, Ohio, R. R. No. 1. (No issue reported, and no reply received.)

[271] **WILLIAM[5] MADLEM,** son of [48] Savilla[4] (Fouse) Madlem and Isaac Madlem, was born June 5, 1847. November 23, 1871, he married *Ducetta Slabaugh,* born September 13, 1851. They reside at Peabody, Kansas.

Children (2):

[1099] Samuel[6], *b* July 9, 1872.
[1100] Minnie[6], *b* June 25, 1877; *d* July 6, 1887.

[274] **ISAAC D.[5] MADLEM,** son of [48] Saville[4] (Fouse) Madlem and Isaac Madlem, was born October 18, 1856. He married *Ann Edie* and resides in Cleveland, Ohio. To this union two children were born, but further details have not been secured.

[276] **MALINDA[5] FOUSE,** daughter of [49] Frederick[4] and Elizabeth (Gearty) Fouse, was born January 8, 1849. July 3, 1879 she married *Philip Fulmer.* Residence, Brimfield, Portage County, Ohio.

Children (4), surname Fulmer:

[1106] Edwin A.[6], *b* May 15, 1880; *d* November 26, 1882.
[1107] + Ida May[6], *b* February 3, 1882; *m Henry More.*
[1108] Emery[6], *b* February 9, 1886.
[1109] Frederick Z.[6], *b* November 11, 1887.

[278] **JOHN M.[5] FOUSE,** son of [49] Frederick[4] and Elizabeth (Gearty) Fouse, was born October 7, 1851, and December 17, 1874, married *Susan Royer,* born August 19, 1886; daughter of *Abraham* and *Rebecca (Ulrich) Royer.* They live on a farm near Tallmage, Summit County, Ohio, and he follows the dairy business for a livelihood.

Mrs. Fouse died suddenly June 7, 1910, which was a great shock to the family, relatives and friends. She was an excellent helpmate, a good, faithful wife and mother. She was a model woman in her community, and was much loved by her family and by all who knew her (Plate 62).

Children (11):

[1112] Bertha[6], *b* July 14, 1876.
[1113] + Mahlon Acquilla[6], *b* June 17, 1878; *m Edna Sprague.*
[1114] + Austin J.[6], *b* November 21, 1880; *m Maud Simmons.*
[1115] + Frederick[6], *b* July 17, 1883; *m Ethel Rouinsky.*

STANDING: EDWIN P.[5] FOUSE [281], FERNANDO F.[5] [284], MANODES W.[5] [283], AND WILLIAM FREDERICK[5] [285].
SITTING: REUBEN F.[5] FOUSE [270], JOHN M.[5] [278], JACOB J.[5] [280]. SONS OF FREDERICK[4] FOUSE [49].

[1116] Clarence[6], *b* August 13, 1885; *m Lottie Beachley.*
[1117] Claude W.[6], *b* April 11, 1888; *m Juanita Waterman.*
[1118] Mable R.[6], *b* November 15, 1890.
[1119] Floyd R.[6], *b* September 28, 1893.
[1120] Gladis[6], *b* July 22, 1895.
[1121] Elton[6], *b* April 25, 1897; *d* April 23, 1898.
[1122] Elva[6], *b* July 31, 1900.

[279] **REUBEN[5] FOUSE,** son of [49] Frederick[4] and Elizabeth (Gearty) Fouse, was born March 4, 1853. December 28, 1875 he married *Salina Royer.* They lived on a farm near Hartville, Stark County, Ohio—the same tract preëmpted by his grandfather John Fouse, October 8, 1818 (see Plate 9). Reuben, being next to the oldest son, became possessor of the farm, but does not live on it. Being mechanically inclined, he followed contracting and building. He lived at Akron, but became paralyzed about eleven years ago, and, unable longer to work, he and his wife went to Kansas City, Missouri, in 1910, with his son Winnefred. The mother died there in 1911, and Reuben took the body back to Akron, where he has since remained (Plate 62).

One son:

[1126] + Winnefred E.[6], *b* December 24, 1877; *m Elva Pearl Corl.*

[280] **JACOB J.[5] FOUSE,** son of [49] Frederick[4] and Elizabeth (Gearty) Fouse, was born January 17, 1855, and November 28, 1878, married *Emma J. Wise.* They reside on North Hill, Akron, Ohio. Occupation, carpenter and joiner. Mr. Fouse is an expert mechanic and builder, and an overseer of contracts, and is a very busy man. He and his wife are very comfortably situated on Tallmadge Street, Akron, Ohio. They are blessed with plenty of this world's goods and are charitably inclined. They are kind to their neighbors, friends and relatives, and ever receive them kindly at their hospitable home. They are members of Trinity Reformed Church. Mrs. Fouse is educating a young man for the ministry. (No children. Plate 62.)

[281] **EDWIN P.[5] FOUSE,** son of [49] Frederick[4] and Elizabeth (Gearty) Fouse, was born May 1, 1857, and married *Mary Rose* on December 24, 1878. They reside in Akron, Ohio, and are members of the Trinity Reformed Church of that place, taking an active interest in all its services.

Mr. Fouse is a handy, all around man and can suit himself to almost any kind of work, as occasion requires. He lives on his own farm, part of the Akron homestead farm, and does some farming but devotes much of his time to other business. At present he is employed with one of the rubber manufactories of the city (Plate 62).

Children (7):

[1127] + Onney May[6], *b* April 14, 1880; *m John Homer Meyers.*
[1128] + Ella[6], *b* March 21, 1882; *m Herbert C. Kauffman.*
[1129] Elizabeth[6], *b* July 16, 1886.
[1130] William Paul[6], *b* January 28, 1888; address, 262 Glenwood Avenue, Akron, Ohio.
[1131] Sarah Ethel[6], *b* December 18, 1891; address, Tallmadge, Ohio, R. D. 18.
[1132] Pearl[6], *b* February 7, 1897.
[1133] Mary Leta[6], *b* March 28, 1898.

[283] **MINODES[5] FOUSE,** son of [49] Frederick[4] and Elizabeth (Gearty) Fouse, was born February 12, 1861, and March 23, 1883, married *Christina Rose.* He follows the carpenter's trade in Akron, Ohio. The family are members of the Reformed Church of that city.

Mrs. Fouse died November 5, 1909. She was an excellent help-mate and a kind, good mother. The family residence is 500 Schiller Avenue, Akron, Ohio (Plate 62).

Children (3):

[1136] + Charles M.[6], *b* March 16, 1883.
[1137] + Esther M.[6], *b* June 15, 1885.
[1138] + John Floyd[6], *b* September 22, 1887; *m Hazel Weaver.*

[284] **FERNANDO[5] FOUSE,** son of [49] Frederick[4] and Elizabeth (Gearty) Fouse, was born December 14, 1864. December 25, 1884, he married *Lydia Rose.* Occupation, carpenter and joiner. They are members of the Reformed Church.

Mr. Fouse from his boyhood has been mechanically inclined and in his youth worked with his brothers at the carpenter trade, but of late years he takes contracts to manage and oversee all kinds of buildings and is considered an expert in erecting and finishing buildings. They reside on Schiller Avenue, Akron, Ohio (Plate 62).

One son:

[1140] William Earl[6], *b* October 28, 1890, address, 506 Schiller Avenue, Akron, Ohio.

[285] **WILLIAM F.[5] FOUSE,** son of [49] Frederick and Elizabeth [Gearty] Fouse was born February 2, 1867, on the original Fouse homestead preempted by John Fouse, his grandfather, in October, 1818, in Stark County, Ohio. A few years after William's birth, his father bought another farm near Akron, Cuyahoga County, Ohio, and moved over there in the spring of 1872 when William was 5 years old. Thus he spent his boyhood days on the farm, and in the country school. After he finished his course in the public schools, he entered Heidelburg College, Tiffin, Ohio. He next entered the University of Ohio, at Wooster, and graduated therefrom in the class of 1893. He then commenced to read law and engaged in teaching school to meet expenses. He followed this occupation for several years, but it did not appeal to him as a profession although the years he spent in teaching were a success. He preferred law to teaching, and kept on reading law. He was examined in June, 1897, and was admitted to the bar in Ohio. He then abandoned teaching, and opened his law office in the city of Akron, Ohio. He has been successful in his practice, and with it handled a lot of real estate and placed mortgages for his clients; and has also interested himself in real estate to some extent in the development of manufacturing interests of the city.

August 26, 1894, Mr. Fouse married *Ada Keller*, daughter of *Joel F.* and *Susannah Keller*, of Sulphur Springs, Ohio. Mr. Fouse and family are members of Trinity Reformed Church of Akron, Ohio. The congregation honored him by electing him a deacon, which office he has held for a number of years. Residence, 576 Schiller Avenue, Akron, Ohio. (Plate 62).

Children (2):

[1142] Howard Keller[6], *b* April 1, 1895.
[1143] James Keller[6], *d* at age 4.

[286] **IRA[5] FOUSE,** son of [49] Frederick[4] and Elizabeth (Gearty) Fouse, was born May 20, 1870. September 30, 1892, he married *Bessie Greenland*, of Jamestown, New York. Mr. Fouse died at Akron, Ohio October 20, 1896. and his wife died December 8, 1897, in the same city.

One daughter:

[1145] Ruth Elizabeth[6], *b* May 13, 1893; address, 2 Stearns Avenue, Jamestown, New York.

[287] **GEORGE W.[5] FOUSE[3]**, son of [51] Theobald ("Dewalt") Adam[4] and Margaret (Duncan) Fouse, was born June 29, 1844. When the Civil War broke out in 1861, he enlisted in the service of the United States among the first calls for troops, at the age of 16 years. Death claimed him December 13, 1861.

[288] **WILLIAM DUNCAN FOUSE[5]**, son of [51] Theobald Adam[4] and Margaret (Duncan) Fouse, was born December 23, 1845, and lived with his father. In the winter he went to school and in the summer he worked on the farm.

On the seventh day of August, 1862, when not 17 years of age, he enlisted in the nine months' service in Co. B, 125th Pa. Vol. Inf. He arrived home on the eighteenth day of May, 1863. On the twenty-fourth day of June, 1863, he again enlisted in Co. D, 22nd Pa. Cav., for a term of six months. In this Company he received the appointment as Sergeant. After serving his full term, he received an honorable discharge on the fifth day of February, 1864. He then remained home and helped his father on the farm until the eighteenth day of August. Then there was another call for more men to serve in the army. He enlisted the third time for one year or during the war, and served in Co. B, 208th Reg. Pa. Vol. Inf. He participated in the engagements at Antietam, Chancelorsville, South Mountain, Fort Steadman, and the three days' fight, April 1, 2, and 3, 1865, in front of Petersburg, Virginia. He was with his command on the march to capture the Confederate Army, under General Lee, when Lee surrendered at Appomattox Courthouse. His command then returned via Petersburg, Virginia, to City Point, where they embarked on a steamer and went to Washington, via the James River, Chesapeake Bay and Potomac River. In Washington, D. C., he lay in camp until the inspection and grand parade, in June, 1865. He there received an honorable discharge and was mustered out of service; returned home and worked with his father on the farm.

January 10, 1878, he married *Linda B. Knode*, born February 26, 1856, and followed farming for many years; later he quit farming and accepted a position in Altoona, Pennsylvania, and moved there with his family about the year 1890, and resides at 410 Fifth Street (Plate 63).

WILLIAM DUNCAN-FOUSE (288) GROUP.

Children (2):

[1146] + Mary Maud[6], *b* October 30, 1878; *m J. Edwin Weber.*
[1147] Anna Grace, *b* October 7, 1883.

[289] **DANIEL D.[5] FOUSE,** son of [51] Theobald Adam[4] and Margaret (Duncan) Fouse, was born May 23, 1847. November 4, 1875, he married *Malinda Bossler,* who was born May 30, 1851. Mr. Fouse resides near Drab, Blair County, Pennsylvania.

Children (5):

[1149] + Lillie May[6], *b* August 4, 1877; *m Harry W. Smith.*
[1150] + Homer B.[6], *b* July 7, 1879; *m Anna[6] Lecrone* [732].
[1151] + Elmer E.[6], *b* October 6, 1882; *m Mary Luella Weber.*
[1152] + Margaret C.[6], *b* January 16, 1885; *m Jacob Clarence Nicodemus.*
[1153] + Dewalt O.[6], *b* September 11, 1887.

[291] **CALVIN SYLVESTER[5] FOUSE,** son of [51] Theobald ("Dewalt") Adam[4] and Elizabeth (Duncan) Fouse, was born December 28, 1851; April 1, 1877, married *Rosanna Fisher,* born July 17, 1859; daughter of *Daniel Henry Fisher.* Mr. Fouse was educated in the common schools and at Pennsylvania State College; is a florist and fruit grower at Mount Union, Huntingdon County, Pennsylvania; and is a member of Methodist Episcopal Church.

Children (3):

[1156] + Marcus M. P.[6], *b* April 8, 1878; *m Ella Marie Kyper.*
[1157] + Mary Elizabeth[6], *b* November 18, 1881; *m James H. Smith.*
[1158] Lulu May[6], *b* October 6, 1888.

[292] **ANNA MALINDA[5] FOUSE,** daughter of [51] Theobald ("Dewalt") Adam[4] and Agnes (Greaser) Fouse, was born January 3, 1855. December 7, 1881, she married *Winfield Scott Garner,* born August 5, 1853; son of *George* and *Rachel (Sorrick) Garner.* Mr. Garner farms the old Garner homestead in Penn Township, Huntingdon County, Pennsylvania.[a] Mrs. Garner died in 1911. Mr. Garner's address is James Creek, Huntingdon County, Pennsylvania.

[a] See [II], page 35 and *Brumbaugh Families,* pages 425–429.

Children (5), surname Garner:

[1161] Mary Agnes[6], *b* November 12, 1882.
[1162] George Winfield[6], *b* July 14, 1885.
[1163] Anna Rachel[6], *b* October 25, 1888.
[1164] Laura Grace[6], *b* October 12, 1890.
[1165] Ruth Susan[6], January 23, 1895.

[293] **MARY ELIZABETH[5] FOUSE,** daughter of [51] Theobald Adam[4] and Agnes (Greaser) Fouse, was born June 26, 1856. August 15, 1882, she married *Charles Winfield Ferry,* who was born July 14, 1862. Mr. Ferry resided in Altoona until his death in a wreck, September 8, 1892.

Mrs. Ferry reared her children in the nurture and admonition of the Lord, when all responsibility was thrown on her by the sad accident that befell her husband. She had her own home, and was permitted to rear and live with her children sixteen years, when the reaper (death) came and called her away, July 20, 1909.

Children (5), surname Ferry:

[1167] Theobald Ross[6], *b* September 19, 1883; address New York City.
[1168] + Ada Blanche[6], *b* September 20, 1886; *m Ernest Byron Sprankle.*
[1169] Charles Arthur[6], *b* November 28, 1887; address Altoona, Pa.
[1170] + Vernice Edna[6], *b* March 7, 1889; *m Arthur Albert McCullum.*
[1171] Clyde Ira[6], *b* August 30, 1891; *d* April 26, 1892.

[294] **SUSAN[5] FOUSE,** daughter of [51] Theobald Adam[4] and Agnes (Greaser) Fouse, was born August 26, 1857. November 11, 1880, she married *William P. Erb,* who was born April 29, 1854. Residence on Clover Creek, on the homestead farm; post office address, Drab, Blair County, Pennsylvania.

Children (6), surname Erb:

[1173] + Laura Elsie[6], *b* October 1, 1884; *m Frederick William Sorrick.*
[1174] Anna Desse[6], *b* May 3, 1886.
[1175] + Jesse Roy[6], *b* June 12, 1888; *m Frances Acker.*
[1176] Martin Clair[6], *b* January 23, 1891; *d* October 9, 1891.
[1177] Daniel Homer[6], *b* August 24, 1892.
[1178] William Levi[6], *b* March 28, 1902.

[297] **MAHLON L.[5] FOUSE,** son of [51] Theobald Adam[4] and Agnes (Greaser) Fouse, was born November 29, 1864, and December 24, 1889, married (1) *Anna Malinda Cooper*, born October 18, 1866, and died July 31, 1890. December 21, 1893, Mahlon married (2) *Ella Jane Bear*, daughter of *George C.* and *Amanda Bear*. Mr. Fouse lives on his farm near Marklesburgh, Huntingdon County, Pennsylvania (James Creek postoffice).

Children (5):

[1181] Carrie Laruhe[6], *b* October 9, 1894.
[1182] George Herman[6], *b* February 28, 1897.
[1183] Frederick Knode[6], *b* June 20, 1899.
[1184] Anna Grace[6], *b* September 12, 1901.
[1185] Viola May[6], *b* October 10, 1903.

[298] **DEWALT H.[5] FOUSE,** son of [51] Theobald Adam[4] and Agnes (Greaser) Fouse, was born March 6, 1868. In early life he became desirous of gaining an education, though his advantages were somewhat limited. During the winter school term he attended the public school at the "Ditch" school house, Huston Township, Blair County, Pennsylvania, where he made good progress in the different branches of study. During the summer months he worked on the farm to help support the family until the age of 20 years. During the summer of the year 1888, he attended a term of school at the Theological Seminary, Greensburg, Pennsylvania. In the fall of the same year he passed a successful examination under the county superintendent, obtained a teacher's certificate, and was appointed teacher of the "Rebecca Furnace" school by the Board of Education in Huston Township. After ending the term successfully he attended the summer term of school at the Juniata Collegiate Institute, Martinsburg, Pennsylvania, teaching again the next winter. He continued this course for a number of years, when he was granted a teacher's professional certificate. With the exception of two years in which he was employed by the Pennsylvania Railroad Company, at Altoona, Pennsylvania, as assistant baggagemaster and clerk, he taught ten continuous terms of school, always being employed in his native township. In the spring of 1900, he resigned his school to accept a position as clerk in the office of the Pittsburgh Limestone Company, Ltd., at Williamsburg, Pennsylvania. In 1903, he was made assistant to the superintendent where he is still employed. Address, Williamsburg, Blair County, Pennsylvania.

He was united in marriage to *Magdalene Lavina Wisgerer*, September 15, 1898.

Children (2):

[1187] Alice Rosina[6], *b* August 3, 1899.
[1188] Paul Dewalt[6], *b* October 1, 1907.

[299] **LAURA A.[5] FOUSE,** daughter of [51] Theobald Adam[4] and Agnes (Greaser) Fouse, was born December 9, 1872. She remained at home with her parents until they departed this life. She assisted her mother in the general care of the house, after which she secured employment at the William F. Gable and Company store, Altoona, Pennsylvania, where she is yet employed.

[302] **WESLEY FOUSE[5] NICODEMUS,** son of [52] Margaret[4] (Fouse) Nicodemus and Jacob A. Nicodemus, was born April 26, 1846, and in 1868 married *Lucinda Acker*, daughter of *John Acker, Jr.* The family resides in Denver, Colorado, where Mr. Nicodemus died in 1906.

Children (4):

[1191] + Margaret Elizabeth[6], *b* January 24, 1870; *m Charles O. Westphal.*
[1192] + Oliver[6], *b* August 5, 1874; *m Maud A. Criswell.*
[1193] + Jacob Earl[6], *b* October 30, 1880; *m Clio Abergaust.*
[1194] + Wesley Roy[6], *b* June 16, 1886; *m Oris Hiatt.*

[303] **SUSANNA FOUSE[5] NICODEMUS,** daughter of [52] Margaret,[4] (Fouse) Nicodemus and Jacob A. Nicodemus, was born December 25, 1847. November 25, 1868, she married *Daniel Acker*, who was born December 10, 1841, and on February 8, 1880, he died, leaving his wife and four children at Forreston, Illinois. He and his wife were members of the Reformed Church.

Mrs. Acker on March 14, 1895, married (2) *George Bowers*, who died in 1912. Mrs. Bowers lives in Polo, Illinois.

Children (4), surname Acker:

[1196] Adie Oliver[6], *b* July 3, 1871; *d* November 13, 1882.
[1197] + Albert[6], *b* November 5, 1872; *m Mabel Judson.*
[1198] + Franklin J.[6], *b* October 10, 1874; *m Nettie May Foy.*
[1199] + Harry W.[6], *b* November 20, 1876; *m Anna Dieffenbach.*

[304] **REUBEN FOUSE[5] NICODEMUS**, son of [52] Margaret[4] (Fouse) Nicodemus and Jacob A. Nicodemus, was born May 16, 1850, and October 16, 1874, married *Mary H. Boydston*, born March 10, 1855. He resided at Swedenburg, Saunders County, Nebraska, and died March 30, 1896. They were members of the Reformed Church.

Children (2):

[1200] + Rachel Almyrta[6], *b* October 4, 1875; *m Bennie Dettle Horne.*
[1201] + Burris Vernon[6], *b* September 29, 1882; *m Helen Eva Hawkins.*

[305] **MARY AGNES[5] NICODEMUS**, daughter of [52] Margaret[4] (Fouse) Nicodemus and Jacob A. Nicodemus, was born June 14, 1852. September 11, 1873 she married *Levi Diehl.* They are members of the Reformed Church. Residence, Maryland, Ogle County, Illinois.

Children (3), surname Diehl:

[1203] + Lusha Elva[6], *b* November 7, 1878; *m O. Stouffer.*
[1204] + Chester Lee[6], *b* April 16, 1886; *m Anna Friseman.*
[1205] + Omah May[6], *b* November 9, 1889; *m Charles W. Yates.*

[306] **FREDERICK FOUSE[5] NICODEMUS**, son of [52] Margaret[4] (Fouse) Nicodemus and Jacob A. Nicodemus, was born September 1, 1854, and December 28, 1876, married *Rebecca Bowman*, who was born August 10, 1854 and died November 9, 1901. They are members of the Reformed Church. The family resides at Forreston, Ogle County, Illinois.

Children (2):

[1207] + Alvernia Bowman[6], *b* December 6, 1878; *m Antonius Aykins.*
[1208] + Frederick Bowman[6], *b* June 19, 1884.

[307] **THEOBALD FOUSE[5] NICODEMUS**, son of [52] Margaret[4] (Fouse) Nicodemus and Jacob A. Nicodemus, was born May 12, 1856. He married *Clara Masse.* They reside at Forreston, Ogle County, Illinois, and belong to the Reformed Church.

Children (3):

[1210] + Inez[6], *b* August 10, 1888; *m J. Harold Campbell.*
[1211] Beatrice[6], *b* January 2, 1890.
[1212] Hazel Ellen[6], *b* December 4, 1896; *d* January 9, 1899.

[308] **ESTHER FOUSE[5] NICODEMUS,** daughter of [52] Margaret[4] (Fouse) Nicodemus and Jacob A. Nicodemus, was born April 24, 1858, and December 18, 1884, married *David M. Diehl,* born June 7, 1857. They were members of the Reformed Church. Residence, Forreston, Ogle County, Illinois.

Children (2), surname Diehl:

[1214] Della May[6], *b* January 30, 1894.
[1215] A son[6], *b* February 21, 1898. Mother died the same day.

[309] **WILLIAM FOUSE[5] NICODEMUS,** son of [52] Margaret[4] (Fouse) Nicodemus and Jacob A. Nicodemus, was born February 27, 1860. March 8, 1881, he married *Anna Mary Myers,* who was born November 15, 1858. They are members of the Reformed Church. They reside at 1421 Adams Street, Chicago, Illinois.

Children (2):

[1217] Edith Anna[6], *b* December 25, 1881.
[1218] Ruth May[6], *b* August 7, 1883.

[310] **JACOB FOUSE[5] NICODEMUS,** son of [52] Margaret[4] (Fouse) Nicodemus and Jacob A. Nicodemus, was born February 6, 1862, and April 17, 1883, married *Mary Clarissa Lantz.* They are members of the Reformed Church, and reside at 1421 Adams Street, Chicago, Illinois. (No issue.)

[311] **CATHERINE FOUSE[5] NICODEMUS,** daughter of [52] Margaret[4] (Fouse) Nicodemus and Jacob A. Nicodemus, was born February 26, 1864. November 13, 1884, she married *John O. Fager,* who was born May 31, 1859. They are members of the Reformed Church; and live in Wichita, Kansas. (No issue.)

[312] **MARGARET ELIZABETH FOUSE[5] NICODEMUS,** daughter of [52] Margaret[4] (Fouse) Nicodemus and Jacob A. Nicodemus, was born June 22, 1866, and November 19, 1886, married *Joseph M. Faber,* who was born February 4, 1857. Residence, Forreston, Ogle County, Illinois.

One son, surname Faber:

[1220] Harry Melvin[6], *b* September 1, 1892.

[313] **ANNMA[6] FOUSE**, daughter of [53] Solomon B.[4] and Matilda (Enyeart) Fouse, was born August 5, 1855. November 24, 1874, she married *George B. Daugherty*, who was born February 14, 1848. She is a member of the Reformed Church, and resides at Scottdale, Westmoreland County, Pennsylvania, where her family are engaged in various occupations.

Children (10), surname Daugherty:

[1222] + John J.[6], *b* October 12, 1875; *m Elizabeth Irwin.*
[1223] Margaret E.[6], *b* December 6, 1876; *d* July 4, 1905.
[1224] Ruth[6], *b* February 13, 1878; *d* March 16, 1878.
[1225] + Charlott J.[6], *b* August 26, 1880; *m Jacob Blystone.*
[1226] + Owen F.[6], *b* August 16, 1882; *m Edith Dale Reed.*
[1227] + Sarah O.[6], *b* April 13, 1884; *m Homer C. Dieffenbaugh.*
[1228] + Anna M.[6], *b* September 30, 1885; *m James McClure Ross.*
[1229] Clarence[6], *b* January 26, 1887; *d* March 9, 1887.
[1230] Viola C.[6], *b* February 2, 1888; *unm.*
[1231] Naomi D.[6], *b* January 21, 1890; *unm.*

[315] **SUSAN[6] FOUSE**, daughter of [54] William Acker[4] and Catharine (Greaser) Fouse, was born February 28, 1849; and in January ——, she married *Henry C. Rhodes* They reside on a farm near Roaring Spring, Blair County, Pennsylvania, which is their address.

Children (4), surname Rhodes:

[1234] Nettie, May[6], *b* March 26, 1876.
[1235] William Calvin[6], *b* September 13, 1877.
[1236] Elmer Garfield[6], *b* July 15, 1882.
[1237] Ralph Palmer[6], *b* July 12, 1887.

[317] **REUBEN[6] FOUSE**, son of [54] William Acker[4] and Catharine (Greaser) Fouse, was born April 5, 1852. January 15, 1878 he married *Anna Collins*, who was born September 21, 1852. Residence, Duncanville, Pennsylvania.

Children (5):

[1240] + Harvey Elmer[6], *b* November 14, 1878; *m Delilah Stephens.*
[1241] + Lola Belle[6], *b* February 2, 1880; *m William Schultz.*

[1242] Betta Roberta[6], *b* August 28, 1881; *d* March 21, 1895.
[1243] + Orville[6], *b* June 30, 1883; *m Adelaide Kindred.*
[1244] Alfred Jones[6], *b* August 22, 1886.

[320] **MARGARET[5] FOUSE,** daughter of [54] William Acker[4] and Catharine (Greaser) Fouse, was born December 23, 1857; and November 4, 1886, married *Joseph Detweiler,* who was born February 1, 1859. Residence, Drab, Blair County, Pennsylvania.

Children (8), surname Detweiler:

[1247] Newton Henry[6], *b* May 20, 1879.
[1248] Effy Gertrude[6], *b* May 12, 1887.
[1249] Warren[6], *b* February 2, 1889.
[1250] Mertie May[6], *b* January 30, 1891; *d* February 2, 1892.
[1251] Luella[6], *b* July 23, 1892.
[1252] William Edward[6], *b* January 31, 1894.
[1253] Harry[6], *b* October 30, 1895.
[1254] Katie Idella[6], *b* October 27, 1898.

[321] **SAMUEL[5] FOUSE,** son of [54] William Acker[4] and Catharine (Greaser) Fouse, was born April 7, 1859. October 9, 1894, he married *Martha Detweiler,* daughter of *Joseph Detweiler.* Address is Drab, Blair County, Pennsylvania.

Children (4):

[1257] Anna Florence[6], *b* August 2, 1896.
[1258] Fanny Pearl[6], *b* May 28, 1898.
[1259] Levi Calvin[6], *b* May 30, 1900.
[1260] William Earl[6], *b* September 4, 1905.

[322] **ELIZABETH[5] FOUSE,** daughter of [54] William Acker[4] and Catharine (Greaser) Fouse, was born September 16, 1860. She married *Martin L. Acker.* Address is Drab, Blair County, Pennsylvania, care Martinsburg, R. R. No. 2.

Children (6), surname Acker:

[1262] + John A.[6], *b* September 16, 1888; *m Mary Olive Rhul.*
[1263] Marvin C.[6], *b* August 19, 1890.
[1264] William Preston[6], *b* July 30, 1893.

[1265] Clara Ferne[6], *b* July 27, 1895.
[1266] Harry Earl[6], *b* October 2, 1897; *d* September 14, 1898.
[1267] Roy Elmer[6], *b* August 12, 1901.

[323] **JANE[5] FOUSE,** daughter of [54] William Acker[4] and Catharine (Greaser) Fouse, was born August 20, 1863, and November 28, 1894, married *Jacob Detweiler.* Residence, Drab, Blair County, Pennsylvania.

Children (5), surname Detweiler:

[1270] Clara Verna[6], *b* February 21, 1895.
[1271] Florence[6], *b* May 10, 1896.
[1272] Howard Newton[6], *b* July 18, 1898.
[1273] Nettie[6], *b* April 2, 1901.
[1274] Mabel Grace[6], *b* February 5, 1905.

[325] **WILLIAM[5] FOUSE,** son of [54] William Acker[4] and Catharine (Greaser) Fouse, was born September 23, 1869, and married *Jane Reiley.* They live at Clover Creek, Blair County, Pennsylvania.

Children (4):

[1276] Lester[6], *b* January 11, 1899.
[1277] Catharine Elizabeth[6], *b* December 26, 1900.
[1278] Daniel Carl[6], *b* March 22, 1903.
[1279] Anna Florence[6], *b* April 11, 1907.

[327] **FREDERICK[5] GREASER,** son of [55] Catharine[4] (Fouse) Greaser and George Greaser, was born February 25, 1851. He married (1) *Christina Weidner,* who died May 12, 1872. April 8, 1873, he married (2) *Elizabeth Acker,* born December 29, 1849; daughter of *Henry Acker,* and sister of *Sarah Acker*—see [330]. Elizabeth died November —, 1907, and Frederick November 15, 1890. Mr. Greaser was a miller, and their home was at Drab, Blair County, Pennsylvania.

Children by second marriage (8):

[1281] + Alice[6], *b* March 31, 1874; *m James Detweiler.*
[1282] + Harvey[6], *b* August 4, 1876; *m Mary Pollock.*
[1283] Anna[6], *b* August 10, 1878; *d* September 17, 1879.
[1284] + Ida May[6], *b* April 4, 1880; *m David Householder.*
[1285] + Fannie Elizabeth[6], *b* April 4, 1882; *m Charles Walker.*

[1286] Homer Ellsworth[6], *b* April 12, 1884.
[1287] Ralph[6], *b* October 1, 1887; *d* April 23, 1894.
[1288] Infant son, *b* May 18, 1889; *d* May 23, 1889.

[328] **LUCINDA[6] GREASER,** daughter of [55] Catharine[4] (Fouse) Greaser and George Greaser, was born November 11, 1852. She married (1) *Byron Monroe.* September 28, 1882, she married (2) *John William Daughinbaugh*, born March 30, 1852; son of *John* and *Catharine* (*Merritts*) *Daughinbaugh.* Residence is Drab, Blair County, Pennsylvania.

Children (5), *surname Daughinbaugh:*

[1290] Cheisaelvie[6], *b* July 17, 1883; *d* March 16, 1885.
[1291] Gilbert[6], *b* December 10, 1887.
[1292] Elsie E.[6], *b* November 4, 1889; teacher.
[1293] Samuel Irwin[6], *b* July 24, 1891.
[1294] Levi Earl[6], *b* February 16, 1896.

[330] **DANIEL FOUSE[6] GREASER,** son of [55] Catharine[4] (Fouse) Greaser and George Greaser, was born April 27, 1856. In 1877 he married *Sarah Acker*, born August 27, 1842; daughter of *Henry Acker*, and sister of *Elizabeth Acker*—see [327]. His address is Martinsburg, Blair County, Pennsylvania, R. R. No. 2 (Plates 41 and 42).

Children (3):

[1296] + Margaret Acker[6], *b* September 19, 1878; *m George W. Garner.*
[1297] + Minnie Grace[6], *b* May 7, 1883; *m Jacob Grimes.*
[1298] + Henry Harrison[6], *b* May 2, 1888; *m Violet Waters.*

[331] **JACOB FOUSE[5] GREASER,** son of [55] Catharine[4] (Fouse) Greaser and George Greaser, was born August 1, 1858. February 12, 1884, he married *Susan Ellen Bassler*, born September 18, 1860; daughter of *Jacob Stern* and *Lydia* (*Shank*) *Bassler.* Mr. Greaser conducts the Martinsburg Hotel, Martinsburg, Blair County, Pennsylvania (Plate 64).

Children (5):

[1301] + Lydia[6], *b* September 8, 1855; *m Homer Umbower Loose.*
[1302] Harry[6], *b* July 10, 1887.
[1303] Levi Blanden[6], *b* February 3, 1890.
[1304] Almeda Rebecca[6], *b* June 22, 1892.
[1305] Jay Merril[6], *b* June 7, 1898.

JACOB FOUSE[9] GREASER [331] AND FAMILY, AND JACOB BASSLER.

[332] **PAUL G.⁵ GREASER,** son of [55] Catharine⁴ (Fouse) Greaser and George Greaser, was born July 4, 1860. December 24, 1887, he married *Eleanore (Weber) Mehrwein*, born February 13, 1861; daughter of *Godfrey* and *Rachel Weber*. Mr. Greaser died February 14, 1903, and his remains were interred at Salem Reformed Church, Clover Creek, Pennsylvania. The family live on the Greaser homestead farm near Clover Creek; address, Martinsburg, Blair County, Pennsylvania, R. R. No. 2.

Children (4):

[1307] + Carrie⁶, *b* January 31, 1889; *m George Rhodes.*
[1308] Edna⁶, *b* November 29, 1891; *m Raymond Rhule.*
[1309] Edith⁶, *b* February 28, 1893.
[1310] Orpha Virginia⁶, *b* May 5, 1899.

[334] **ROSAN⁵ GREASER,** daughter of [55] Catharine⁴ (Fouse) Greaser and George Greaser, was born April 14, 1866. December 9, 1886 at Newry, Pennsylvania, she married *William Henry Kemberlin*, born in Martinsburg, Pennsylvania, February 6, 1858; son of *John Geesey* and *Susanna (Geist) Kemberlin.* Mr. and Mrs. Kemberlin live at Martinsburg, Pennsylvania.

Children (5), surname Kemberlin:

[1312] Maud Gertrude⁶, *b* July 10, 1887.
[1313] Idella May⁶, *b* November 9, 1889.
[1314] George Royer⁶, *b* February 7, 1893; *d* February 4, 1894.
[1315] Blanch Edna⁶, *b* April 20, 1895.
[1316] Lloyd Melvin⁶, *b* February 7, 1898.

[335] **SUSAN F.⁵ GREASER,** daughter of [55] Catharine⁴ (Fouse) Greaser and George Greaser, was born April 16, 1868, and December 24, 1891, married *Jacob Obenour*, born October 24, 1859; son of *Christian* and *Mary Elizabeth (Hess) Obenour.* Mr. Obenour is a musician, but is mechanically inclined, a good workman in wood or iron; and does general repairing to buildings and implements, as well as the making of brooms. His address is Martinsburg, Pennsylvania, R. F. D. No. 2, Box 51.

Children (3), surname Obenour:

[1318] George Grover⁶, *b* November 14, 1892.
[1319] Homer Lloyd⁶, *b* December 28, 1894.
[1320] Anna Mary⁶, *b* March 30, 1897.

[336] **MARY ELIZABETH[5] GREASER,** daughter of [55] Catharine[4] (Fouse) Greaser and George Greaser, was born September 15, 1871. November 12, 1890, she married *William Snowberger Wagner*, born June 20, 1864; son of *John* and *Susan* (*Snowberger*) *Wagner*. They live at Martinsburg, Blair County, Pennsylvania.

Children (7), *surname Wagner:*

[1322] Otis Warren[6], *b* November 24, 1891.
[1323] Ruth Ella[6], *b* November 13, 1894.
[1324] Lona[6], *b* October 12, 1897.
[1325] Jacob[6], *b* November 9, 1900.
[1326] Irwin[6], *b* March 11, 1903.
[1327] Carl[6], *b* February 15, 1906.
[1328] Levi[6], *b* April 20, 1909.

[337] **MARY CATHARINE[6] BOYD,** daughter of [56] Elizabeth[4] (Fouse) Boyd and Albert G. Boyd, was born October 15, 1870. August 7, 1888, she married (1) *Harry C. Boerner*. This union was not congenial, and a separation followed. July 7, 1895, Mary Catharine Boerner married (2) *Thomas F. Miller*. They live near Hackettstown, New Jersey, where they purchased a home; address, care R. R. No. 1.

Children (2), *by first marriage, surname Boerner:*

[1330] + Bessie Rubel[7], *b* October 25, 1889; *m Alfred Rader*.
[1331] Paul Boyd[7], *b* January 14, 1892.

Children (2), *by second marriage, surname Miller:*

[1332] Ruth Lenox[7], *b* October 20, 1898.
[1333] Thomas Wesley[7], *b* November 1, 1905.

[338] **JACOB R.[5] FOUSE,** son of [57] Jacob Acker[4] and Margaret Shontz (Grove) Fouse, was born January 7, 1858. April 18, 1900, he married Mrs. *Lavenia* (*Blackburn*) *Good*, born February 10, 1869; daughter of *Moses* and *Agnes* (*McFarland*) *Blackburn*, of Piney Creek, Blair County, Pennsylvania. Mr. Fouse attended school at Roaring Spring, Blair County, Pennsylvania; farmed in his early life, but during the past fourteen years has been in the employ of the Pennsylvania Railroad Company. Address is 1112 Church Street, Hollidaysburg, Blair County, Pennsylvania.

Mrs. Good's children are named Laura, Henry and Arthur Good.

BENJAMIN SIMONTON[5] FOUSE [343].

[339] **MARY ALICE[5] FOUSE,** daughter of [57] Jacob Acker[4] and Margaret Shontz (Grove) Fouse, was born August 16, 1860. February 6, 1879, she married *Samuel Grubb Lininger,* born April 7, 1852; son of *George* and *Sarah (Grubb) Lininger.* Residence, 718 Warm Spring Avenue, Huntingdon, Pennsylvania.

Children (2), surname Lininger:

[1335] Maggie May[6], *b* January 21, 1881; *unm.*
[1336] + Edgar Harry[6], *b* March 19, 1883; *m Margaretta Peightel.*

[340] **HARRY BRUMBAUGH[5] FOUSE,** son of [57] Jacob Acker[4] and Margaret Shontz (Grove) Fouse, was born May 22, 1864. February 21, 1901, he married *Mary Louise Wicke,* born February 25, 1864, and daughter of *Casper* and *Elizabeth (Rietze) Wicke.*

Mr. Fouse is proprietor of a general merchandise store, is a Republican, and a member of the Reformed Church. He has furnished considerable information concerning his general family lines, and is much interested in securing a permanent record of the extensive families embraced in this work. Address is Huntingdon, Pennsylvania.

One son:

[1338] Ralph Wicke[6], *b* August 19, 1902.

[341] **ANNA GRACE[5] FOUSE,** daughter of [57] Jacob Acker[4] and Margaret Shontz (Grove) Fouse, was born May 30, 1870; June 9, 1910, married *Lemuel Lawrence Vanorman,* born April 11, 1866.

He is a traveling salesman, member German Reformed Church, and a Republican. Address, 714 Warm Spring Avenue, Huntingdon, Huntingdon County, Pennsylvania.

One daughter, surname Vanorman:

[1340] Margaret Grace[6], *b* January 16, 1911.

[343] **BENJAMIN SIMONTON[5] FOUSE,** son of [60] Adam[4] and Elizabeth Jane (Simonton) Fouse, was born October 10, 1851. October 24, 1867, he married *Mary M. Knode,* born December 8, 1854. He is engaged in the meat business and is one of the successful business men of Huntingdon, Pennsylvania. He is the owner of his father's homestead farm, which he manages. His mother and youngest sister live there and occupy the house. He and his wife are consistent members of the Reformed

Church and take an active part in all church work. He has been teacher of the Bible class for many years; is one of the active elders of their congregation, and invariably is the elder on the floor of classis and Synod. They are charitable to all good causes and support both home and foreign mission work. Not blessed with any children of their own, they have adopted and reared several children (Plate 65).

[344] **WILLIAM SIMONTON⁶ FOUSE,** son of [60] Adam⁴ and Elizabeth Jane (Simonton) Fouse, was born June 6, 1853, in Lincoln Township, Huntingdon County, Pennsylvania; learned the tanning trade in his father's tannery; remained on his father's farm until about 1875, when he rented a farm of 100 acres in Penn Township. That year he married *Martha Jane Schell*, born June 30, 1853; daughter of *Samuel Schell* of Marklesburg, Pennsylvania, and sister of *Annie Rachel Schell*, who married *Benjamin Greaser Fouse* [378].

Mr. Fouse continued farming in Penn Township, upon several farms, until 1888, when he returned to the paternal farm and continued there for eight years; rented a farm in Penn Township for two years; and then bought a 700-acre farm in Lincoln Township. Address is Entriken, Huntingdon County, Pennsylvania.

"Mr. Fouse has been a member of the school board of this township, and filled the office of supervisor. He is a Republican. He is a deacon in the Reformed Church; was trained in the Sunday school, and has been a teacher there. Following his father's example, he has been no visitor or patron of saloons, and endeavors to maintain a consistent course in life, enjoying the respect and good will of the community."[a]

Children (*4*):

[1342] + Samuel Herman⁶, *b* February 16, 1878; *m Harriet Cunningham.*
[1343] + Mary Jane⁶, *b* October 5, 1882; *m Anthony Howard Russell.*
[1344] + Keturah Pearl⁶, *b* November 16, 1887; *m John H. Ketterman.*
[1345] William Lester⁶, *b* May 20, 1896; address, Entriken, Pennsylvania.

[345] **NANCY SIMONTON⁶ FOUSE,** daughter of [60] Adam⁴ and Elizabeth Jane (Simonton) Fouse, was born July 18, 1855; January 5, 1879, married *John C. Greaser.* They live near Shellsburg, Benton County, Iowa, which is their address.

[a] *Biological Encyclopaedia of Juniata Valley*, Runk & Co., 1897, p. 247.

Children (8), surname Greaser:

[1347] + Mary Bertha[6], *b* November 16, 1879; *m Frank Wilmer Shultz.*
[1348] + George F.[6], *b* January 15, 1881; *m Edna Viola McKean.*
[1349] + Martha Jane[6], *b* May 13, 1882; *m George Edgar King.*
[1350] Adam[6], *b* August 22, 1883; *unm.*
[1351] Wilmer[6], *b* October 17, 1884; *unm.*
[1352] + Ella[6], *b* December 4, 1885; *m Clifford I. Shomler.*
[1353] + Agnes Ruth[6], *b* June 10, 1890; *m Joseph Arthur Budd.*
[1354] Anna Edith[6], *b* November 29, 1892.

[347] **SARAH ANN[5] FOUSE,** daughter of [61] Christian[4] and Barbara (Summers) Fouse, was born October 20, 1846; in 1870 married *James Stone,* born in 1845. Mrs. Stone died March 2, 1896. Mr. Stone is in the furniture business at Sebastopal, California.

Children (6), surname Stone:

[1356] + Ira[6], *b* January 31, 1872; *m Ida Catharine McCall.*
[1357] + Elizabeth A.[6], *b* May 21, 1874; *m Robert E. Galbraith.*
[1358] + William[6], *b* August 6, 1877; *m Anna May Kyle.*
[1359] + Margaret F.[6], *b* January 7, 1880; *m I. Warren Louder.*
[1360] + M. Ella[6], *b* January 31, 1882; *m J. William Louder.*
[1361] + Laura Catherine[6], August 26, 1883; *m John Wintrode Shontz.*

[349] **JOSEPH[5] FOUSE,** son of [61] Christian[4] and Barbara (Summers) Fouse, was born June 18, 1849; October 27, 1874, he married *Anna B. Fisher,* born May 20, 1850. Address, Rohrerstown, Lancaster County, Pennsylvania.

Children (4):

[1363] + Harry F.[6], *b* October 16, 1875; *m Amelia Baker.*
[1364] + Mary M[6], *b* March 14, 1877; *m William Lichty.*
[1365] Barbara[6], *b* April 10, 1879; *unm.*
[1366] George[6], *b* December 12, 1881; *unm.*

[350] **HENRY SUMMERS[5] FOUSE,** son of [61] Christian[4] and Barbara (Summers) Fouse, was born November 12, 1850; and October 25, 1877, married *Emma May Grove,* born February 8, 1858; daughter of *Daniel Hoover* and *Mary Catherine (Domer) Grove.* Mr. Fouse died July 10, 1905, and was interred at Alexandria, Huntingdon County, Pennsylvania.

Children (4):

[1369] Howard Grove[6], *b* February 15, 1879; *d y.*
[1370] + Anna Grace[6], *b* August 10, 1881; *m Thomas J. Stone.*
[1371] Henry Blair[6], *b* March 14, 1884; *d* July 29, 1904.
[1372] Mary Ella[6], *b* May 27, 1898.

[352] **DEWALT[6] FOUSE,** son of [61] Christian[4] and Barbara (Summers) Fouse, was born July 17, 1853. December 28, 1876, he married *Eliza Jane Lininger,* born March 13, 1852; daughter of *Jacob* and *Mary (Speck) Lininger.* Address, Juniata, Pennsylvania.

Children (2):

[1374] + Benjamin[6], *b* March 29, 1884; *m Jennie Elizabeth Wilson.*
[1375] Anna Lena[6], *b* April 16, 1892; *unm.*

[353] **CATHERINE[6] FOUSE,** daughter of [61] Christian[4] and Barbara (Summers) Fouse, was born December 22, 1854; July 24, 1895, married *Lewis Schoch,* born December 12, 1844, and died July, 1908. His widow lives at 221 Park Avenue, Punxsutawney, Pennsylvania.

One daughter, surname Schoch:

[1377] Ella Dorathy[6], *b* June 23, 1896.

[357] **MARGARET[6] FOUSE,** daughter of [61] Christian[4] and Barbara (Summers) Fouse, was born June 28, 1862; August 28, 1884, married *Samuel Gilliland Rudy,* born April 9, 1855.

Mr. Rudy for a number of years was county superintendent of the public schools of Huntingdon County, Pennsylvania; and is a member of the Huntingdon County Bar, being actively engaged in the practice of his profession. He graduated from the Normal English course of Juniata College in 1882. Address, Huntingdon, Pennsylvania.

Children (7), surname Rudy:

[1381] Harry Fouse[6], *b* March 17, 1885; *d* August 24, 1886.
[1382] + Mary Viola[6], *b* May 2, 1887; *m Lewis George Snell.*
[1383] + Alvin Walter[6], *b* January 1, 1890; *m Gretta Milligan.*
[1384] Raymond Bruce[6], *b* February 12, 1893.
[1385] Edwin Hayes[6], *b* May 6, 1896; *d* February 2, 1904.
[1386] Frederick Ralph[6], *d* May 17, 1900.
[1387] Gerald Burket[6], *b* March 22, 1904.

ELLA GRACE[9] (FOUSE) JACKSON [361], THEODORE CUNNINGHAM JACKSON, AND CHILDREN.

[358] **FRANK[5] FOUSE,** son of [61] Christian[4] and Eliza (Frank-Shontz) Fouse, was born March 27, 1886. August 18, 1891, he married *Ida May Aultman*, born about 1870; daughter of *Gustave* and *Margaret Aultman*. Occupation is brickmoulder, and address is Alexandria, Huntingdon County, Pennsylvania.

Children (6):

[1390] Chester Gustave[6], *b* October 28, 1892.
[1391] Harry William[6], *b* January 15, 1895.
[1392] Blanch Margaret[6], *b* May 24, 1897.
[1393] Ella May[6], *b* April 26, 1900.
[1394] Fred Hutchinson[6], *b* April 18, 1903.
[1395] Frank Jr.[6], *b* April 16, 1906.

[360] **MARY ELIZABETH[5] FOUSE,** daughter of [61] Christian[4] and Eliza (Frank-Shontz) Fouse, was born June 27, 1873; August 26, 1896, married *Henry Musser Hosterman*, born about 1875, son of *Adam* and *Susan Hosterman*. Address, Boalsburg, Center County, Pennsylvania.

Children (2), surname Hosterman:

[1398] Charles, *b* June 7, 1900.
[1399] Frank, *b* June 6, 1904.

[361] **ELLA GRACE[5] FOUSE,** daughter of [61] Christian[4] and Eliza (Frank-Shontz) Fouse, was born July 31, 1877; April 9, 1903, married *Theodore Cunningham Jackson*, born June 30, 1877, at McAlevey's Fort, Pennsylvania; son of *Hugh Alexander* and *Mary Elizabeth (Forrest) Jackson*. The Jacksons came from New Jersey and settled on the Raystown Branch of the Juniata River; later near Barre; and later were amongst the early settlers of Jackson Township, Huntingdon County, Pennsylvania. Hugh Alexander Jackson's mother was an Alexander of Mifflin County, Pennsylvania, and was a direct descendant of Hugh Alexander, Delegate to Provincial Conference, and Convention of 1776, from Cumberland County, Pennsylvania[a]; and of Alexander Brown, Lieutenant-Colonel 1777-1780, Cumberland County, Pennsylvania.[b]

Theodore Cunningham Jackson was educated in the common schools of Pennsylvania, attended Juniata College for two years; read law with

[a] *Penna. Archives*, 2d Ser., Vol. 3, p. 679, 680.

[b] *Penna. Archives*, 2d Ser., Vol. 10, p. 177; Vol. 15, p. 467; Vol. 14, pp. 90, 405, 430; Vol. 14, p. 466.

Thomas Fisher Bailey, and was admitted to the Huntingdon County Bar, October 14, 1901. He continues in the practice of law, and also is teller of the First National Bank of Huntingdon, Pennsylvania—one of the early national banks of the state. He is member of the Presbyterian Church, and of its board of trustees. Address, 725 Portland Avenue, Huntingdon, Pennsylvania (Plate 66).

Children (2), surname Jackson:

[1401] Charles Herbert[6], *b* December 28, 1903.
[1402] Robert Hugh[6], *b* June 11, 1908.

[362] **JACOB SUMMERS[5] FOUSE,** son of [62] John[4] and Rebecca (Summers) Fouse, was born May 28, 1855; April 22, 1879, married *Martha Ellen Donnelson;* daughter of *John* and *Margaret (Shultz) Donnelson.* They lived and died at James Creek, Huntingdon County, Pennsylvania. Mr. Fouse died January 27, 1881, and Mrs. Fouse March 30, 1898.

Children (5):

[1404] + John Nevin[6], *b* October 31, 1880; *m Agnes Anmen.*
[1405] + Jacob Rupley[6], *b* May 27, 1882; *m Margaret Ada Snare.*
[1406] + Theobald Kieffer[6], *b* October 2, 1884; *m Elsie M. Shultz.*
[1407] + Margaret Rebecca[6], *b* October 15, 1886; *m James Monroe Allison.*
[1408] Samuel Hoy[6], *b* July 2, 1890; *d.*

[363] **DEWALT FOUSE[5] SHULTZ,** son of [64] Elizabeth[4] (Fouse) Shultz and Anthony Beaver Shultz, was born August 26, 1848. November 14, 1872, he married *Margaret Greaser,* born March 11, 1842; daughter of *George* and *Agnes (Katzelmoyer) Greaser* [see 55]. Mr. Shultz lived at James Creek, Huntingdon County, Pennsylvania; was a farmer until 1897, when he moved to Entriken, Pennsylvania. He there engaged in mercantile business, and was postmaster for a number of years—until his death, May 6, 1913; buried at the Reformed Cemetery, James Creek, Pennsylvania.

Children (8), surname Shultz:

[1410] + Elmer Ellsworth[6], *b* June 14, 1874.
[1411] + Anthony Harvey[6], *b* March 2, 1876; *m Anna Catharine Frank.*
[1412] Elizabeth Agnes[6], *b* May 19, 1878; *unm.*; address, Entriken, Pennsylvania.
[1413] + Clarence Greaser[6], *b* December 5, 1879; address, Huntingdon, Pennsylvania.

[1414] + George Greaser[6], *b* May 23, 1881; *m Jennie Jackson Johnson.*
[1415] + Henry Franklin[6], *b* August 29, 1883; *m Lena Verona Myers.*
[1416] Dewalt[6], *b* August 3, 1885; *d* August 12, 1885.
[1417] Benjamin Reuben[6], *b* August 7, 1887; *d* January 29, 1888.

[364] **NANCY[5] SHULTZ,** daughter of [64] Elizabeth[4] (Fouse) Shultz and Anthony Beaver Shultz, was born September 11, 1851. September 12, 1869, she married *John Russell Lynn,* born April 16, 1845; son of *David* and *Catharine (Russell) Lynn.* Mr. Lynn has a common school education, is a Democrat, member Reformed Church, and a farmer. Address, Entriken, Pennsylvania.

Children (7), surname Lynn:

[1419] + Laura[6], *b* September 10, 1870; *m Samuel Calvin Weller.*
[1420] + Catharine[6], *b* May 22, 1872; *m Dewalt Robert Shultz.*
[1421] Reuben Shultz[6], *b* May 14, 1874; *d* June, 1876.
[1422] + Cora Elizabeth[6], *b* March 24, 1876; *m George Washington Shontz.*
[1423] + John Shultz[6], *b* March 14, 1880; *m Anna Mary Snare.*
[1424] + Nancy Jane[6], *b* February 5, 1887; *m William H. Ford.*
[1425] Andrew Charles[6], *b* February 8, 1895; *unm.*

[365] **ELIZABETH[5] SHULTZ,** daughter of [64] Elizabeth[4] (Fouse) Shultz and Anthony Beaver Shultz, was born February 5, 1853. March 20, 1873, she married *Andrew Russell Lynn, b* February 20, 1848; son of *David* and *Catharine (Russell) Lynn.* Mr. Shultz taught public schools for three years, farmed near Entriken, Huntingdon County, Pennsylvania, and recently moved to Fairfield, Greene County, Ohio. He is there overseer for a cemetery.

Children (6), surname Lynn:

[1428] + Frances[6], *b* February 17, 1874; *m Sanuel Albert Weaver.*
[1429] + Dewalt Shultz[6], *b* October 14, 1876; *m Clara Tobias.*
[1430] Mary Ann[6], *b* October 13, 1879; *d* October, 1898.
[1431] + Anthony Claude[6], *b* May 8, 1881; *m Jessie Huffman.*
[1432] + William Henry[6], *b* January 25, 1886; *unm.*
[1433] + Andrew Russell, Jr.[6], *b* July 10, 1890; *m Irene Bell.*

[366] **DAVID FOUSE[5] SHULTZ,** son of [64] Elizabeth[4] (Fouse) Shultz and Anthony Beaver Shultz, was born August 5, 1854; February 14, 1878,

married *Sarah Catharine Brumbaugh*,* born February 24, 1857; daughter of *Daniel* and *Mary* (*Hoover*) *Brumbaugh.* Mr. Shultz served as Justice of the Peace in 1906, and was reelected in 1913 for a term of six years. The family live on a farm near Entriken, Huntingdon County, Pennsylvania, which is their address.

Children (10), surname Shultz:

[1436] + Chester Arthur[6], *b* June 23, 1878; *m Flora May Weaver.*
[1437] + Ida Bertha[6], *b* June 12, 1880; *m Frank Homer Cypher.*
[1438] Clyde B.[6], *b* March 14, 1882.
[1439] + Mary Elva[6], *b* June 6, 1884; *m Milton Sangree Isenberg.*
[1440] Lizzie Cora[6], *b* May 13, 1886; *d* September 20, 1892.
[1441] + Laura Dessie[6], *b* May 21, 1888; *m John Nevin Isenberg.*
[1442] Della Hazel[6], *b* April 4, 1890.
[1443] David Gailen[6], *b* December 27, 1891.
[1444] Reuben Franklin[6], *b* September 13, 1893; *d* January 29, 1895.
[1445] Rupley Carl[6], *b* February 9, 1897.

[367] **REUBEN FOUSE[6] SHULTZ,** son of [64] Elizabeth[4] (Fouse) Shultz and Anthony Beaver Shultz, was born October 31, 1855, and May 24, 1887 married *Erminie Cook* of Phillipsburg, Montgomery County, Ohio; born September 22, 1866.

Mr. Shultz worked on his father's farm and attended school in the old log school-house on the Summer's farm. At the age of 15 he entered Juniata Collegiate Institute, Martinsburg, Blair County, Pennsylvania, where he prepared himself for teaching. In 1872 he began the latter work and continued until June, 1880, when he went to Montgomery County, Ohio, and there taught six years. He also taught music, sometimes having as many as four classes at a time. He was also active in Sunday school work, as superintendent, etc. He continued teaching until 1885; when he entered Heidelberg Theological Seminary, Tiffin, Ohio, taking a two years' course and graduating with the class of 1887.

Rev. Reuben Fouse Shultz has filled pastorates as follows: Reedsburg, Wayne County, Ohio, 1887-1889; Fairfield, Ohio, 1889-1896; Springfield, 1896-1906. Mission work at Freeport, Illinois and Akron, Ohio, July, 1906-January, 1907; Germantown, Ohio, 1907-March, 1909. On the latter date he became field secretary of the board of trustees of the Central

*No. [E 287] *Brumbach Families*, page 565.

REV. REUBEN FOUSE[5] SHULTZ (367).

Theological Seminary. Address, 1226 Hoffman Avenue, Dayton, Ohio (Plate 67).

Children (5):

[1448] Charles Emil[6], *b* March 23, 1888; *d* August 7, 1888.
[1449] Lois Naomi[6], *b* October 3, 1889.
[1450] Herman[6], *b* May 5, 1892.
[1451] Catharine[6], *b* May 2, 1894.
[1452] Thisbe Elizabeth[6], May 22, 1901.

[368] **MARY ANN[5] SHULTZ,** daughter of [64] Elizabeth[4] (Fouse) Shultz and Anthony Beaver Shultz, was born April 24, 1857; April 5, 1885, she married *John Shirley Beaver*, born February 10, 1854; son of *John* and *Catharine (Garner) Beaver.* They reside on a farm near Entriken, Huntingdon County, Pennsylvania.

Children (6), surname Beaver:

[1454] + Nannie Shultz[6], *b* April 11, 1886; *m Harry Clayton Speck.*
[1455] + Catherine Elizabeth[6], *b* December 20, 1887; *m Harry Cleveland Lorenz.*
[1456] Almeda Gertrude[6], *b* September 2, 1889; *unm.*
[1457] John Nevan[6], *b* October 7, 1891; *unm.*
[1458] Mary Ann[6], *b* April 10, 1894; *unm.*
[1459] Mabel G.[6], *b* March 23, 1897; *unm.*

[370] **CATHARINE[5] SHULTZ,** daughter of [64] Elizabeth[4] (Fouse) Shultz and Anthony Beaver Shultz, was born December 17, 1859, and December 25, 1887, married *Jacob Bowser Russell,* who was born February 28, 1853; son of *John H.* and *Delilah (Bowser) Russell.* Mr. Russell is a farmer. Address; Martinsburg, Blair County, Pennsylvania.

Children (11), surname Russell:

[1462] Martin Luther[6], *b* April 22, 1878; *d* April 8, 1901.
[1463] + Delilah[6], *b* February 7, 1881; *m John Carmack.*
[1464] + Elizabeth[6], *b* June 6, 1883; *m John Phillips.*
[1465] + Anthony Howard[6], *b* December 19, 1884; *m Mary Jane Fouse.*
[1466] Henrietta[6], *b* November 8, 1886; *d* February 27, 1897.
[1467] + Laura Helen[6], *b* February 11, 1888; *m Henry Esco Walker.*
[1468] John Homer[6], *b* July 29, 1889; address, Entriken, Pennsylvania.

[1469] Maggie Catherine[6], *b* February 18, 1891.
[1470] Jacob Charles[6], *b* December 10, 1892; *d* July 19, 1893.
[1471] William Henry[6], *b* May 9, 1894; address, Curryville, Pennsylvania.
[1472] Reuben Chester[6], *b* March 5, 1896.

[371] **WILLIAM HENRY[5] SHULTZ,** son of [64] Elizabeth[4] (Fouse) Shultz and Anthony Beaver Shultz, was born September 17, 1861. July 24, 1887, he married (1) *Margaret Summers*, daughter of *Jacob* and *Elizabeth (Enyeart) Summers*. Margaret died December 10, 1887.

February 7, 1892, Mr. Shultz married (2) *Minnie Simpson*, born February 14, 1874, and died November 5, 1904.

October 13, 1906, Mr. Shultz married (3) *Malinda Detweiler*, born September 10, 1863; daughter of *Joseph* and *Elizabeth (Kinger) Detweiler*. Malinda had previously married (1) William Shontz and (2) Davis Glasgow Enyeart. (No issue to the third marriage.) The address of Mr. Shultz is Entriken, Huntingdon County, Pennsylvania.

One daughter by first marriage:

[1475] + Margaret[6], *b* October 26, 1887; *m Jesse Rodgers*,

Children (3) by second marriage:

[1476] Ollie May[6], *b* August 1, 1897.
[1477] William Henry[6], *b* November 9, 1901.
[1478] Carrie[6], *b* March 25, 1904.

[374] **MARGARET[5] SHULTZ,** daughter of [64] Elizabeth[4] (Fouse) Shultz and Anthony Shultz, was born June 28, 1867. September 21, 1890, she married *Albert Criswell*, born June 10, 1866; son of *Joseph* and *Sarah (Fisher) Criswell.* Mr. Criswell is a plasterer, and his address is Entriken, Huntingdon County, Pennsylvania.

Children (6), surname Criswell::

[1481] Chester Arthur Reed[6], *b* March 9, 1888.
[1482] Anthony Howard[6], *b* April 21, 1892; *d* August 4, 1896.
[1483] + Lena Catharine[6], *b* April 25, 1897; *m George W. Hess.*
[1484] Charles H.[6], *b* April 25, 1897.
[1485] A. Ross[6], *b* April 22, 1899.
[1486] Margaret[6], *b* February 5, 1904.

[375] **ANTHONY HOWARD[5] SHULTZ,** son of [64] Elizabeth[4] (Fouse) Shultz and Anthony Beaver Shultz was born May 23, 1870. He attended Juniata College, Huntingdon, Pennsylvania, taught five terms in the public schools; was a member of German Reformed Church; died May 2, 1893; was unmarried.

[376] **MARY AGNES[5] FOUSE,** daughter of [65] Benjamin[4] and Anna (Greaser) Fouse, was born November 17, 1862; December 19, 1887, married *Levi Lininger,* born January 30, 1856; son of *Jacob* and *Mary* (*Speck*) *Lininger.* Mr. Lininger is a farmer, and the family live on the Fouse homestead, Clover Creek, Pennsylvania; are members of the Reformed Church; Republican. Address is Drab, Blair County, Pennsylvania.

Children (3), surname Lininger:

[1489] Frederick Fouse[6], *b* July 29, 1892.
[1490] Anna May[6], *b* February 15, 1894.
[1491] Harriet Kathryn[6], *b* March 21, 1900.

[377] **MARTHA JANE[5] FOUSE,** daughter of [65] Benjamin[4] and Anna (Greaser) Fouse, was born November 3, 1863. December 24, 1890, she married *Edward Elwood Haffley,* born March 10, 1858, and who died May 31, 1893. During his short career in life, he followed farming. Mrs. Haffley resides at Drab, Blair County, Pennsylvania.

One daughter, surname Haffley:

[1494] Ella Grace[6], *b* December 27, 1891.

[378] **BENJAMIN GREASER[5] FOUSE,** son of [65] Benjamin[4] and Ann (Greaser) Fouse, was born August 29, 1865. December, 1886, he married *Annie Rachel Schell,* born July 23, 1865, in Lincoln Township, Huntingdon County, Pennsylvania, sister of *Martha Jane Schell,* who married *William Simonton[5] Fouse* [344]; daughter of *Samuel Schell.* Mr. Fouse is a merchant at Marklesburg, Huntingdon County, Pennsylvania (James Creek post-office), where the family have long lived, and where Mrs. Fouse died, September, 1913, from apoplexy. The services were conducted by Rev. E. R. Hamme, pastor of Mr. and Mrs. Fouse, and the body was laid away in the Reformed Church Cemetery near Marklesburg.

Children (3):

[1496] Homer Ellsworth[6], *b* March 14, 1888; address, Altoona, Pennsylvania.

[1497] Ada Grace[6], *b* November 2, 1891; address, James Creek, Pennsylvania.

[1498] Ruth Mildred[6], *b* June 24, 1897; *m Clair Boyer*, Aitch, Pennsylvania.

[380] **JOHN F.[5] GROVE,** son of [66] Catherine[4] (Fouse) Grove and Samuel H. Grove, was born August 12, 1855. September 30, 1875, he married *Mary E. Summers*, who was born August 15, 1857. Address, Huntingdon, Pennsylvania.

Children (5):

[1500] Flora E.[6], *b* August 11, 1876; *d* January 10, 1899.
[1501] Alburtis[6], *b* September 9, 1879.
[1502] Huron P.[6], *b* May 26, 1881.
[1503] Maud M.[6], *b* December 29, 1882.
[1504] Hurshell C.[6], *b* July 18, 1884.

[381] **MARTHA J.[5] GROVE,** daughter of [66] Catherine[4] (Fouse) Grove and Samuel H. Grove, was born April 14, 1857; and in 1877 married *Henry Irwin Harris*, born February 10, 1859.

Children (4), surname Harris:

[1507] Clara B[6], *b* October 13, 1878; *d* March 29, 1880.
[1508] John G.[6], *b* September 4, 1881; *d* March 15, 1882.
[1509] Henry B.[6], *b* August 28, 1883; *d* January 31, 1884.
[1510] Ann C.[6], *b* January 19, 1886; *d* March 10, 1886.

[382] **MARGARET ELLEN[5] GROVE,** daughter of [66] Catherine[4] (Fouse) Grove and Samuel H. Grove, was born August 24, 1858. January 1, 1876, she married *Anthony Wayne Beaver*, born July 15, 1856; son of *John* and *Catharine (Garner) Beaver*. Mr. Beaver is a farmer, and his address is Entriken, Huntingdon County, Pennsylvania.

Children (8), surname Beaver:

[1513] Rachel[6], *b* January 18, 1877.
[1514] Benjamin[6], *b* November 26, 1878.

[1515] Samuel T.[6], *b* May 6, 1880.
[1516] Franklin C.[6], *b* February 8, 1883.
[1517] Reuben S.[6], *b* July 16, 1884.
[1518] Edna Grace[6], *b* August 3, 1886.
[1519] Henry S.[6], *b* September 14, 1893; *d* December 29, 1903.
[1520] Martha J.[6], *b* February 3, 1896.

[383] **BENJAMIN F.[5] GROVE,** son of [66] Catherine[4] (Fouse) Grove and Samuel H. Grove, was born January 7, 1860. March 11, 1880, he was united in marriage to Miss *C. A. Reed,* who was born January 31, 1862; daughter of *William Reed* of Marklesburg, Huntingdon County, Pennsylvania.

Children (8):

[1523] Nancy[6], *b* May 3, 1882; *d* November 19, 1889.
[1524] Viona May[6], *b* May 8, 1884; *d* November 29, 1889.
[1525] Grace[6], *b* March 29, 1886; *d* December 30, 1889.
[1526] James H.[6], *b* May 15, 1890.
[1527] Blanche[6], *b* March 4, 1893.
[1528] Martha[6], *b* January 17, 1898; *d* March 2, 1899.
[1529] William[6], *b* September 22, 1901.
[1530] George[6], *b* December 22, 1903.

[384] **RACHEL[5] GROVE,** daughter of [66] Catherine[4] (Fouse) Grove and Samuel H. Grove, was born April 29, 1861; March 8, 1888, she married *Blair S. Summers,* who was born November 23, 1859, and died August 3, or 21, 1890; son of *Henry H. Summers.*[a] Mrs. Summers died August 17, 1905.

Children (2), surname Summers:

[1533] Henry[6], *b* February 1, 1889; *d* February 4, 1889.
[1534] + Clara May[6], *b* February 10, 1890.

[385] **DEWALT F.[5] GROVE,** son of [66] Catherine[4] (Fouse) Grove and Samuel H. Grove, was born August 15, 1862; and June 22, 1887, married *Edith Blanche Sheckler,* who was born January 1, 1867. Last address, Plymouth, Richland County, Ohio.

[a] Henry H. Summers was son of Henry and Sarah Boyer Summers. See [35], [61], and [62] this volume.

Children (8):

[1536] Mabel Elmira⁶, *b* March 20, 1888.
[1537] Edith Grace⁶, *b* October 30, 1891.
[1538] Lois Lucile⁶, *b* March 27, 1892.
[1539] John Homer⁶, *b* January 19, 1896.
[1540] James Russell⁶, *b* October 24, 1897.
[1541] Frank Sheckler⁶, *b* February 17, 1901; *d* January 12, 1904.
[1542] Samuel Elymor⁶, *b* September 26, 1902.
[1543] Robert Ellsworth⁶, *b* November 19, 1906.

[386] **GEORGE S.⁵ GROVE,** son of [66] Catherine⁴ (Fouse) Grove and Samuel H. Grove, was born March 5, 1864. December 22, 1887, he married *Emma R. Stover*, who was born November 1, 1865. His address is Altoona, Pennsylvania.

Children (3):

[1547] Homer L.⁶, *b* October 17, 1888.
[1548] Ella May⁶, *b* August 26, 1889.
[1549] Alda Martha⁶, *b* November 1, 1893.

[390] **REUBEN FOUSE⁵ HOOVER,** son of [68] Mary⁴ (Fouse) Hoover and Benjamin Hoover, was born September 6, 1859, and married *Anna M. Fenstermaker*, of Grafton, Pennsylvania, on March 2, 1882. Address, Grafton, Huntingdon County, Pennsylvania.

Children (2):

[1552] Benjamin Clyde⁶, *b* July 20, 1883; *d* April 3, 1885.
[1553] Elsie May⁶, *b* January 18, 1885.

[391] **CATHERINE FOUSE⁵ HOOVER,** daughter of [68] Mary⁴ (Fouse) Hoover and Benjamin Hoover, was born July 26, 1861, at Grafton, Huntingdon County, Pennsylvania, and was educated in the common schools of Penn Township, that county. April 26, 1898, she married *Benjamin Franklin Fink*, born April 2, 1858, at Colfax, Huntingdon County, Pennsylvania; son of *Daniel W.* and *Catharine Elizabeth (Tool) Fink.* Daniel W. Fink was born in Penn Township, Huntingdon County, Pennsylvania, February 10, 1823, and died February 18, 1904; and his wife was born in Blair County, Pennsylvania, June 16, 1820, and died August 24, 1892.

CATHERINE FOUSE[5] (HOOVER) FINK [391], FRANK HAROLD[6] FINK [1556], AND BENJAMIN FRANKLIN FINK.

These parents spent their life on the farm, and of their six children, two died in infancy.

Benjamin Franklin Fink passed his boyhood on his father's farm, acquiring his education in the common schools of Union Township; at age of 20 he began teaching in Henderson Township, and taught in the public schools of Henderson, Union and Cass Townships from 1878 to 1885. He remained at home from 1885 to April 1, 1889, when he went to Huntingdon and there engaged in the working of sheetiron. In 1892 he removed to Orbisonia, Huntingdon County, Pennsylvania, where he engaged in the business of roofing, spouting and hardware. In 1895, Mr. Fink returned to Huntingdon, engaging in the same business. In 1902 he built the three story brick building at 704-706 Washington Street, that place, which he occupies as a hardware store, etc.; and he is also interested in other real estate, having been quite successful in business. He is Republican in politics, and a member of the Presbyterian Church. Mrs. Fink is a member of the Reformed Church (Plate 68).

One son:

[1556] Frank Harold^6, *b* February 24, 1902.

[392] **NANCY F.^{5} HOOVER,** daughter of [68] Mary^4 (Fouse) Hoover and Benjamin Hoover, was born October 10, 1863; and on February 25, 1897, married *William Heffner*, of McConnellstown, Pennsylvania, son of *Benjamin Heffner*. Their address is McConnellstown, Huntingdon County, Pennsylvania. (No issue reported.)

[393] **ELIZABETH F.^{5} HOOVER,** daughter of [68] Mary^4 (Fouse) Hoover and Benjamin Hoover, was born July 1, 1866. February 28, 1895, she married *John Keith^6 Brumbaugh*,[a] of Huntingdon County, Pennsylvania; son of *Peter^5* and *Mary (Keith) Brumbaugh*. Mr. Brumbaugh is engaged in the industrial life insurance business at Charleroi, Washington County, Pennsylvania.

Children (2), surname Brumbaugh:

[1562] Glenn H.^{6}, *b* June 28, 1898.
[1563] John Blaine^6, *b* August 18, 1900.

[a] No. [E 575] in *Brumbach Families*, 1913, page 598.

[394] **BENJAMIN FRANKLIN[6] HOOVER,** son of [68] Mary[4] (Fouse) Hoover and Benjamin Hoover, was born in Penn Township, Huntingdon County, Pennsylvania, July 18, 1873. He was educated in the public schools and also attended one term in Juniata College He has always been active in support of educational work and is serving as a school director. "The Democratic party has his strong support in political matters and he has held a number of local offices, filling them to the entire satisfaction of the community. He is a consistent member of the Reformed Church."[a]

December 13, 1894, Mr. Hoover married *Lucy Hellyer*, daughter of *Edward* and *Elizabeth (Putt) Hellyer.* In 1895, he purchased 154 acres of land near Grafton, Huntingdon County, Pennsylvania, his address, and he is there engaged in dairy farming.

Children (3):

[1565] Charles Edward[6], *b* August 31, 1895.
[1566] Reuben Merle[6], *b* November 27, 1896.
[1567] Benjamin Carl[6], *b* December 2, 1900; *d* September 3, 1901.

[395] **DAVID HENRY[5] FOUSE,** son of [71] Dewalt Shontz[4] and Sarah Ann (Geissinger) Fouse, was born July 1, 1869. He graduated at the Lisbon High School in 1886. In the fall of the same year he entered Cornell College, at Mt. Vernon, Iowa, and took the classical course; graduated from said college in June, 1890. In September of the same year he entered the Theological Seminary of the Reformed Church at Lancaster, Pennsylvania, and graduated from the same in 1893. He at once took charge of the churches at Columbus Junction and St. Pauls, in Louisa County, Iowa. He continued to serve this charge until 1901, when he took charge of the English Mission at Denver, Colorado, where he has been for the past eleven years, and at the First Reformed Church of that city. He is an able and interesting preacher and a good writer on matters of piety and religion.

October 21, 1896, Mr. Fouse was united in marriage with *Margaret Owen*, born March 30, 1873, daughter of *Robert White* and *Mary Jane (Duncan) Owen.* Mrs. Fouse graduated from the Columbus Junction High School (1891), and from the Cornell Conservatory of Music (1896). Address, 2530 Ash Street, Denver, Colorado (Plate 69).

[a] *History of Juniata Valley, Jordan,* 1913, page 1057.

REV. DAVID HENRY[9] FOUSE [395].

Children (4):

[1570] Frederick David[6], *b* September 6, 1898.
[1571] Robert Dewalt[6], *b* August 12, 1900.
[1572] Mary Elizabeth[6], *b* February 8, 1909.
[1573] Kathryn Margaret[6], *b* December 11, 1911.

[396] **SAMUEL GEISSINGER[5] FOUSE**, son of [71] Dewalt Shontz[4] and Sarah Ann (Geissinger) Fouse, was born February 27, 1871. June 27, 1906, he married *Helen Chambers* of New Hampton, Iowa, born August 19, 1880; daughter of *Edwin Lawrence* and *Mary Jane (Pauley) Chambers.* Mrs. Fouse graduated from the Clarksville High School (1897), Cornell College (A.B., 1901; A.M., 1904), and attended the University of Chicago (1901-1902).

Mr. Fouse is a merchant at Lisbon, Iowa. He has followed that pursuit with success, for more than sixteen years in his home town where he bears the reputation of being honest and upright in all his dealings. He also takes quite an interest in church work, and is a consistent member of the Reformed Church. (No children.)

[397] **JOHN DEWALT[5] FOUSE**, son of [71] Dewalt Shontz[4] and Sarah Ann (Geissinger) Fouse, was born June 1, 1873. He married *Bertha Mae Gauby* of Lisbon, Iowa, daughter of Captain *Jonas S.* and *Miltilda (Cook) Gauby.* Mr. Fouse graduated from Lisbon High School in 1891, and his wife in 1893; and from Cornell Conservatory of Music in 1896, and his wife in 1897. He is western representative of Schoenbrun and Company, merchant tailors of Chicago, and lives in Lisbon, Iowa.

Children (2):

[1575] Sevendolin Gauby[6], *b* January 1, 1904.
[1576] Hortense Geissinger[6], *b* December 11, 1911.

[398] **MARY NAOMI[5] FOUSE**, daughter of [71] Dewalt Shontz[4] and Sarah Ann (Geissinger) Fouse, was born April 18, 1879. June 3, 1903, she married *Jason Daniel Kinsley* of McGregor, Iowa, born December 16, 1875; son of *Guy* and *Lucinda (Ellsworth) Kinsley.* Dr. Kinsley graduated from Breckenridge Normal (1893), and from Dental Department of State University of Iowa (1898). Mrs. Kinsley graduated from Lisbon High School (1896) and Cornell College (1900) Address, Lisbon, Iowa.

Children (2), surname Kinsley:

[1579] Guy Dewalt[6], *b* November 17, 1904.
[1580] Bruce Whitney[6], *b* December 1, 1906.

[401] **CLYDE EVERETT[5] FOUSE,** son of [73] Frederick Shontz[4] and Harriet Emma (Long) Fouse, was born May 1, 1871, at Huntingdon, Pennsylvania. He was educated in the public schools of Pennsylvania, Central Manual Training School, Philadelphia, Pennsylvania; Veterinary Department of the University of Pennsylvania (V.M.D., 1894). He served as assistant demonstrator of veterinary anatomy, University of Pennsylvania, 1895-1896; inspection and efficiency expert for American Bridge Company, 1900; elected to board of auditors, Borough of Ambridge.

December 21, 1900, Mr. Fouse married *Elsie Irene Deike* of Ottawa, Ontario, born March 12, 1879; daughter of *August Herman* and *Elizabeth Jane (Sweetman) Deike.* Mrs. Fouse died —— 1913. The family live at 235 Maplewood Avenue, Ambridge, Beaver County, Pennsylvania.

Children (2):

[1582] Dorathea Caroline[6], *b* October 25, 1901.
[1583] Frederick Everett[6], *b* October 8, 1907.

[404] **CAROLINE EDITH[5] FOUSE,** daughter of [73] Frederick Shontz[4] and Harriet Emma (Long) Fouse, was born January 19, 1881. She was educated in the Girls' Commercial High School, Philadelphia, Pennsylvania, graduating 1898. December 17, 1913, she married *Albert Bailey Megrew,* Philadelphia. The latter is manager Macbeth-Evans Glass Company. Address, 25 N. 61st Street, Philadelphia, Pennsylvania.

[407] **ADAM SUMMERS[5] FOUSE,** son of [75] David[4] and Margaret Ann (Summers) Fouse, was born November 20, 1856. February 6, 1889, he married *Ann Huff,* daughter of *Henry* and *Sarah (Hillyer) Huff.* Mr. Fouse is a farmer, and his address is Aitch, Huntingdon County, Pennsylvania. (No issue reported.)

[409] **ALFRED S.[5] FOUSE,** son of [75] David[4] and Margaret Ann (Summers) Fouse, was born April 12, 1861. December 25, 1881, he married *Margaret Hood,* who was born in 1861.

Mrs. Margaret Hood Fouse died about 1900. She was a good, kind helpmate; and an excellent wife, and a good mother to her children. Her loss was very much felt in her family and amongst her neighbors and friends.

Mr. Fouse is a farmer and his address is Aitch, Huntingdon County, Pennsylvania.

Children (6):

[1589] + Annie Mary[6], *b* November 18, 1882; *m Galbraith Lang.*
[1590] + Emma Susan[6], *b* November 14, 1885; *m Frederick Householder.*
[1591] John Wilmer[6], *b* March 15, 1893.
[1592] Clarence Hood[6], *b* July 27, 1895.
[1593] Alice Catherine[6], *b* September 21, 1897.
[1594] Margaret Grace[6], *b* May 8, 1899.

[410] **FRANKLIN SUMMERS[5] FOUSE,** son of [75] David[4] and Margaret Ann (Summers) Fouse, was born June 15, 1862. December 25, 1888, he married *Alice Shultz*; daughter of *Henry* and *Catharine (Cypher) Shultz.* Mr. Fouse for a number of years followed the profession of school teaching. In later years he entered the insurance business, and devotes most of his time to the latter. They reside at Marklesburg (James Creek postoffice), Huntingdon County, Pennsylvania, where they are comfortably situated in their own home. (No children.)

[411] **JOHN SUMMERS[5] FOUSE,** son of [75] David[4] and Margaret Ann (Summers) Fouse, was born December 2, 1864, in Hopewell Township, Huntingdon County, Pennsylvania. He worked on the farm until his majority, then did "job work" and attended school, until the fall of 1888, when he received a teacher's certificate and taught a public school near Saxton, Bedford County, Pennsylvania. Entering his uncle's insurance company, The Alta Friendly Society, he continued in it for nine years. He then, with other agents of the company, founded The Gibraltar Beneficial Society. He was quite successful in the insurance business; he owned a number of houses in Pittsburgh, Pennsylvania, and also his father's homestead. Mr. Fouse died after a brief illness June 3, 1913.

June 6, 1893, Mr. Fouse married *Catharine Horni*, born December 13, 1863; daughter of *Urich* and *Catharine Horni*, of Zurich, Switzerland. Mrs. Fouse is a lady of exceptional sweetness and nobleness of character. The family address is Kingcade Street, Pittsburgh, Pennsylvania.

Children (4):

[1597] Marguerite[6], *b* August 31, 1896.
[1598] Raymond[6], *d* at age six.
[1599] Hazel[6], *b* February 6, 1902.
[1600] Clyde[6], *b* August 7, 1907.

[412] **SUSAN[5] FOUSE**, daughter of [75] David[4] and Margaret Ann (Summers) Fouse, was born July 13, 1866. She was reared on the farm and attended the public schools in the country, through which she received a fair education. She is well versed in the art of housekeeping and is one amongst the best housekeepers in the country. She is cheerful, kind hearted and true, and greets everyone with kindness. She always remained home with her parents, and cared for them in their last days when their health failed and they were unable to care for themselves. She has been so attentive to work that she never took time to do any visiting, and never was over twenty miles from home. Since her parents' death she is keeping house for her brother Alfred[5] Fouse [409] on their old homestead, one and one-half miles south of Marklesburg, Pennsylvania. Her address, is Aitch, Huntingdon County, Pennsylvania.

[413] **SUSAN[5] NICODEMUS**, daughter of [76] Margaret[4] (Fouse) Nicodemus and George Nicodemus, was born February 15, 1853. She married *Daniel Hoffa*, January 17, 1879. He died March 25, 1909. Mrs. Hoffa's address is Sanborn, Iowa.

Children (12), surname Hoffa:

[1603] + Roselda Loretta[6], *b* August 9, 1872; *m Frank E. Wells.*
[1604] + Calvin O.[6], *b* September 13, 1873; *m Lena Croson.*
[1605] + Vernia Irene[6], *b* June 26, 1875; *m August Frederick Telkamp.*
[1606] Lizzie M.[6], *b* February 9, 1877.
[1607] William G.[6], *b* October 8, 1878.
[1608] + Elmer C.[6], *b* June 5, 1880; *m Agnes Baile.*
[1609] + Charles N.[6], *b* December 13, 1882; *m Sadie Vesta Dean.*
[1610] + Porter C.[6], *b* February 19, 1885; *m Edith A. Smith.*
[1611] Vesta E.[6], *b* March 16, 1887.
[1612] Jacob D.[6], *b* April 21, 1890.
[1613] Emery[6], *b* October 1, 1892.
[1614] Lloyd L.[6], *b* December 29, 1895.

[414] **MARY ELIZABETH[5] NICODEMUS,** daughter of [76] Margaret[4] (Fouse) Nicodemus and George Nicodemus, was born October 4, 1854, and married *August Marr* in March, 1876. Their address is Iola, Allen County, Kansas.

Children (7), surname Marr:

[1617] + Lillie May[6], *b* May 29, 1877; *m Richard H. Bushgens.*
[1618] + Rose Elva[6], *b* December 13, 1878; *unm.*
[1619] + George Jacob[6], *b* December 8, 1880; *m Mary E. Cooper.*
[1620] + Anna Amelia[6], *b* January 7, 1883; *m Walter A. Decker.*
[1621] + Grace Augusta[6], *b* November 30, 1887.
[1622] + Edith Fern[6], *b* April 16, 1892.
[1623] + Bernice Elrene[6], *b* September 28, 1894.

[415] **SARAH[5] NICODEMUS,** daughter of [76] Margaret[4] (Fouse) Nicodemus and George Nicodemus, was born November 21, 1856. August 24, 1876, she married *Philip Schadt*, who was born at Hesse Darmstadt, August 24, 1847. They resided near Hartley, O'Brien County, Iowa. Mrs. Sarah Schadt died March 22, 1898, and Philip Schadt died June 1, 1901.

Children (7), surname Schadt:

[1626] George Harvey[6], *b* January 4, 1877; *d* August 18, 1877.
[1627] + Charles William[6], *b* April 7, 1878.
[1628] + Nettie Angelina[6], *b* June 2, 1880; *m Adam Meehlhouse.*
[1629] + Philip Calvin[6], *b* December 4, 1881; *m Jennie Bell Illard.*
[1630] + Harry Rogers[6], *b* February 11, 1883; *m Kitty Myrtle Van Hassen.*
[1631] Margaret Louisa[6], *b* December 17, 1884.
[1632] Alta Catherine[6], *b* June 22, 1897.

[416] **ADAM F.[5] NICODEMUS,** son of [76] Margaret[4] (Fouse) Nicodemus and George Nicodemus, was born May 6, 1858, and married *Lizzie Lambly* October 13, 1889. They reside at Friend, Nebraska.

Children (3):

[1634] Alta Grace[6], *b* July 26, 1890.
[1635] Walter Irwing[6], *b* December 6, 1894.
[1636] Alfa Lavina[6], *b* April 8, 1897.

[418] **EDWIN[5] NICODEMUS,** son of [76] Margaret[4] (Fouse) Nicodemus and George Nicodemus, was born August 22, 1863. June 22, 1885,

he married *Kate Lambly,* who was born February 15, 1865. They reside at Columbus, Nebraska.

Children (5):

[1639] Jacob Edwin[6], *b* December 9, 1890.
[1640] Verna Rose[6], *b* March 5, 1893.
[1641] Barbara Ellen[6], *b* December 15, 1895.
[1642] Nellie Margaret[6], *b* August 24, 1897.
[1643] Bertha Maud[6], *b* October 29, 1900.

[419] **JOHN H.[6] NICODEMUS,** son of [76] Margaret[4] (Fouse) Nicodemus and George Nicodemus, was born August 13, 1866. July 2, 1892, he married (1) *Della Dart Walker,* born July 10, 1869, and died May 30, 1893. February 18, 1895, he married (2) *Mary Amanda Vinson,* born June 29, 1866. Residence is Columbus, Nebraska.

Children (2):

[1646] Rosa Belle[6], *b* September 25, 1895.
[1647] George Henry[6], *b* January 4, 1898.

[420] **ISAAC C.[6] NICODEMUS,** son of [76] Margaret[4] (Fouse) Nicodemus and George Nicodemus, was born March 17, 1869. September 29, 1889, he married *Myrtle L. Walt,* born March 3, 1868.

Mr. Nicodemus died May 25, 1898, and the funeral services on May 27 were largely attended, filling the Presbyterian Church (where the family usually worshiped) to overflowing. One of those in attendance said: "Everybody mourned his death, for we all loved him. He was a fine man, and good to his mother." His remains were laid away in the cemetery on the hill south of Hartley, Iowa.

Mrs. Nicodemus married the following year (1899), and the family moved to South Dakota.

Children (5):

[1650] Grace J.[6], *b* July 22, 1890.
[1651] Elsie M.[6], *b* July 30, 1891.
[1652] Mary Ruth[6], *b* August 13, 1893.
[1653] Veda[6], *b* July 25, 1895.
[1654] Mamie[6], *b* August 15, 1897.

[421] **MARGARET IDA[5] NICODEMUS,** daughter of [76] Margaret[4] (Fouse) Nicodemus and George Nicodemus, was born January 15, 1872; and on December 24, 1899, she married *Edward Hugill*. They reside in Columbus, Nebraska. (No issue.)

[423] **SARAH JANE[5] RHODES,** daughter of [79] Barbara[4] (Fouse) Rhodes and John M. Rhodes, was born September 15, 1862. January 6, 1887, she married *David Barchley Barnett*. They reside at Martinsburg, Blair County, Pennsylvania. Mr. Barnett is section boss on the Morrison's Cove Branch of the Pennsylvania Railroad. (No issue.)

[424] **JOHN F.[5] RHODES,** son of [79] Barbara[4] (Fouse) Rhodes and John McGraw Rhodes, was born April 15, 1868. He married (1) *Lemma Nenomia Hazzard*, of Saxton, Bedford County, Pennsylvania, on December 29, 1890. His wife died ——, and he married (2) *Daisy Maud E. Koon*, of Asheville, North Carolina. Address is Barbara, Blair County, Pennsylvania.

Children (2), by the first marriage—(None by second marriage):

[1657] + John Chesterfield[6], *b* November 13, 1891; *m Grace Belle Harding*.
[1658] Cyrus Blain[6], *b* January 14, 1894.

[425] **EMMA GETTY[5] FOUSE,** daughter of [80] John Garner[4] and Mary Ellen (Shoemaker) Fouse, was born July 7, 1867. She was educated in the public schools, and, after moving to Pittsburgh in 1888, was her father's bookkeeper and cashier. In 1890 she was appointed bookkeeper and cashier for the city office of the Fidelity Mutual Life Insurance Company, and held that position until August 1, 1893, the date of her marriage to *Isaac Kagarise Bechtel*. The latter was born December 14, 1865, is son of *David S.* and *Salome Kagarise Bechtel* (grandparents, *Peter* and *Elizabeth Snowberger Bechtel* and *Daniel Kagarise*).

Mr. Bechtel attended the public schools, 1871-1882; Juniata College, 1883-1886; Iron City Commercial College, 1887-1888, graduating in 1888, and teaching in that institution 1888-1896. He engaged in real estate and insurance business 1896-1905, and since 1906 has been manager of a glass sand business at Berkeley Springs, West Virginia. Mr. Bechtel was deacon in Grace Reformed Church, 1896-1911, and treasurer of that church 1896-1908. Address, 5218 Friendship Avenue, Pittsburgh, Pennsylvania (Plate 45).

Children (2), surname Bechtel:

[1660] + Ida Florence[6], *b* October 2, 1896.
[1661] + Mary Elizabeth[6], *b* March 31, 1898.

[426] **MARY MATILDA[5] FOUSE,** daughter of [80] John Garner[4] and Mary Ellen (Shoemaker) Fouse, was born February 23, 1869. She was educated in the public schools, and followed the art of dress making—is an expert fitter. Besides this, she thoroughly understands the art of good housekeeping; was her mother's principal nurse in the last eight months of her illness. She is single and lives with her father at 300 Orchard Place, Knoxville, Pennsylvania, Mt. Oliver Station (Plate 45).

[427] **ELLA ELIZABETH[5] FOUSE,** daughter of [80] John Garner[4] and Mary Ellen (Shoemaker) Fouse, was born September 6, 1871. She was educated in the public schools of Pittsburgh, Pennsylvania; was appointed clerk and cashier for the Fidelity Mutual Life Insurance Company office in 1893, and held that position until March, 1911. She then abandoned office work and became housekeeper, and helped to care for her mother. She is single and lives with her father, 300 Orchard Place, Knoxville, Pennsylvania, Mt. Oliver Station (Plate 45).

[428] **HARVEY SHOEMAKER[5] FOUSE,** son of [80] John Garner[4] and Mary Ellen (Shoemaker) Fouse, was born September 21, 1873. October 16, 1901, he married *Susan Gillmore Chambers*. Mr. Fouse was educated in public schools, and went to Volant College, and Iron City College from which he graduated. He is employed as assistant manager and clerk, as well as cashier, in his father's office at 404 Ross Street, Pittsburgh, Pennsylvania. They reside at 5480 Broad Street, Pittsburgh, Pennsylvania (Plate 45).

One son:

[1663] Robert Chambers[6], *b* December 12, 1913.

[430] **ORLANDO[5] FOUSE,** son of [80] John Garner[4] and Mary Ellen (Shoemaker) Fouse, was born May 6, 1878. He was educated in the Pittsburgh public and high schools, from which he graduated in 1898. He then entered Washington and Jefferson College, and graduated (B.S., 1901). After graduation, he became manager of a distillery which position he held about 10 years. He always had a desire to study medicine,

and finally gave up his position at the distillery, and entered the University of Pittsburgh with the class of 1915.

September 22, 1913, Mr. Fouse married *Laura Helen O'Conner* (at Pittsburgh), born in Guelph, Canada, April 3, 1879; youngest daughter of *John* and *Mary* (*Neagle*) *O'Conner.* Mrs. Fouse was educated at the Lorello Convent, Guelph; 1901 entered the Training School for Nurses, South Side Hospital, Pittsburgh, graduating in class of 1904. Address 219 Summit St., Mt. Oliver Station, Knoxville, Pennsylvania (Plate 45).

[431] **IRA SHOEMAKER**[5] **FOUSE,** son of [80] John Garner[4] and Mary Ellen (Shoemaker) Fouse, was born September 22, 1880. He was educated in the public and high schools of Pittsburgh, from which he graduated in 1901. He has been in the employ of the Pressed and Standard Steel Car Company almost continuously since he left school, occupying various positions. For a number of years he has been connected with the purchasing department of that company, and was recently made buyer for its Hammond, Indiana, plant. He resides with his father at 300 Orchard Place, Knoxville, Pennsylvania, Mt. Oliver Station (Plate 45).

[432] **JOHN MARVIN**[5] **FOUSE,** son of [80] John Garner[4] and Mary Ellen (Shoemaker) Fouse, was born September 28, 1881. He went to the public and high schools of Pittsburgh and graduated in 1901. He entered Lehigh University and was graduated with the class of 1905, as a mining engineer. His work has taken him to a number of places. He was employed in Dutch Guiana in South America for eighteen months, and then on the Island of Cuba for six months. He was employed by the Carnegie Steel Company, holding a position in the technical end of the sales department. He is at Montreal, Canada, holding a similar position with the Dominion Bridge Company (Plate 45).

[433] **EDITH LILLIAN**[5] **FOUSE,** daughter of [80] John Garner[4] and Mary Ellen (Shoemaker) Fouse, was born August 1, 1885; was educated in the public schools of Pittsburgh, Pennsylvania, and she was assistant clerk in her father's insurance office for a number of years. June 4, 1908, Edith married *Hagey Harry Campbell,* son of *Lawrence Finley* and *Laura Jane* (*Hagey*) *Campbell.* Mr. Campbell attended the public schools of Martinsburgh, Blair County, Pennsylvania, graduating from its high school in 1904. They began housekeeping at New Salem, Pennsylvania, but moved to Pittsburgh in April, 1911, to assist in nursing Mrs. Fouse

in her last illness. Mr. Campbell is District Agent for Fidelity and Casualty Company. Residence, 1314 West Chestnut Street; office, 78 Altoona Trust Company Building, Altoona, Pennsylvania (Plate 45).

Children, surname Campbell:

[1666] Laura Mary[6], *b* October 25, 1911.
[1667] Hagey Fouse[6], *b* June 7, 1914.

[434] **FLORA FOUSE[6] HOOVER,** daughter of [81] Sarah Ann[4] (Fouse) Hoover and Benjamin Franklin Hoover, was born September 3, 1869, and married *Albert B. Miller*, March 20, 1890. Address, East Freedom, Pennsylvania (Plate 46).

Children (9), surname Miller:

[1669] Daisy Irene[6], *b* April 24, 1892; *d* January 20, 1893.
[1670] Bessie Lucinda[6], *b* November 28, 1893.
[1671] Homer Willard[6], *b* February 16, 1896.
[1672] Clara Edith[6], *b* May 1, 1898.
[1673] Marvin McKinley[6], *b* October 2, 1900.
[1674] Charles Percy[6], *b* January 18, 1903.
[1675] Martha Ethel[6], *b* August 15, 1905.
[1676] Lilly Marguerite[6], *b* December 27, 1907.
[1677] Nelson Albert[6], *b* July 4, 1911.

[435] **MINERVA FOUSE[5] HOOVER,** daughter of [81] Sarah Ann[4] (Fouse) Hoover and Benjamin Franklin Hoover, was born August 23, 1871. She was educated in the Millersville State Normal School from which she graduated, as also from the Mechanicsburg Normal School. She follows the profession of teaching with success and has her home with her parents, near Martinsburg, Blair County, Pennsylvania (Plate 46).

[436] **JANETTA FOUSE[6] HOOVER,** daughter of [81] Sarah Ann[4] (Fouse) Hoover and Benjamin Franklin Hoover, was born September 1, 1873. She was educated in the public schools and received a good, practical education. She is single and lives with her parents near Martinsburg, Pennsylvania, assisting her mother in housekeeping (Plate 46).

[437] **ADAM FOUSE[6] HOOVER,** son of [81] Sarah Ann[4] (Fouse) Hoover and Benjamin Franklin Hoover, was born September 5, 1877. He was educated in the public schools. After his majority, he went to

Chicago and learned the trade of barbering, and now follows that as his business. October 19, 1909, he married *Virginia Bowl*, born February 12, 1873, at Hampshire, Kane County, Illinois. Their address is Chicago, Illinois (Plate 46).

[439] **CLARA FRANK[5] FOUSE**, daughter of [82] Adam Garner[4] and Sarah (Frank) Fouse was born July 10, 1872; was educated in the common and high schools of Philadelphia, Pennsylvania, but on account of ill health was obliged to discontinue her studies and devoted her time to household duties. Being very industrious she also became expert in china decorating. During the serious illness of her mother she was most devoted and continuous in her ministrations, as becometh a faithful daughter. She has traveled extensively throughout the United States, is a member of Livingston Manor Chapter, Daughters of the American Revolution, and has been a page at several of the national congresses of that organization; is unmarried. Address 838 North Forty-first Street, Philadelphia, Pennsylvania. Martinsburg, Pennsylvania, after December, 1914 (Plate 47).

[441] **ADAM IRVING[5] FOUSE**, son of [82] Adam Garner[4] and Sarah (Frank) Fouse, was born in Philadelphia, Pennsylvania, September 29, 1877; March 1, 1878, the family returned to "Clover Plains" farm, his father's birthplace and the Fouse homestead, where he attended school during the winter months; March, 1888, the family returned to Philadelphia and he entered its public schools; graduated June, 1892, from the E. Spencer Miller Grammar school; graduated June, 1896, from Central High School for Boys (A.B.), and from Wharton School of Finance, University of Pennsylvania (B.S. in Economics—June, 1900). He followed the life insurance business for a number of years, and April 1, 1913, actively took charge of the "Clover Plains" farm; address, Martinsburg, Blair County, Pennsylvania, R. F. D. No. 2 (Plate 47).

January 15, 1913 Adam Irving married *Xenia Awilda Hampton*, born November 20, 1884; daughter of *Stacy Watson* and *Mary* (*Heaton*) *Hampton* of Germantown, Pennsylvania. Mrs. Fouse attended the public school at Johnsville, Bucks County, Pennsylvania, entered the Millersville State Normal School and remained there a year, until her father's death. She later took a course at Banks Business College, Philadelphia, Pennsylvania, and occupied a clerical position in the office of the Fidelity Mutual Life Insurance Company until her marriage.

One son:

[1679] Eugene Garner[6], *b* January 20, 1914.

[442] **DAVID MILTON⁶ FOUSE,** son of [83] Henry Smith[4] and Mary, Jane (Aurandt) Fouse, was born September 23, 1868. He married (1) *Nancy Bechtel*, December 22, 1891. She died June 22, 1906. May 20, 1909, he married (2) *Lizzie Falkender*, who was born April 15, 1872. Mr. Fouse follows farming. Address is Drab, Pennsylvania.

To the first union five children were born:

[1682] + Blanche[6], *b* December 16, 1892; *m Homer Shenefelt.*
[1683] Lester[6], *b* May 1, 1896.
[1684] Edison I.[6], *b* August 2, 1898; *d* March 12, 1899.
[1685] Mary Florence[6], *b* February 15, 1900.
[1686] Harold B.[6], *b* June 8, 1903.

To the second union one child was born:

[1687] Clarence Aden[6], *b* September 23, 1910, *d.*

[443] **ADAM FRANKLIN[6] FOUSE,** son of [83] Henry Smith[4] and Mary Jane (Aurandt) Fouse, was born March 27, 1870. He married (1) *Bertha Kunes.* This marriage was not congenial and a divorce followed. He then married (2) *Martha Johnson* of Huntington, West Virginia. He is overseer of a railroad in Central America, where they now live. There were no children born to either union.

[448] **ORA ELIZABETH[6] FOUSE,** daughter of [83] Henry Smith[4] and Mary Jane (Aurandt) Fouse, was born July 31, 1878. May 10, 1906, she married *Samuel Nicodemus*, who was born January 26, 1880. Mr. Nicodemus is a mechanic, and works in the Pennsylvania Railroad shops at Altoona. They reside at Curryville, Pennsylvania.

Children (4), surname Nicodemus:

[1691] Helen[6] *b* February 21, 1907.
[1692] Robert[6], *b* July 20, 1908.
[1693] Mary Dorothy[6], *b* July 2, 1910.
[1694] Charles Samuel[6], *b* December 30, 1911.

[449] **FREDERICK AUGUSTUS[6] FOUSE,** son of [83] Henry Smith[4] and Mary Jane (Aurandt) Fouse, was born October 12, 1880. December 28, 1904, he married *Matilda Miller*, born November 21, 1881. Mr. Fouse is the owner of a farm near Petersburg, Huntingdon County, Pennsylvania.

He works on the farm during the summer, and in the winter works in the car shops at Altoona. He is a mechanic and a good car builder; post-office address, Shaver's Creek, Pennsylvania.

Children (2):

[1697] George Henry⁶, *b* February 18, 1905.
[1698] Mary Elizabeth⁶, *b* May 28, 1909.

[450] **MARY ENDORA⁵ FOUSE,** daughter of [83] Henry Smith⁴ and Mary J. (Aurandt) Fouse, was born March 20, 1884. September 15, 1904, she married *Andrew C. Karns,* who was born November 2, 1884. Their address is Altoona, Pennsylvania.

Children (3), surname Karns:

[1700] Ella Elizabeth⁶, *b* September 15, 1905.
[1701] Mary Lovenia⁶, *b* August 14, 1907.
[1702] James Andrew⁶, *b* September 10, 1909.

[451] **ELLA MELISSA⁵ FOUSE,** daughter of [83] Henry Smith⁴ and Mary Jane (Aurandt) Fouse, was born September 15, 1888. She completed a course as a trained nurse; was lately at the Altoona, Pennsylvania, Hospital, but recently went to the Woman's Hospital, Philadelphia, Pennsylvania.

[455] **HARRY HAUSE⁵ FOUSE,** son of [84] Levi Garner⁴ and Mary Belle (Hause) Fouse, was born May 12, 1874. April 10, 1900, he married *Mary Ella Steese,* from St. Paul, Minnesota, who was born April 4, 1877. Mr. Fouse is engaged in the garage and automobile business in Philadelphia, Pennsylvania.

One son:

[1705] John Alfred Steese⁶, *b* December 31, 1908.

Families of The Sixth Generation

[500] **MINERVA MAUD⁶ MILLER,** daughter of [86] Adam Lewis⁵ and Sarah Etta (Cocklin) Miller, was born March 18, 1869, and on September 22, 1902, she married *Abner Kreamer Hamm,* born February 14, 1864; son of *Jacob* and *Sarah Eliza* (*Lamerson*) *Hamm.* Mr. Hamm is a railroad employee, Republican, and his address is Denton, Kansas.

Children (*3*), *surname Hamm:*

[1725] Ruth Etta⁷, *b* October 11, 1903; *d* October 13, 1903.
[1726] Beatrice Trevillian⁷, *b* June 23, 1905.
[1727] Gladys Lucile⁷, *b* October 30, 1907.

[501] **WALTER SCOTT⁶ MILLER,** son of [86] Adam Lewis⁵ and Sarah Etta (Cocklin) Miller, was born May 26, 1871. April 25, 1900, he married *Mary Ann Johnson,* born January 15, 1874; daughter of *William Nicholas* and *Eveline* (*Bowers*) *Johnson.* Mr. Miller and his wife were educated in the public schools of Buchanan County, Missouri. He is engaged in general construction work, is a Democrat, and member of Cumberland Presbyterian Church, and his wife is a member of Disciples of Christ. Address, Clinton, Missouri, R. F. D. No. 4.

Children (*6*):

[1729] Mildred Maurene⁷, *b* June 25, 1901.
[1730] William Forrest⁷ *b* October 8, 1902.
[1731] Hazel Eveline⁷, *b* September 27, 1904.
[1732] Beulah Opal⁷, *b* October 27, 1906.
[1733] Curtis Clifford⁷, *b* September 13, 1908.
[1734] Harry Homer⁷, *b* January 11, 1911.

[502] **RAWLINS ADAM⁶ MILLER,** son of [86] Adam Lewis⁶ and Sarah Etta (Cocklin) Miller, was born December 24, 1872; June 18, 1902, married *Luemma Estella Donaldson,* who was born September 30, 1880; daughter of *Thomas Larkin* and *Mary* (*Aniser*) *Donaldson.* Mr. and Mrs. Miller were educated in the public schools of Buchanan County, Missouri.

They belonged to the Methodist Episcopal Church, and she died in 1911, He is a Democrat, salesman in a store, and his address is Deer Park, Washington.

Children (3):

[1736] Delbert Donaldson[7], *b* April 28, 1903.
[1737] Lester Rawlins[7], *b* October 25, 1904.
[1738] Edith May[7], *b* October 25, 1909.

[503] **FRANCIS PRESTON[6] MILLER,** son of [86] Adam Lewis[5] and Sarah Etta (Cocklin) Miller, was born November 15, 1875; October 5, 1898, married *Laura May Williams,* born June 27, 1878; daughter of *William Henry* and *Eliza Jane (Smith) Williams.* They were educated in the public schools of Buchanan County, Missouri; are members of the Cumberland Presbyterian Church, and he is a Democrat, and section foreman on the Rock Island Railroad. Address, Easton, Missouri, R. F. D. No. 3.

Children (6):

[1740] Harold Burt[7], *b* August 18, 1899.
[1741] Ralph Dale[7], *b* May 12, 1902.
[1742] Stella May[7], *b* March 22, 1905.
[1743] Guy Preston[7], *b* August 27, 1907.
[1744] Sadie Adaline[7], *b* August 26, 1910.
[1745] William Lewis[7], *b* April 14, 1914.

[504] **OLIVE MAY[6] MILLER,** daughter of [86] Adam Lewis[5] and Sarah Etta (Cocklin) Miller, was born September 29, 1877; February 16, 1898, married *Stephen Edgar De Vore,* born June 7, 1871; son of *Joseph Benjamin* and *Harriet Priscilla (Ewin) De Vore.* Mr. Miller is Republican, a farmer, 5 miles southeast of St. Joseph; and both he and his wife were educated in the public schools of Buchanan County, Missouri, and they are members of the Cumberland Presbyterian Church. Address, St. Joseph, Missouri. R. F. D. No. 4.

Children (6) surname De Vore:

[1746] Victor Emory[7], *b* January 31, 1899.
[1747] Ruth Esther[6], *b* October 22, 1900.
[1748] Hilda Estella[7], *b* June 7, 1902.

[1749] Raymond Earl[7], *b* March 2, 1904.
[1750] Dale Clifford[7], *b* December 26, 1908.
[1751] Lester Edgar[7], *b* March 16, 1911; *d* December 16, 1911.

[505] **IRENE STELLA[6] MILLER,** daughter of [86] Adam Lewis[5] and Sarah Etta (Cocklin) Miller, was born October 1, 1879; March 30, 1898, married *Christian Henry Zysset,* born February 24, 1875; son of *Christian* and *Magdalena (Ozenberger) Zysset.* Mr. Zysset owns two farms, 6 and 8 miles east of St. Joseph; is a farmer, and a Republican; and both he and his wife are members of the Cumberland Presbyterian Church. Address, St. Joseph, Missouri. R. F. D. No. 4.

Children (5), surname Zysset:

[1753] Fern Stella[7], *b* August 22, 1899.
[1754] Esther May[7], *b* April 27, 1902.
[1755] Faye Luella[7], *b* April 24, 1906.
[1756] Opal Lee[7], *b* July 14, 1908.
[1757] Clifford Christian[7], *b* September 28, 1911.

[506] **STANLEY COCKLIN[6] MILLER,** son of [86] Adam Lewis[5] and Sarah Etta (Cocklin) Miller, was born December 22, 1882; February 28, 1907, married *Lola Richter* in Nelson, British Columbia. He is a telegraph operator, Democrat, and his address is Seattle, Washington. (No children.)

[512] **FLORENCE MABEL[6] MILLER,** daughter of [88] John Cassler[5] and Dora Emeline (Anderson) Miller, was born September 7, 1888; December 8, 1907, married *Charles William Driscoll,* who was born July 14, 1887. Address, Springton, Idaho. (No children.)

[521] **CORA LYDIA[6] HOPPEL,** daughter of [91] Mary[5] (Miller) Hoppel and Jacob Hoppel, was born August 18, 1877. March 7, 1898, she married *James Richard Heffley,* born February 5, 1873. Address is Deer Park, Spokane County, Washington.

Children (4), surname Heffley:

[1760] Charles Jacob[7], *b* November 20, 1898.
[1761] Forrest Alva[7], *b* June 7, 1903.

[1762] Floyd Richard[7], *b* April 28, 1906.
[1763] Ruth Agnes[7], *b* July 1, 1909.

[522] **ELMER LEE[6] HOPPEL,** son of [91] Mary[5] (Miller) Hoppel and Jacob Hoppel, was born May 5, 1880; and April 21, 1909, married *Bertha Grace Roberts*, born October 6, 1885. Address is Deer Park, Route No. 2, Spokane County, Washington. (No issue.)

[526] **LYDIA MAY[6] WHITMORE,** daughter of [92] Fyanna[5] (Miller) Whitmore and Sampson Sollars Whitmore, was born November 23, 1881; and July 2, 1900, married *Francis Sigel Atterberry*, born August 12, 1862. Address, Osborne, Missouri, R. F. D. No. 3.

Children (3), surname Atterberry:

[1766] Lena Leota[7], *b* July 8, 1901.
[1767] Ruby Frances[7], *b* January 29, 1904; *d* July 9, 1904.
[1768] Mary Fyanna[7], *b* March 21, 1906.

[528] **OCTAVIA DELL[6] WHITMORE,** daughter of [92] Fyanna[5] (Miller) Whitmore and Sampson Sollars Whitmore, was born March 23, 1886; March 12, 1905, married *Edward Joseph Hinderks*, born May 2, 1883. Address Stewardsville, Missouri, R. F. D. No. 4.

Children (2), surname Hinderks:

[1770] Gladys Lucile[7], *b* June 15, 1906.
[1771] Norval Leroy[7], *b* August 20, 1908.

[529] **OLIVE GOLDIE[6] WHITMORE,** daughter of [92] Fyanna[5] (Miller) Whitmore and Sampson Sollars Whitmore, was born November 19, 1888; and June 17, 1908, married *Walter Leroy Hall*, who was born May 14, 1885. Address is Stewardsville, Missouri.

One son, surname Hall:

[1773] Herbert Whitmore[7], *b* December 27, 1909.

[534] **ELMER ELLSWORTH[6] MILLER,** son of [96] Elizabeth[5] (Bair) Miller and Jacob Solomon Miller, was born in Plain Township, Stark County, Ohio, December 9, 1861. He was married August 16, 1883, at Randolph, Portage County, Ohio, to *Florence Carline Henry*, daughter of *Jacob* and *Elizabeth (Mootz) Henry*, and she was born in Lake Township,

Stark County, Ohio, October 5, 1861. Mr Miller was educated in private and academic schools; is manufacturer, inventor, mechanical engineer, and at present is proprietor of the Canton Grate Company. He is German Reformed in religion, as are the entire family, except the youngest child; and Progressive in politics. Address is 1706 Woodland Avenue, N.W., Canton, Ohio (Plate 53).

Children (6):

[1775] + Pearl Bell[7], *b* July 2, 1884; *m George E. Robinson.*
[1776] + Bessie Irene[7], *b* May 7, 1886.
[1777] Eva Myrtle[7], *b* October 8, 1887; artist; address, 14825 Detroit Avenue, Lakewood, Ohio.
[1778] + Anna Bolander[7], *b* January 13, 1890; *m Mordicai McK. Walker.*
[1779] Dorothy Christina[7], *b* December 25, 1901.
[1780] Mildred Florence[7], *b* January 19, 1904.

[535] **MORRIS MONROE[6] MILLER,** son of [96] Elizabeth[5] (Bair) Miller and Jacob Solomon Miller, was born August 22, 1863. December 31, 1884, he married *Amanda Byerly*, born March 7, 1867; daughter of *Elida ("Lyde")* and *Elizabeth (Brumbaugh) Byerly.* Mr. Miller is a farmer; a Democrat in politics; and a member of the United Brethren Church. Address is Atwood, Indiana.

Children (2):

[1782] Daughter, *b* January 5, 1886; *d* January 13, 1886.
[1783] Son, *b* January 27, 1901; *d* February 3, 1901.

[536] **MARY MINTIE[6] MILLER,** daughter of [96] Elizabeth[5] (Bair) Miller, and Jacob Solomon Miller, was born April 16, 1865; December 25, 1887, married *John Ellsworth Steffe*, son of *Peter* and *Mary Ann Benjamin Steffe.* Mr. Steffe is a farmer and breeder, a Democrat; and he and his wife are members of United Brethren Church. Address, Etna Green, Kosciusko County, Indiana.[a]

Children (2) surname Steffe:

[1785] Ruth Iola[7], *b* February 5, 1893.
[1786] Erra Glen[7], *b* December 19, 1894.

[a] Mrs. Steffe has materially assisted with facts gathered from various sources, concerning her general family lines, and cordial thanks are hereby returned to her for such assistance.

[537] **AMELIA MANDILLA[6] MILLER,** daughter of [96] Elizabeth[5] (Bair) Miller and Jacob Solomon Miller, was born September 9, 1867, and on January 20, 1889, she married *William McCoy*, son of *David* and *Misanier (Walker) McCoy*. Mr. Miller is a farmer, a Democrat and member United Brethren Church. Address, Columbia City, Indiana, R. F. D. No. 5.

Children (8), surname McCoy:

[1788] Quinby Francis[7], *b* May 9, 1889.
[1789] Clerda Mae[7], *b* December 4, 1890; *d* August 30, 1906.
[1790] Clela Elizabeth[7], *b* July 14, 1892; *d* October 24, 1907.
[1791] Orrin Hubert[7], *b* March 28, 1894; *m Edna Mae Schinbeckler.*
[1792] Mary Irena[7], *b* February 3, 1897.
[1793] Carley Roy[7], *b* August 10, 1899.
[1794] Parley Jay[7], *b* August 10, 1899; *d* August 26, 1899.
[1795] Thomas Franklin[7], *b* December 5, 1901.

[538] **THOMAS JEFFERSON[6] MILLER,** son of [96] Elizabeth[5] (Bair) Miller and Jacob Solomon Miller, was born December 14, 1869. April 19, 1894, he married *Ida May Larne*, daughter of *James* and *Emily Oram Larne.* Mr. Miller is a farmer, and his address is Etna Green, Kosciusko County, Indiana.

Children (2):

[1798] Echo Fairy[7], *b* August 1, 1895.
[1799] Emma Elizabeth[7], *b* November 2, 1902.

[539] **ORPHA ALICE[6] MILLER,** daughter of [96] Elizabeth[5] (Bair) Miller and Jacob Solomon Miller, was born July 3, 1872; and August 28, 1890, married *William Bowman*, son of *Michael* and *Laura Waggomon Bowman.* To them one son [1800] was born and died March 23, 1893. Mrs. Bowman died 7 days later. Mr. Bowman is a member of the Christian Church, Republican, laborer, and resides in Minnesota.

[540] **FRANK JAY[6] MILLER,** son of [96] Elizabeth[5] (Bair) Miller and Jacob Solomon Miller, was born August 3, 1874. December 20, 1897, he married (1) *Nora Boone*, daughter of *Martin* and *Catharine (Cripe) Boone.* Mrs. Miller died September 30, 1901. Mr. Miller on September 23, 1904, married (2) *Nettie Fiene*, daughter of *Frank* and *Arma Zanzirge*

Fiene. Mrs. Nettie Miller died August 14, 1907. April, 1910, Mr. Miller married (3) *Margaret Ludwig*, daughter of *August* and *Salome Miedenbeck Ludwig.* Mr. Miller in politics is a Democrat and is vice president of the Elkhart Bridge Works. Address is 814 Strong Avenue, Elkhart, Indiana.

Children (3), by first marriage:

[1801] Mary⁷, *b* September 3, 1898; *d* December 30, 1898.
[1802] George Harris⁷, *b* November 9, 1899.
[1803] Charles Edward⁷, *b* September 18, 1901.

[541] **CORWIN J-.⁶ MILLER,** son of [96] Elizabeth⁶ (Bair) Miller and Jacob Solomon Miller, was born in Plain Township, Stark County, Ohio, October 12, 1876. May 31, 1900, at Canton, Ohio, he married *Ada Irene Youtzy*, born April 12, 1877, in Pike Township, Stark County, Ohio; daughter of *Jacob J.* and *Sarah Ann (Stands) Youtzy.* Mr. Miller is an electrical engineer, connected with the Canton branch of the United Engineering and Foundry Company; in politics Progressive; and he and his wife are active workers in the United Brethren Church.

Children (2):

[1806] Atlee Russell⁷, *b* March 23, 1901; address, Canton, Ohio.
[1807] Margaret Pauline⁷, *b* May 5, 1908; address, Canton, Ohio.

[542] **ORIN ENEW⁶ MILLER,** son of [96] Elizabeth⁶ (Bair) Miller and Jacob Solomon Miller, was born December 28, 1878. February 23, 1902, he married *Nancy Jane Yazel*, born December 14, 1880; daughter of *Henry* and *Sarah Aikens Yazel.* Mr. Miller is a farmer, Democrat and member of United Brethren Church; address Etna Green, Indiana.

Children (4):

[1809] Lester Glendon⁷, *b* July 31, 1904; *d* February 26, 1905.
[1810] Pauline Rosella⁶, *b* April 8, 1907; *d* April 25, 1909.
[1811] Eva Mae⁷, *b* August 9, 1909.
[1812] Herbert Donald⁷, *b* March 17, 1911.

[543] **MINNIE ESTELLA⁶ MILLER,** daughter of [96] Elizabeth⁶ (Bair) Miller and Jacob Solomon Miller, was born October 19, 1880. September 22, 1902, she married *Charles N. Jordan*, born December 26, 1878; son of *Aurolis* and *Ella Allen Jordan.* Mr. Jordan is a Presbyterian, Republican,

and meat inspector in the service of the Bureau of Animal Industry, United States Department of Agriculture. His address is 219 Pope Street, Louisville, Kentucky.

One daughter, surname Jordan:

[1814] Ella Elizabeth[7], *b* March 2, 1908.

[544] **GROVER LEE[6] MILLER,** son of [96] Elizabeth (Bair) Miller and Jacob Solomon Miller, was born November 18, 1884. February 7, 1903, she married *Laoma E. Bliss*, born November 28, 1885; daughter of *Herbert* and *Clara (Walker) Bliss*. Mr. Miller is a farmer, Democrat, and his address is Onondaga, Michigan.

Children (4):

[1816] Gladys Estella[7], *b* February 7, 1905.
[1817] Vera Irene[7], *b* December 2, 1906.
[1818] Lether Mae[7], *b* January 15, 1911.
[1819] Echo Elnora[7], *b* March 29, 1912.

[547] **MINERVA[6] SNYDER,** daughter of [98] Mary Ann[5] (Bair) Snyder and George Snyder, was born March 17, 1868. June 27, 1888, she married *Simon Nolt*, who was born October 31, 1864. Address, Columbia City, Indiana, R. D. No. 4, Box 125.

Children (4), surname Nolt:

[1821] Mary Elizabeth, *b* March 16, 1889; *d* December 13, 1889.
[1822] Hugo Arvitus[7], *b* September 3, 1897.
[1823] Turah May[7], *b* July 16, 1901.
[1824] Cletus Jay[7], *b* May 20, 1904.

[548] **JEFFERSON JAY[6] SNYDER,** son of [98] Mary Ann[5] (Bair) Snyder and George Snyder, was born July 18, 1876. July 26, 1898, he married *Dora C. Guster*, who was born May 12, 1878. Address, Columbia City, Indiana.

One daughter:

[1846] Mary Lena[7], *b* June 27, 1900.

[550] **MARTHA JANE[6] BAIR,** daughter of [99] Franklin Bair[5] and Sarah (Lesher) Bair, was born December 1, 1869. August 21, 1887, she married *Monroe C. Weaver*, born November 10, 1864. Address, New Berlin, Stark County, Ohio.

Children (5), surname Weaver:

[1848] Viola May⁷, *b* July 20, 1889.
[1849] Paul Ray⁷, *b* May 5, 1892.
[1850] Ruth Irene⁷, *b* October 24, 1896.
[1851] Stanford Dewig⁷, *b* April 10, 1900.
[1852] Ferne E.⁷, *b* December 28, 1904.

[551] **OTTO LEE⁶ BAIR**, son of [99] Franklin⁵ Bair and Sarah (Lesher) Bair, was born June 4, 1875. December 16, 1899, he married *Alice Brown.* Address, Middle Branch, Ohio.

One son:

[1854] John Franklin⁷, *b* July 19, 1900; *d* September 28, 1900.

[552] **MARY MANDILLA⁶ BAIR**, daughter of [99] Franklin Bair⁵ and Sarah (Lesher) Bair, was born May 20, 1877. On October 23, 1895, she married *John B. Bloomfield.* Address Harrisburg, Stark County, Ohio.

Children (2), surname Bloomfield:

[1856] Carl Bryan⁷, *b* August 15, 1896.
[1857] Roy Benton⁷, *b* September 18, 1898.

[567] **JOHN CHARLES⁶ CASSLER**, son of [104] Nancy Cassler⁵ Corey and John C. Corey, was born December 29, 1876. August 9, 1898, he married *Inez Everetta Adams*, born August 6, 1880.

One son:

[1860] Whitney LaVerzna⁷, *b* June 17, 1899.

[574] **EDWARD LEE⁶ MACHAMER**, son of [105] Lavina⁵ (Cassler) Machamer and P. D. Machamer, was born September 25, 1870. He married *Fanny Wetzel.* They reside at Middle Branch, Ohio. To this union one child was born, and it died in infancy.

[575] **JOHN S.⁶ MACHAMER**, son of [105] Lavina⁵ (Cassler) Machamer and P. D. Machamer, was born April 4, 1874. September 29, 1895, he married *Pearl Lantzer.*

[576] **GERTY**[6] **MACHAMER**, daughter of [105] Lavina[5] (Cassler) Machamer and P. D. Machamer, was born July 1, 1880. She married *Edward Wilamam* of New Berlin, Ohio. No issue reported. Address, Middle Branch, Ohio.

[580] **CHARLOTTE ELIZABETH**[6] **CASSLER**, daughter of [106] La Fayette[5] and Melvina Amelia (Weaver) Cassler, was born April 7, 1871. April 14, 1891, she married *Harvey Augustus Geer*, born July 24, 1857; son of *Horatio Nelson* and *Mary Bowdine* (*Freeman*) *Geer*. Mr. Geer is a Democrat, member of Church of Nazarene, and the family live at Foss, Washita County, Oklahoma.

Children (9), surname Geer:

[1866] Infant son[7], *b* December 28, 1891; *d* January 13, 1892.
[1867] Irma Augusta[7], *b* June 2, 1893.
[1868] Ralph Nelson[7], *b* January 11, 1896.
[1869] Mary Eloise[7], *b* February 28, 1898.
[1870] Grace Amelia[7], *b* August 12, 1900.
[1871] Roy Harvey[7], *b* January 24, 1905.
[1872] Edith Charlotte[7], *b* July 16, 1907; *d* November 4, 1909.
[1873] Florence Anna[7], *b* November 17, 1909.
[1874] Paul Cassler[7], *b* October 7, 1913.

[581] **BERTHA MILLICENT**[6] **CASSLER**, daughter of [106] La Fayette[5] and Melvina Amelia (Weaver) Cassler, was born November 4, 1873. September 8, 1895, she married *William Arley Gardner*, born November 4, 1872; son of *Walter Nathan* and *Mary Eliza* (*Latham*) *Gardner*. Mr. Gardner, in politics is a Democrat, in religion is Methodist; and his address is Gainesville, Cooke County, Texas, R. R. No. 3.

Children (5), surname Gardner:

[1876] William Harold[7], *b* June 10, 1896.
[1877] Oma Letris[7], *b* March 22, 1898.
[1878] Lillian Pearl[7], *b* December 30, 1899.
[1879] Cecil Ray[7], *b* April 21, 1903.
[1880] Maud Lorene[7], *b* November 19, 1905.

[582] **CELESTA GRACE**[6] **CASSLER**, daughter of [106] La Fayette[5] and Melvina Amelia (Weaver) Cassler, was born October 6, 1877. June 29, 1901, she married *Hiram Weeks Newcomb*, born July 28, 1873; son of

Hiram H. and *Hattie M.* (*Bowles*) *Newcomb.* In politics Mr. Newcomb is Independent; address, Clinton, Oklahoma, R. R. No. 2.

Children (4), surname Newcomb:

[1882] Leona Ruth, *b* March 24, 1903.
[1883] Lloyd Leon[7], *b* April 30, 1905.
[1884] Cliff Paul[7], *b* May 26, 1906.
[1885] Ralph Bethuel[7], *b* December 13, 1907.

[583] **PHILIP BLISS[6] CASSLER,** son of [106] La Fayette[5] and Melvina Amelia (Weaver) Cassler, was born July 10, 1883. November 18, 1903, he married *Melvina Goins,* born April 12, 1880; daughter *Frank M.* and *Nancy* (*Cadell*) *Goins.* Mr. Cassler took a business course in Peniel University. He started home from Sullivan, Illinois, and apparently died from violence about September 30, 1904. Melvina (Goins) Cassler married (2) *C. W. Hundley,* and they live at Durham, Roger Mills County, Oklahoma.

One daughter, surname Cassler:

[1887] Alma Pearl[7], *b* August 22, 1904.

[584] **RUTH IRENE[6] CASSLER,** daughter of [106] La Fayette[5] and Melvina Amelia (Weaver) Cassler, was born March 17, 1887. March 14, 1908, she married *Clarence Dryden Girton,* born March 2, 1882; son of *Minard F.* and *Esther* (*Springer*) *Girton.* Mr. Girton and his wife are members of the Pentecostal Church of the Nazarene; he is Independent in politics, and their address is Valley, Oklahoma. Mr. and Mrs. Girton were engaged in missionary work in Mexico before their marriage, and after the settlement of existing Mexican difficulties they may return to work in that country.

One daughter, surname Girton:

[1889] Mary Melvina[7], *b* September 27, 1911.

[590] **WILLIAM FREDERICK[6] CASSLER,** son of [108] Lewis David[5] and Lucinda Allis (Henney) Cassler, was born November 17, 1875. November 27, 1902, he married *Zetta Cole,* born September 11, 1887; daughter of *Thornton C. J.* and *Drue* (*Showalter*) *Cole*; occupation, hardware and implement dealer at Moundridge, Kansas.

One son:

[1891] Winston Glenn[7], *b* September 2, 1906.

[592] **CHESTER DEVAIN[6] CASSLER,** son of [108] Lewis David[5] and Lucinda Allis (Henney) Cassler, was born March 2, 1885. December 2, 1912, he married *Anna Sinclair,* born July 27, 1886; daughter of *John* and *Elizabeth (Reel) Sinclair*; occupation, miller, Stafford, Kansas.

[596] **MINERVA CELESTA[6] MACHAMER,** daughter of [109] Elizabeth[5] (Cassler) Machamer and Anthony Wayne Machamer, was born August 25, 1876. October 15, 1895, she married *Elmer E. Markley.* They reside near Cairo, Ohio. (No children.)

[597] **ERMA LUCILLE[6] MACHAMER,** daughter of [109] Elizabeth[5] (Cassler) Machamer and Anthony Wayne Machamer, was born May 15, 1878. February 28, 1897, she married *Arthur E. Wise.*

Children (4), surname Wise:

[1893] Glen Machamer[7], *b* September 19, 1897.
[1894] Williard Eugene[7], *b* November 11, 1901.
[1895] Ruth Mozella[7], *b* October 18, 1909.
[1896] Zella Grace[7], *b* November 4, 1912.

[600] **WALTER A.[6] WISE,** son of [110] Ottilla[5] (Miller) Wise and William Wise, was born January 21, 1870. February 15, 1906, he married *Jessie Thursby.*

One daughter:

[1898] Flossie May[7], *b* July 11, 1908.

[601] **BYRON P.[6] WISE,** son of [110] Ottilla[5] (Miller) Wise and William Wise, was born November 3, 1873. June 6, 1900, he married *Lela Smith.*

Children (2):

[1899] Royale C.[7] *b* April 29, 1902.
[1900] Clark J.[7], *b* November 14, 1905.

[603] **BERTHA ESTELLA[6] LAMBERSON,** daughter of [111] Jemima[5] (Miller) Lamberson and George Lamberson, was born March 8, 1881. She married *Charles DeWalt* September 25, 1906.

One child, surname DeWalt:

[1902] Twila Pola[7], *b* July 24, 1907.

[613] **CLARA E.[6] FULMER,** daughter of [118] Lucinda[5] (Snyder) Fulmer and Christian Fulmer, was born August 17, 1872 Address is 1213 West Lake Street, Canton, Ohio.

[614] **ARLINGTON C.[6] FULMER,** son of [118] Lucinda[5] (Snyder) Fulmer and Christian Fulmer, was born January 25, 1874. December 18, 1898, he married *Artie Hess*, born July 17, 1876. Address is Oxford Street, Canton, Ohio.

One son:

[1904] Roy J.[7], *b* August 10, 1902.

[617] **CARRIE S.[6] FULMER** daughter of [118] Lucinda[5] (Snyder) Fulmer and Christian Fulmer, was born October 9, 1877. June 28, 1896, she married *Henry Brown*, born July 12, 1877. Address, Middle Branch, Ohio, R. R. No. 1.

Children (2), surname Brown:

[1905] Leto May[7], *b* May 2, 1898.
[1906] Vera Pauline[8], *b* July 19, 1909.

[618] **OMAH ALICE[6] FULMER,** daughter of [118] Lucinda[5] (Snyder) Fulmer and Christian Fulmer, was born September 23, 1880. September 15, 1898, she married *Ezra Hubley*, born April 4, 1876. Address, 1526 Navarre Street, Canton, Ohio.

Children (2), surname Hubley:

[1908] Helen[7], *b* February 6, 1901.
[1909] Hilda Birdem[7], *b* May 28, 1906.

[621] **WINNIFRED CLOY[7] FULMER,** daughter of [118] Lucinda[5] (Snyder) Fulmer and Christian Fulmer, was born October 14, 1886. February 24, 1904, she married *Calvin A. Grove*, born September 28, 1880. Address is New Berlin, Ohio, R. R. No. 1.

Children (2), surname Grove:

[1911] Edith Viola[7], born October 16, 1905.
[1912] Walter Leroy[7], *b* January 3, 1908.

[625] **MARVIN F.[7] FULMER,** son of [120] Elizabeth[6] (Snyder) Fulmer and Henry Fulmer, was born June 27, 1873. November 14, 1897, he married *Emma Belle Rettig*, born May 26, 1874. Address is Greentown, Ohio.

One child:

[1914] Merl[7], *b* January 16, 1899.

[626] **DORA CELESTA[6] FULMER,** daughter of [120] Elizabeth[6] (Snyder) Fulmer and Henry Fulmer, was born March 21, 1877. February 28, 1895, she married *Sherman Hildebrand*, who was born June 27, 1895. Address, Altman, Ohio, R. R. No. 1.

Children (2), surname Hildebrand:

[1916] Ruth Lucille[7], *b* September 24, 1899.
[1917] Carl[7], *b* June 13, 1902.

[627] **ARTIE MAY[6] FULMER,** daughter of [120] Elizabeth[6] (Snyder) Fulmer and Henry Fulmer, was born April 1, 1880. March 4, 1900, she married *Albert Allison*, who was born December 10, 1876. Address, New Berlin, Ohio, R. R. No. 1.

One daughter, surname Allison:

[1918] Blanche Viola[7], *b* October 15, 1900.

[630] **JOHN ALBERT[6] GUILEY,** son of [121] Sarah[6] (Snyder) Guiley and Milton Guiley, was born August 15, 1877. On October 5, 1902, he married *Ratcura L. Wolf*, who was born May 3, 1873. Address, 529 West Ninth Street, Canton, Ohio.

One son:

[1920] George M.[7], *b* September 8, 1907.

[631] **ROBERT PETER[6] GUILEY,** son of [121] Sarah[6] (Snyder) Guiley and Milton Guiley, was born March 25, 1879. June 20, 1908, he married *Winona Jane Banks*, who was born January 22, 1871. Address, 1175 Bittner Place, Akron, Ohio.

[632] **ARTHUR J.[6] GUILEY,** son of [121] Sarah[6] (Snyder) Guiley and Milton Guiley, was born April 22, 1881. August 25, 1904, he married

Hannah M. Strickler, who was born August 11, 1884. Address, Hartville, Stark County, Ohio.

One child:

[1922] Parmaley Doyle, *b* April 4, 1905.

[633] **WALDO LEE[6] GUILEY**, son of [121] Sarah[5] (Snyder) Guiley and Milton Guiley, was born July 7, 1883. December 25, 1904, he married *Edna F. Haverstack*, who was born November 26, 1886. Address, Dewalt Street, Canton, Ohio.

Children (2):

[1923] Beulah Frances, *b* June 3, 1906.
[1924] Joseph Donald, *b* November 22, 1907.

[637] **CORWIN JOHN[6] BROUSE**, son of [122] Savilla[5] (Snyder) Brouse and Rufus Brouse, was born March 31, 1876. He was educated in the public schools, is a rubber worker, member of the Reformed Church, and his address is Cuyahoga Falls, Ohio. October 17, 1895, he married *Laura B. Bair*, born March 7, 1878.

Children (3):

[1926] Helen Maud[7], *b* April 10, 1896.
[1927] Howard Earl[7], *b* April 5, 1897.
[1928] Beulah Pauline[7], *b* December 16, 1900.

[638] **CHARLES FREDERICK[6] BROUSE**, son of [122] Savilla[5] (Snyder) Brouse and Rufus Brouse, was born June 27, 1884, in Lake Township, 2 miles northeast of Greentown, Stark County, Ohio. His early life was spent in the country. He secured an elementary education at the public school at Chapel Hill. Gifted with a good mind, and studious habits, he made rapid progress in his studies and entered upon a thorough course of preparation. From the public school he went to the High School at Greentown, thence in 1901 to the preparatory department at Heidelberg University at Tiffin, Ohio, and graduated from this University (A.B. 1906). In the fall of 1906, he entered the Central Theological Seminary of the Reformed Church at Dayton, Ohio, at which institution he finished the prescribed course of study in 1909. Having accepted the call from the Reformed Church at Marshallville, Wayne County, Ohio, at once he

REV. CHARLES FREDERICK[8] BROUSE [638].

entered upon the active duties of his office, and he continues faithfully and acceptably to serve the people over which he is placed as spiritual guide and overseer.

September 28, 1911, Mr. Brouse married *Mary Helen Pease* of Massillon, Ohio, who was born July 9, 1882; daughter of *Edmund Noxon* and *Ida May (Weimer) Pease.* Mrs. Brouse was educated in the common and high schools, and in Buckingham Seminary for young women. Address, Marshallville, Wayne County, Ohio (Plate 70).

[1930] One daughter *b* and *d* October 7, 1912.

[640] **ORA HADASSA[6] BISHOP,** daughter of [124] Catharine[5] (Snyder) Bishop and Harvey Clinton Bishop, was born July 31, 1880. March 11, 1900, she married *Ira Jacob Werstler,* born September 9, 1874; son of *Louis* and *Carolina (Wagner) Werstler.* Mr. Werstler is a farmer; he and his wife are members of the Lutheran Church; and their address is Hartville, Stark County, Ohio, R. F. D.

Children (5):

[1932] Dessa Bernice[7], *b* October 16, 1900.
[1933] Mabel May[7], *b* October 21, 1903.
[1934] Harley Leroy[7], *b* April 11, 1904.
[1935] Carrie Catharine[7], *b* February 3, 1907.
[1936] Leona Charlotte[7], *b* May 1, 1909.

[641] **HENRY ADAM[6] BISHOP,** son of [124] Catharine[5] (Snyder) Bishop and Harvey Clinton Bishop, was born November 8, 1882. March 29, 1904, he married *Bertha Kanel,* born April 26, 1883; daughter of *Gottfried* and *Anna (Reitz) Kanel.* Mr. Bishop is a grower of celery; he is a member of the Lutheran Church and his wife is a member of the Reformed Church; address, Altman, Ohio.

One son:

[1938] Lester Leroy[7], *b* January 25, 1909.

[642] **LAWRENCE LEROY[6] BISHOP,** son of [124] Catharine[5] (Snyder) Bishop and Harvey Clinton Bishop, was born November 1, 1884. May 12, 1906, he married *Martha Ellen Suffecool,* born April 30, 1885; daughter of *William Harrison* and *Catherine Suffecool.* Address is New Berlin, Stark County, Ohio.

Children (4):

[1940] William Harvey[7], *b* December 12, 1906.
[1941] Catherine Grace[7], *b* April 3, 1909.
[1942] Roger Burdette[7], *b* January 10, 1911.
[1943] Paul Leroy[7], *b* January 24, 1913, *d* January 28, 1913.

[654] **ORIN SAGE[6] INGOLD,** son of [125] Celesta[5] (Snyder) Ingold and George Ingold, was born March 16, 1887. August 14, 1910, he married *Elizabeth Emma Cordin,* who was born May 28, 1890. Address, Mogadore, Summit County, Ohio.

[655] **MARY E[6]. INGOLD,** daughter of [125] Celesta[5] Snyder Ingold, was born April 11, 1889. August 18, 1910, she married *Russell Leroy[6] Fouse* [see 1023], son of *Daniel* [249] and *Minnie Jane (Shanafelt) Fouse.* Address, Alliance, Stark County, Ohio.

[667] **HARVEY WEBSTER[6] MILLER,** son of [132] Malez S.[5] and Ellen (Walters) Miller, was born April 20, 1884. On September 18, 1906, he married *Evelyn M. Germget.* Address, Gibbs and Washington Avenues, Canton, Ohio.

Children (2):

[1947] Harold H.[7], *b* June 28, 1908.
[1948] Charles.[7]

[669] **BERTHA MAY[6] MILLER,** daughter of [132] Malez S.[5] and Ellen (Walters) Miller, was born September 15, 1887. February 23, 1906, she married *Erwin Faber.*

Children (2), surname Faber:

[1949] Nellie Miller[7], *b* May 16, 1905.
[1950] Paul L.[7], *b* March 5, 1907.

[672] **RUFUS[6] BAIR,** son of [136] Mary M.[5] (Miller) Bair and Ozias Bair, was born July 23, 1879. November 6, 1900, he married *Emma Indermuehle.* Address, Middle Branch, Ohio.

Children (3):

[1953] Arthur LeRoy[7], *b* July 2, 1902.
[1954] Helen Margaret[7], *b* July 31, 1904.
[1955] Grace Lucile[7], *b* June 19, 1908.

[678] **CHESTER ARTHUR⁶ HILL,** son of [137] Martha M.⁵ (Miller) Hill and Charles F. Hill, was born March 28, 1881. December 15, 1901, he married *Eva S. Meekes*, who was born June 25, 1882.

[684] **MINA P. STORMFELT⁶ FRY,** daughter of [139] Mandana⁵ (Miller) Fry and Zenas Fry, was born December 1, 1880. March 24, 1903, she married *Charles Heiser*.

One daughter, surname Heiser:

[1960] Thelma Janette⁷, *b* November 29, 1907.

[685] **MARY P.⁶ FRY,** daughter of [139] Mandana⁵ (Miller) Fry and Zenas Fry, was born December 8, 1884. May 2, 1903, she married *Lloyd Ream*.

Children (2), surname Ream:

[1961] Lowell⁷, *b* October 20, 1903.
[1962] Martha Mandana⁷, *b* January 5, 1910.

[686] **BERTHA⁶ FRY,** daughter of [139] Mandana⁵ (Miller) Fry and Zenas Fry, was born November 23, 1886. March 17, 1906, she married *Elmer Haverstock*.

Children (3), surname Haverstock:

[1963] Lee Roy⁷, *b* March 20, 1907; *d* April 3, 1907.
[1964] Claud Fry⁷, *b* July 23, 1908.
[1965] Ralph Glenn⁷, *b* June 21, 1911.

[688] **EVA M.⁶ FRY,** daughter of [139] Mandana⁵ (Miller) Fry and Zenas Fry, was born February 13, 1890. She married *Albert Moore*. One son is said to have been born to them, but details have not been secured.

[714] **JOHN A.⁶ MYERS,** son of [147] Susan⁵ (Acker) Myers and Daniel Myers, was born February 25, 1857. August 14, 1890, he married *Sarah A. Markel*. Address is 1901 Mission Avenue, Spokane, Washington.

Children (5):

[1970] Ada F.⁷, *b* April 9, 1892.
[1971] Edgar⁷, *b* June 20, 1894.

[1972] Irene[7], *b* March 17, 1898.
[1973] Caroline[7], *b* October 27, 1903.
[1974] Lena[7], *b* March 19, 1908.

[716] **ELIZABETH[6] MYERS,** daughter of [147] Susan[5] (Acker) Myers and Daniel Myers, was born April 6, 1860. October 19, 1879, she married *Edwin W. Curtis.* Residence, Versailles, Morgan County, Missouri.

Children (4), surname Curtis:

[1976] Edwin John[7], *b* in Jefferson, Iowa, July 27, 1880.
[1977] Lester Myers[7], *b* in Jefferson, Iowa, May 30, 1883.
[1978] Rosina[7], *b* in Versailles, Missouri, January 20, 1893.
[1979] Sarah Elizabeth[7], *b* in Versailles, Missouri, August 9, 1896.

[719] **DEWALT[6] MYERS,** son of [147] Susan[5] (Acker) Myers and Daniel Myers, was born November 20, 1866. December 28, 1886, he married *Minnie B. Southern.* Residence, 1717 Mission Avenue, Spokane, Washington.

Children (3):

[1981] Sidney S.[7], *b* November 17, 1887.
[1982] Arlie D.[7], *b* September 7, 1890.
[1983] Virginia Mae[7], *b* May 15, 1893.

[722] **SARAH[6] MYERS,** daughter of [147] Susan[5] (Acker) Myers and Daniel Myers, was born near Oxford, Iowa, December 21, 1870. September 21, 1890, at Spokane, Washington, she married *Robert E. Hall,* born in Glass County, Missouri, October 29, 1864. Address is Colby, Thomas County, Kansas.

Children (11), surname Hall:

[1991] Minnie Elizabeth[7], *b* August 4, 1891, at Ballard, Washington.
[1992] Wilfred Thompson[7], *b* January 5, 1894, at Spokane, Washington.
[1993] Annie Mae[7], *b* February 28, 1896, near Atwood, Kansas.
[1994] Iona Pearl[7], *b* August 18, 1897, near Atwood, Kansas.
[1995] Sarah Ethel[7], *b* February 14, 1899, near Atwood, Kansas.
[1996] Susan Emily[7], *b* April 11, 1901, near Atwood, Kansas.
[1997] Mabel Irene[7], *b* May 18, 1904, at Goodland, Kansas.
[1998] Robert Ellsworth[7], *b* November 25, 1904, at Goodland, Kansas.

[1999] Wendell Gladstone[7], *b* April 25, 1907, at Goodland, Kansas.
[2000] Edmond Antonio[7], *b* April 16, 1909, at San Antonio, Texas.
[2001] Harold Curtis[7], *b* June 7, 1911, near Colby, Kansas.

[727] **SUSANNA E.[6] MYERS,** daughter of [147] Susan[5] (Acker) Myers and Daniel Myers, was born April 15, 1878. In Spokane, Washington, October 23, 1895, she married *Robert Kennedy*, of Pleasanton, Kansas. Address, Mica, Washington.

Children (6):

[2004] Susan Eliza[7], *b* October 15, 1897.
[2005] Jesse Daniel[7], *b* August 3, 1900.
[2006] Hyla Hawthorne[7], *b* August 3, 1900.
[2007] Robert Dewalt[7], *b* August 23, 1903.
[2008] Kenneth Sylvester[7], *b* February 16, 1906.
[2009] Quincy Myers[7], *b* September 15, 1910.

[732] **ANNA[6] LECRONE,** daughter of [149] Sarah[5] (Acker) Lecrone and Jacob Lecrone, was born September 24, 1875. December 14, 1907, she married *Homer B.[6] Fouse* [1150], *b* July 7, 1879; son of *Daniel D.[5]* [289] and *Malinda (Bossler) Fouse.* Residence, Drab, Pennsylvania.

[733] **DORA JANE[6] LECRONE,** daughter of [149] Sarah[5] (Acker) Lecrone and Jacob Lecrone, was born April 7, 1881. December 14, 1902, she married *Charles O. Acker*, born February 4, 1875. Address is Martinsburg, Blair County, Pennsylvania, R. F. D. No. 2.

Children (3), surname Acker:

[2013] Anna May[7], *b* February 26, 1904; *d* October 13, 1905.
[2014] Emma Malinda[7], *b* November 17, 1905.
[2015] Verna Alice[7], *b* July 1, 1908.

[735] **ELIZABETH[6] ACKER,** daughter of [151] Adam[5] Acker and Agnes (Greaser) Acker, was born February 18, 1871. November, 1898, she married *George F. Swartz*, born October 31, 1871. Address, Altoona, Pennsylvania. (No issue.)

[736] **CATHARINE[6] ACKER,** daughter of [151] Adam[5] Acker and Agnes (Greaser) Acker, was born October 2, 1873. She married *Charles*

L. Metzgar, born August 27, 1873. Address, Roaring Spring, Blair County, Pennsylvania.

One daughter, surname Metzgar:

[2017] C. Lillian^7, *b* November 24, 1892.

[737] **NETTIE^6 ACKER,** daughter of [151] Adam^5 Acker and Agnes (Greaser) Acker, was born November 28, 1877. September 5, 1903, she married *William C. Fagle*, born February 23, 1876. Address, Altoona, Pennsylvania.

Children (3), surname Fagle:

[2019] Jessie Belle^7, *b* May 25, 1904.
[2020] William Melvin^7, *b* December 13, 1905.
[2021] Dorothy Mae^7, *b* August 26, 1907.

[739] **MARGARET^6 ACKER,** daughter of [151] Adam^5 Acker and Agnes (Greaser) Acker, was born January 13, 1882. March 16, 1904, she married *Daniel B. Noel*, born January 26, 1874. Address, Altoona, Pennsylvania.

Children (4), surname Noel:

[2024] Clarence Edwin^7, *b* August 30, 1904.
[2025] Clyde Albert^7, *b* September 11, 1905.
[2026] Edna Mae^7, *b* May 1, 1908.
[2027] Violet Beatrice^7, *b* February 4, 1910.

[740] **HARRIET M.^{6} ACKER,** daughter of [151] Adam^5 Acker and Agnes (Greaser) Acker, was born October 3, 1885; and, on September 11, 1907, she married *Calvin Prough*, born August 11, 1883. Address, Altoona, Pennsylvania. (No issue.)

[741] **ELSIE MAE^6 ACKER,** daughter of [151] Adam^5 Acker and Agnes (Greaser) Acker, was born February 2, 1888. July 3, 1907, she married *Ernest Brindle*, born August 16, 1885. Address, Altoona, Pennsylvania. (No issue.)

[744] **ESSINGTON R.^{6} HOOVER,** son of [153] Daniel^5 and Eliza Jane (Rhodes) Hoover, was born April 14, 1869. He married *Della Shoen-*

felt, born April 12, 1872. Address, Martinsburg, Blair County, Pennsylvania.

Children (7):

[2031] Ralph Edmond^{7}, *b* May 9, 1894; *d* May 6, 1895.
[2032] John Hubbard^{7}, *b* May 18, 1898.
[2033] Charles Ernest^{7}, *b* May 16, 1900.
[2034] Lilly May^{7}, *b* August 1, 1902.
[2035] Grace Anna^{7}, *b* October 14, 1904.
[2036] Daniel Shoenfelt, *b* August 20, 1906.
[2037] Kathryn Jane^{7}, *b* June 26, 1908.

[745] **JACOB NEWTON^{6} HOOVER,** son of [153] Daniel^{5} Hoover and Eliza Jane (Rhodes) Hoover, was born December 8, 1870. He married *Jennie Quarry*, born August 10, 1869. Address, Martinsburg, Blair County, Pennsylvania, Box 271.

Children (7):

[2041] Elrene^{7} May, *b* October 5, 1892.
[2042] Arthur Fillmore^{7}, *b* April 16, 1895.
[2043] Melvin McKinley^{7}, *b* November 14, 1896.
[2044] Mary Eliza^{7}, *b* April 7, 1900.
[2045] Carrie Edith^{7}, *b* October 23, 1902.
[2046] Charles Edon^{7}, *b* July 23, 1905.
[2047] Martha Jane^{7}, *b* July 9, 1909.

[746] **JOHN EDWIN^{6} HOOVER,** son of [153] Daniel^{5} and Eliza Jane (Rhodes) Hoover, was born June 6, 1872. March 9, 1911, he married *Lola Vanallman*, born October 14, 1876. Residence, Roaring Spring, Blair County, Pennsylvania. (No issue reported.)

[747] **LILLY EDITH^{6} HOOVER,** daughter of [153] Daniel^{5} and Eliza Jane (Rhodes) Hoover, was born August 15, 1875. March 16, 1897, she married *George W. Mock*, born June 24, 1869. Address, Roaring Spring, Blair County, Pennsylvania.

Children (2), *surname Mock:*

[2050] Daniel Raymond^{7}, *b* December 25, 1897.
[2051] May Josephine^{7}, *b* November 3, 1899.

[756] **NEVIN[6] PEIGHTEL,** son of [155] John[5] and Margaret (Hamer) Peightel, was born August 25, 1863. September 12, 1893, he married *Laura Alice[5] Myers* [226], who was born April 1, 1866, daughter of [40] *Catharine (Garner) Myers* and *Abraham Myers.* Mr. Peightel is a building contractor at Huntingdon, Pennsylvania.

Children (4):

[2054] Ada Ruth[7], *b* December 28, 1894.
[2055] Sarah Catharine[7], *b* April 12, 1898.
[2056] Dorothy May[7], *b* May 20, 1900.
[2057] Ellen Bertha[7], *b* November 4, 1904.

[759] **WILLIAM E.[6] PEIGHTEL,** son of [155] John[5] and Margaret (Hamer) Peightel, was born November 18, 1872; and on November 5, 1896, married *Margaret T. Lincoln.* Mr. Peightel died April 13, 1905, aged 33 years. Mrs. Peightel's address is McConnellstown, Huntingdon County, Pennsylvania.

Children (4):

[2059] Harry John[7], *b* May 20, 1898.
[2060] Thelma Grace[7], *b* July 1, 1900.
[2061] William Edgar[7], *b* April 28, 1902.
[2062] Martha Catharine[7], *b* October 21, 1904.

[764] **DAISY MAY[6] HEFFNER,** daughter of [159] Mary Jane[5] (Peightel) Heffner and Samuel Dean Heffner, was born February 17, 1873. November 3, 1897, she married Hon. *Robert Patton Habgood,* born at Bellefonte, Center County, Pennsylvania, May 21, 1871; son of *William Henry* and *Sarah (Sircombe) Habgood.* Mr. and Mrs. Habgood were educated in the public schools of Pennsylvania. His additional training for business was received in railroad and newspaper offices. He was employed upon the *Evening Star*, Bradford, Pennsylvania. in 1899; was appointed manager of the same in 1900; became its owner in 1903; and February 1, 1909, merged the *Bradford Daily Record* with the *Bradford Evening Star,* continuing the same as the *Star and Record,* an evening paper. He was president of the Pennsylvania State Republican League, 1907-1908, member of the State Legislature, 1907; secretary Pennsylvania State Editorial Association; and postmaster of Bradford, Pennsylvania, 1911——. Mr. Habgood is a Republican, and both he and his wife

ROBERT PATTON HABGOOD, DAISY MAY[7] HEFFNER HABGOOD [764], AND CHILDREN.

REV. ERNEST NEWTON[8] EVANS [767].

were together members of the Presbyterian Church, until her death, March 10, 1910. Address, The Star Publishing Company, 12-14 St. James Place, Bradford, McKean County, Pennsylvania (Plate 71).

Children (2), surname Habgood:

[2064] Stuart[7], *b* May 18, 1900.
[2065] Dorothy Gladys[7], *b* October 10, 1906.

[765] **HENRY CLAY[6] HEFFNER,** son of [159] Mary Jane[5] (Peightel) Heffner and Samuel Dean Heffner, was born August 8, 1874. May 4, 1897, he married *Minnie Hane,* of Bradford, Pennsylvania, born June 6, 1876; daughter of *Frank Oscar* and *Clara (Kuhn) Hane.* Mr. and Mrs. Heffner were educated in the public schools of Pennsylvania; and are members of the Presbyterian Church. He is an oil well driller and contractor; and served as a member of Co. C, National Guard of Pennsylvania, having been mustered out as sergeant. Residence is Bradford, Pennsylvania.

Children (2):

[2067] Henry Clay[7], *b* March 16, 1898.
[2068] Samuel Frank[7], *b* February 6, 1906.

[767] **ERNEST NEWTON[6] EVANS,** son of [161] Sarah Alice[5] (Peightel) Evans and Dr. Micaiah R. Evans, was born at the Henry Peightel homestead (his mother's parental home) near McConnellstown, Pennsylvania, December 16, 1876. He spent his childhood and youth at Saxton, Bedford County, Pennsylvania, where he attended the public schools. After his family settled at Huntingdon, Pennsylvania, he completed the prescribed course of study in the Huntingdon High School graduating as salutatorian in 1894. In 1895 he entered Franklin and Marshall College, at Lancaster, Pennsylvania, from which institution he graduated with the class of 1899. On this occasion he was the valedictorian. During his collegiate course he filled the position of president of the Y. M. C. A. and president of the State Inter-Collegiate Oratorical Union. He captured the third prize in the state oratorical contest of 1899. During the summer vacations he employed his time in the lumber camps of his native state, under the direction of Pennsylvania State Y. M. C. A. He also has been contributing editor of the *Christian World* since 1910.

He took a three years' course in theology at the Seminary at Lancaster, Pennsylvania, graduating in 1902. He at once entered upon the pastorate of the mission at Abilene, Kansas. After a successful pastorate of five years at that place, he entered upon pastoral work at Xenia, Ohio. He has had decided success in this field of labor in bringing the unchurched into the Kingdom, the additions numbering 220 members. There has also been material progress during these five years. A church edifice costing $40,000 was erected and paid for.

June 14, 1905, at Siloam Springs, Arkansas, Mr. Evans married *Elizabeth Helen Vincent*, born January 16, 1878, at Brighton, Iowa; daughter of Rev. *Alvan Stuart Vincent*, D.D., Ph.D. and *Susan (Walker) Vincent*. Elizabeth Helen Vincent graduated from the high school of Paxton, Illinois; attended Monmouth College two years, and graduated from Emporia (Kansas) College. Address, Xenia, Greene County, Ohio (Plate 72).

Children (4):

[2070] Robert Vincent[7], *b* March 12, 1907.
[2071] Elizabeth Vincent[7], *b* August 1, 1909.
[2072] John Vincent[7], *b* January 29, 1911; *d* February 1, 1911.
[2073] Ernest Vincent[7], *b* June 8, 1914.

[771] **DANIEL ADAM[6] SMITH,** son of [164] Mary A.[5] (Garner) Smith and Henry Smith, was born March 8, 1862. September 30, 1890, he married *Anna G. Schmidt*, who was born November 25, 1869. Mr. Smith is a farmer, and his address is Fenimore, Grant County, Wisconsin.

Children (5):

[2074] Urban Ulysses[7], *b* May 2, 1892.
[2075] Orilla C.[7], *b* November 19, 1895.
[2076] Daniel D.[7], *b* November 8, 1897.
[2077] Landis[7], *b* July 22, 1903.
[2078] Lowell, *b* July 22, 1903; *d* October 16, 1903.

[773] **CHARLES HENRY[6] SMITH,** son of [164] Mary A.[5] (Garner) Smith and Henry Smith, was born in Grant County, Wisconsin, December 24, 1865. November 14, 1896, in Boscobel, Wisconsin, he married *Mary Sweeney*, born February 20, 1873, also in Grant County, Wisconsin. Mrs. Smith died August 28, 1913. Mr. Smith is a farmer; address Platteville, Wisconsin.

Children (3):

[2081] Earl[7], *b* January 7, 1898.
[2082] Kathleen[7], *b* October 31, 1899.
[2083] Lauretta[7], *b* March 6, 1907.

[774] **MARGARET ANGELINA^{6} SMITH,** daughter of [164] Mary A.^{5} (Garner) Smith and Henry Smith, was born December 12, 1867. October 15, 1890, at Stitzer, Wisconsin, she married *Louis W. Schuppener*, born in Grant County, Wisconsin, 1865. Mr. Schuppener is a merchant. Address, Stitzer, Wisconsin.

Children (3), surname Schuppener:

[2085] Portia Lee^{7}, *b* May 26, 1892.
[2086] Laverna Virgil^{7}, *b* February 27, 1894.
[2087] Dewey Daniel^{7}, *b* April 18, 1898.

[775] **HENRIETTA MAY^{6} SMITH,** daughter of [164] Mary Ann^{5} (Garner) Smith and Henry Smith, was born in Grant County, Wisconsin, December 12, 1869. April 4, 1904, in Freeport, Illinois, she married *Frederick Kirk*, born in Hazel Green, Wisconsin, June 14, 1867. Mr. Kirk is a conductor on the Great Northern Railroad; the family address is Stockton, Illinois.

Children (5), surname Kirk:

[2090] Donovan Converse^{7}, *b* in Dubuque, Iowa, June 6, 1906.
[2091] Clifford Frederick^{7}, *b* in Dubuque, Iowa, November 16, 1907.
[2092] Frederick^{7}, *b* in Dubuque, Iowa, March 8, 1909.
[2093] Rush W.^{7}, *b* in Dubuque, Iowa, August 16, 1910.
[2094] Marjorie Henrietta^{7}, *b* in Stockton, Illinois, November 14, 1911.

[776] **LOUIS ALVIN^{6} SMITH,** son of [164] Mary Ann^{5} (Garner) Smith and Henry Smith, was born October 24, 1871. October 2, 1895, in Fennimore, Wisconsin, he married *Gertie Smith*, born in Patch Grove, Wisconsin, August 19, 1876. Address, Stitzer, Wisconsin.

Children (6):

[2096] Tarence^{7}, *b* May 2, 1897.
[2097] Gladys Pearl^{7}, *b* June 24, 1899.
[2098] Bernice Georgia^{7}, *b* January 19, 1902.
[2099] Kenneth Henry^{7}, *b* October 16, 1904.
[2100] Beulah^{7}, *b* November 8, 1906.
[2101] Mona L.^{7}, *b* May 6, 1912.

[778] **IDA MATILDA^{6} SMITH,** daughter of [164] Mary Ann^{5} (Garner) Smith and Henry Smith, was born May 26, 1876. March 10, 1902, she

married *Converse Winson*, born in Juneau County, Wisconsin, April 19, 1875. Mr. Winson is a buttermaker; address, Stitzer, Wisconsin. (No issue reported.)

[779] **OSCAR MARTIN[6] SMITH,** son of [164] Mary Ann[5] (Garner) Smith and Henry Smith, was born May 3, 1878. April 15, 1902, in Davis, Illinois, he married *Anna Pittenger*, born in North Lancaster, Wisconsin, April 5, 1881. Mr. Smith is a farmer, and his address is Fennimore, Wisconsin.

Children (2):

[2103] Delos[7], *b* January 31, 1903.
[2104] Garner[7], *b* April 14, 1909.

[780] **TRESSIE LAURA[6] SMITH,** daughter of [164] Mary Ann[5] (Garner) Smith and Henry Smith, was born in Grant County, Wisconsin, April 12, 1881. In Dubuque, Iowa, October 12, 1909, she married *Benjamin W. Kirk*, born in Hazel Green, Wisconsin, July 18, 1877; a painter. Address, Stitzer, Wisconsin.

[785] **GEORGE D.[6] GARNER,** son of [165] Dewalt[5] and Mary Ann (Hedges) Garner, was born September 20, 1871. November 4, 1896, he married *Matilda C. E. Schmidt.* Address, Lancaster, Wisconsin.

One son:

[2103] Robert M.[7], *b* April 23, 1905.

[786] **FLORENCE ELENORA[6] GARNER,** daughter of [165] Dewalt[5] and Mary Ann (Hedges) Garner, was born Aug ıst 4, 1873. She was educated in the public schools, and prepared herself for teaching, which she followed until her marriage, April 7, 1896, to *Edward W. Schmidt*, born December 30, 1873. Address, Lancaster, Wisconsin.

One son, surname Schmidt:

[2104] Dalton V.[7], *b* June 26, 1902.

[787] **NELLIE S.[6] GARNER,** daughter of [165] Dewalt[5] and Mary Ann (Hedges) Garner, was born March 27, 1875. November 25, 1897, she married *Harry C. Craig*, born November 25, 1873. Address, Lancaster, Wisconsin.

Children (2) surname Craig:

[2106] Florence A.[7], *b* February 8, 1901.
[2107] Dewalt J.[7], *b* June 23, 1904.

[790] **FLORA ETTA[6] SHAFFER,** daughter of [166] Margaret[5] (Garner) Shaffer and Edward Shaffer, was born June 28, 1878; graduated from the State Normal School of Platteville; teacher in public schools; Congregationalist; address, Platteville, Grant County, Wisconsin.

[791] **CHARLES MELVIN[6] SHAFFER,** son of [166] Margaret[5] (Garner) Shaffer and Edward Shaffer, was born August 13, 1881; educated in the High School of Platteville, Wisconsin; member Congregational Church; merchant, St. Paul, Minnesota. July 29, 1908, he married *Maria Shatka,* born April 11, 1886.

One son:

[2109] Edward Thomas[7], *b* July 29, 1909.

[793] **MAGGIE ETTA[6] LEIBERT,** daughter of [167] Catharine[5] (Garner) Leibert and Fred Leibert, was born June 30, 1867; graduated from State Normal School and was a teacher; member of Methodist Church. She married *William Frederick Dawley;* farmer; address, Sioux Falls, South Dakota, R. R. No. 6.

Children (2), surname Dawley:

[2111] Fred William[7], *b* June 17, 1897.
[2112] Kathryn Neoma Windsor[7], *b* September 29, 1899.

[795] **NELLIE RETTA[6] LEIBERT,** daughter of [167] Catharine[5] (Garner) Leibert and Fred Leibert, was born September 6, 1871; educated in the public schools; member Methodist Church. She married *Adolph Spink,* a merchant; address, 554 Arundel Street, St. Paul, Minnesota.

Children (2), surname Spink:

[2113] Frederick Bernard[7], *b* June 15, 1894.
[2114] Meta Deloris[7], *b* December 15, 1896.

[797] **ELSIE BELLE[6] LEIBERT,** daughter of [167] Catharine[5] (Garner) Leibert and Fred Leibert, was born December 13, 1875; and March 1, 1900, married *John William Akins.* Mrs. Akins attended the public

schools, and the State Normal School; is a member of the Methodist Church. Mr. Akins is a barber. Address, Sioux Falls, South Dakota, R. R. No. 1.

Children (2), surname Akins:

[2117] Bernice Frances[7], *b* November 29, 1906.
[2118] William E.[7], *b* September 1906.

[798] **SADIE MAE[6] LEIBERT,** daughter of [167] Catharine[5] (Garner) Leibert and Fred Leibert, was born September 16, 1881. November 27, 1906, she married *Dennis Albert Roselip*, son of *Charles Roselip*; farmer; Methodists; address, Broadway, Platteville, Wisconsin.

Children (2) surname Roselip:

[2119] Robert[7], *b* December 11, 1907.
[2120] Dorothy Elizabeth[7], *b* October 23, 1909.

[802] **WILLIAM GARNER[6] WADDLE,** son of [168] Elizabeth Ann[5] (Garner) Waddle and William Warren Waddle, was born in Grant County, Wisconsin, June 29, 1870. He is a practicing attorney, firm name Anderson and Waddle, of Webster, South Dakota.

July 3, 1900, Mr. Waddle married *Eliza Mae Otis*, who was born March 4, 1873, in Union County, South Dakota.

Children (3):

[2122] Sterling William[7], *b* in Clay County, South Dakota, July 4, 1903.
[2123] Garner J.[7], *b* in Marshall County, South Dakota, April 13, 1905.
[2124] Kenneth Lorraine[7], *b* in Day County, South Dakota, April 23, 1907.

[803] **THOMAS WARREN[6] WADDLE,** son of [168] Elizabeth Ann[5] (Garner) Waddle and William Warren Waddle, was born in Grant County, Wisconsin, December 30, 1871. October 28, 1906, he married *Tillie Mathwig* of Plymouth County, Iowa, born in said county June 14, 1882. Residence and address, Merrill, Iowa. (No issue reported.)

[804] **ARTHUR[6] WADDLE,** son of [168] Elizabeth Ann[5] (Garner) Waddle and William Warren Waddle, was born in Grant County, Wisconsin, June 18, 1874. February 12, 1900, at Sioux City, Iowa, he married *Sylvia Pearl Crow*, who was born in Marshall County, West Virginia, January 1, 1878. Residence and address, Webster, South Dakota.

Children (3), surname Waddle:

[2126] Fae Margaret⁷, *b* in Plymouth County, Iowa, November 4, 1901.
[2127] Raymond Arthur⁷, *b* in Plymouth County, Iowa, July 25, 1904.
[2128] Wesley Warren⁷, *b* in Day County, South Dakota, December 6, 1907.

[805] **NELLIE MAE⁶ WADDLE,** daughter of [168] Elizabeth Ann⁵ (Garner) Waddle and William Warren Waddle, was born in Plymouth County, Iowa, July 16, 1877. March 15, 1900, she married *Myron Elmer Kanago,* who was born in Plymouth County, Iowa, December 1, 1873. Residence, Webster, South Dakota.

Children (4), surname Kanago:

[2131] Archie Bernard⁷, *b* in Plymouth County, Iowa, December 18, 1900.
[2132] Vivian Mae⁷, *b* in Plymouth County, Iowa, March 15, 1903.
[2133] Elmer Perry⁷, *b* in Plymouth County, Iowa, August 30, 1905.
[2134] Lloyd, *b* in Day County, Iowa, January 26, 1909.

[806] **REUBEN⁶ WADDLE,** son of [168] Elizabeth Ann⁵ (Garner) Waddle and William Warren Waddle, was born in Plymouth County, Iowa, September 15, 1879. January 1, 1906, in Plymouth County, Iowa, he married *Maude Myrtle Ramsbotham,* who was born in McCook County, South Dakota, May 13, 1883. Residence, Webster, South Dakota.

One daughter:

[2136] Lula Evelyn⁷, *b* in Plymouth County, Iowa, November 4, 1906.

[807] **FREDERICK⁶ WADDLE,** son of [168] Elizabeth Ann⁵ (Garner) Waddle and William Warren Waddle, was born in Plymouth County, Iowa, May 27, 1881. December 27, 1906, in Plymouth County, Iowa, he married *Mattie Brown,* who was born December 27, 1887. Residence and address, Webster, South Dakota.

[808] **EDWARD DEWALT⁶ WADDLE,** son of [168] Elizabeth Ann⁵ (Garner) Waddle and William Warren Waddle, was born in Plymouth County, Iowa, February 22, 1883. July 17, 1907, he married *Alburta Mae Baldwin,* in Plymouth County, Iowa, who was born in Jones County, Iowa, November 19, 1886. Residence and address, Webster, South Dakota.

[809] **LAURA E.[6] WADDLE,** daughter of [168] Elizabeth Ann[5] (Garner) Waddle and William Warren Waddle, was born in Plymouth County, Iowa, June 7, 1885. On July 15, 1908, she married *John William Grebner* of Plymouth County, Iowa, also born in Plymouth County, Iowa, April 19, 1884. Address of the family is Lisbon, North Dakota.

[812] **ARCHIE ROY[6] CLIFTON,** son of [169] Mariah Jane[5] (Garner) Clifton and Watson Elihugh Clifton, was born July 17, 1874. June 18, 1903, he married *Sarah Winnifred Goodnough,* at Evansville, Wisconsin. His education is high school, normal, and university; and he is a teacher, Address, Reedsburg, Wisconsin.

Children (2):

[2140] Orin Watson[7], *b* August 12, 1906.
[2141] Dorothy Evelyn[7], *b* August 12, 1906.

[813] **LESTER EUGENE[6] CLIFTON,** son of [169] Mariah Jane[5] (Garner) Clifton and Watson Elihugh Clifton, was born April 12, 1879. December 24, 1902, he married *Jennie M. Irish* of Bloomington, Wisconsin. Mr. Clifton was educated in the common schools; is a farmer; Republican; address Lancaster, Wisconsin.

Children (3):

[2142] Melvin Lunem[7], *b* June 15, 1904.
[2143] Margaret Lucile[7], *b* September 21, 1905.
[2144] Stanley Brehania[7], *b* October 17, 1907.

[815] **LAURA MARIE[6] GARNER,** daughter of [171] Reuben Peter Philip[5] and Fannie L. (Starr) Garner, was born December 11, 1881. December 30, 1903, she married *Clarence Hinch.*

One son, surname Hinch:

[2146] Harold Garner[7], *b* January 12, 1905.

[836] **CALVIN L.[6] GARNER,** son of [176] Alfred[5] and Celinda (Schlodtt) Garner, was born August 23, 1870. March 20, 1894, he married *Sallie E. Patterson,* born September 15, 1870. They live in Canton, Ohio, where he is secretary of the Peoples Savings Bank.

Children (2):

[2149] Alfred Galvin^{7}, *b* December 1894.
[2150] Ruth Evelyn^{7}, *b* July 6, 1897.

[846] **GRACE TARRANT^{6} GARNER,** daughter of [180] Harrison^{5} and Lou A. (Maclaskey) Garner, was born April 11, 1880. February 25, 1903, she married *Merle E. Robinson, D.D.S.*, born June 17, 1881. Dr. Robinson follows his profession of dentistry, and the family live at 6326 Lincoln Street, Chicago, Illinois.

Children (2), surname Robinson:

[2152] James Steward^{7}, *b* October 19, 1904.
[2153] Merric Eldridge^{7}, *b* December 4, 1905.

[847] **LESLIE HENRY^{6} GARNER,** son of [180] Harrison^{5} and Lou A. (Maclaskey) Garner, was born August 10, 1881. June 8, —— he married *Ethel Weisbroett*, born September 2, 1881. Mr. Garner is employed by the Pullman Company; address 4314 Haight Avenue, Cincinnati, Ohio.

Children (2):

[2155] Helen Virginia^{7}, *b* November 22, 1906.
[2156] Mary Louise^{7}, *b* June 5, 1910.

[854] **ELMER^{6} GARNER,** son of [186] Benjamin F.^{5} and Emma (Keister) Garner, was born January 24, 1880. May 18, 1899, he married *Matilda Liesveld*, who was born at Hickman, Nebraska, January 19, 1882. Address, Hickman, Nebraska.

Children (4):

[2158] Bessie L.^{7}, *b* July 15, 1900.
[2159] Sadie Emma^{7}, *b* August 22, 1902.
[2160] Gerald Lynn^{7}, *b* February 11, 1905.
[2161] Mary Helen^{7}, *b* September 8, 1906.

[855] **SARAH^{6} GARNER,** daughter of [186] Benjamin F.^{5} and Emma Keister Garner, was born December 15, 1884. September 2, 1903, she married *Charles William Lafler*, who was born March 21, 1874. Address, Hickman, Nebraska.

One daughter, surname Lafler:

[2163] Gladys Blanche^7, *b* June 2, 1904.

[879] **EMMA ELLEN^6 ACKER,** daughter of [199] Julia Ann^5 (Garner) Acker and Emanuel B. Acker, was born January 16, 1874. She married *John Wolfgang Sommers*, who was born November 10, 1866. He is a native of Bavaria, Germany, and came to America August 17, 1883. Address, Holton, Jackson County, Kansas, R. F. D. No. 1.

Children (9), surname Sommers:

[2165] John Henry^7, *b* and *d* December 15, 1892.
[2166] Anna Katherine^7, *b* December 16, 1893.
[2167] George Calvin^7, *b* July 8, 1895.
[2168] Walter Henry^7, *b* July 17, 1897.
[2169] Margaritta Elizabeth^7, *b* December 15, 1901.
[2170] Florantine Carl^7, *b* April 26, 1904.
[2171] Lillie Eva^7, *b* November 11, 1905.
[2172] Emma Ellen^7, *b* October 10, 1908.
[2173] Lyda Lona^7, *b* August 1, 1910.

[880] **HARVEY MAHLEN^6 ACKER,** son of [199] Julia Ann^5 (Garner) Acker and Emanuel B. Acker, was born September 7, 1875. March 9, 1898, he married *Mary Margaret Linville.* Address, Wiley, Colorado.

Children (5):

[2175] Katharine May^7 *b* December 23, 1898.
[2176] Clara Belle^7, *b* March 23, 1900.
[2177] Helen Frances^7, *b* April 2, 1902; *d* April 4, 1905.
[2178] Harvey Linville^7, *b* October 29, 1904.
[2179] John Calvin^7, *b* May 3, 1908.

[881] **DAVID CALVIN^6 ACKER,** son of [199] Julia Ann^5 (Garner) Acker and Emanuel B. Acker, was born June 3, 1877. June 3, 1908, he married *Ruth Mueller*, who was born August 10, 1881, at Rock Island, Illinois. Address, Eureka, Kansas, R. D. No. 4.

One son:

[2181] Richard Calvin^7, *b* August 26, 1909.

[882] **LILLIE ELIZABETH[6] ACKER,** daughter of [199] Julia Ann[5] (Garner) Acker and Emanuel B. Acker, was born November 16, 1879. April 12, 1905, she married *Oliver Francis Simmons*, who was born in Minard County, Illinois, March 7, 1878. They were married at Holton Kansas, by Rev. C. E. Platz. Address, Holton, Kansas.

[888] **HARRISON R.[6] SATERFIELD,** son of [202] Mary Jane[5] (Garner) Saterfield and J. L. Saterfield, was born September 27, 1890. In 1911, he married *Alice Mae Bell Pointer*, who was born in Tennessee, November 27, 1888. Address, Holton, Kansas.

One son:

[2183] Basil Glenn[7], *b* November 6, 1912.

[951] **HERMAN H.[6] SHULTZ,** son of [224] Mary Jane[5] (Myers) Shultz and Daniel Shultz, was born October 13, 1883. September 20, 1905, he married *Clara Emigh.* Address, Aitch, Huntingdon County, Pennsylvania. (No issue.)

[967] **JACOB ELIAS[6] HEIMBAUGH[a],** son of [233] Abraham[5] and Adaline (Reed) Heimbaugh, was born November 23, 1861. October 16, 1883, he married *Amanda Catharine Schreiner*, born June 3, 1862; daughter *Michael* and *Almira Schreiner.* Mr. Heimbaugh is a miller and dealer in all kinds of grain, is a Democrat, and his address is East Akron, Ohio, R. D. No. 22. (No children.)

[968] **SAMUEL E.[6] HEIMBAUGH[a],** son of [233] Abraham[5] and Adaline (Reed) Heimbaugh, was born November 14, 1863. He lives in Akron, Ohio, but repeated letters have failed to secure further facts.

Children (2):

[2186] Arthur[7].
[2187] Jasper[7].

[970] **MARY[6] HEIMBAUGH[a],** daughter of [233] Abraham[5] and Adaline (Reid) Heimbaugh, was born December 25, 1874, in Suffield Township, Portage County, Ohio. October 14, 1894, she married *Edwin Ambrose Wengert*, born November 24, 1864 at Martinsburg, Blair County, Pennsylvania. The family live at 374 Cleveland Street, Akron, Ohio.

[a] Spelled also "Himebaugh."

Children (8), surname Wengert:

[2189] Lucinda Edna[7], *b* in Suffield, Portage County, Ohio, August 28, 1895.
[2190] Mary Adaline[7], *b* in Suffield, Portage County, Ohio, October 19, 1896.
[2191] Ruth Edna[7], *b* in Lake, Ohio, September 15, 1898.
[2192] Doris Mae[7], *b* in Lake, Ohio, September 30, 1901.
[2193] George Edward[7], *b* in Lake, Ohio, June 3, 1903.
[2194] Grace Catherine[7], *b* in Akron, Ohio, May 16, 1906.
[2195] Earl Ambrose[7], *b* in Akron, Ohio, May 23, 1911.
[2196] Geraldine Blandie[7], *b* Akron, Ohio, August 14, 1913.

[975] **MARY[6] BOWSER,** daughter of [234] Elizabeth[5] (Heimbaugh) Bowser and Samuel Bowser, was born November 6, 1862. November 23, 1879, she married *Daniel M. Brubaker*, son of *Daniel* and *Harriet (Martin) Brubaker.*

Mr. Brubaker is a minister and an elder in the Church of the Brethren. For eleven years he was at different mission points in the West, but the family returned to the paternal farm in order that Mrs. Elizabeth (Heimbaugh) Bowser [234] might continue on the farm—the sons all being employed on the railroad.

Mrs. Brubaker has kindly furnished considerable information fcr this volume, and also secured a number of pictures for the same. Address is Weilersville, Wayne County, Ohio.

Children (6), surname Brubaker:

[2200] + Della[7], *b* September 9, 1880; *m Scott Long.*
[2201] + Jessie[7], *b* September 17, 1882; *m John Austin Collins, Jr.*
[2202] + Anna[7], *b* October 10, 1886; *m Otto Ulrich, M.D.*
[2203] + Nettie[7], *b* September 5, 1889, *m Louis Boyer.*
[2204] Elizabeth[7], *b* October 3, 1894.
[2205] Paul[7], *b* December 2, 1897.

[976] **SAMUEL[6] BOWSER,** son of [234] Elizabeth[5] (Heimbaugh) Bowser and Samuel Bowser, was born March 28, 1864. He married *Sarah E. Moore*, born September 9, 1869; daughter of *Huston* and *Mary Jane Moore.* Mr. Moore is a locomotive engineer on the M. K. & T. R. R. Address is Sedalia, Missouri.

Children (4):

[2207] Jessie[7], *b* January 8, 1889.
[2208] John[7], *b* October 23, 1891.
[2209] Sadie Hariston[7], *b* February 28, 1893.
[2210] Samuel Jr.[7], *b* September 13, 1900.

[977] **DANIEL[6] BOWSER,** son of [234] Elizabeth[5] (Heimbaugh) Bowser and Samuel Bowser, was born March 28, 1864. He married *Melvina Ober*, born February 11, 1867; daughter of *George* and *Lydia Ober*. Mr. Bowser is a fireman on the M. K. & T. R. R. and the family live at Parsons, Kansas.

Children (8):

[2212] Ira S.[7], *b* January 19, 1887; *d* November 3, 1890.
[2213] Elsworth[7], *b* November 8, 1888.
[2214] Arthur[7], *b* May 6, 1890.
[2215] Myrtle[7], *b* February 21, 1892; *m Arthur Akins.*
[2216] Grace[7], *b* November 11, 1893; *m Ross Franklin.*
[2217] Daughter[7], *b* and *d* February 22, 1899.
[2218] Crede[7], *b* May 24, 1900.
[2219] Elizabeth[7], *b* September 27, 1906.

[978] **ERASTUS[6] BOWSER,** son of [234] Elizabeth[6] (Heimbaugh) Bowser and Samuel Bowser, was born December 12, 1869. In 1910 he married *Victoria Bowser*; occupation, brakeman; residence Chicago, Illinois.

One daughter:

[2221] Marion[7], *b* December 8, 1912.

[979] **LUCINDA[6] BOWSER,** daughter of [234] Elizabeth[6] (Heimbaugh) Bowser and Samuel Bowser, was born February 4, 1875. February 4, 1900, she married *Aaron Kurtz*, born August 23, 1875; son of *John* and *Mary Kurtz*. Mr. Kurtz is a butcher, and his address is Hartville, Stark County, Ohio.

Children (3), surname Kurtz:

[2223] Ada[7], *b* August 10, 1901.
[2224] Samuel[7], *b* October 7, 1903.
[2225] Ruth[7], *b* March 6, 1906.

[981] **ANDREW JACKSON[6] PONTIOUS,** son of [235] Christina[5] (Heimbaugh) Pontious and Lewis Pontious, was born April 2, 1861. August 22, 1883, by Rev. David Young, he was married to *Amelia E. Swartz.* He is a contractor for moving buildings and heavy machinery, and his address is 34 Royal Place, Akron, Ohio.

Children (2)[6]

[2227] Melvin[7].
[2228] Maud[7].

[982] **SARAH ELIZABETH[6] PONTIOUS,** daughter of [235] Christina[5] (Heimbaugh) Pontious and Lewis Pontious, was born January 19, 1863. October 25, 1890, by Rev. J. H. Hollingshead, she was married to *Jacob Scheefer.* Address, 1619 Clark Avenue, Canton, Ohio.

Children (2), surname Scheefer:

[2231] Bertha M.[7], *b* March 21, 1892.
[2232] Minnie A.[7], *b* May 21, 1894.

[988] **JENNIE CANDAS[6] BRUMBAUGH,**[a] daughter of [237] Mary[5] (Heimbaugh) Brumbaugh and Samuel[5] Brumbaugh, was born October 26, 1869, in Suffield, Ohio; March 18, 1888, she married *Cyrus Franklin Dulabahn,* born June 7, 1860; son of *Cyrus* and *Rachel Dulabahn.* They live on a farm near New Baltimore, Stark County, Ohio; Post office address, Hartville, Ohio, R. R. No. 2.

Children (5), surname Dulabahn:

[2235] Lamar Harrison[7], *b* March 10, 1890.
[2236] Bessie Jane[7], *b* February 21, 1892.
[2237] Estella Ruth[7], *b* May 20, 1895.
[2238] Chauncey E.[7], *b* January 17, 1898; *d* May 4, 1898.
[2239] Mary Rosalia[7], *b* May 29, 1900.

[989] **ALVERNA[6] BRUMBAUGH,**[b] daughter of [237] Mary[5] (Heimbaugh) Brumbaugh and Samuel[5] Brumbaugh, was born in Suffield, Ohio, March 29, 1872; June 11, 1891, she married *Israel Steffy,* born November 22, 1870; son of *David* and *Christena (Snyder) Steffy.* They live on a farm near New Baltimore, Stark County, Ohio; address Hartville, Ohio, R. R. No. 2.

[a] No. [E960], p. 634 and 682, *Brumbach Families,* 1913.
[b] No. [E961] on p. 634 and 582 of *Brumbach Families.*

Children (3), surname Steffy:

[2241] Melvin Edward[7], *b* January 24, 1892.
[2242] Leon Wilford[7], *b* February 23, 1897.
[2243] Clarence Donald[7], *b* August 15, 1907.

[990] **IRA ALVIN[6] BRUMBAUGH,**[a] son of [237]. Mary[5] (Heimbaugh) Brumbaugh and Samuel Brumbaugh, was born in Marlboro, Ohio, Spetember 28, 1875; December 25, 1897, married *Viola Austin*, born December 14, 1875; daughter of *David* and *Eunice Austin*. They live near New Baltimore, Stark County, Ohio. (No children.)

[991] **HOWARD[6] BRUMBAUGH,**[b] son of [237] Mary (Heimbaugh) Brumbaugh and Samuel Brumbaugh, was born March 5, 1882. January 21, 1904, he married *Effie May Fall*, born July 25, 1883 in Suffield, Ohio; daughter of *Isaac* and *Leah Fall*, and sister of Edgar Eugene Fall who married [E 965] Nellie[6] Brumbaugh, daughter of Henry P.[5] Brumbaugh. Howard Brumbaugh is a farmer; address Hartville, Stark County, Ohio, R. R. 2.

Children (3):

[2245] Grace Lucile[7], *b* October 30, 1905.
[2246] Thelma Marie[7], *b* July 4, 1908.
[2247] Florence Margaret[7], *b* May 7, 1911.

[1013] **LYDIA LEOTA[6] FOUSE,** daughter of [247] Franklin[5] and Laura E. (Bishop) Fouse, was born April 5, 1885. June 2, 1901, she married *Iran F. Coulson*, who was born November 18, 1869.

One daughter, surname Coulson:

[2250] Mary Laura[7], *b* May 30, 1908.

[1023] **RUSSEL LEROY[6] FOUSE,** son of [249] Daniel[5] and Minnie Jane (Shanafelt) Fouse, was born January 18, 1889. August 18, 1910, he married *Mary E.*[6] *Ingold*, [655] daughter of *Celesta*[5] *(Snyder) Ingold* already noted. Address, Alliance, Ohio.

[a] No. [E962] on pp. 634 and 582 of *Brumbach Families*.
[b] No. [E963] on pp. 634 and 582 of *Brumbach Families*.

[1028] **VERNA⁶ HOOVER,** daughter of [250] Franklin D.⁵ and Mollie (Zentz) Hoover, was born July 29, 1871. November 27, 1890, she married *Charles Shoner*, who was born January 20, 1887. Mrs. Shoner died September 10, 1897. Residence of Mr. Shoner is Lake, Stark County, Ohio.

One son, surname Shoner:

[2251] Earl Henry[7], *b* November 13, 1896.

[1029] **CLEON[6] HOOVER,** son of [250] Franklin D.[5] and Mollie (Zentz) Hoover, was born April 18, 1873. October 11, 1898, he married *Laura Schneider*. Address, 508 Elwood Avenue, Akron, Ohio.

Children (2):

[2253] Cleon Donald[7], *b* July 28, 1907.
[2254] Catharine Eliza[7], *b* May 7, 1908.

[1031] **ELLA E.[6] HOOVER,** daughter of [251] William[5] and Emma C. (Heimbaugh) Hoover, was born November 28, 1868; and married *Walter Gillmore*, June 3, 1908. Residence, Aqueduct Street, Akron, Ohio.

[1032] **CLIFFORD[6] HOOVER,** son of [251] William[5] and Emma C. (Heimbaugh) Hoover, was born June 26, 1877, and married *Mabel Cowan*, December 25, 1907. Residence, Carol Street, Akron, Ohio.

[1034] **SADIE[6] STROSACKER,** daughter of [252] Elizabeth[5] (Hoover) Strosacker and John Strosacker, was born May 18, 1875. March 13, 1889, she married *Norman Weyrick*. Mrs. Weyrick died June 20, 1889.

One son, surname Weyrick:

[2258] Russell[7], *b* December 20, 1898.

[1035] **HARRY[6] STROSACKER,** son of [252] Elizabeth[5] (Hoover) Strosacker and John Strosacker, was born May 15, 1878. He married *Birdie Greenhoe*, October 28, 1903.

One son:

[2259] John Nervin[7], *b* September 2, 1904.

[1091] **DILLA C.[6] MADLEM,** daughter of [267] Hiram B.[5] and Mary A. (Zentz) Madlem, was born April 28, 1865. July 2, 1882, she married *Isaac C. Kent*, who was born August 6, 1858.

To this union three children were born, but only one lives:

[2262] Leo James[7], *b* September 3, 1887.

[1107] **IDA MAY[6] FULMER,** daughter of [276] Malinda[6] (Fouse) Fulmer and Phillip Fulmer, was born February 3, 1882. June 24, 1900, she married *Henry More,* who was born September 22, 1877. Address, Brimfield (?), Portage County, Ohio.

Children (6), surname More:

[2266] Perry P.[7], *b* December 30, 1900.
[2267] Son[7], *b* and *d* October 22, 1902.
[2268] Dilla Myra[7], *b* December 27, 1903.
[2269] William E.[7], *b* October 4, 1905.
[2270] John B.[7], *b* April 17, 1907; *d* September 16, 1907.
[2271] Pearl Estella[7], *b* November 7, 1908.

[1113] **MAHLON ACQUILLA[6] FOUSE,** son of [278] John M.[6] and Susan (Royer) Fouse, was born June 17, 1878. May 9, he married *Edna Sprague,* who was born May 22, 1878. Address, 1405 Main Street, Houston, Texas.

Children (3):

[2274] Ruth[7], *b* April 14, 1900.
[2275] Helen[7], *b* September 19, 1901.
[2276] Harold[7], *b* June 12, 1905.

[1114] **AUSTIN J.[6] FOUSE,** son of [278] John M.[6] and Susan (Royer) Fouse, was born November 21, 1880; October 16, 1907, married *Maud Simmons,* who was born September 23, 1884.

[1115] **FREDERICK[6] FOUSE,** son of [278] John M.[6] and Susan (Royer) Fouse, was born July 17, 1883. November 3, 1904, he married *Ethel Rouinsky,* who was born August 25, 1885.

Children (2):

[2279] Irene Adele[7], *b* March 29, 1905.
[2280] Esther Lillian[7], *b* January 10, 1907.

[1126] **WINNEFRED E.[6] FOUSE,** son of [279] Reuben[5] and Salida (Royer) Fouse, was born December 24, 1877. March 29, 1902, he married *Elva Pearl Corl,* who was born June 23, 1876. Address, Kansas City, Missouri.

Children (3):

[2283] Harlan Corl[7], *b* March 21, 1903.
[2284] Irene Lucile[7], *b* March 6, 1905.
[2285] Eugene Kennith[7], *b* September 11, 1906.

[1127] **ONNEY MAY[6] FOUSE,** daughter of [281] Edwin P.[5] and Mary (Rose) Fouse, was born April 14, 1880. March 21, 1899, she married *John Homer Meyers,* who was born September 14, 1877. They resided at Ravenna, Portage County, Ohio, where Mr. Meyers had a factory in which he manufactured granite and marble monuments; present address, 365 Glenn Avenue, Youngstown, Ohio.

Children (3), surname Meyers:

[2287] Melin Louise[7], *b* February 8, 1902.
[2288] Beulah May[7], *b* August 13, 1903.
[2289] Leland Kenneth[7], *b* February 13, 1906.

[1128] **ELLA[6] FOUSE,** daughter of [281] Edwin P.[5] and Mary (Rose) Fouse, was born March 21, 1882. September 7, 1899, she married *Herbert C. Kauffman,* who was born January 28, 1876. They also lived at Ravenna, Portage County, Ohio, and Mr. Kauffman was connected with his brother-in-law in the granite and marble monument business. Present address, Kansas City, Missouri.

Children (2), surname Kauffman:

[2291] Mary Grace[7], *b* March 23, 1900.
[2292] Eva[7], *b* August 9, 1902.

[1136] **CHARLES M.[6] FOUSE,** son of [283] Minodes[5] and Christina (Rose) Fouse, was born March 16, 1883. Address, 26 Robert Street, Toronto, Canada.

Children (2):

[2294] Charles Nevin[7], *b* April 1, 1907.
[2295] Bruce Cleo[7], *b* October 14, 1908.

[1137] **ESTHER M.**[6] **FOUSE,** daughter of [283] Minodes[5] and Christina (Rose) Fouse, was born June 15, 1885. She has been her father's housekeeper since the death of her mother November 5, 1909. Address, 500 Schiller Avenue, Akron, Ohio.

[1138] **JOHN FLOYD**[6] **FOUSE,** son of [283] Minodes[5] and Christina (Rose) Fouse, was born September 22, 1887. December 24, 1908, he married *Hazel Weaver*, born March 16, 1892; and who died May 18, 1910. Address, 500 Schiller Avenue, Akron, Ohio.

[1146] **MARY MAUD**[6] **FOUSE,** daughter of [288] William Duncan[5] and Linda B. (Knode) Fouse, was born on Clover Creek, in Blair County, Pennsylvania, October 30, 1878. March 15, 1901, she married *J. Edwin Weber*, born June 26, 1868. Address, Huntingdon, Huntingdon County Pennsylvania (Plate 63).

One daughter, surname Weber:

[2298] Emma Grace[7], *b* April 11, 1902.

[1149] **LILLIE MAY**[6] **FOUSE,** daughter of [289] Daniel D.[5] and Malinda (Bossler) Fouse, was born on Clover Creek, in Blair County, Pennsylvania, August 4, 1877. December 14, 1899, she married *Harry W. Smith.* Mrs. Smith died February 1, 1910, and was buried at the Beavertown cemetery, on the old Fouse homestead. Mr. Smith's address is Drab, Blair County, Pennsylvania.

One daughter, surname Smith:

[2300] Florence Cathline[7], *b* June 28, 1902.

[1150] **HOMER B.**[6] **FOUSE,** son of [289] Daniel D.[5] and Malinda (Bossler) Fouse, was born July 7, 1879. December 14, 1907, he married *Anna Lecrone* [732], born September 24, 1875; daughter of *Sarah (Acker) Lecrone* [149] and *Jacob Lecrone.* Address, Drab, Blair Counry, Pennsylvania.

One daughter:

[2301] Mabel Pearle[7], *b* September 20, 1904.

[1151] **ELMER E.**[6] **FOUSE,** son of [289] Daniel D.[5] and Malinda (Bossler) Fouse, was born October 6, 1882. November 25, 1909, at Harrisburg, Pennsylvania, he married *Mary Luella Weber*, born February 1, 1885.

[1152] **MARGARET C.^{6} FOUSE,** daughter of [289] Daniel D.^{5} and Malinda (Bossler) Fouse, was born January 16, 1885. December 19, 1907, she married *Jacob Clarence Nicodemus.* Address, Drab, Pa.

One son, surname Nicodemus:

[2305] Harold Richard^{7}, *b* September 12, 1908.

[1153] **DEWALT O.^{6} FOUSE,** son of [289] Daniel D.^{5} and Malinda (Bossler) Fouse, was born September 11, 1887. His address is Drab, Blair County, Pennsylvania.

[1156] **MARCUS M. P.^{6} FOUSE,** son of [291] Calvin S.^{5} and Rosanna (Fisher) Fouse, was born April 8, 1878; and August 10, 1901, married *Ella Marie Kyper.* Address, is Mount Union, Huntingdon County, Pennsylvania.

One son:

[2307] Gaver P.^{7}, *b* July 16, 1903.

[1157] **MARY ELIZABETH^{6} FOUSE,** daughter of [291] Calvin S.^{5} and Rosanna (Fisher) Fouse, was born November 18, 1881. September 3, 1902, she married *James H. Smith.*

Children (2):

[2309] Edna M.^{7} *b* June 10, 1904.
[2301] Herbert Elisses^{7}, *b* January 8, 1906.

[1168] **ADA BLANCHE^{6} FERRY,** daughter of [293] Mary Elisabeth^{5} (Fouse) Ferry and Charles W. Ferry, was born September 20, 1886. September 20, 1906, she married *Ernest Bryan Sprankle.* Mrs. Sprankle is reported as deceased, and Mr. Sprankle as residing in Altoona, Pennsylvania. (No issue reported.)

[1170] **VERNICE EDNA^{6} FERRY,** daughter of [293] Mary Elizabeth^{5} (Fouse) Ferry and Charles W. Ferry, was born March 7, 1889; and, on December 5, 1907, married *Arthur Albert McCullum.* Mrs. McCullum died June 11, 1908.

[1173] **LAURA ELSIE^{6} ERB,** daughter of [294] Susan^{5} (Fouse) Erb and William P. Erb, was born October 1, 1884; and January 3, 1906, married *Frederick William Sorrick.* Address, Drab, Pennsylvania.

Children (2), surname Sorrick:

[2313] Frederick Wiliam[7], *b* January 1, 1907.
[2314] Josephine Lenora[7], *b* December 3, 1908.

[1175] **JESSE ROY[6] ERB,** son of [294] Susan[5] (Fouse) Erb and William P. Erb, was born June 12, 1888, and December 24, 1908, married *Frances Acker.* Address, Drab, Pennsylvania. (No issue reported.)

[1191] **MARGARET ELIZABETH[6] NICODEMUS,** daughter of [302] Wesley Fouse[5] and Lucinda (Acker) Nicodemus, was born January 24, 1870. October 23, 1895, she married *Charles O. Westphal* of Chicago, Illinois. No issue reported. Address, 2934 Juin Street, Denver, Colorado.

[1192] **OLIVER[6] NICODEMUS,** son of [302] Wesley Fouse[5] and Lucinda (Acker) Nicodemus, was born August 5, 1874. June 29, 1898, he married *Maud A. Criswell.* Last address, 182 W. Madison Street, Chicago, Illinois. (No issue reported.)

[1193] **JACOB EARL[6] NICODEMUS,** son of [302] Wesley Fouse[5] and Lucinda (Acker) Nicodemus, was born October 30, 1879. October 29, 1906, he married *Clio Abergaust* of Denver, Colorado. Residence, 118 11th Street, Oakland, California.

[1194] **WESLEY ROY[6] NICODEMUS,** son of [302] Wesley Fouse[5] and Lucinda (Acker) Nicodemus, was born June 16, 1886. September 16, 1907, he married *Oris Hiatt.*

Children (2):

[2317] Viola Iris[7], *b* April 4, 1909.
[2318] Wesley Raymond[7], *b* March 8, 1910.

[1197] **ALBERT[6] ACKER,** son of [303] Susanna Fouse[5] (Nicodemus) Acker and Daniel Acker, was born November 5, 1872. September 20, 1893, he married *Mabel Judson,* who was born May 4, 1872. Address, Foreston, Illinois.

Children (2):

[2320] George Henry[7], *b* August 15, 1903.
[2321] Ella Retta[7], *b* August 2, 1906.

[1198] **FRANKLIN J.[6] ACKER,** son of [303] Susana Fouse[6] (Nicodemus) Acker and Daniel Acker, was born October 10, 1874. May 25, 1904, he married *Nettie May Foy,* who was born September 28, 1876. Address, Forestan, Illinois.

One daughter:

[2323] Susan[7], *b* June 13, 1905.

[1199] **HARRY W.[6] ACKER,** son of [303] Susana Fouse[5] (Nicodemus) Acker and Daniel Acker, was born November 20, 1876. January 6, 1897, he married *Anna Dieffenbach,* who was born August 20, 1874. Address, Foreston, Illinois.

Children (2):

[2325] Beulah May[7], *b* November 5, 1898.
[2326] Benjamin F.[7], *b* May 1, 1900.

[1200] **RACHEL ALMYRTA[6] NICODEMUS,** daughter of [304] Reuben Fouse[5] and Mary H. (Boydston) Nicodemus, was born October 4, 1875, and on February 25, 1903, married *Bennie Dettle Horne.* Address, Foreston, Illinois.

Children (2), surname Horne:

[2327] Gladys Marie[7], *b* May 10, 1907.
[2328] Vera Ardis[7], *b* January 13, 1909.

[1201] **BURRIS VERNON[6] NICODEMUS,** son of [304] Reuben Fouse[5] and Mary H. (Boydston) Nicodemus, was born September 29, 1882. March 28, 1906, he married *Helen Eva Hawkins.* Address, Foreston, Illinois.

Children (2):

[2330] John Vernon[7], *b* December 28, 1906.
[2331] Burris Leonard[7], *b* March 31, 1909.

[1203] **LUSHA ELVA[6] DIEHL,** daughter of [305] Mary Agnes[5] (Nicodemus) Diehl and Levi Diehl, was born November 7, 1878; and, on November 24, 1879, married *O. Stouffer.* Address, Foreston, Illinois.

Children (2), *surname Stouffer:*

[2333] Lester[7], *b* December 24, 1898.
[2334] LeRoy Otis[7], *b* June 25, 1907.

[1204] **CHESTER LEE[6] DIEHL,** son of [305] Mary Agnes[5] (Nicodemus) Diehl and Levi Diehl, was born April 16, 1886. February 10, 1908, he married *Anna Friseman.* Address, Foreston, Illinois. (No issue reported.)

[1205] **OMAH MAY[6] DIEHL,** daughter of [305] Mary Agnes[5] (Nicodemus) Diehl and Levi Diehl, was born November 9, 1889. May 14, 1907, she married *Charles W. Yates.* Address, Foreston, Illinois.

One son, surname Yates:

[2336] Laverna Melvin[7], *b* September 28, 1907.

[1207] **ALVERNIA BOWMAN[6] NICODEMUS,** daughter of [306] Frederick Fouse[5] and Rebecca (Bowman) Nicodemus, was born December 6, 1878. May 31, 1899, she married *Antonius Aykins*, born May 30, 1873. Address, Battle Creek, Michigan.

Children (2), *surname Aykins:*

[2338] Marguerite Marie[7], *b* June 6, 1900.
[2339] Robert Kenneth[7], *b* March 31, 1906.

[1208] **FREDERICK BOWMAN[6] NICODEMUS,** son of [306] Frederick Fouse[5] and Rebecca (Bowman) Nicodemus, was born June 19, 1884. He is engaged in Mission work in Japan, and sailed for that land August 16, 1909.

[1210] **INEZ[6] NICODEMUS,** daughter of [307] Theobald Fouse[5] and Clara (Masse) Nicodemus, was born August 10, 1888. July 18, 1907, she married *J. Harold Campbell.* Address, Foreston, Illinois.

One son, surname Campbell:

[2341] Arelia Theobald[7], *b* July 18, 1908.

[1222] **JOHN J.[6] DAUGHERTY,** son of [313] Anma[5] (Fouse) Daugherty and George B. Daugherty, was born October 12, 1875. July 3, 1898, he married *Elizabeth Irwin*, who was born July 1, 1874; died August 19, 1906. Address, Scottdale, Pennsylvania.

Children (2):

[2343] George Irwin^7, *b* July 6, 1900.
[2344] Albert Lawrence^7, *b* July 26, 1904.

[1225] **CHARLOTTE J.^{6} DAUGHERTY,** daughter of [313] Anna^5 (Fouse) Daugherty and George B. Daugherty, was born August 26, 1880. November 17, 1901, she married *Jacob Blystone*, who was born March 8, 1880. Address, Scottdale, Pennsylvania.

Children (5), surname Blystone:

[2346] Walter Eugene^7, *b* March 27, 1903.
[2347] Marshall Mackline^7, *b* February 12, 1905.
[2348] Gilbert George^7, *b* February 28, 1906.
[2349] Charles Leroy^7, *b* May 25, 1907.
[2350] Raymond Ross^7, *b* August 23, 1908.

[1226] **OWEN F.^{6} DAUGHERTY,** son of [313] Anna^5 (Fouse) Daugherty and George B. Daugherty, was born August 16, 1882. April 4, 1908, he married *Edith Dale Reed*, born February 6, 1880. Address, Scottdale, Pennsylvania.

One son:

[2353] Wayne F.^{7}, *b* December 29, 1908.

[1227] **SARAH O.^{6} DAUGHERTY,** daughter of [313] Anna^5 (Fouse) Daugherty and George B. Daugherty, was born April 13, 1884. November 17, 1909, she married *Homer C. Dieffenbaugh*, born June 28, 1882. Address, Scottdale, Pennsylvania.

[1228] **ANNA M.^{6} DAUGHERTY,** daughter of [313] Anna^5 (Fouse) Daugherty and George B. Daugherty, was born September 30, 1885. November 19, 1902, she married *James McClure Ross*, born February 13, 1881. Address, Scottdale, Pennsylvania.

Children (3), surname Ross:

[2355] Homer Alfred^7, *b* July 26, 1904.
[2356] Kenneth Albert^7, *b* January 29, 1906.
[2357] Vernon Elroy^7, *b* December 30, 1907.

[1240] **HARVEY ELMER[6] FOUSE,** son of [317] Reuben[5] and Anna (Collins) Fouse, was born November 14, 1878. September 5, 1905, he married *Delilah Stephens.* Address, Duncansville, Pennsylvania.

Children (2):

[2360] Harvey Stephens,[7] *b* August 11, 1906.
[2361] Thelma[7], *b* July 13, 1908.

[1241] **LOLA BELLE[6] FOUSE,** daughter of [317] Reuben[5] and Anna (Collins) Fouse, was born February 2, 1880. February 11, 1898, she married *William Schultz.* Address, Duncansville, Pennsylvania.

One daughter, surname Schultz:

[2363] Pearl Elizabeth[7], *b* April 25, 1899.

[1242] **ORVILLE[6] FOUSE,** son of [317] Reuben[5] and Anna (Collins) Fouse, was born June 30, 1883. August 7, 1907, he married *Adelaide Kindred.* Address, Duncansville, Pennsylvania.

One son:

[2365] Orville, Jr.[7], *b* June 17, 1908.

[1262] **JOHN A.[6] ACKER,** son of [322] Elizabeth[5] (Fouse) Acker and Martin Acker, was born September 16, 1888. September 12, 1907, he married *Mary Olive Rhul,* who was born April 30, 1891. Address, Williamsburg, Pennsylvania.

Children (2):

[2368] Ethel Ferne[7], *b* January 2, 1908.
[2369] Ernest Erle[7], *b* August 26, 1909.

[1281] **ALICE[6] GREASER,** daughter of [327] Frederick[5] and Elizabeth (Acker) Greaser, was born March 31, 1874. July 8, 1894, she married *James Detweiler,* born January 25, 1872. Address is Williamsburg, Blair County, Pennsylvania.

Children (9), surname Detwiler:

[2371] Emma May[7], *b* September 5, 1894.
[2372] Lester Charles[7], *b* December 14, 1896.
[2373] Harry McKinley[7], *b* September 15, 1898.

[2374] John Roosevelt[7], *b* September 8, 1900.
[2375] Mildred Eliza[7], *b* December 4, 1902.
[2376] Anna Elizabeth[7], *b* July 15, 1904.
[2377] Dorothy Lenora[7], *b* August 13, 1906.
[2378] Margaret Victoria[7], *b* August 7, 1909.
[2379] James Homer[7], *b* November 24, 1911.

[1282] **HARVEY GREASER**[6], son of [327] Frederick[5] and Elizabeth (Acker) Greaser, was born August 4, 1876. April 30, 1903, he married *Mary Pollock*, born March 19, 1876, in Ireland. Mr. Greaser went to New York City about 1901 and learned the plumbing trade. Address, Dumont, New Jersey.

One son:

[2381] Frederick Robert[7], *b* February 9, 1904.

[1284] **IDA MAY**[6] **GREASER,** daughter of [327] Frederick[5] and Elizabeth (Acker) Greaser, was born April 4, 1880. February 14, 1904, she married *David Householder*, born September 6, 1873.

Children (2), surname Householder:

[2384] Lucile[7], *b* December 10, 1904; *d* December 12, 1907.
[2385] Alice[7], *b* August 12, 1906.

[1285] **FANNIE ELIZABETH**[6] **GREASER,** daughter of [327] Frederick[5] and Elizabeth (Acker) Greaser, was born April 4, 1882. May 16, 1906, she married *Charles Walker*, born May 16, 1881. Address, Sevierville, Sevier County, Tennessee, R. R. No. 3.

One daughter (1), surname Walker:

[2387] Mary Elizabeth[7], *b* July 14, 1907.

[1296] **MARGARET ACKER**[6] **GREASER,** daughter of [330] Daniel F.[5] and Sarah (Acker) Greaser, was born September 19, 1878. February 24, 1904, she married *George W. Garner*, born November 24, 1875—a great-grandson of *John Mathew Garner*, born September 21, 1776, and *Mary (Brumbaugh) Garner*, born August 26, 1791 ([E 18] pp. 424-429, *Brumbach Families*). Mr. Garner is a prosperous merchant at Fredericksburg, Pennsylvania; address, Martinsburg, Blair County, Pennsylvania, R. F. D. No. 2. (Plate 73, shows an interesting group at the time of their wedding.)

GROUP AT WEDDING OF MARGARET ACKER[8] GREASER [1296] AND GEORGE W. GARNER FEBRUARY 24, 1904, CLOVER CREEK, PA.

Children (4), surname Garner:

[2390] Walter G.[7], *b* December 3, 1904.
[2391] Daniel G.[7], *b* March 27, 1906.
[2392] Rose Anna[7], *b* February 16, 1908.
[2393] John Mathew[7], *b* January 19, 1910.

[1297] **MINNIE GRACE[6] GREASER,** daughter of [330] Daniel F.[5] and Sarah (Acker) Greaser, was born May 7, 1883. October 10, 1903, she married *Jacob Grimes.* Address, Saxton, Bedford County, Pennsylvania.

Children (3), surname Grimes:

[2396] Marie[7], *b* July 10, 1903.
[2397] Gladys[7], *b* March, 1905.
[2398] George[7], *b* October 1907.

[1298] **HENRY HARRISON[6] GREASER,** son of [330] Daniel F.[5] and Sarah (Acker) Greaser, was born May 2, 1888. November 23, 1909, at Beaver, Pennsylvania, he married *Violet Waters*, born April, 1890. Address, Beaver Falls, Pennsylvania. (No children reported.)

[1301] **LYDIA[6] GREASER,** daughter of [331] Jacob Fouse[5] and Ellen B. (Bossler) Greaser, was born September 8, 1885. April 27, 1904, she married *Homer Umbower Loose*, born November 5, 1882. Address, Martinsburg, Blair County, Pennsylvania.

Children (3), surname Loose:

[2400] Fred, *b* July 2, 1905; *d* September 18, 1905.
[2401] Jesse, *b* May 31, 1907; *d* September 26, 1907.
[2402] Madaline, *b* January 18, 1909; *d* July 22, 1909.

[1307] **CARRIE[6] GREASER,** daughter of [332] Paul G.[5] and Laura (Mehrvine) Greaser, was born January 31, 1889. September 18, 1907, she married *George Rhodes*, born February 8, 1884. Address, Martinsburg, Blair County, Pennsylvania, R. R. No. 2.

One son, surname Rhodes:

[2404] Paul[7], *b* January 25, 1908.

[1330] **BESSIE RUBEL[6] BOERNER**, daughter of [337] Mary Catharine[5] (Boyd) Boerner and Harry C. Boerner, was born October 25, 1889. June 22, 1911, she married *Alfred Rader*. Address, Pearl City, Illinois. (No issue reported.)

[1336] **EDGAR HARRY[6] LININGER**, son of [339] Mary Alice[5] (Fouse) Lininger and Samuel Grubb Lininger, was born March 19, 1883; May 18, 1910, married *Margaretta Peightel*, daughter of *W. M.* and *Martha (Hamer) Peightel.* Address, Huntingdon, Huntingdon County, Pennsylvania.

[1342] **SAMUEL HERMAN[6] FOUSE**, son of [344] Wm. Simonton[5] and Martha J. (Schell) Fouse, was born February 16, 1878; married *Harriet Cunningham*; address, Wireton, Allegheny County, Pennsylvania.

Children (2):

[2409] Frederick Qwingh[7], *b* April 16, 1901.
[2410] Grace Catharine[7], *b* January 18, 1903.

[1343] **MARY JANE[6] FOUSE**, daughter of [344] Wm. Simonton[5] and Martha J. (Schell) Fouse, was born October 5, 1882. January 10, 1905, she married *Anthony Howard Russell*, born December 19, 1884; son of *Jacob Bowser* [370] and *Catharine (Shultz) Russell.*[a] Mr. Russell is a farmer; Republican; member Reformed Church; and his address is Entriken, Huntingdon County, Pennsylvania.

Children (2), surname Russell:

[2412] Helen Catharine[7], *b* October 19, 1905.
[2413] Martha Elma[7], *b* August 15, 1907.

[1344] **KETURAH PEARL[6] FOUSE**, daughter of [344] Wm. Simonton[5] and Martha J. (Schell) Fouse, was born November 16, 1887. She married *John H. Ketterman.* Address, Entriken, Huntingdon County, Pennsylvania.

Children (3), surname Ketterman:

[2415] Ruth Gladys[7], *b* January 11, 1907.
[2416] John William[7], *b* September 25, 1908.
[2417] Anna May[7], *b* August 2, 1910.

[a] See p. 261, [No. 1405].

[1347] **MARY BERTHA[6] GREASER,** daughter of [345] Nancy Simonton[5] (Fouse) Greaser and John C. Greaser, was born November 16, 1879, on Clover Creek, Blair County, Pennsylvania. June 15, 1898, she married *Frank Wilmer Shultz,* at Marklesburg, Huntingdon County, Pennsylvania. He was born in Huntingdon County, Pennsylvania on February 14, 1879. They reside at 614 Thompson Street, Pittsburgh, Pennsylvania.

Children (3), surname Shultz:

[2419] Carrie Olive[7], *b* October 18, 1899, at Marklesburg, Pennsylvania.
[2420] Florence May[7], *b* December 15, 1902, at Pittsburgh, Pennsylvania.
[2421] Anna Eva[7], *b* March 9, 1906, at Pittsburgh, Pennsylvania.

[1348] **GEORGE F.[6] GREASER,** son of [345] Nancy Simonton[5] (Fouse) Greaser and John C. Greaser, was born January 15, 1881. November 17, 1903, in Pittsburgh, Pennsylvania, he married *Edna Viola McKean,* daughter of Arthur McKean and she was born in Pittsburgh, Pennsylvania, September 27, 1883. Mr. and Mrs. Greaser moved April, 1912, to a farm near Shellsburg, Iowa.

Children (5):

[2423] Thelma Georgia[7], *b* September 5, 1904, at Pittsburgh, Pennsylvania.
[2424] Fern Dorothy[7], *b* February 5, 1906, at Pitcairn, Pennsylvania.
[2425] Elmer Ellsworth[7], *b* December 14, 1907, at Pitcairn, Pennsylvania.
[2426] George[7], *b* April 13, 1909, at Pitcairn, Pennsylvania.
[2427] Mary Melrose[7], *b* February 5, 1911, at Pitcairn, Pennsylvania.

[1349] **MARTHA JANE[6] GREASER,** daughter of [345] Nancy Simonton[5] (Fouse) Greaser and John C. Greaser, was born May 13, 1882. July 15, 1903, she married *George Edgar King* at Vinton, Benton County, Iowa—he was born at Shellsburg, Iowa, October 10, 1882. Mr. and Mrs. King live on their own farm near Shellsburg, Benton County, Iowa, where all their children were born.

Children (6), surname King:

[2430] Edgar Ray[7], *b* February 3, 1904.
[2431] Edith Marie[7], *b* April 12, 1905.
[2432] Clara Ethel[7], *b* March 31, 1906.
[2433] Della Esto[7], *b* December 11, 1908.
[2434] Daniel Clair[7], *b* April 15, 1911.
[2435] Harold Myron[7], *b* August 14, 1912.

[1350] **ELLA[6] GREASER,** daughter of [345] Nancy Simonton[5] (Fouse) Greaser and John C. Greaser, was born December 4, 1885. May 30, 1907, she married *Clifford I. Shomler*, born at Shellsburg, Iowa, February 14, 1880. Mr. and Mrs. Shomler live at Rockwell City, Calhoun County, Iowa, where the former is in business.

Children (3), surname Shomler:

[2437] Darle Cleone[7], *b* January 21, 1908, at Livermore, Humboldt County, Iowa.
[2438] Leta Fern[7], *b* August 11, 1909, at Rockwell City, Iowa.
[2439] Mary Elizabeth[7], *b* October 28, 1911, at Rockwell City, Iowa.

[1353] **AGNES RUTH[6] GREASER,** daughter of [345] Nancy Simonton[5] (Fouse) Greaser and John C. Greaser, was born June 10, 1890. October 6, 1907, she married *Joseph Arthur Budd*, at Shellsburg, Iowa, where he was born July 29, 1886. Mr. and Mrs. Budd live on a farm near Shellsburg, Benton County, Iowa.

Children (3), surname Budd:

[2441] Dortha Mayo[7], *b* March 20, 1908.
[2442] Wilda Joseph Lancaster[7], *b* November 10, 1910.
[2443] Annie[7], *b* November 29, 1912.

[1356] **IRA[6] STONE,** son of [347] Sarah Ann[5] (Fouse) Stone and James Stone, was born January 31, 1872. October 6, 1892, he married *Ida Catharine McCall*, who was born June 29, 1874. Address, Entriken, Huntingdon County, Pennsylvania.

Children (5):

[2446] Elva Catharine[7], *b* December 5, 1894; *d* April 22, 1906.
[2447] Harvey Glen[7], *b* October 22, 1897.
[2448] Sarah Grace[7], *b* July 5, 1903.
[2449] Mary Elizabeth[7], *b* June 3, 1905.
[2450] James Orville[7], *b* February 21, 1908.

[1357] **ELIZABETH A.[6] STONE,** daughter of [347] Sarah Ann[5] (Fouse) Stone and James Stone, was born May 31, 1874. March 3, 1892, she married *Robert E Galbraith*, who was born January 28, 1870. Address, Waynesboro, Pennsylvania.

Children (8), surname Galbraith:

[2452] Mae B.[7], *b* February 16, 1893.
[2453] Viola[7], *b* February 27, 1895.
[2454] Walter[7], *b* June 21, 1896.
[2455] Edna[7], *b* December 30, 1897.
[2456] John[7], *b* September 17, 1900.
[2457] Elmer[7], *b* March 27, 1902.
[2458] Mary[7], *b* June 15, 1904.
[2459] Sarah[7], *b* May 13, 1907.

[1358] **WILLIAM[6] STONE,** son of [347] Sarah Ann[5] (Fouse) Stone and James Stone, was born August, 1877. He married *Anna May Kyle* about 1900. Mr. Stone died ——.

One daughter:

[2461] Ethel Viola[7], *b* August 6, 1902.

[1359] **MARGARET F.[6] STONE,** daughter of [347] Sarah Ann[5] (Fouse) Stone and James Stone, was born January 7, 1880. May 2, 1900, she married *I. Warren Louder*, born August 8, 1876. Address, Seanor, Somerset County, Pennsylvania.

Children (3), surname Louder:

[2463-4] Joseph H.[7] and Jean G.[7], twins, *b* December 6, 1901.
[2465] Ruth A. B.[7], *b* March 23, 1910.

[1360] **M. ELLA[6] STONE,** daughter of [347] Sarah Ann[5] (Fouse) Stone and James Stone, was born January 31, 1882. August 29, 1902, she married *J. William Louder*, born September 8, 1879. Address, Seanor, Pennsylvania.

Children (2), surname Louder:

[2467] Warren I.[7], *b* January 30, 1903.
[2468] Dean S.[7], *b* May 14, 1906.

[1361] **LAURA CATHARINE[6] STONE,** daughter of [347] Sarah Ann[5] (Fouse) Stone and James Stone, was born August 26, 1883. September 13, 1900, she married *John Wintrode Shontz*, born November 17, 1880. Address, Yeagertown, Mifflin County, Pennsylvania.

Children (2), surname Shontz:

[2470] Dessie Margaret[7], *b* November 25, 1900; *d* May 1, 1903.
[2471] Ralph Milton[7], *b* November 22, 1903.

[1363] **HARRY F.[6] FOUSE,** son of [349] Joseph[5] and Anna B. (Fisher) Fouse, was born October 16, 1875. October 10, 1905, he married *Amelia Baker* of Silver Springs, Lancaster County, Pennsylvania, born March 3, 1880.

Children (2):

[2473] Jennie May Baker[7], *b* April 1, 1906.
[2474] Joseph Roy Baker[7], *b* October 20, 1907.

[1364] **MARY M.[6] FOUSE,** daughter of [349] Joseph[5] and Anna B. (Fisher) Fouse, was born March 14, 1877. December 9, 1897, she married *William Lichty*, of East Petersburg, Pennsylvania, born May 25, 1873.

Children (3), surname Lichty:

[2476] Charles F.[7], *b* December 31, 1899.
[2477] Walter F.[7], *b* April 19, 1904.
[2478] Herbert F.[7], *b* May 1, 1908.

[1370] **ANNA GRACE[6] FOUSE,** daughter of [350] Henry Summers[5] and Emma May (Grove) Fouse, was born August 10, 1881. March 22, 1905, she married *Thomas J. Stone.* Address, Alexandria, Huntingdon County, Pennsylvania.

Children (2), surname Stone:

[2480] Mary Catharine[7], *b* February 9, 1907.
[2481] Helen Elizabeth[7], *b* May 1, 1908.

[1374] **BENJAMIN[6] FOUSE,** son of [352] Dewalt[5] and Eliza Jane (Lininger) Fouse, was born March 29, 1884. September 28, 1905, he married *Jennie Elizabeth Wilson,* who was born September 11, 1884. No issue reported. Address, Juniata, Pennsylvania.

[1382] **MARY VIOLA[6] RUDY,** daughter of [357] Margaret[5] (Fouse) Rudy and Samuel Gilliland Rudy, was born in Huntingdon, Pennsylvania, May 2, 1887. August 28, 1911, she married *Lewis George Snell,* born October 12, 1882; son of *John Addison* and *Louise (Mochel) Snell.* Residence, Niagara Falls, New York.

One daughter, surname Snell:

[2484] Margaret Louise⁷, *b* September 10, 1913.

[1383] **ALVIN WALTER⁶ RUDY,** son of [357] Margaret⁶ (Fouse) Rudy and Samuel Gilliland Rudy, was born in Huntingdon, Pennsylvania, January 1, 1890; September 15, 1908, he married *Gretta Milligan,* born August 20, 1880. Address, Huntingdon, Pennsylvania.

One son:

[2486] William Henry⁷, *b* February 2, 1909.

[1404] **JOHN NEVIN⁶ FOUSE,** son of [362] Jacob Summers⁶ and Martha Ellen (Donnelson) Fouse, was born October 31, 1880. September, 1905, he married *Agnes Anmen,* born 1883; daughter of *Jacob* and *Agnes Burket Anmen,* of Aitch, Huntingdon County, Pennsylvania. Mr. Fouse has conducted the "Marklesburg Normal and Select School" for some years. Address, James Creek, Huntingdon County, Pennsylvania.

Children (3):

[2490] Dorothy⁷, *b* June 22, 1906.
[2491] Thelma⁷, *b* April 6, 1908.
[2492] Mirium⁷, *b* —— 1910.

[1405] **JACOB RUPLEY⁶ FOUSE,** son of [362] Jacob Summers⁶ and Martha Ellen (Donnelson) Fouse, was born May 27, 1882. June, 1905, he married *Margaret Ada Snare,* born 1886; daughter of *William* and *Margaret Snare.* Address, James Creek, Huntingdon County, Pennsylvania.

[2494] Margaret Blanche⁷, *b* May 15, 1906.
[2495] Lina Ellen⁷, *b* January 18, 1908.
[2496] Kenneth R.⁷, *b* February 15, 1910.
[2497] ————.

[1406] **THEOBALD KIEFFER⁶ FOUSE,** son of [362] Jacob Summers⁶ and Martha Ellen (Donnelson) Fouse, was born October 2, 1884; October, 1907, he married *Elsie M. Shultz,* born 1885; daughter of *Luther* and *Dessa Shultz.* Address, James Creek, Huntingdon County, Pennsylvania.

One son:

[2499] Allen[7], *b* 1908.

[1407] **MARGARET REBECCA[6] FOUSE,** daughter of [362] Jacob Summers[5] and Martha Ellen (Donnelson) Fouse, was born October 15, 1886. June 14, 1911, at West 23d Street, New York City, she married *James Monroe Allison*, of Donation, Pennsylvania.

[1410] **ELMER ELLSWORTH[6] SHULTZ,** son of [363] Dewalt Fouse[5] and Margaret (Greaser) Fouse, was born June 14, 1874, at Marklesburg, Huntingdon County, Pennsylvania. He attended the "Fouse School" seven terms, Ursinus Academy one term; worked on a farm until 1898; clerked in his father's store and in the James Creek postoffice ten years in all; worked two years in the Westinghouse Electrical and Manufacturing Company.

Mr. Shultz is a township committeeman; secretary Board of Supervisors, also field and corresponding secretary Y. M. C. A., both since 1911; secretary Woodcock Valley Telephone Company since 1905; deacon and secretary of Reformed Church since 1903; superintendent Sunday school 1910, and assistant superintendent since 1914; president District Sunday School Association 1913. He was appointed postmaster at Entriken, Huntingdon County, Pennsylvania, July 26, 1913, succeeding his late father. He is unmarried, and has shown decided interest and activity in gathering facts in his locality for this publication.

[1411] **ANTHONY HARVEY[6] SHULTZ,** son of [363] Dewalt Fouse[6] and Margaret (Greaser) Shultz, was born March 2, 1876. April 29, 1903, he married *Anna Catharine Frank*, born in Huntingdon County, Pennsylvania, May 25, 1877; daughter of *Andrew Baer* and *Mary* (*Householder*) *Frank*. Mr. Shultz is assistant cashier Turtle Creek Savings and Trust Company. Address, Turtle Creek, Allegheny County, Pennsylvania, Box 595. (No children.)

[1413] **CLARENCE GREASER[6] SHULTZ,** son of [363] Dewalt Fouse[6] and Margaret (Greaser) Shultz, was born December 5, 1879; educated in the common schools, in which he taught one year; clerk in Railway Mail Service for over 12 years; unmarried; address, Huntingdon, Pennsylvania.

[1414] **GEORGE GREASER**[6] **SHULTZ**, son of [363] Dewalt Fouse[5] and Margaret (Greaser) Shultz, was born May 23, 1881; educated in the common schools; was in the grocery business for several years, and recently entered the selling of real estate and insurance at Pitcairn, Pennsylvania. July 30, 1913, he married *Jennie Jackson Johnson*, born April 2, 1886; daughter of *William Hunter* and *Susan (Foster) Johnson*.

[1415] **HENRY FRANKLIN**[6] **SHULTZ**, son of [363] Dewalt Fouse[5] and Margaret (Greaser) Shultz, was born August 29, 1883; educated in the common schools; bank clerk. Mr. Shultz married *Leona Verona Myers*. Address, Turtle Creek, Pennsylvania, Box 595.

[1419] **LAURA**[6] **LYNN**, daughter of [364] Nancy[5] (Shultz) Lynn and John Russell Lynn, was born September 10, 1870. December 30, 1888, she married *Samuel Calvin Weller*, born February 9, 1866; son of *Edward David* and *Catharine (Prough) Weller*. Mr. Weller is a farmer, and lives near Entriken, Huntingdon County, Pennsylvania.

Children (7), surname Weller:

[2500] Minnie Catharine[7], *b* August 15, 1890.
[2501] John Howard[7], *b* August 13, 1894.
[2502] Nancy Margaret[7], *b* June 24, 1897.
[2503] James Allen[7], *b* June 9, 1899.
[2504] Laura Dorothy[7], *b* January 15, 1907.
[2505] Frances Rhoda[7], *b* February 3, 1911.
[2506] Florence Lynn[7], *b* February 3, 1911.

[1420] **CATHARINE**[6] **LYNN**, daughter of [364] Nancy[5] (Shultz) Lynn and John Russell Lynn, was born May 22, 1872. January 18, 1891, she married *Dewalt Robert Shultz*, born March 28, 1858; son of *Martin* and *Martha (Heffner) Shultz*. Mr. Shultz is a laborer; member Reformed Church; and his address is Williamsburg, Blair County, Pennsylvania.

Children (4), surname Shultz:

[2509] Nancy Beatrice[7], *b* January 14, 1892.
[2510] Frederick Warren[7], *b* February 14, 1894.
[2511] Ralph Herbert[7], *b* October 1, 1901.
[2512] Cloyd Robert[7], *b* February 28, 1905.

[1422] **CORA ELIZABETH[6] LYNN,** daughter of [364] Nancy[6] (Shultz) Lynn and John Russell Lynn, was born March 24, 1876. She married *George Washington Shontz*, born May 8, 1870; son of *George* and *Margaret (Clapper) Shontz.* Address, 222 Camp Avenue, Braddock, Pennsylvania.

Children (6), surname Shontz:

[2515] Nellie Blanch[7], *b* April 27, 1893.
[2516] Catharine Myers[7], *b* January 27, 1895.
[2517] Grace Nora[7], *b* April 2, 1898.
[2518] Charles Roy[7], *b* April 15, 1900.
[2519] John H.[7], *b* February 26, 1902.
[2520] George Arthur[7], *b* February 1, 1907.

[1423] **JOHN SHULTZ[6] LYNN,** son of [364] Nancy[6] (Shultz) Lynn and John Russell Lynn, was born March 14, 1880. January 1, 1908, he married *Anna Mary Snare*, born January 2, 1888; daughter of *Frank* and *Jane (Beaver) Snare* of Aitch, Pennsylvania. Farmer—address, Entriken, Pennsylvania.

Two children:

[2522] William Harold[7], *b* December 21, 1908.
[2523] Hazel Marie[7], *b* March 13, 1913.

[1424] **NANCY JANE[6] LYNN,** daughter of [364] Nancy[6] (Shultz) Lynn and John Russell Lynn, was born February 5, 1887. February 1, 1911, she married *William H. Ford*, born September 7, 1883; son of *Robert* and *Mary Ford.*

One daughter, surname Ford:

[2525] Mary Beulah[7], *b* August 21, 1911.

[1428] **FRANCES[6] LYNN,** daughter of [365] Elizabeth[6] (Shultz) Lynn and Andrew Russell Lynn, was born February 17, 1874. November 16, 1908, she married *Samuel Albert Weaver*, born January 8, 1874; son of *George* and *Lydia Weaver.* Mr. Weaver is a farmer; address, Fairfield, Ohio.

Children (2), surname Weaver:

[2527] Elizabeth May[7], *b* May 7, 1912.
[2528] Lynn Albert[7], *b* December 24, 1913.

[1429] **DEWALT SHULTZ**[6] **LYNN,** son of [365] Elizabeth[5] (Shultz) Lynn and Andrew Russell Lynn, was born October 14, 1876. June 18, 1906, he married *Clara Tobias*, daughter of *Martin* and *Mary Tobias*. Mr. Lynn is township superintendent of schools; address, "Ellerton, Ohio."[a]

One son:

[2530] Harry Leroy[7], *b* 1909.

[1431] **ANTHONY CLAUDE**[6] **LYNN,** son of [365] Elizabeth[5] (Shultz) Lynn and Andrew Russell Lynn, was born May 8, 1881. June 30, 1904, he married *Jessie Huffman*, daughter of *Silas* and *Martha Jane* (*Shank*) *Huffman*. Mr. Huffman is an engineer on the Pennsylvania Railroad—address, Xenia, Ohio.

Children (2), surname Huffman:

[2532] Roger Paul[7], *b* March 20, 1905.
[2533] Raymond Walter[7], *b* March 17, 1909.

[1432] **WILLIAM HENRY**[6] **LYNN,** son of [365] Elizabeth[5] (Shultz) Lynn and Andrew Russell Lynn, was born January 25, 1886; member Reformed Church; laborer; unmarried; address Fairfield, Ohio.

[1433] **ANDREW RUSSELL**[6] **LYNN, JR.,** son of [365] Elizabeth[5] (Shultz) Lynn and Andrew Russell Lynn, was born July 10, 1890; married *Irene Bell*, born 1890; fireman on Pennsylvania Railroad; address, Xenia, Ohio.

One son:

[2535] Robert Bell[7], *b* 1913.

[1436] **CHESTER ARTHUR**[6] **SHULTZ,** son of [366] David Fouse[5] and Sarah Catharine (Brumbaugh)[b] Shultz, was born June 23, 1878. June 21, 1901, he married *Flora May Weaver*, born October 15, 1878; daughter of *Caleb* and *Anna Weaver*. Address, Saxton, Bedford County, Pennsylvania. (No children.)

[1437] **IDA BERTHA**[6] **SHULTZ,** daughter of [366] David Fouse[5] and Sarah Catharine (Brumbaugh) Shultz, was born June 12, 1880. June 30,

[a] No such office, and no reply to letters.
[b] No. [E287] p. 565, *Brumbach Families*.

1902, she married *Frank Homer Cypher*, born April 27, 1879. Address, 912 Beckford Street, New Castle, Lawrence County, Pennsylvania.

One son, surname Cypher:

[2537] Cloyd M.[7], *b* November 19, 1902.

[1439] **MARY ELVA[6] SHULTZ,** daughter of [366] David Fouse[6] and Sarah Catharine (Brumbaugh) Shultz, was born June 6, 1884. June 17, 1908, she married *Milton Sangree Isenberg*, born February 11, 1884; son of *William Huyett* and *Ester* (*Smith*) *Isenberg*. Address, 1118 19th Street, Altoona, Pennsylvania.

Children (2), *surname Isenberg:*

[2539] Milton Shultz[7], *b* September 18, 1909; *d. y.*
[2540] Ester Kathryn[7], *b* August 10, 1912.

[1441] **LAURA DESSIE[6] SHULTZ,** daughter of [366] David Fouse[5] and Sarah Catharine (Brumbaugh) Shultz, was born May 21, 1888. November 25, 1909, she married *John Nevin Isenberg*, brother of Milton Sangree Isenberg [1439]; address 1118 19th Street, Altoona, Pennsylvania.

One son, surname Isenberg:

[2542] Clyde Milton[7], *b* September 20, 1910.

[1454] **NANNIE SHULTZ[6] BEAVER,** daughter of [368] Mary Ann[5] (Shultz) Beaver and John Shirley Beaver, was born April 11, 1886. May 1, 1907, she married *Harry Clayton Speck*, born October 3, 1872; son of *Felix* and *Ann* (*Huff*) *Speck*. Mr. Speck is a barber at Entriken, Huntingdon County, Pennsylvania.

One daughter, surname Speck:

[2545] Mildred Almeda[7], *b* December 18, 1907.

[1455] **CATHERINE ELIZABETH[6] BEAVER,** daughter of [368] Mary Ann[5] (Shultz) Beaver and John Shirley Beaver, was born December 20, 1887. She married *Harry Cleveland Lorenz*, son of *Harman* and *Mary* (*Haines*) *Lorenz*. Mr. Lorenz is an electrician; address, 727 Franklin Street, Wilkinsburg, Allegheny County, Pennsylvania.

One daughter, surname Lorenz:

[2547] Mary Alberta[7], *b* July 7, 1910.

[1463] **DELILAH[6] RUSSELL,** daughter of [370] Catharine[5] (Shultz) Russell and Jacob Bowser Russell, was born February 7, 1881. May 30, 1901, she married *John Carmack*, born June 20, 1878; son of *William* and *Maria (Kyler) Carmack*. Mr. Carmack is an engineer; he and his wife are members Reformed Church; and they live at 423 Camp Avenue, Braddock, Pennsylvania.

One son, surname Carmack:

[2550] Harry Hartman[7], *b* June 15, 1902.

[1464] **ELIZABETH[6] RUSSELL,** daughter of [370] Catharine[5] (Shultz) Russell and Jacob Bowser Russell, was born June 6, 1883. September 24, 1903, she married *John Phillips*, born February 24, 1878; son of *James* and *Martha (Britton) Phillips*. Mr. Phillips was educated in the common school of Hopewell Township, Huntingdon County, Pennsylvania; Republican; member Reformed Church; laborer, address, Saxton, Bedford County, Pennsylvania.

Children (5), surname Phillips:

[2552] James H.[7], *b* July 29, 1904.
[2553] D. Catharine[7], *b* January 6, 1905.
[2554] Charles I.[7], *b* February 19, 1906.
[2555] Emma Grace[7], *b* December 17, 1907.
[2556] Martha Helen[7], *b* November 15, 1913.

[1465] **ANTHONY HOWARD[6] RUSSELL,** son of [370] Catharine[5] (Shultz) Russell and Jacob Bowser Russell, was born December 19, 1884. January 10, 1905, he married *Mary Jane Fouse* [1343], born October 5, 1882; daughter *William Simonton* and *Martha Jane (Schell) Fouse* [344]. There are two children—see page 250. Address, Saxton, Pennsylvania.

[1467] **LAURA HELEN[6] RUSSELL,** daughter of [370] Catharine[5] [Shultz] Russell and Jacob Bowser Russell, was born February 11, 1888. September 16, 1908, she married *Henry Esco Walker*, born November 1, 1882; son of *David* and *Leah (Dell) Walker*. Mr. Walker was educated at the Latta Grove school, Cass Township, Huntingdon County, Pennsylvania; member Reformed Church; carpenter; address, Smithfield Street, Huntingdon, Pennsylvania.

Children (2), surname Walker:

[2560] Closter Harold[7], *b* April 28, 1909.
[2561] Fred Russell[7], *b* December 24, 1913.

[1475] **MARGARET[6] SHULTZ,** daughter of [371] William Henry[5] and Margaret (Summers) Shultz, was born October 26, 1887. November 20, 1903, she married *Jesse Rodgers,* born July 17, 1880; son of *William Ashcombe* and *Mary (Fleck) Rodgers*; address, Aitch, Huntingdon County, Pennsylvania.

One son, surname Rodgers:

[2565] Lee[7], *b* April 1904.

[1483] **LENA CATHARINE[6] CRISWELL,** daughter of [374] Margaret[5] (Shultz) Criswell and Albert Criswell, was born April 25, 1897; May 28, 1892, married *George W. Hess,* son of *Samuel* and *Martha (Inery) Hess.* Mr. Hess is a carpenter; member Reformed Church; address, Entriken, Huntingdon County, Pennsylvania.

[1534] **CLARA MAY[6] SUMMERS,** daughter of [384] Rachel[5] (Grove) Summers and Blair S. Summers, was born February 10, 1890. Clara May was left an orphan when she was but 15 years of age, her father having died when she was but 7 months old. After the death of the father, the mother was obliged to make a living for herself and daughter. The grandparents then took Clara May to rear and to educate. They lived in the village of Marklesburg, Huntingdon County, Pennsylvania, where she received a public school education. Her grandfather, H. H. Summers, being an invalid, she is of great benefit to them and is rewarding them for the kindness they showed to her in her infancy. Her address is James Creek, Pennsylvania.

[1589] **ANNIE MARY[6] FOUSE,** daughter of [409] Alfred S.[5] and Margaret (Hood) Fouse, was born November 18, 1882. January 10, 1901, she married *Galbraith Lang,* born October 30, 1876. Address, Huntingdon, Pennsylvania.

Children (5), surname Lang:

[2570] Harry Raymond[7], *b* July 10, 1902.
[2571] Emma Edith[7], *b* July 2, 1904.

[2572] Margaret Lillian[7], *b* July 31, 1906; *d* December 4, 1910.
[2573] Carl Galbraith[7], *b* May 6, 1908.
[2574] Gertrude Susan[7], *b* June 21, 1910.

[1590] **EMMA SUSAN[6] FOUSE**, daughter of [409] Alfred S.[5] and Margaret (Hood) Fouse, was born November 14, 1885. January 20, 1904, she married *Frederick Householder*, born 1881. Address, McConnellstown, Huntingdon County, Pennsylvania.

One son, surname Householder:

[2576] Earl Frederick[7], *b* June 26, 1906.

[1603] **ROSELDA LORETTA[6] HOFFA**, daughter of [413] Susan[5] (Nicodemus) Hoffa and Daniel Hoffa, was born August 9, 1872. May 10, 1892, she married *Frank E. Wells*. Address, Stonewall, Canada.

Children (10), surname Wells:

[2581] Arthur Elois[7], *b* April 12, 1893.
[2582] Blanche Irene[7], *b* January 20, 1896.
[2583] Harlan Newton[7], *b* October 17, 1898.
[2584] Wayne Ellie[7] *b* April 20, 1900.
[2585] Pearl Elizabeth[7], *b* August 6, 1901.
[2586] Ralph Emerson[7], *b* December 23, 1902.
[2587] Beulah Loretta[7], *b* September 8, 1904.
[2588] Gilbert Daniel[7], *b* September 16, 1906.
[2589] ———— *b* June 18, 1909.
[2590] Neva Gladys[7], *b* April 21, 1912.

[1604] **CALVIN O.[6] HOFFA**, son of [413] Susan[5] (Nicodemus) Hoffa and Daniel Hoffa, was born September 13, 1873. December 11, 1895, he married *Lena Croson*, born August 30, 1876. Address, Lisbon, North Dakota.

Children (8):

[2592] Neva May[7], *b* November 15, 1896; *d* March, 1897.
[2593] Earl Daniel[7], *b* April 8, 1898.
[2594] Merle Thomas[7], *b* April 8, 1898.
[2595] Lucius[7], *b* December 4, 1899.
[2596] Ray Everett[7], *b* April 19, 1901; *d* April, 1903.

[2597] Ruth Ethel[7], *b* September 26, 1902; *d* May, 1903.
[2598] Frank Lester[7], *b* ——, 1906.
[2599] Pearl Edith[7], *b* January, 1908.

[1605] **VERNIA IRENE[6] HOFFA,** daughter of [413] Susan[5] (Nicodemus) Hoffa and Daniel Hoffa, was born June 26, 1875. February 26, 1896, she married *August Frederick Telkamp.* Address, Brookings, South Dakota.

Children (9), surname Telkamp:

[2601] Emmet William[7], *b* April 27, 1897.
[2602] Edna Martha[7], *b* June 28, 1898.
[2603] Alida[7], *b* January 19, 1900; *d* February 11, 1906.
[2604] Lizzie Mary[7], *b* April 26, 1901.
[2605] Irene Augusta[7], *b* June 20, 1902.
[2606] Frederick Basil[7], *b* May 13, 1904.
[2607] Harold Isaac[7], *b* December 1, 1905.
[2608] Roy Bertin[7], *b* January 27, 1909.
[2609] Vida Loretta[7], *b* April 24, 1912.

[1608] **ELMER C.[6] HOFFA,** son of [413] Susan[5] (Nicodemus) Hoffa and Daniel Hoffa, was born June 5, 1880. December 20, 1906, he married *Agnes Baile,* born March 19, 1885. Address, Steamboat Rock, Hardin County, Iowa.

One daughter:

[2611] Hattie Susan[7], *b* September 20, 1910.

[1609] **CHARLES N.[6] HOFFA,** son of [413] Susan[5] (Nicodemus) Hoffa and Daniel Hoffa, was born December 13, 1882. June 29, 1905, he married *Sadie Vesta Dean,* born August 7, 1883.

Children (3):

[2613] Harold Francis[7], *b* July 20, 1906.
[2614] Lucile Noreni[7], *b* June 29, 1908.
[2615] Eldon[7], *b* November 30, 1910.

[1610] **PORTER C.[6] HOFFA,** son of Susan (Nicodemus) Hoffa and Daniel Hoffa, was born February 19, 1885. July 14, 1909, he married

Edith A. Smith, born June 21, 1884. Address, Sanborn, Iowa. (No issue reported.)

[1617] **LILLIE MAY[6] MARR**, daughter of [414] Mary Elizabeth[5] (Nicodemus) Marr and August Marr, was born May 29, 1877. January 28, 1896, she married *Richard H. Bushgens*, born September 26, 1872; occupation, cigar maker; address, Iola, Kansas.

Children (3), surname Bushgens:

[2618] Irene Lillian[7], *b* July 21, 1897.
[2619] Harold Marr[7], *b* January 1, 1900.
[2620] Cayle Albert[7], *b* June 25, 1903.

[1618] **ROSE ELVA[6] MARR**, daughter of [414] Mary Elizabeth[5] (Nicodemus) Marr and August Marr, was born December 13, 1878; clerk, unmarried; address, Iola, Kansas.

[1619] **GEORGE JACOB[6] MARR**, son of [414] Mary Elizabeth[5] (Nicodemus) Marr and August Marr, was born December 8, 1880. November 12, 1903, he married *Mary E. Cooper*, born May 24, 1884. Mr. Marr is a manager of a bakery; address, Iola, Kansas. (No issue reported.)

[1620] **ANNA AMELIA[6] MARR**, daughter of [414] Mary Elizabeth[5] (Nicodemus) Marr and August Marr, was born January 7, 1883. June 5, 1904, she married *Walter A. Decker*, born August 2, 1885; occupation foreman of a pipe line; address, Iola, Kansas. (No issue reported.)

[1621] **GRACE AUGUSTA[6] MARR**, daughter of [414] Mary Elizabeth[5] (Nicodemus) Marr and August Marr, was born November 30, 1887; clerk; unmarried; address, Iola, Kansas.

[1622] **EDITH FERN[6] MARR**, daughter of [414] Mary Elizabeth[5] (Nicodemus) Marr and August Marr, was born April 16, 1892; unmarried; stenographer; address, Iola, Kansas.

[1623] **BERNICE ELRENE[6] MARR**, daughter of [414] Mary Elizabeth[5] (Nicodemus) Marr and August Marr, was born September 28, 1894; high school student; address, Iola, Kansas.

[1627] **CHARLES WILLIAM**[6] **SCHADT,** son of [415] Sarah[5] (Nicodemus) Schadt and Philip Schadt, was born April 7, 1878. January 30, 1901, he married *Christina* ————, born October 9, 1879.

Children (2):

[2625] Roy Schadt[7], *b* November 6, 1902.
[2626] Helen[7], *b* July 12, 1905.

[1628] **NETTIE ANGELINA**[6] **SCHADT,** daughter of [415] Sarah[5] (Nicodemus) Schadt and Philip Schadt, was born June 2, 1880. April 30, 1899, she married *Adam Meehlhouse,* born July 15, 1870. Address, Hartley, Iowa.

Children (4), surname Meehlhouse:

[2628] Maria Catharine[7], *b* August 12, 1901.
[2629] Anna Martha[7], *b* April 28, 1903.
[2630] Bernice Christian[7], *b* October 30, 1905.
[2631] Lillian Florence[7], *b* January 19, 1910.

[1629] **PHILIP CALVIN**[6] **SCHADT,** son of [415] Sarah[5] (Nicodemus) Schadt and Philip Schadt, was born December 4, 1881. November 12, 1906, he married *Jennie Bell Illard,* born November 25, 1889. Address, Ocheyedan, Osceola County, Iowa, R. F. D. No. 2.

[1630] **HARRY ROGERS**[6] **SCHADT,** son of [415] Sarah[5] (Nicodemus) Schadt and Philip Schadt, was born February 11, 1883. March 16, 1904, he married *Kitty Myrtle van Hassen.* Mr. Schadt is a butcher; address Wilmot, Minnesota.

One child:

[2633] Silvia Iradell[7], *b* April 16, 1905.

[1657] **JOHN CHESTERFIELD**[6] **RHODES,** son of [424] John F.[5] and Lemma Nenomia (Hazzard) Rhodes, was born November 13, 1891. September 6, 1910, he married *Grace Belle Harding,* of Iowa, born October 3, 1883. Address, Ollie, Iowa.

One son:

[2640] John Ganreve[7], *b* December 4, 1911.

[1660] **IDA FLORENCE[6] BECHTEL,** daughter of [425] Emma Getty[5] (Fouse) Bechtel and Isaac Kagarise Bechtel, was born October 2, 1896; high school student; address, 5218 Friendship Avenue, Pittsburgh, Pennsylvania.

[1661] **MARY ELIZABETH[6] BECHTEL,** daughter of [425] Emma Getty[5] (Fouse) Bechtel and Isaac Kagarise Bechtel, was born March 31, 1898; high school student; address, 5218 Friendship Avenue, Pittsburgh, Pennsylvania.

[1682] **BLANCHE[6] FOUSE,** daughter of [442] David Milton[5] and Nancy (Bechtel) Fouse, was born December 16, 1892. January 30, 1912, she married *Homer Shenefelt*, born September 28, 1880. Address, Drab, Blair County, Pennsylvania.

One son, surname Shenefelt:

[2645] Franklin Fouse[7], *b* May 13, 1912.

[1775] **PEARL BELL[7] MILLER,** daughter of [534] Elmer Ellsworth[6] and Florence Carline (Henry) Miller, was born at Middlebranch, Ohio, July 2, 1884; married *George E. Robinson*, July 3, 1906, at St. Louis, Missouri; son of *William E.* and *Jane A. Robinson.* Mr. Robinson is a commercial traveler; Republican; member United Brethren Church; residence 14,825 Detroit Avenue, Lakewood, Ohio (Plate 52).

One son, surname Robinson:

[2647] Charles Elmer[8], *b* May 5, 1908, at Washington, Pennsylvania.

[1776] **BESSIE IRENE[7] MILLER,** daughter of [534] Elmer Ellsworth[6] and Florence Carline (Henry) Miller, was born at Middlebranch, Ohio, May 7, 1886; graduated from the Canton, Ohio, high school, and from the Ingleside Hospital training school; professional nurse; address, 11,225 Detroit Avenue, Cleveland, Ohio.

[1778] **ANNA BOLANDER[7] MILLER,** daughter of [534] Elmer Ellsworth[6] and Florence Carline (Henry) Miller, was born January 13, 1890, at Canton, Ohio; graduated from Canton high school; has been society editor of daily papers, and, under the name "Jane Ellis," is women's editor of the *Akron* (Ohio) *Press*; is a Daughter of the American Revolution.

Anna Berdella Miller was married January 24, 1914, at Akron, Ohio, to *Mordicai McKinney Welker*, born August 21, 1891, at Howard, Knox County, Ohio; son of *Shipley* and *Mary (Ryan) Welker*. Mr. Welker has lived in Akron since childhood; is a Progressive in politics; member of the First Christian Church at Akron; and is connected with the Firestone Rubber Company, in the collection and credit department. Residence, 968 Jefferson Avenue, Akron, Ohio.

[2200] **DELLA[7] BRUBAKER,** daughter of [975] Mary[6] (Bowser) Brubaker and Daniel Brubaker, was born September 9, 1880. December, 1899, she married *Scott Long*, at Williamsport, Indiana; and he died November 22, 1908.

Children (2), surname Long:

[2650] Valcena[8], *b* November 4, 1902.
[2651] Theressia[8], *b* July 6, 1905.

[2201] **JESSIE[7] BRUBAKER,** daughter of [975] Mary[6] (Bowser) Brubaker and Daniel Brubaker, was born September 17, 1882. She married *John Austin Collins, Jr.*, born March 10, 1884; son of *John Austin* and *Ella (McDonald) Collins*; Mr. Collins is a liveryman; address, 408 East 4th Street, Sedalia, Missouri. (No children.)

[2202] **ANNA[7] BRUBAKER,** daughter of [975] Mary[6] (Bowser) Brubaker and Daniel Brubaker, was born October 10, 1886. She graduated from the Liberty, Illinois, High School; and May 26, 1908, married *Otto Ulrich*, M.D., born at Keokuk, Iowa; son of *Emil Charles Ulrich*, of Germany. Dr. Ulrich served as house physician in the Oconomow Sanitarium (Wisconsin); intern at St. Joseph's Hospital, Keokuk, Iowa; and engaged in private practice in Liberty, Illinois, where he married. He moved to Orrville, Wayne County, Ohio, in 1913, and there practices his profession.

One son, surname Ulrich:

[2654] Myron Wilbur[8], *b* January 31, 1912.

[2203] **NETTIE[7] BRUBAKER,** daughter of [975] Mary[6] (Bowser) Brubaker and Daniel Brubaker, was born September 5, 1889. March, 1907, in Illinois, she married *Louis Boyer*; son of *John* and *Louise Boyer*. Nettie (Brubaker) Boyer died February 13, 1908. (No children.)

Index

Numbers refer to pages, except when preceded by "Pl." (Plate).

A

Abergaust, Clio, 162, 243.
Acker, Adam, 58, 124.
Albert, 162, 243.
Anna May, 219.
Benjamin F., 244.
Beulah May, 244.
Catharine, 23, 36, 39, 50, 64–58–124, 219.
Charles O., 124, 219.
Christian, 9, 27.
Clara Belle, 232.
Clara Ferne, 167.
Daniel, 74, 162.
David Calvin, 140, 232.
Dewalt, 58, 124.
Elizabeth, 76, 167, 168, 124, 219.
Ella Retta, 243.
Elsie Mae, 124, 220.
Emanuel B., 67, 140.
Emma Ellen, 140, 232.
Emma Malinda, 219.
Ernest Erle, 247.
Ethel Ferne, 247.
Frances, 160, 243.
Franklin J., 162, 244.
George Henry, 243.
Harriet M., 124, 220.
Harry Earl, 167.
Harry W., 162, 244.
Harvey Linville, 232.
Harvey Mahlen, 140, 232.
Helen Frances, 232.
Henry, 14, Pl. 15–Jr. Pl. 15–167, 168—Henry and Susanna (Ditch), 58.
Jacob, Pl. 15–58.
John, 34, 37, 58, 65, Pl. 15—John Jr., Pl. 15–162.
John A., 166, 247.
Acker, John Calvin, 232.
John, E., 124.
Katharine May, 232.
Leonard, 23, 39.
Lillie Elizabeth, 140, 232.
Lucinda, 74, 162.
Margaret, 58–124, 220.
Martin L., 75, 166.
Marvin C., 166.
Nancy, 58, 124.
Nettie, 124, 220.
Richard Calvin, 232.
Roy Elmer, 167.
Sarah (Lecrone), 58, 124, 241–76, 167, 168.
Susan (Garner), 140–58, 123–244.
Susanna, 37, 65, Pl. 22.
Verna Alice, 219.
William Preston, 166.
Adams, Elizabeth, 17.
Inez Everetta, 114, 208.
Joshua, 18—Mary, 18—Thomas, 18.
Address, Memorial, Rev. W. C. Robinson, 102.
Aerlenbaugh, 73, 90.
Akins, Arthur, 235.
Bernice Frances, 228.
John William, 131, 227.
William E., 228.
Akron (O.) *Press*, 267.
Allison, Albert, 118, 213.
Blanche Viola, 213.
James Monroe, 176, 256.
Anderson, Dora Emeline, 55, 111.
Robert G. and Elizabeth, 111.
Aniser, Mary (Donaldson), 200.
Anmen, Agnes, 176, 255.
Jacob and Agnes B., 255.
Assn. of Life Ins. Pres's, 102.
Atterberry, Francis Sigel, 112, 203. Lena Leota, 203—Mary Fyanna, 203—Ruby Frances, 203.
Aultman, Elizabeth Tawney, 29.
Gustave and Margaret, 175.
Ida May, 80, 175.
Aungst, Ada, 57, 120.
Aupperley, Margaret, 37, 61.
Aurandt David and Elizabeth (Kemp), 97.
John Dietrich, 16, 40, 63.
Mary Jane, 53, 97, Pl. 48.
Austin, Addie—
David and Eunice, 237.
Viola, 147, 237.
Aykins, Antonius, 163, 245—Marguerite Marie, 245—Robert Kenneth, 245.

B

Baer, Elizabeth (Frank), 95.
Mary Mandilla, 114, 208.
Baile, Agnes, 190, 264.
Bailey, Thomas Fisher, 176.
Bair, Abraham, 55.
Amanda, 69, 147, Pl. 59.
Arthur LeRoy, 216.
Carl C., 114.
Clara E., 57, 120.
Edward F., 114.
Elizabeth, 55, 113, Pl. 53.
Franklin, 55, 113.
Grace Lucile, 216.
Helen Margaret, 216.
Hubert J., 114.
Jacob H., 33, 55.
Jefferson, 55, 114.
John and Mary, 147.
John Franklin, 208.

Bair, Laura B., 119, 214.
Mandilla, 55.
Manodes, 121.
Martha Jane, 113, 207.
Mary (Brouse), 119.
Mary Ann, 55, 113.
Elizabeth, 114.
Mandilla, 114, 208.
Maude Alice, 114.
Otto Lee, 113, 2c8.
Ozias, 57, 121.
Paul, 114.
Priscilla, 55.
Roy L., 114.
Rufus, 121, 216.
Solomon, 55.
William J., 114.
Baker, Amelia, 173, 254.
Baldwin, Alburta Mae, 131, 229.
Banks, Winona Jane, 118, 213.
Barnett, David Barchley, 91, 193.
Barrick, Jane (Geissinger), 84.
Basser, Jacob Stern and Lydia, 168, Pl. 64.
Susan Ellen, 76, 168.
Bauer, Catharine (Greaser), 126.
Johannes, Pl. 15.
Peter, Pl. 15.
Bavaria, 1, 25.
Bear, Ella Jane, 73, 161.
George C. and Amanda, 161.
Beaver, Almeda Gertrude, 179.
Anthony, 5.
Wayne, 82, 182.
Benjamin, 182.
Catherine Elizabeth, 179, 260.
Edna Grace, 183.
Elizabeth (Summers), 79.
Franklin C., 183.
Henry, 1, Pl. 15.
S., 183.
Jane (Snare), 258.
John Nevan, 179.
John and Catharine, 179, 182.
John Shirley, 81, 179.
Mabel G., 179.
Martha J., 183.
Mary Ann, 179—Mary Grace, 69, 144.
Beaver, Nannie Shultz, 179, 260.
Rachel, 182.
Reuben S., 183.
Samuel T., 183.
Bechtel, David S. and Salome, 193.
Ida Florence, 194, 267.
Isaac Kagarise, 93, 193.
Mary Elizabeth, 194, 267.
Nancy, 97, 198.
Peter and Elizabeth, 193.
Susan Snowberger, 145.
Beisel, Henry, 65, 139.
Bell, Irene, 177, 259.
Benjamin, Mary Ann (Steffe), 204.
Berkhart, George, Pl. 15.
Betrick, Lizzie A., 69, 145.
Beyers, Margaret, 89.
Bible Record, Abraham Miller, Pls. 6 and 7; 29.
Biog. Encyc. Juniata Valley, 78, 172.
Bishop, Carrie Catherine, 215.
Catherine Grace, 216.
Dessa Bernice, 215.
Edith Grace, 119.
Elizabeth, 33, 56.
Harley Leroy, 215.
Harvey Clinton, 57, 119.
Henry Adam, 119, 215.
Hubert Carl, 119.
Kermit Jay, 119.
Laura E., 70, 148.
Lawrence Leroy, 119, 215.
Lela Byril, 119.
Leona Charlotte, 215.
Lester Leroy, 215.
Mabel May, 215.
Martin Glenn, 119.
Mildred Catharine, 119.
Ora Hadassa, 119, 215.
Paul Ester, 119—Paul Leroy, 216—Roger Burdette, 216—William Harvey, 216.
Bixler, Ada, 71, 151.
Black, Louisa, 57, 121.
Blackburn, Lavenia, 170.
Moses and Agnes, 170.
Bliss, Herbert and Clara, 207.
Bliss, Laoma E., 113, 207.
Bloomfield, Carl Bryan, 208.
John B., 114, 208.
Roy Benton, 208.
Blystone, Charles Leroy, 246.
Gilbert George, 246.
Jacob, 165, 246.
Marshall Mackline, 246.
Raymond Ross, 246.
Walter Eugene, 246.
Board of Home Missions, 84.
Boerner, Bessie Rubel, 170, 250.
Harry C., 76, 170.
Paul Boyd, 170.
Bond, Virginia (Hoover), 94, 197.
Boone, Martin and Catharine, 205.
Nora, 113, 205.
Booth, Daisy J., 67, 142.
George P., 61, 127.
Bossler, Malinda, 73, 159, 219.
Bowers, Eveline (Johnson) 200.
George, 74, 162.
Peter, 22, 38, Pl. 15.
Susanna, 22, 38, 65.
Bowl, Virginia, 94, 197.
Bowles, Hattie M. (Newcomb), 210.
Bowman, Michael and Laura, 205.
Rebecca, 74, 163.
William, 113, 205.
Bowser, Anna, 146.
Arthur, 235.
Crede, 235.
Daniel, 146—Daniel and Anna, 146.
Delilah (Russell), 179.
Elizabeth, 235.
Elsworth, 235.
Erastus, 146, 235.
Grace, 235.
Ira S., 235.
Jessie, 235.
John, 235.
Lucetta, 146.
Lucinda, 146, 235.
Marion, 235.
Mary, 146, 234.

Bowser, Myrtle, 235.
Sadie Hariston, 235.
Samuel, 69, 146, Pl. 24—146, 234—Samuel, Jr. 235.
Victoria, 146, 235.
Boyd, Albert G., 39, 76, Pl. 33.
Mary Catherine, 76, Pl. 33.
Boydston, Mary H., 74, 163.
Boyer, Clair, 182.
Elizabeth, 80, 90.
Henry, 79.
John and Louise, 268.
Louis, 234, 268.
Sarah (Summers), 63, 78, 79, 136, 183.
Bradford Daily Record (Pa.), 222.
Bridenstine, Christina, 153.
Dawn Marie, 153.
Irene, 153.
John, 71, 153.
John Herman, 153.
Mary Evelyn, 153.
Brindle, Ernest, 124, 220.
Britton, Martha (Phillips), 261.
Brouse, Adam and Mary, 119.
Beulah Pauline, 214.
Charles Frederick, 119, 214, Pl. 70.
Corwin John, 119, 214.
Helen Maud, 214.
Howard Earl, 214.
Rufus, 56, 119.
Browen, Frederick, 17, 18.
Brown, Alice, 113, 208.
Henry, 118, 212.
Leto May, 212.
Mattie, 131, 229.
Vera Pauline, 212
Brubaker, Anna, 234, 268.
Daniel M., 146, 234—Daniel and Harriet, 234
Della, 234, 168.
Elizabeth, 234.
Jessie, 234, 168.
Nettie, 234, 268
Paul, 234.
Brumback Families, 1, 4, 14, 33, 50, 76, 79, 145, 147, 178, 185, 236, 237, 248, 259, Pls. and Introduction.
Brumbaugh, Alverna, 147, 236.
Andrew Boelus, M.D., 79, 83, 92, 94, 95, 125.
Anna Agnes, 69, 145.
Daniel and Mary (Hoover), 178.
David Boyer and Susan, 145.
Elizabeth (Byerly), 204.
Florence Margaret, 237.
Gaius Marcus, M.D., Title page and Introduction.
Glenn, H., 185.
Grace Lucile, 237.
Henry, 76—Henry and Catharine, 147.
Henry P., 237.
Howard, 147, 237.
Ira Alvin, 147, 237.
Jacob, 4, 5, 14.
Johannes Henrich, 4.
Jennie Candas, 147, 236.
John, 5; John Blaine, 185—John Keith, 83, 185.
Margaret, 1, 4.
Mary (Garner), 33, 36, 50, 248.
Nellie (Fall), 237.
Peter and Mary, 185.
Samuel, 69, 147, Pl. 60.
Sarah Catharine, 81, 178.
Thelma Marie, 237.
Budd, Annie, 252.
Dortha Mayo, 252
Joseph Arthur, 173, 252.
Wilda, J. L., 252.
Bushgens, Cayle Albert, 265.
Harold Marr, 265.
Irene Lillian, 265.
Richard H., 191, 265.
Byerly, Amanda, 113, 204.
Elida and Elizabeth, 204.
Byers, Margaret, 50, 89.

C

Cadell, Nancy (Goins), 210.
Campbell, Arelia Theobald, 245—Hagey Harry, 94, 195—Hagey Fouse, 196.
J. Harold, 163, 245.
Laura Mary, 196.
Campbell, Lawrence Finley, 195.
Carmack, Harry Hartman, 261.
John, 179, 261.
William and Maria, 261.
Cassler, Alma Pearl, 210.
Bertha Millicent, 116, 209.
Celesta Grace, 116, 209.
Charlotte Elizabeth, 116, 209.
Chester Devain, 116, 211.
Elizabeth, 56, 117.
Ivan Margrett, 116.
James Arthur, 114—James Abraham, 116.
John Charles, 114, 208.
LaFayette, 56, 115, Pl. 54.
Lewis and Nancy (Wise), 54, 55—Lewis David, 56, 116—Lewis Franklin, 114.
Lovina, 55, 114.
Lydia, 33, 54, Pl. 16.
Margaret, 56, 116.
Mary Elizabeth, 114.
Nancy, 55, 114.
Philip Bliss, 116, 210.
Ruth Irene, 116, 210.
Whitney LaVerzna, 208.
William, 33, 54, 55—William Edwin, 114—William Frederick, 116, 210.
Winston Glenn, 210.
Census of 1790, 5, 17, 26, 79.
Chambers, Edwin Lawrence, 187.
Helen, 87, 187.
Susan Gillmore, 93, 194.
Christian World, 223.
Church, Lutheran, 15, 16, 27, 44.
Reformed, 2, 9, 27, 44, 50, Pls. 14, 15.
Snyders, 52.
Union, 9, 15, 26, 27, 44, 52.
Civil War Records of Fouses, 106.
Clapper, Elizabeth (Miller), 25, 26, 27, 29, 37.
Henry, Pl. 15.
Margaret (Shontz), 258.
Clay, Catharine, 33, 54.
Clifton, Archie Roy, 131, 230.
Dorothy Evelyn, 230.
Lester Eugene, 131, 230.

Clapper, Margaret Lucile, 230.
Melvin Lunem, 230.
Orin Watson, 230.
Stanley Brehania, 230.
Watson Elihugh, 62, 131.
William and Frances. 131.
Clover Creek Reformed Church, 50, Pls. 14, 15.
Cocklin, Adam and Barbara, 110.
Sarah Etta, 110.
Cole, Thornton C. J., and Drue, 210.
Zetta, 116, 210.
Collins, Anna, 75, 165.
John Austin and Ella, 268—John Austin, Jr. 234, 268.
Connor, Eliza (Shaffer), 130.
Cook, Erminie, 81, 178.
Matilda (Gauby), 187.
Cooper, Anna Malinda, 73, 161.
Mary E., 191, 265.
Corbin, Mary Ann (Evans), 128.
Cordin, Elizabeth Emma, 120, 216.
Corey, John C.; 114.
Corl, Elva Pearl, 155, 240.
Coulson, Iran F., 148, 237.
Mary Laura, 237.
Cowan, Mabel, 150, 238.
Craft, John Michael, George, Mathias, 18.
Craig, Caroline Emma, 88
Florence, A., 227.
Dewalt J., 227.
Harry C., 130, 226.
Cramer, Abraham, 71, 151.
Catherine O., 71, 153.
Elizabeth, 71, 151.
Frankie, 152.
Isaac, 71, 152.
James Emil, 152.
Mary E., 71, 152.
Ollie, 152.
Samuel, 37, 71, Pl. 27.
Susanna (Wertenberger), 148.
William H., 71, 152.
Cripe, Catharine (Boone), 205.
Criswell, A. Ross, 180.
Albert, 81, 180.
Anthony Howard, 180.
Criswell, Charles H., 180.
Chester Arthur Reed, 180.
Joseph and Sarah, 180.
Lena Catharine, 180, 262.
Margaret, 180.
Maud A., 162, 243.
Croft, Abraham, 27.
Croson, Lena, 190. 263.
Crow, Sylva Pearl, 131, 228.
Cunningham, Harriet, 172, 250.
Curtis, Edwin John, 218.
Edward W., 123, 218.
Lester Myers, 218.
Rosina, 218.
Sarah Elizabeth, 218.
Cypher, Catharine (Shultz), 189.
Clody M., 260.
Frank Homer, 178, 260.

D

Daugherty, Albert Lawrence, 246
Anna M., 165, 246.
Charlotte J., 165, 246.
Clarence, 165.
George B., 74, 165—Geo. Irwin, 246
John J., 165, 245.
Margaret E., 165.
Naomi D., 165.
Owen F., 165, 246.
Ruth, 165.
Sarah O., 165, 246.
Voila C., 165.
Wayne F., 246.
Daughinbaugh, Cheisaelvie, 168.
Elsie E., 168.
Gilbert, 168.
John, 76, 168—John William, 168.
Levi Earl, 168.
Samuel Irwin, 168.
Daughters of American Revolution, 3, 197, 267.
Dawley, Fred Wm., 227.
Kathryn Neoma Windsor, 227.
Wm. Frederick, 130, 227.
Dean, John ("Judge"), 94.
Sadie Vesta, 190, 264.
Decker, Walter A., 191, 265.
Deike, August Herman, 188.
Deike, Elsie Irene, 88, 188.
Deisel, Bennie Arthur, 139.
Dell, Leah (Walker), 261.
DeVore, Stephen Edgar, 111, 201
Joseph Benjamin, 201.
DeWalt, Charles, 211.
Detweiler, Anna Elizabeth, 248.
Clara Verna, 167.
Dorothy Lenora, 248.
Effy Gertrude, 166.
Emma May, 147.
Florence, 167.
Harry, 166—Harry McKinley, 247.
Howard Newton, 167.
Jacob, 75, 167.
James. 167, 247—James Homer, 248.
John Roosevelt, 248.
Joseph, 75, 166—Joseph and Elizabeth, 180.
Katie Idella, 166.
Lester Charles, 247.
Luella, 166.
Mable Grace, 167.
Malinda (Shultz) 81, 180.
Margaret Victoria, 248.
Martha, 75, 166.
Mertie May, 166.
Mildred Eliza, 248.
Nettie, 167.
Newton Henry, 166.
Warren, 166.
William Edward. 166.
DeVore, Dale Clifford, 202.
Hilda Estella, 201.
Joseph Benjamin and Harriet, 201.
Lester Edgar, 202.
Raymond Earl, 202.
Ruth Esther, 201.
Stephen Edgar, 111, 201.
Victor Emory, 201.
DeWalt, Twila Pola, 211.
Dieffenbach, Anna, 162, 244.
Dieffenbaugh, Homer C., 165, 246.
Diehl, Chester Lee, 163, 245.
David M., 74, 164.
Della May, 164.

Diehl, Levi, 74, 163.
Lusha Elva, 163, 244.
Omah May, 163, 245.
Dimond, Patrick, 13.
Dipple, Mary, 100.
Ditch, Susanna (Acker), 58.
Domer, Mary Catherine (Grove), 173.
Donaldson, Luemma Estella, 110, 200.
Thomas Larkin, 200.
Donnelson, John and Margaret, 176.
Donneldson, Martha Ellen, 80, 176.
Driscoll, Charles William, 111, 202.
Duerner, John, 58, 124.
Dulabahn, Bessie Jane, 236.
Chauncey E., 236.
Cyrus and Rachel, 236—Cyrus Franklin, 147, 236.
Estella Ruth, 236.
Lamar Harrison, 236.
Mary Rosalia, 236.
Duncan, Edward, 73.
Elizabeth, 39, 73.
Margaret, 39, 73.
Mary Jane (Owen), 186.

E

Eberly, John, 75.
Eddy, Mary, 17, 18.
Edie, Ann, 72, 154.
Ellsworth, Lucinda (Kinsley), 187.
Emigh, Clara, 144, 233.
Enyeart, Elizabeth (Summers), 79, 180.
Davis Glasgow, 180.
Matilda 39, 74.
Thomas and Mary, 74.
William, 74.
Erb, Anna Desse, 160.
Daniel Homer, 160.
Jesse Roy, 160, 243.
Laura Elsie, 160, 242.
Martin Clair, 160.
William Levi, 160—Wm. P., 73, 160.
Essig, Ellen, 57, 120.
Evans, Abraham and Mary Ann, 128.
Elizabeth Vincent, 224.
Ernest Newton, 128, 223, Pl. 72.
Ernest Vincent, 224.
Harriet, Henry, Jacob, 18.
John Vincent, 224.
Lillian May, 128.
Mary Bertha, 128.
Micaiah Reden, M.D., 61, 128.
Robert Vincent, 224.
Roland and Mary, 128.
Evening Star, Bradford, Pa., 222.
Ewin, Harriet Priscilla, 201.

F

Faass, Fauss,—see Fouse, 1.
Faber, Erwin, 121, 216.
Harry Melvin, 164.
Joseph M., 74, 164.
Nellie Miller, 216.
Paul L., 216.
Fager, John O., 74, 164.
Fagle, Dorothy Mae, 220.
Jessie Belle, 220.
Wm. C., 124, 220—Wm. Melvin, 220.
Fall, Edgar Eugene, 237.
Effie May, 147, 237.
Isaac and Leah, 237.
Falkender, Lizzie, 97, 198.
Fenstermaker, Alice, 37, 67.
Anna M., 82, 184.
Ferrero, Maj. Gen., 92, 95.
Ferry, Ada Blanche, 160, 242.
Charles Arthur, 160—Chas. Winfield, 73, 160.
Clyde Ira, 160.
Theobald Ross, 160.
Vernice Edna, 160, 242.
Fidelity Mutual Life Ins. Co., 96, 98–106, Pls. 49, 50; 194, 197.
Fiene, Frank and Arma Z., 205.
Nettie, 205.
Fink, Benj. Franklin, 83, 184, Pl. 68.
Daniel W., 184.
Frank Harold, 185.
Fisher, Anna B., 79, 173.
Daniel Henry, 159.
Rosanna, 73, 159.
Sarah (Criswell), 180.
Fleck, Mary (Rodgers), 262.
Ford, Mary Beulah, 258.
Robert and Mary, 258.
William H., 177, 258.
Forrest, Mary Elizabeth, 175.
Foster, Susan (Johnson), 257.
Founder and President, *L. G. Fouse*, 98–106.

FOUSE

A

Abraham, 37, 70, Pl. 25.
Ada Grace, 182.
Adam, 7, 17, 21, 36, 50, Pl. 13, 66, 108–49, 77–72—Adam Franklin, 97, 198—Adam Garner, 51, 53, Pl. 2; 79, 94; Pl. 47, 108—Adam Irving, 96, Pl. 47; 197—Adam Summers, 90, 188.
Alfred Jones, 166—Alfred S., 90, 188, 190.
Alice Catherine, 189—Alice Rosina, 162.
Allen, 256.
Amy Elizabeth, 96.
Andrew, 79.
Anna Florence, 166, 167—Anna Grace, 77, 171–159–161–174, 254—Anna Lena, 174—Anna Malinda, 73, 159.
Annie Mary, 189, 262.
Annma, 74, 165.
Austin, J., 154, 239.

B

Barbara, 53, 91, Pl. 43–173—Barbara Ann, 70, 148—Barbara S., 91.
Benjamin, 49, 81, Pl. 36; 108–174, 254—Benjamin Greaser, 81, 172, 181—Benjamin Simonton, 78, 171, Pl. 65.
Bertha, 154.
Betta Roberta, 166.
Blanch Margaret, 175.

Blanche, 198, 267.
Bruce Cleo, 240.

C

Calvin, 75—Calvin Sylvester, 73, 159.
Caroline, of Theobald, 17, 18—Caroline Edith, 88, 188.
Carrie J., — —Carrie Laruhe, 161.
Catharine, 5, 17, 21, 33, 36, 52—Catharine of Theobald, 17, 18-37, 70, Pl. 26-30, 75, Pl. 32; 91-49, 82-80, 174—Catharine Elizabeth, 167.
Charles M., 156, 240—Charles Nevin, 240.
Chester Gustave, 175.
Christena, 37, 71, Pl. 27.
Christian, 49, 78, Pl. 35; 79, 108.
Clara, 80—Clara Frank, 96, Pl. 47; 197.
Clarence, 155—Clarence Aden, 198—Clarence Hood, 189.
Claud Long, 88—Claude W., 155.
Clyde, 190—Clyde Everett, 88, 188.

D

Daniel, 53-70, 149, Pl. 61; 216—Daniel Carl, 167—Daniel Duncan, 73, 159, 219.
David, 49-53, 80, 89, Pl. 39—David Henry, 87, 186, Pl. 69—David Milton, 97, 198, Pl. 48—David S., 80.
Dewalt, 79, 174—Dewalt A.—see Theobald A.—Dewalt H., 73, 161—Dewalt O., 159, 242—Dewalt Shontz, 49, 83, Pl. 38; 108.
Dorathea Caroline, 188.
Dorothy, 255.

E

Easton Leroy, 148.
Edison I., 198.
Edith Lillian, 94, 195, Pl. 45.
Edwin P., 72, 155, Pl. 62.
Eleanor, 97.
Elizabeth, 5, 17, 22, Pl. 5; 25, 28, 29, 52—Elizabeth of Theobald, 17, 18-33, 55-39, 76, Pl. 33-49, 80-53, 91, Pl. 41-75, 166-156—Elizabeth A., 70.
Ella, 156, 240—Ella Elizabeth, 93, 194, Pl. 45—Ella Grace, 79, 80, 175, Pl. 66—Ella May, 175—Ella Melissa, 97, 199.
Ellen, 70, 149-75.
Elmer Aurandt, 97—Elmer E., 159, 241.
Elton, 155.
Elva, 155.
Emma Getty, 93, 193, Pl. 45—Emma Susan, 189, 263.
Esther Lillian, 239—Esther M., 156, 241.
Etha Pearl, 149.
Eugene Garner, 197—Eugene Kennith, 240.

F

Fanny Pearl, 166.
Fernando, 72, 156, Pl. 62.
Flora, 97.
Floyd R., 155.
Frank, 80, 175—Frank, Jr., 175.
Franklin, 70, 148—Franklin Summers, 90, 189.
Fred Hutchinson, 175.
Frederick, 7, 14, 17, 23, Pls. 11 and 15; 39, 50, 52-38, 72, Pls. 28 and 62, 39-154, 239—Frederick Augustus, 97, 198—Frederick David, 187—Frederick Everett, 188—Frederick Knode, 161—Frederick Lowman, 88—Frederick Qwingh, 250—Frederick Shontz, 50, 87, 108.
Freeman Burdett, 149, Pl. 61.

G

Gaver P., 242.
George, 75-173—George Barton, 88—George W., 73, 108, 158.
George Henry, 199—George Herman, 161.
Gilbert Eugene, 149, Pl. 61.
Gladis, 155.
Grace Catherine, 250.

H

Harlan Corl, 240.
Harold, 239—Harold B., 198.
Harry, of Theobald, 17, 18—Harry Brumbaugh, 77, 171—Harry F., 173, 254—Harry Hause, 106, 199—Harry William, 175.
Harvey Elmer, 165, 247—Harvey Shoemaker, 93, 194, Pl. 45—Harvey Stephens, 247.
Hattie May, 88.
Hazel, 190.
Helen, 239.
Henry, 49—Henry Blair, 174—Henry Smith, 53, 96, Pl. 48; 108—Henry Summers, 79, 173.
Homer B., 124, 159, 219, 241—Homer Ellsworth, 182.
Howard Grove, 174.
Hortense Geissinger, 187.
Howard Keller, 157.

I

Ida Belle, 94.
Ira, 72, 157—Ira Shoemaker, 94, 195, Pl. 45.
Irene Adele, 239—Irene Lucile, 240.
Isaac, 80.

J

Jacob, 2, 4-5, 17, 22, 29, 31, 37, 38, 52—Jacob of Theobald, 17, 18-70—Jacob Acker, 39, 76, Pl. 34—Jacob J., 72, 155, Pl. 62—Jacob M., 17—Jacob Rhodes, 77, 170—Jacob Rupley, 176, 255—Jacob Summers, 80, 176.
James Keller, 157.
Jane, 75, 167.
Jennie May Baker, 254.

John, 7, 17, 22, 27, 29, 31, 32, 38, Pl. 9; 52-39-49, 80, 90, 108—John Alfred Steese, 199—John Dewalt, 87, 187—John Floyd, 156, 241—John Garner, Title Page and Introduction, 1, 5, 16, 21, 52, 53, 91, Pls. 44 and 45; 108—John M., 72, 154—John Marvin, 94, 195, Pl. 45—John Nevin, 176, 255—John S., 90, 189—John Wilmer, 189.
Jonathan, 7, 17, 59, 52, 53.
Joseph, 79, 173—Joseph Roy Baker, 254.

K

Kathryn Margaret, 187.
Kenneth R., 255.
Keturah Pearl, 172, 250.

L

Laura A., 73, 162.
Leon Franklin, 149.
Lester, 167-198.
Levi Calvin, 166—Levi Garner, 53, 98, Pls. 49 and 50—Levi R., 73.
Lillie May, 159, 241.
Lina Ellen, 255.
Lloyd Elbert, 149.
Lola Belle, 165, 247.
Lula May, 159.
Lydia Leota, 148, 237.

M

Mabel Pearle, 241—Mable R., 155.
Magdalena of Theobald, 17, 19.
Mahlon Acquilla, 154, 239—Mahlon L., 73, 161.
Malinda, 72, 154.
Marcus, M. P., 159, 242.
Margaret, 2, 4-2, 17, 23, 50, Pl. 15; 52-37, 70-39, 73, Pl. 30-49-53, 90, Pl. 40-75, 166-80, 174—Margaret Blanche, 255—Margaret C., 159, 242—Margaret Grace, 189—Margaret Rebecca, 176, 256.
Marguerite, 190.
Martha Jane, 81, 181.
Martin G., 73.
Mary of Theobald, 17, 18.
Mary, 37, 69, Pl. 24-49, 82, Pl. 37—Mary Agnes, 75-81, 181—Mary Alice, 77, 171—Mary Ann, 78—Mary E., 90—Mary Elizabeth, 73, 160-80, 175-159, 242-187-199—Mary Ella, 174—Mary Endora, 97, 190—Mary Florence, 198—Mary Jane, 172, 250-179, 261—Mary Leta, 156—Mary M., 173, 254—Mary Matilda, 93, 194, Pl. 45—Mary Maud, 159, 241, Pl. 63—Mary Naomi, 87, 187.
Mildred May, 149.
Milton, 80.
Minodes, 72, 156, Pl. 62.
Mirium, 255.

N

Nancy, 79—Nancy Simonton, 78, 172.
Naomi, 78.
Nicholas, 1, 2, 4, 9, 17, Pls. 1, 2 and 4, 52-38.

O

Oliver, 97.
Onney May, 156, 240.
Ora Elizabeth, 97, 198.
Orlando, 94, 194, Pl. 45.
Orville, 97-166, 247—Orville, Jr., 247.

P

Paul, 39—Paul Dewalt, 162.
Pearl, 156.
Philip, 76.
Priscilla, 38.

R

Ralph Wicke, 171—Ralph Wiestling, 88.
Raymond, 190.
Reuben, 72, 155, Pl. 62-75, 165, Reuben Shontz, 49, 87, 108.
Robert Chambers, 194—Robert Dewalt, 187.
Rozilla, 73.
Russel Leroy, 120, 149, 216, 237, Pl. 61.
Ruth, 74—Ruth Mildred, 182—Ruth, 239.

S

Samuel, 75, 166—Samuel Geissinger, 87, 187—Samuel Herman, 172, 250—Samuel Hoy, 176—Samuel Shontz, 50, 83, 89, 108.
Sarah Ann, 53, 94, Pl. 46—Sarah Ethel, 156.
Savilla, 22, 38, 71.
Sarah Ann, 70, 173.
Sevendolin Gauby, 187.
Solomon B., 39, 74.
Susan, 75, 165—73, 160, 90, 190.

T

Thelma, 247-255.
Theobald, 1 to 4, Theobald, J. 2, 4, 17—Theobald ("Dewalt"), 7, 14, 17, 23, Pl. 12; 39, 40, 50, 51, 52, 68, 79, 108—Theobald A. ("Dewalt"), 39, Pl. 29; 73—Theobald Kieffer, 176, 255.

V

Valentine, 2, 4.
Vera Elizabeth, 149.
Viola May, 161.

W

William, 7, 14, Pl. 3 (Deed of Nicholas to Wm., Pl. 3), 17, 22, 38, Pls. 10 and 15; 52, 66-75, 167—William Acker, 39, 75, Pl. 31—Wm. Duncan, 73, 108, 158, Pl. 63—Wm. Earl, 157-166—Wm. Frederick, 72, 157, Pl. 62—Wm. Lester, 172—Wm. Paul, 156—Wm. Simonton, 78, 172, 181, 261.
Winnefred E., 155, 240.

Foust, Bertha M., 71, 151.
David L., 70, 148.
Foy, Nettie May, 162, 244.
Andrew B. and Mary, 256.
Frank, Anna Catherine, 176, 256.
Cemetery, 35.
Elizabeth, 49, 79, Pl. 35; 95.
Jacob and Elizabeth, 95.
Maria, 79, 95.
Sarah, 53, 79, 95.
Franklin, Ross, 235.
Fread, Mary, 36.
Frederick, Laura, 71, 152.
Freeman, Mary Bodine (Geer), 209.
Friseman, Anna, 163, 245.
Fry, Anna, 114.
Bertha, 122, 217.
Edna, 122.
Emma M., 122.
Eva M., 122, 217.
Hilda, 122.
Lucy, 122.
Mary P., 122, 217.
Martha, 122.
Mina P. Stormfelt, 122, 217.
William E., 122.
Zenas, 57, 122.
Fulmer, Arlington C., 118, 212.
Artie May, 118, 213.
Calvin, 118.
Carrie S., 118, 212.
Christian, 56, 118.
Clara E., 118, 212.
Dora Celesta, 118, 213.
Edwin A., 154.
Emery, 154.
Frederick Z., 154.
Henry, 56, 118.
Ida May, 154, 239.
Marvin F., 118, 213.
Mary L., 118.
Merl, 213.
Omah Alice, 118, 212.
Philip, 72, 154.
Roy J., 212.
Sarah S., 118.
Winnified Cloy, 118, 212.
Furnaces, 13—Paradise, 43—Rebecca, 66.

G

Gaerte Gearty, Barbara, 72, 110.
Elizabeth, 22, 38, 72, Pl. 28; 110.
Caspar, 72, 110.
Galbraith, Edna, 253.
Elmer, 253.
John, 253.
Mae B., 253.
Mary, 253.
Robert E., 173, 252.
Sarah, 253.
Viola, 253.
Walter, 253.
Gammill, Elfa, 139.
William, 65, 139.
Gardner, Lillian Pearl, 209.
Oma Letris, 209.
Walter Nathan, 209.
William Atley, 116, 209.
Gardner, Wm. Harold, 209.
Garner Family, 33, 36.
Abigail Landa, 62, 132.
Abraham, 68.
Adam, 37, 63, 79—Adam, Jr. 64—Adam, 68, 142.
Agnes Leotia, 142.
Alfred, 63, 108, 133—Alfred Galvin, 231.
Alice, 67, 141.
Allen Norman—.
Angeline Alveretta, 62, Pl. 20.
Anna Mary, etc., 36—Anna Rachel, 160.
Annetta, 66, 139.
Arthur Raymond, 142.
Benjamin, 37, 64, Pl. 21—Benjamin F., 65, 138, Pl. 57—Benjamin J., 138.
Bessie L., 231.
Calvin L., 133, 230.
Catharine (Myers), 37, 68, 222—Catharine, 62, 130-63-67, 141.
Catharine (Beaver), 179, 182.
Chalmer H., 142.
Clara E., 67.
Cora May, 140.
Daniel, 37, 61, Pl. 20; 108—Daniel G., 249.
Garner, Dawald, 62, 108, 129.
Earl W., 141.
Edward Melvin, 132.
Eli, 63, 133.
Elizabeth, 37, 58—Elizabeth Ann, 62, 131—Elizabeth Caroline, 133.
Ellen, 67.
Elmer, 138, 231—Elmer D., 67, 142—Elmer Ellsworth, 142—Elmer Harris, 141.
Emma, 67—Emma Luella, 62, 132.
Florence Elenore, 130, 226.
Frank W., 130.
Franklin, 63, 134-66-67-140.
Frederick, 37, 62, 108.
George, etc., 35, 36—George and Rachel, 159—George D., 130, 226—George W., 168, 248, Pl. 73—George Winfield, 160.
Gerald Lynn, 231.
Grace May, 142—Grace Tarrant, 135, 231.
Harrison, 64, 134-67, 142-68—Harrison C., 66, 140.
Harry, 139.
Hazel Garnett, 142.
Helen Virginia, 231.
Henry Edward, 68, 143—Henry Summers, 64, 78, 135, Pl. 56.
Homer, 142.
Howard, 134.
Isabel, 66, 140.
Jacob, 64.
James Calvin, 68, 143.
John, 36—John Mathew, 33, 36, 50, 248-249—John Michael (Sr.), and Catharine (Seiss), 33, 34, 36—John Michael, Jr., 21, 36, 50, 64—John Nevin, 138—John Philip, 17, 21, 33, 36, 59.
Jonathan, 36, 37.
Joseph Frank, 68.
Julia Ann, 67, 140.
Laura Grace, 160—Laura Marie, 132, 230.

Garner, Lawrence Harold, 133—Lawrence Henry, 142.
Leslie Henry, 135, 231.
Leverne Franklin, 138.
Levi, 65, 139.
Lillie, 139.
Lizzie, 65, 139–67.
Lloyd M., 139.
Lucinda, 66, 139, Pl. 58.
Mabel Rosine, 133.
Margaret, 37, 58–62, 130–68, 142.
Mariah J., 61, 62, 131.
Martha Amanda, 66.
Mary Agnes, 160—Mary Ann, 62, 129—Mary Ann, 65–68—Mary Helen, 231—Mary Jane, 67, 141—Mary Louise, 231—Mary Vida, 138.
Matilda, 65.
Michle, 5—Michael F., 37, 67.
Myron Elnathan, 138.
Nellie S., 130, 226.
Paul, 134—Paul Henry, 133.
Percy Glenn, 142.
Philip, 37, 65, Pl. 22.
Reuben, 65–66, 140—Reuben Peter P., 62, 132.
Rilla May, 66.
Robert M., 226.
Rose Anna, 249.
Ruth Agnes, 133—Ruth Evelyn, 231—Ruth Susan, 160.
Sadie Emma, 231.
Sarah, 37, 59, Pl. 19–138, 231—Sarah Grace, 252—Sarah Jane, 65, 139.
Solomon, 65.
Susan, 36.
Susanna, 17, 21, 50, Pl. 13.
Ulysses Grant, 62, 133.
Virgil Ulysses, 133.
Walter F., 141—Walter G., 249.
Wilbur L., 134.
William, 34, 37, 66, Pl. 23–65—Wm. Daniel, 62, 132—Wm., Jr., 67, 141—Wm. S., 68, 142.
Winfield Scott, 35, 73, 159.
Gauby, Bertha May, 87, 187.
Jonas S. and Matilda, 187.
Gearty—see Gaerte, Gaerty.
Geer, Cecil Ray, 209.
Edith Charlotte, 209.
Florence Anna, 209.
Grace Amelia, 209.
Harvey Augustus, 116, 209.
Horatio Nelson, 209.
Irma Augusta, 209.
Mary Eloise, 209.
Maud Lorene, 209.
Paul Cassler, 209.
Ralph Nelson, 209.
Roy Harvey, 209.
Geissinger, H. B., 87.
John and Jane (Barrick), 84.
Sarah Ann, 49, 84.
Geist, Susanna, 169.
Generations, Fouse, First, 1—Second, 4—Third, 21—Fourth, 54—Fifth, 109—Sixth, 200—Seventh, 267.
Germget, Evelyn M., 121, 216.
Gibble, Hettie A., 33, 56.
Gillmore, Walter, 150, 238.
Ginther, Charlotte (Weaver), 115.
Girton, Clarence Dryden, 116, 210.
Minard F., and Esther, 210.
Mary Melvina, 210.
Glasgow, Samuel and Mary, 74.
Goins, Frank M., and Nancy, 210.
Melvina, 116, 210.
Good, Arthur, Henry, Laura, 170.
Lavenia (Blackburn), 77, 170.
Goodnough, Sarah Winnifred, 131, 230.
Graffius, Elizabeth, Pl. 15.
Jacob, Pl. 15.
Greaser, Adam, 173.
Agnes, 39, 73–58, 124—Agnes, Ruth, 173, 252.
Alice, 167, 247.
Almeda Rebecca, 168.
Anna, 167—Anna Edith, 173—Anna (Fouse), 81, Pl. 36.
Greaser, Carrie, 169, 249.
Catharine, 39, 75, Pl. 31.
Daniel Fouse, 76, 168.
Edith, 169.
Edna, 169.
Ella, 173, 252.
Elmer Ellsworth, 251.
Fannie Elizabeth, 167, 248.
Fern Dorothy, 251.
Frederick, 76, 167—Frederick Robert, 248.
George, 39, 53, Pls. 32 and 42; 81, 91—George and Agnes, 75, 176—George, 251—George B., 51—Geo. F., 173, 251.
Harry, 168.
Harvey, 167, 248.
Henry Harrison, 168, 249.
Homer Ellsworth, 168.
Ida May, 167, 248.
Jacob and Catharine, 126—Jacob Fouse, 76, 168, Pl. 64.
Jay Merril, 168.
John C., 78, 172.
Levi, 76—Levi Blanden, 168.
Lucinda, 76, 168.
Lydia, 168, 249.
Margaret, 81, 176—Margaret Acker, 168, 248, Pl. 73—Margaret Bauer, 60, 126.
Martha Jane, 173, 251.
Mary Bertha, 173, 251—Mary Elizabeth, 76, 170—Mary Melrose, 251.
Minnie Grace, 168, 249.
Orpha Virginia, 169.
Paul G., 76, 169.
Philip, 76.
Ralph, 168.
Rosan, 76, 169.
Susan F., 76, 169.
Thelma Georgia, 251.
Wilmer, 173.
Grebner, John William, 131, 230.
Greenhoe, Birdie, 150, 238.
Greenland, Bessie, 72, 157.
Grimes, George, 249.
Gladys, 249.
Jacob, 168, 249.

Grimes, Marie, 249.
Grove, Alburtis, 182.
Alda Martha, 184.
Anna E., 82.
Benjamin, 82—Benjamin F., 82, 183.
Blanche, 183.
Calvin A., 118, 212.
Carrie Elizabeth, 143.
Charles Andrew, 143.
Clara M., 144.
Daniel, 69, 143—Daniel Hoover and Mary C., 173.
David H., 144.
Dewalt F., 82, 183.
Edith Grace, 184—Edith Viola, 212.
Ella May, 184.
Emma May, 79, 173.
Flora E., 182.
Frank Sheckler, 184.
George, 183.—George S., 82, 184.
Grace, 183.
Homer L., 184.
Huron P., 182.
Hurshell C., 182.
James H., 183—James Russell, 184.
John and Catharine (Shontz), 76—John F., 82, 182—John Homer, 184.
Lloyd M., 144.
Lois Lucile, 184.
Mabel Elmira, 184.
Margaret Ellen, 82, 182—Margaret (Shontz), 39, 76.
Martha, 183—Martha J., 82, 182.
Martin, 69, 144.
Mary Alice, 143.
Maud M., 182.
Nancy, 76, 183.
Rachel, 82, 183.
Robert Ellsworth, 184.
Samuel Elymor, 184—Samuel H., 49, 82, 108—Samuel T., 82.
Susannah (Hoover), 82.
Viona May, 183.
Grove, Walter Leroy, 212.
William, 183—Wm. R., 82.
Grubb, Jacob, etc., 36.
Sarah (Lininger), 171.
Guiley, Arthur J., 118, 213.
Beulah Frances, 214.
George M., 213.
John Albert, 118, 213.
Joseph Donald, 214.
Milton M., 56, 118—Milton Roy, 118.
Parmaley Doyle, 214.
Robert Peter, 118, 213.
Waldo Lee, 118, 214.
Guster, Dora C., 113, 207.
Guthrie, Eloise (Reese), 53, 96.

H

Habgood, Dorothy Gladys, 223.
Robert Patton, 127, 222, Pl. 71.
Stuart, 223.
Wm. Henry and Sarah, 222.
Haffley, Edward Ellwood, 81, 181.
Ella Grace, 181.
Hagey, Laura Jane, 195.
Haines, Mary (Lorenz), 260.
Hainley, Tobias, 9.
Hall, Annie Mae, 218.
Edmond Antonio, 219.
Harold Curtis, 219.
Herbert Whitmore, 203.
Iona Pearl, 218.
Mabel Irene, 218.
Minnie Elizabeth, 218.
Robert E., 123, 218—Robert Ellsworth, 218.
Sarah Ethel, 218.
Susan Emily, 218.
Walter Leroy, 112, 203.
Wendell Gladstone, 219.
Wilfred Thompson, 218.
Halman, Wm. S., 61, 128.
Halm, Abraham, 32.
Hamer, Margaret, 60, 126, 144.
Martha (Peightel), 250.
Hamm, Abner Kreamer, 110, 200.
Beatrice Trevillian, 200.
Hamm, Gladys Lucile, 200.
Jacob and Sarah Eliza, 200.
Ruth Etta, 200.
Hamme, E. R. (Rev.), 181.
Hampton, Stacy Watson and Mary, 197.
Xenia Awilda, 96, 197.
Hancock, Wm. Scott, 83.
Hane, Frank Oscar and Clara, 223.
Minnie, 127, 223.
Harbaugh, Henry, 51.
Harding, Grace Belle, 193, 266.
Hardman, Henry (Capt.), 25, 35.
Harnish, Rachel, 69, 143.
Harris, Ann C., 182.
Clara B., 182.
Daniel, 79.
Henry B., 182—Henry Irwin, 82, 182.
John G., 182.
Harter, Melvina, 57, 123.
Hause, Harmon and Susan (Minnich), 99.
Mary Bell, 53, 99.
Haverstack, Edna F., 118, 214.
Haverstock, Claud Fry, 217.
Elmer, 122, 217.
Lee Roy, 217.
Ralph Glenn, 217.
Hawkins, Helen Eva, 163, 244.
Hazzard, Lemma Nenomia, 91, 193.
Heaton, Mary (Hampton), 197.
Hedges, Mary A., 62, 129.
Heffley, Charles Jacob, 202.
Floyd Richard, 203.
Forrest Alva, 202.
James Richard, 112, 202.
Ruth Agnes, 203.
Heffner, Benjamin, 185.
Daisy May, 127, 222, Pl. 71.
Henry Clay, 127, 223—Junior, 223.
Martha (Shultz), 257.
Samuel Dean, 60, 127, Pl. 55—Samuel Frank, 223.
William, 83, 185.
Heimbaugh—Himebaugh, Abraham, 69, 145.

Heimbaugh, Arthur, 233.
Catherine, 70.
Christina, 69, 146.
D. Franklin, 146.
David, 69, 146, Pl. 59; 108.
Elizabeth, 69, 146, 234, Pl. 24.
Emanuel, 69, 147.
Emma C., 71, 149.
J. Wm., 146.
Jacob, 37, 69, 70, 108-70, 108—Jacob Elias, 146, 233.
Jasper, 233.
John, 147.
Mary, 69, 147, Pl. 60-146, 233.
Michael, 37, 70.
Oscar, 148.
Pierce, 70, 148.
Samuel E., 146, 233.
Sevilla, 70, 148.
William H., 70.
Heiser, Charles, 122, 217.
Thelma Janette, 217.
Hellyer, Edward and Elizabeth, 186.
Lucy, 83, 186.
Henney, Abraham and Margaret, 116.
Christopher, 29, 31.
Elizabeth, 29.
Lucinda Allis, 116.
Philip, 29, 31.
Henry, Florence, Caroline, 113, 203.
Jacob and Elizabeth, 203.
Herde, Martha, 67, 141.
Hershberger, Mabel Grace, 68, 143.
Hess, Artie, 118, 212.
George W., 180, 262.
Mary Elizabeth, 169.
Samuel and Martha, 262.
Hiatt, Oris, 162, 243.
Higgins, Jacob, 125.
Hildebrand, Carl, 213.
Ruth Lucile, 213.
Sherman, 118, 213.
Hill, Charles F., 57, 121.
Chester Arthur, 121, 217.
Hillyer, Sarah (Huff), 188.
Hinch, Clarence, 132, 230.
Harold Garner, 230.
Hinderks, Edward Joseph, 112, 203.
Gladys Lucile, 203.
Norval Leroy, 203.
Hinkel, Elizabeth (Smith), 129.
History of Juniata Valley, Jordan, 186.
Hodges, Unpublished Manuscript, 3.
Hoeffner, Caroline, 62, 133.
Leonard Rosine, 133.
Hoffa, Calvin O., 190, 263.
Charles N., 190, 264.
Daniel, 90, 190.
Earl Daniel, 263.
Eldon, 164.
Elmer C., 190, 264.
Emery, 190.
Frank Lester, 264.
Harold Francis, 264.
Hattie Susan, 264.
Jacob D., 190.
Lizzie M., 190.
Lloyd, L., 190.
Lucile Noreni, 264.
Lucius, 263.
Merle Thomas, 263.
Neva May, 263.
Pearl Edith, 264.
Porter C., 190, 264.
Ray Everett, 263.
Roselda Loretta, 190, 263.
Ruth Ethel, 164.
Vernia Irene, 190, 264.
Vesta E., 190.
William G., 190.
Homestead, Fouse, Pl. 2; 13.
Hood, Margaret, 90, 188.
Hoover, Adam, 58—Adam Fouse, 94, 196, Pl. 46.
Arthur Fillmore, 221.
B. Paul, 126.
Benjamin, 49, 82, Pl. 37—Benjamin Carl, 186—Benjamin Clyde, 184—Benjamin Franklin, 53, 94, Pl. 46-83, 186.
Carrie Edith, 221.
Catherine, 59—Catherine Eliza, 238—Catherine Fouse, 83, 184, Pl. 68.
Hoover, Charles Edon, 221—Charles Edward, 186—Charles Ernest, 221.
Cleon, 149, 238—Cleon Donald, 238.
Clifford, 150, 238.
Daniel, 59, 108, 125—Daniel C., 71, 151—Daniel H., 126—Daniel Shoenfelt, 221.
David, 94—David Mahlon, 94.
Elizabeth, 71, 150—Elizabeth F., 83, 185.
Ella F., 150, 238.
Ellen, M., 71, 151.
Elrene May, 221.
Elsie May, 184.
Essington R., 126, 220.
Ethel E., 151.
Flora Fouse, 94, 196, Pl. 46.
Floyd W., 151.
Francis A., 126.
Franklin D., 71, 149.
Grace Anna, 221.
Homer G., 126.
Ida A., 71, 151.
Jacob, Pl. 15—Jacob C., 37, 58, 70, 108-71—Jacob Newton, 126, 221.
Janetta Fouse, 94, 196, Pl. 46.
John Edwin, 126, 221—John Hobard, 221.
Jonathan, 37, 70, Pl. 26; 108-71.
Josephine, 126.
Kathryn Jane, 221.
Lilly Edith, 126, 221—Lilly May, 221.
Ludwig and Susannah (Grove), 82.
Martha Jane, 221.
Mary Eliza, 221.
Melvin McKinley, 221.
Minerva Fouse, 94, 196, Pl. 46.
Nancy F., 83, 185.
Priscilla, 71, 150.
Ralph Edmond, 221.
Raymond L., 126.
Reuben Fouse, 82, 184—Reuben Merle, 186.
Samuel, 21, 50, 70, 58.

Hoover, Sarah A., 71, 150—Sarah Jane, 82.
Vera Loretta, 151.
Verna, 149, 238.
William, 71, 108, 149.
Wilson, 71, 151.
Hoppel, Cora Lydia, 112, 202.
Edwin M., 112.
Elmer Lee, 112, 203.
Jacob, 55, 108, 112.
Mary Elvira, 112.
Raymond Jacob, 112.
Horne, Bennie Dettle, 163, 244.
Gladys Marie, 244.
Vera Ardis, 244.
Horni, Catharine, 90, 189.
Urich and Catharine, 189.
Hosterman, Adam and Susan, 175.
Charles, 175.
Frank, 175.
Henry Musser, 80, 175.
Houck, Wm. A., 83, 92.
Householder, Alice, 248.
David, 167, 248.
Earl Frederick, 263.
Frederick, 189, 263.
Lucile, 248.
Mary (Frank), 256.
Housel, Katie, 71, 149.
Huber, Margaret (Shontz), 41.
Hubley, Ezra, 118, 212.
Helen, 212.
Hilda Birdem, 212.
Huff, Ann (Speck), 260.
Anna, 90, 188.
Henry and Sarah, 188.
Huffman, Jessie, 177, 259.
Raymond Walter, 259.
Roger Paul, 259.
Silas and Martha Jane, 259.
Hugill, Edward, 91, 193.

I

Illard, Jennie, Bell, 191, 266.
Imler, Sadie, 58, 124.
Indermuehle, Emma, 121, 216.
Inery, Martha (Hess), 262.
Ingold, George, 57, 120.
Gilbert R., 120.
Ingold, Mary E., 120, 149, 237.
Maud, 120.
Orin Sage, 120, 216.
Ralph Henry, 120.
Willard Jason. 120.
Irish, Jennie M, 230.
Iron Industry, 13.
Irwin, Elizabeth, 165, 246.
Isenberg, Clyde Milton, 260.
Ester Kathryn, 260.
John Nevin, 178, 260.
Milton Sangree, 178, 260—Milton Shultz, 260.
S. B., 51.
Wm. Huyett and Ester, 260.

J

Jackson, Charles Herbert, 176, Pl. 66.
Hugh Alexander, 175.
Robert Hugh, 176, Pl. 66.
Theodore C., 80, 175, Pl. 66.
Thomas, 23.
Jacobs, Edna, 140.
Harrison, 140.
John P., 66, 139.
Lillie, 140.
"Jane Ellis," 267.
Johnson, Alexander, 20.
James H., 146.
Jennie Jackson, 177, 257.
Martha, 97, 198.
Mary Ann, 110, 200.
Wm. Hunter and Susan, 257—Wm. Nicholas, 200.
Jordan (?), Aurolis and Ella A., 206—Charles N., 113, 206—Ella Elizabeth, 207.
Judson, Mabel, 162, 243.
Juniata River, 12.

K

Kagarise, Daniel, 193—Salome (Bechtel), 193.
Kanago, Archie Bernard, Elmer Perry, Lloyd, 229—Myron Elmer, 131, 229—Vivian Mae, 229.
Kanel, Bertha, 119, 215—Gottfried and Anna, 215.
Karns, Andrew C., 97, Ella Elizabeth, James Andrew, Mary Lovenia, 199.
Katzelmoyer, Agnes (Greaser), 75, 176.
Kauffman, Eva, 240—Herbert C., 156, 240—Mary Grace, 240.
Keely, Susan, 17, 38.
Keeth, Michael, Pl. 15.
Keister, Emma, 65, 138, Pl. 57.
Keller, Ada, 72, 157—Joel F. and Susannah, 157.
Kemberlin, John Geesy, Blanch Edna, George Royer, Idella May, Lloyd Melvin, Maud Gertrude, 169—William Henry, 76, 169.
Kemp, Elizabeth (Aurandt), 97.
Kennedy, Hyla Hawthorne, 218—Jesse Daniel, Kenneth, Sylvester, Quincy Myers, 219—Robert, 124, 219—Robert Dewalt, 219—Susan Eliza, 219.
Kent, Isaac C., 153, 238—Leo James, 239.
Kephart, Theophilus (Col.), 95.
Kerr, Bernard Irwin, 62, 132—Guy Garner, Irene Martha, Wm. Daniel, Wm. and Martha, 132.
Ketterman, Anna May, John H., 172, 250—John Wm., Ruth Gladys, 250.
Key, Joseph (Bishop), 115.
Kieffer, Moses, 42, 48.
Kindred, Adelaide, 166, 247.
King, Clara Ethel, Daniel Clair, Della Esto, Edgar Ray, Edith Marie, 251—George Edgar, 173, 251—Harold Myron, 251.
Kinger, Elizabeth, 180.
Kinsley, Bruce Whitney, 188—Guy and Lucinda, 187—Guy Dewalt, 188—Jason Daul, 87, 187.

Kirk, Benjamin W., 129, 226—Clifford Frederick, 225—Donovan Converse, 225—Frederick, 129, 225—Marjorie Henrietta, 225—Rush W., 225.
Knepper, Sarah, 68, 142.
Knode, Linda B., 73, 158, Pl. 63—Mary M., 78, 171.
Kohlenburg, Allen Gotlieb, 132—August, 62, 132—Ethel May, 132—Gotlieb and Bertha, 132—Kail Kohlen, 132—Reuben Hugo, 132.
Koon, Daisy Maud E., 193.
Kreighbaum, Alice, 71, 152.
Kryder, John, 32.
Kuhn, Clara (Hane), 223.
Kunes, Bertha, 97, 198.
Kunkle, Anna Mary, 64, 138.
Franklin, 138.
Kurtz, Aaron, 146, 235—Ada, 235—John and Mary, 235—Ruth, 235—Samuel, 235.
Kyle, Anna May, 173, 253.
Kyler, Maria (Carmack), 261.
Kyper, Ella Marie, 159, 242.

L

Lafler, Charles William, 138, 231.
Gladys Blanche, 232.
Lamberson, Bertha Estella, 117, 211.
George, 56, 117.
Lambly, Kate, 91, 192—Lizzie, 91, 191.
Lamerson, Sarah Eliza, 200.
Lanberance, Mildred, 57, 123.
Lancer—see Lantzer.
Lang, Carl Galbraith, 263—Emma Edith, 262—Galbraith, 189, 262—Gertrude Susan, 263—Harry Raymond, 262—Margaret Lillian, 263.
Lantz, Mary Clarissa, 74, 164.
Lantzer, Abraham, 29, 31—Pearl, 115, 208.
Larew, Larue, James, 17, 18—James and Emily, 205—Ida May, 113, 205.
Latham, Mary Eliza, 209.
Lecrone, Alice, 124.
Anna, 124, 159, 219, 241.
Dora Jane, 124, 219.
Jacob, 58, 124, 241.
Leibert, Clara Luella, 131—Elsie Belle, 131, 227—Fred, 62, 108, 130—Frederick E., 130—Maggie Etta, 130, 227—Nellie Retta, 131, 227—Sadie Mae, 131, 228.
Leinbach, Paul S., 85.
Lesber, Sarah, 113.
Leveringhouse, Sarah (Hoppel), 112.
Lichty, Charles F., Herbert F., Walter F., 254—William, 173, 254.
Liesveld, Matilda, 138, 231.
Limerick, Katie, 70, 148.
Lincoln, Abraham (Pres.), 36, 84, 106.
Margaret T., 127, 222.
Lininger, Annie May, 181—Edgar Harry, 171, 250—Eliza Jane, 79, 174—Frederick Fouse, 181—George and Sarah, 171—Harriet Kathryn, 181—Jacob and Mary, 174, 181—Levi, 81, 181—Maggie May, 171—Samuel Grubb, 77, 171.
Linville, Mary Margaret, 140, 232.
Lippincott's Gazetteer, 1.
Long, George and Caroline Emma, 88—Harriet Emma, 50, 88—Scott, 234, 268—Theresia, 268—Valcena, 268—W. C., 134.
Longenecker, Elizabeth, 17, 38.
Loose, Fred, 249—Homer Umbower, 168, 249—Jessie, 249—Madaline, 249.
Lorenz, Harry Cleveland, 179, 260—Ha.man and Mary, 260—Mary Alberta, 260.
Louder, Dean S., 253—I. Warren, 173, 253—J. William, 173, 253—Joseph H., Jean G., Ruth A. B., Warren I., 253.
Lovett, Charles E., 65, 139.
Lower, Sibilla, 27, 29, 38.
Lowry—see Lower.
Ludwig, August and Salome M., 206—Margaret, 206.
Lynn, Andrew Charles, 177—Andrew Russell, 81, 177—Andrew Russell, Jr., 177, 259—Anthony Claude, 177, 259—Catharine, 177, 257—Cora Elizabeth, 177, 258—David and Catharine, 177—Dewalt Shultz, 177, 259—Frances, 177, 258—John Russell, 81, 177—Harry Leroy, 259—Hazel Marie, 258—John Shultz, 187, 258—Laura, 177, 257—Mary Ann, 177—Nancy Jane, 177, 258—Reuben Shultz, 177—Robert Bell, 159—William Harold, 258—Wm. Henry, 177, 259.
Lyons, Elizabeth (Anderson), 111.

M

McCall, Ida Catharine, 173, 252.
McCartney, Maggie, 63, 134.
McCoy, David and Misanier, Carley Roy, Clela Elizabeth, Clerda Mae, Mary Irena, Orrin Hubert, Parley Jay, Quinby Francis, Thomas Franklin, 205—William, 113, 205.
McCullum, Arthur Albert, 160, 242.
McDonald, Ella (Collins), 268.
McFarland, Agnes (Blackburn), 170.
McGraw, Eliza (Rhodes), 91.
McKean, Edna Viola, 173, 251.
McKibben, Brig. Gen., 92, 95.
McMahan, Sarah, 65, 139.

Machamer, Anthony Wayne, 56, 117—David Todd and Hannah (Wertenberger), 117—Edward Lee, 114, 208—Erma Lucille, 117, 211—Gerty, 115, 209—John S., 115, 208—John and Rachel (Miller), 114—Kirby, 115—Margaret, 114—Minerva Celesta, 117, 211—Polk Dallas, 114.
Maclaskey, Lou A., 64, 135.
Madlem, Adam, 72—Dilla C., 153, 238—Franklin, 73, 153, 238—Ellen C., 153—Fyanna, 72—Hiram B., 72, 153—Isaac, 22, 38, 71—Isaac D., 154—Mary Ann., 72, 153—Minnie, 154—Samuel, 154—Sarah, 72—Savilla E., 72—William, 72, 154.
Magee, Mary (O'Conner), 195.
Manners, Mary, 18.
Maria Forges, 14.
Markel, Sarah A., 123, 217.
Marker, Albert, 57.
Markley, Elmer E., 117, 211.
Marr, Anna Amelia, 191, 265—August, 90, 191—Bernice Elrene, Edith Fern, George Jacob, Grace Augusta, Lillie May, Rose Elva, 191, 265.
Martin, D. L., 51.
Harriet (Brubaker), 234.
Maryland, Baltimore, 3, 4, 12, 17, 18, 25.
Funkstown, 4, 25.
Hagerstown, 4, 78.
Sharpsburg, 4.
Washington Co., 3.
Masse, Clara, 74, 163.
Mathwig, Tillie, 131, 228.
May, Lydia, 68, 142.
Meekes, Eva S., 121, 217.
Meehlhouse, Adam, 191, 266—Annie Martha, Bernice Christian, Lillian Florence, Maria Catharine, 266.
Megraw, Albert Bailey, 88, 188.
Mehrwein, Laura, 76, 169.
Mennonite, 45.
Merritts, Catharine, 168.
Metzgar, C. Lillian, 220.
Charles L., 124, 219.
Meyers, Beulah May, 240.
John Hoover, 156, 240.
Leland Kenneth, 240.
Melvin Louise, 240.
Miller, Bible record of, 29, Pls. 6, 7—72, 153.
Abraham, 5, 9, 17, 22, 25, 27, 29, 37, Pls. 6 and 7—25, 54, 108, 109, Pl. 51.
Adam, 70, 149—Adam Lewis, 29, 55, 110, Pls. 17 and 52.
Albert B., 94, 196.
Alice, 57.
Alonzo Lee, 57, 120.
Alva Edison, 111.
Anna Bolander, 204, 267.
Amelia Mandilla, 113, 205.
Atlee Russell, 206.
Bertha May, 121, 216.
Bessie Irene, 204, 267—Bessie Lucinda, 196.
Beulah Opal, 200.
Blanche Ethel, 122.
Catharine, 29, 31, 33, 55.
Charles E., 152—Charles Percy, 196.
Charlotte, 117.
Charles, 216—Charles Augustus, 111—Chas. E., 85—Chas. Edwd., 206—Chas. Webster, 57.
Christina, 17, 22, Pl. 5; 27, 29, 31, 38—Christina (Snyder), 33, 56, Pl. 18—Christena, 152.
Clara Edith, 196.
Claud Wilbert, 122.
Clifford Alton, 123—Clifford Omega, 111.
Cora, 152.
Corwin J., 113, 206.
Curtis Clifford, 200.
Daisy D., 117—Daisy Irene, 196.
Daniel C., 152.
Delbert Donaldson, 201.
Miller, Dorothy Christena, 204.
Echo Elnora, 207—Echo Fairy, 205.
Edith May, 201.
Elias, Pl. 7.
Elizabeth, 17, 22, 29, 31, Pl. 8; 37, 38–33, 35–55, 111, 113, Pl. 17.
Ella, 57, 122.
Elmer Ellsworth, 113, Pl. 53; 203—Elmer Lee, 120.
Emma, 68, 143—Emma Elizabeth, 205.
Etta Irene, 117.
Eva Mae, 206—Eva Myrtle, 204.
Florence Mabel, 111, 202.
Francis Preston, 111, 201.
Frank Jay, 113, 205.
Fyanna, 55, 112, Pl. 17.
George Harris, 206.
Gertrude B., 122.
Gladys Estella, 207.
Grover Lee, 113, 207.
Guy Preston, 201.
Harold Burt, 201—Harold H., 216.
Harry Homer, 200.
Harvey Webster, 121, 216.
Hazel Eveline, 200.
Henry, 29, 30.
Herbert Donald, 206.
Hilda May, 122.
Homer Adam, 111—Homer Willard, 196.
Hubert Clair, 122.
Ida M., 57.
Ina, 117.
Ira Clyde, 111—Ira S., 57, 121.
Irene Stella, 111, 202.
J. David, 51.
Jacob Solomon, 55, 113.
Jemmima, 56, 117.
John, 33–29, 30, 33, 54, 108—John Cassler, 55, 111, Pl. 17; 112.
Jonathan, 33, 54, Pl. 16; 108.
Joseph, Pl. 7.

Miller, Lester Glendon, 206—Lester Lee, 122—Lester Rawling, 201.
Lether Mae, 207.
Lewis, 29, 30.
Lilly Marguerite, 196.
Lyba, 56.
Lydia, 55, Pl. 17; 113.
Magnus M., 57, 122.
Mahlon, 57.
Malez S., 57, 121.
Mandana, 57, 122.
Manodes, 57, 121.
Margaret, 33, 54—Margaret Pauline, 206.
Marie Dorothy, 122.
Martha Ethel, 196—Martha M., 57, 121.
Martin C., 57, 123.
Marvin McKinley, 196—Marvin M., 57, 122.
Mary Ann, 33, 57—Mary, 29, 31, 110–55, 112, Pl. 17–206—Mary M., 57, 121—Mary Mintie, 113, 204.
Mason E., 57, 120.
Matilda, 97, 198.
Maude Grace, 121.
Mildred, 122—Mildred Florence, 204—Mildred Maurene, 200.
Minerva Maud, 110, 200—Minerva May, 123.
Minnie Estella, 113, 206.
Morris Monroe, 113, 204.
Nancy, 55.
Nathaniel, 56, 117.
Nelson Albert, 196.
Olive May, 111, 201.
Orin Albert, 111—Orin Enew, 113, 206.
Orpha Alice, 113, 205.
Otilla, 56, 117.
Pauline Rosella, 206.
Pearl Bell, 204, 267, Pl. 53.
Perry Anderson, 111—Perry L., 152.
Priscilla, 33, 57.
Rachel (Machamer), 114.
Ralph, 122—Ralph Dale, 201.
Miller, Rawlins Adam, 110, 200.
Robert, 56.
Rolley, 56.
Rolley S., 117.
Rosa B., 152.
Rose L., 29.
Ruth Lenox, 170.
Sadie Adaline, 201.
Samuel C., 56—Samuel J., 33, 57.
Sarah Alfareta, 111.
Solomon, 33, 56.
Stanley Cocklin, 111, 202.
Stella May, 201.
Susanna, 29, 31, 33.
Theodore W., 57.
Thomas F., 76, 170—Thomas Jefferson, 113, 205—Thomas Wesley, 170.
Vera Irene, 207.
Vernon, 56.
Walter Scott, 110, 200.
William, 71, 152—Wm. Forrest, 200—Wm. L., 33, 57—Wm. Lewis, 201—Wm. Murray, 29, 57, 123.
Zella E., 120.
Zora J., 120.
Milligan, Gretta, 174, 255.
Minam, Minnie, 66, 140.
Minnich, Susan (Hause), 99.
Missions, Board of Home, 84.
Mitchell, James, 18.
Mock, Daniel Raymond, 221—George W., 126, 221—May Josephine, 221.
Monroe, Byron, 168.
Moore, Albert, 122, 217—Cecilia, 146—Huston and Mary Jane, 234—Sarah E., 146, 234.—William, 146.
Moots, Elizabeth (Henry), 203.
More, Dilla Myra, 239—Henry, 154, 239—John B., 239—Pearl Estella, 239—Perry P., 239—Wm. E., 239.
Morrison's Cove, Pa., 5, 9, 14, 27.
Morrow, Julia, 20.
Mueller, Ruth, 140, 232.
Myers, Abraham, 37, 68, 222–123–143—Ada F., 217—Ada Ruth, 144—Adam, 123—Amanda 71, 151—Anna Mary, 74, 164—Anna May, 143—Arlie D., 218—Benjamin, 69, 145—Bertha Pearl, 143—Brison W., 71, 150—Caroline, 218—Clara Eleanor, 145—Clinton, 150—Daniel, 58, 123—Daniel M., 143—David Sylvester, 124—Della May, 144—Dewalt, 123, 218—Dorothy Mae, 145—Earl McKinley, 143—Edgar, 217—Edward 124—Eleanor, 20—Elizabeth, 69, 143–123, 218—Elizabeth Catharine, 144—Ellen, 150—Franklin, 69, 145—Ida May, 69, 145—Irene, 218—Jacob, 123—Jesse, 150—John, 32, 33—John A., 123, 217—Laura Alice, 69, 127—144, 222,—Lena, 218—Lena Verona, 177, 257—Margaret 69, 145—Martin Luther, 124—Mary Jane, 69, 144—Milton, 69, 144—Ora Blanche, 144—Reuben, 69, 143—Reuben H., 143—Robert, 124—Royal Leonard, 144—Sarah, 123, 218—Sarah Catherine, 69, 144—143–Sidney S., 218—Susanna E., 124, 219—Virginia Mae, 218—William, 150—Wm. C. 123—Wm. H., 69, 144—Wm. N., 143—Wilmer Brumbaugh, 145.

N

Neagle, Mary (O'Conner), 195.
Neuroth, Christopher and Anna, 132—Emma Jane, 62, 132—Newcomb, Cliff Paul, 210—Hiram Weeks, 116, 209—Hiram H. and Hattie M., 210—Leona Ruth, 210—Lloyd Leon, 210—Ralph Bethuel, 210.

Newhouse, Maggie, 147.
Nicholson, Henry, Thomas, William, 18.
Nicodemus, Adam F., 91, 191—Alta Grace, 191—Alfa Lavinia, 191—Alvernia Bowman, 163, 245—Barbara Ellen, 192—Barbara S., 91—Beatrice, 163—Bertha Maud, 192—Burris Leonard, 244—Burris Vernon, 163, 244—Catharine Fouse, 74, 164—Charles Samuel, 198—Conrad, 3, 8—Edith Anna, 164—Edwin, 91, 191—Elsie M., 192—Esther Fouse, 74, 164—Frederick, 3, 5—Frederick Bowman, 163, 245—Frederick Fouse, 74, 163—George, 53, 90, Pl. 40; 108—George Henry, 192—Grace J.. 192—Harold Richard, 242—Hazel Ellen, 163—Helen, 198—Inez, 163, 245—Isaac C., 91, 192—Jacob and —— (Aerlenbaugh), 73, 90—Jacob A., 39, 73, Pl. 30—Jacob Clarence, 159, 242—Jacob Earl, 162, 243—Jacob Edwin, 192—Jacob Fouse, 74, 164—John H., 91, 192—John Vernon, 244—Mamie, 192—Margaret Elizabeth, 162, 243—Margaret Elizabeth Fouse, 74, 164—Margaret Ida, 91, 193—Mary Agnes, 74, 163—Mary Dorothy, 198—Mary Elizabeth, 90, 191—Mary Ruth, 192—Nellie Margaret, 192—Oliver, 162, 243—Rachel Alymrta, 163, 244—Reuben Fouse, 74, 163—Robert, 198—Rosa Belle, 192—Ruth May, 164—Samuel, 97, 198—Sarah, 91, 191—Susan, 90, 190—Susanna Fouse, 74, 162—Theobald Fouse, 74, 163—Veda, 192—Verna Rose, 192—Viola Iris, 243—Walter Irwing, 191—Wesley Fouse, 74, 162—Wesley Raymond, 243—Wesley Roy, 162, 243—William Fouse, 74, 164.
Noel, Clarence Edwin, 220—Clyde Albert, 220—Daniel B., 124, 220—Edna Mae, 220—Violet Beatrice, 220.
Nolt, Cletus Jay, 207—Hugo Arvitus, 207—Mary Elizabeth, 207—Simon, 113, 207—Turah May, 207.
Nussear, Helen, 20.

O

Obenour, Anna Mary, 169—Christian, 169—David, Pl. 15—George Grover, 169—Homer Lloyd, 169—Jacob, 76, 169.
Ober, Melvina, 146, 236.
O'Conner, John and Mary, 195—Laura Helen, 94, 195.
Otis, Eliza Mae, 131, 228.
Owen, Margaret, 87, 186—Robert White, 186.
Ozenberger, Magdalena, 202.

P

Patriot's Oath of Fidelity, 3.
Patterson, Sallie E., 133, 230.
Pauley, Mary Jane, 187.
Paulus, John, 14.
Pease, Edmund Noxen, 215—Mary Helen, 119, 215.
Peightel, Ada Ruth, 222—Catherine, 60—Dorothy May, 222—Elizabeth, 60—Ellen Bertha, 222—Harry, 127—Harry John, 222—Henry, 37, 59, Pl. 19—Rev. I. N., 51—Isaac, 60—John, 60, 108, 126, 144—Lydia Ida, 61, 128—Margaret, 127—Margaret Ann, 61, 127—Margaretta, 171, 250—Martha Catharine, 222—Mary E., 127—Mary Jane, 60, 127, Pl. 55—Nevin, 69, 127, 144, 222—Sarah Alice, 61, 108, 127—Sarah Catharine, 222—Susanna, 61, 128—Thelma Grace, 222—Thomas H., 127—W. M. and Martha, 250—Wm. E., 127, 222—Wm. Edgar, 222.
Pennsylvania Archives, 175.
Huntingdon Co., 6, 9, 12, 14, 26.
Lancaster Co., 13.
Pittsburgh, 12, 14.
Pero, Lovina, 70, 148.
Phillips, Charles I., 261—D. Catherine, 261—Emma Grace, 261—James and Martha, 261—James H., 261—John, 179, 261—Martha Helen, 261—William, 26, 27.
Pittenger, Anna, 129, 226.
Platz, C. E. (Rev.), 233.
Plummer, John, 80.
Pointer, Alice, Mae Bell, 141, 233.
Pollock, Mary, 167, 248.
Pontious. Andrew Jackson, 146, 236—Daniel Otis, 146—Lewis, 69, 146—Maud, 236—May Cora, 146—Melvin, 236—Sarah Elizabeth, 146, 236—Sevilla C., 146—William N., 146.
Portage Railroad, 14.
Prough, Calvin, 124, 220—Catharine (Weller), 257.
Prugh, J. H. (Rev.), 93.
Pugh, David, 17, 19—Elizabeth A., 19, 20—James G., 20—John David, 20—John H., 19—Joseph, 19—Margaret Stevenson, 20—Mary, 18—Mary F., 19—William, 18—Wm. G. 19, 20—Wm. Morrow, 20.
Putt, Elizabeth (Hellyer), 186.

Q

Quarry, Jennie, 126, 221.

R

Rader, Alfred, 170, 250.
Ramsbotham, Maude Myrtle, 131, 229.
Rapp, George and Elizabeth, 111—John Franklin, 111.
Ream, Frank, 72, 153—Irwin F., 153—Isaac H., 153—Lloyd, 122, 217—Lowell, 217—Martha Mandana, 217—Sarah E., 153.
Rebecca Furnace, 14.
Records of Md. Troops, 25.
Records, Miller Bible, Pls. 6, 7; 29.
Reed, Adaline, 69, 145—C. A., 82, 183—Edith Dale, 165, 246—William, 183.
Reel, Elizabeth (Sinclair), 211—Henry, 57, 122—Lottie May, 123—Priscilla Catharine, 123—Roy Martin, 123.
Reese, Benjamin Thomas and Anna M., 96—Eloise, 53, 96.
Reformed Church, 2, 9, 27, 44, 50, Pls. 14, 15; 51, 96—*Messenger*, 84.
Reiley, Jane, 75, 167.
Rentch, Andrew, 3.
Resolutions, Assn. of Life Ins. Presidents, 102—Fidelity Mutual Life, 100—Board of Home Missions, 84.
Rettig, Emma Belle, 118, 213.
Revolution, Sons of American, 25.
Rheinfelz, Rheinville, 1.
Rhodes, A. D. and Eliza Ann, 125—Abraham and Eliza (McGraw), 76, 91—Adam, 91—Cyrus Blain, 193—Eliza Jane, 59, 125—Elmer Garfield, 165—George, 169, 249—Henry C., 75, 165—John Chesterfield, 193, 266—John Ganreve, 266—John F., 91, 193—John McGraw, 51, 91, Pl. 43—Nettie, 165—Paul, 249—Ralph Palmer, 165—Sarah, 39, 76—Sarah Jane, 91, 193—Wm. Calvin, 165.
Rhudy, Mary, 37, 70.
Rhul, Mary Olive, 166, 247.
Richie, Catharine, 121—George, 57, 121—Laura May, 121.
Richter, Lola, 111, 202.
Rietze, Elizabeth (Wicke), 171.
Ritz, Anna (Kanel), 215.
River, Juniata, 12—Susquehanna, 12.
Roath, Melissa, 63, 134.
Robb, Lewis (Rev.), 93.
Roberts, Bertha Grace, 112, 203—Levi, 7.
Robinson, Charles Elmer, 267, Pl. 53—George E., 240, 267—James Steward, 231—Merle E., 135—Merric Eldridge, 231—W. Courtland (Memorial Address), 102—Wm. E. and Jane A., 267.
Rodgers, Jesse, 180, 262—Lee, 262—Wm. Ashcombe, 262.
Roop, Jacob, Pl. 15.
Rose, Christina, 72, 156—Lydia, 72, 156—Mary, 72, 155.
Roselip, Dennis Albert, 131, 228—Dorothy Elizabeth, 228—Robert, 228.
Ross, Homer Alfred, 246—James McClure, 165, 246—Kenneth Albert, 246—Vernon Elroy, 246.
Roth, John, 66, 139, Pl. 58.
Rouinsky, Ethel, 154, 239.
Royer, John, 13—Salina, 72, 155—Susan, 72, 154.
Rudy, Alvin Walter, 174, 255—Edwin Hayes, 174—Frederick Ralph, 174—Gerald Burket, 174—Harry Fouse, 174—Mary Viola, 174, 254—Raymond Bruce, 174—Samuel Gilliland, 80, 174—Wm. Henry, 255.
Rupley, F. A., 51.
Russell, Anthony Howard, 172, 179, 250, 261—Catharine (Lynn), 177—Delilah, 179, 261—Elizabeth, 179, 261—Helen Catherine, 250—Henrietta, 179—Jacob Bowser, 81, 179, 250, 261—Jacob Charles, 180—John H. and Delilah, 179—John Homer, 179—Laura Helen, 179, 261—Maggie Catherine, 180—Martha Elma, 250—Martin Luther, 179—Reuben Chester, 180—Wm. Henry, 180.
Ryan, Mary (Welker), 268.

S

Salem Reformed Church, 51, 96.
Sanders, Charles H., 67, 141.
Saterfield, Basil Glenn, 233—Charles Henry, 141—Harrison R., 141, 233—J. L., 67, 141—Murtie A., 141. Sevilla G., 141.
Schadt, Alta Catherine, 191—Charles William, 191, 266—George Harvey, 191—Harry Rogers, 191, 266—Helen, 266—Margaret Louisa, 191—Nettie Angelina, 191, 266—Philip, 91, 191—Philip Calvin, 191, 266—Roy, 266—Silvia Iradell, 266.
Scheckler, Edith Blanche, 82, 183.
Scheefer, Bertha M., 236—Jacob, 146, 236—Minnie A., 236.
Schell, Annie Rachel, 81, 172. 181—Martha Jane, 78, 172, 181—Martha Jane (Fouse). 261—Samuel, 172, 181.
Schermer, Lawrence Frederick, 141—Myrtle, 141—William, 67, 141.
Schick, Albert, 71, 151 - Esther. 151.
Schleicht, G., 17.
Schlodtt, Celinda, 63, 133.
Schmidt, Anna G., 129, 224—Dalton V., 226—Edward W., 130, 226—Matilda E.. 130, 226.
Schneck, B. S., 42.
Schneider, Elizabeth (Rapp). 111—Laura, 149, 238.
Schock, Ella Dorathy, 174 Lewis, 80, 174.
Schoenberger, Peter, 13.

Schomer, Henry F., 147.
Schreiner, Amanda Catharine, 146, 233—Michael and Almira, 233.
Schultz, Pearl Elizabeth, 247—William, 165, 247.
Schumaker, David, 57, 120.
Schuman, Catharine Wakeman, 17.
Schuppener, Dewey Daniel, 225—Louis W., 129, 225—Laverna Virgil, 225—Portia Lee, 225.
Seiss, Catharine (Garner), 33.
Shaffer, Charles Melvin, 130, 227—Edward, 62, 130—Edward Thomas, 227—Flora Etta, 130, 227—William and Eliza, 130.
Shanafelt, John, 149—Minnie Jane, 70, 149, Pl. 61; 216.
Shank, Lydia (Bassler), 168—Martha Jane, 259.
Shatka, Maria, 130, 227.
Sheckler, Edith Blanche, 82, 183.
Shenefelt, Franklin Fouse, 267—Homer, 198, 267.
Shiffler, Fanny, 37, 62.
Shock, Caroline, 62.
Shoemaker, Henry and Matilda (Snyder), 92—Mary Ellen, 53, 92, Pls. 44 and 45.
Shoenberger, Peter, 93.
Shoenfelt, Della, 126, 220.
Shomler, Clifford I., 173, 252—Darle Cleone, 252—Leta Fern, 252—Mary Elizabeth, 252.
Shoner, Charles, 140, 238.
Shontz, Catharine Myers, 258—Charles Roy, 258—Christian and Margaret, 23, 41—Dessie Margaret, 254—Eliza 79, 49, Pl. 55; 95 (Elizabeth)—George Arthur, 258—George Washington, 177, 258—George and Margaret 258—Grace Nora, 258—John H., 258—John Wintrode, 173, 253—Nancy (Fouse), 17, 23, 41—Nellie Blanch, 258—Ralph Milton, 254—William, 180—Wm. D., 79.
Shoner, Earl Henry, 238.
Showalter, Drue (Cole), 210—Elizabeth S., 37, 67.
Shryock, Henry, 25.
Shultz, Alice, 90, 189—Anna Eva, 251—Anna Maria, 81—Anthony Beaver, 49, 80, 108—Anthony Harvey, 176, 256—Anthony Howard, 81, 181—Benjamin Reuben, 177—Carrie, 180—Carrie Olive, 251—Catharine, 179—Catharine (Russell), 81, 179, 250—Charles Emil, 179—Chester Arthur, 178, 259—Clarence Greaser, 176, 256—Christina, 81—Cloyd Robert, 257—Clyde B., 178—Daniel, 69, 144—David and Elizabeth (Beaver), 80—David Fouse, 81, 177—David Gailen, 178—Della Hazel, 178—Dewalt, 177—Dewalt, Fouse, 81, 176—Dewalt, Robert, 177, 257—Elizabeth, 81, 177—Elizabeth Agnes, 176—Elmer Ellsworth, 176, 256—Elsie M., 176, 255—Florence May 251—Frank Wilmer, 173, 251—Frederick Warren, 257—George Greaser, 177—Henry and Catharine, 189—Henry Franklin, 177, 257—Herman, 179—Herman H., 144, 233—Ida Bertha, 178, 259—Laura Dessie, 178, 260—Lizzie Cora, 178—Lois Naomi, 179—Luther and Dessa, 255—Margaret, 81, 180, 262—Margaret (Donnelson), 176—Martin and Martha, 257—Mary Ann, 81, 179—Mary Elva, 178, 260 Nancy, 81, 177—Nancy, Beatrice, 257—Ollie May, 180—Ralph Herbert, 257—Reuben Fouse, 81, 178, Pl. 67—Reuben Franklin, 178—Rupley Carl, 178—Sarah, 81—William Henry, 81, 180—Thisbe Elizabeth, 179—Wm. Henry, 180.
Simmons, Maud, 154, 239—Oliver Francis, 140, 233.
Simonton, Elizabeth Jane, 49, 77—Jefferson, 77.
Simpson, Minnie, 81, 180.
Sinclair, Anna, 116, 211—John and Elizabeth, 211.
Sircombe, Sarah (Habgood), 222.
Slabaugh, Ducetta, 72, 154.
Smith, Abigail Lusinda, 129—Adam and Elizabeth, 129—Adolph Donald, 129—Bernice Georgia, 225—Beulah, 225—Catherine, 36—Charles Henry, 129, 224—Daniel Adam, 129, 224—Daniel D., 224—Delos, 226—Earl, 224—Edith A., 190, 265—Eli, 68, 142—Edna M., 242—Eliza Jane (Williams), 201—Elizabeth Elsie, 129—Ester (Isenberg), 160—Florence Cathline, 241—Garner, 226—Gertie, 129, 225—Gladys Pearl, 225—Harry W., 159, 241—Henrietta May, 129, 225—Henry, 62, 129—Herbert Elisses, 242—Homer T. G., 143—Ida Matilda, 129, 225—Ida May G., 143—James H., 159, 242—Kathleen 224—Kenneth Henry, 225—Landis, 224—Lowell, 224—Lauretta, 224—Lela, 117, 211—Louis Alvin, 129, 225—Margaret (Henney), 116—Margaret Angelina, 129, 225—Mary (Miller), 110—Mona L., 225—Orilla C., 224—Oscar Martin, 129, 226—Raymond G., 143—Tarence, 225—Tressie Laura 129, 226—Urban Ulysses, 224.

Snare, Anna Mary, 177, 258—Frank and Jane, 258—Margaret Ada, 176, 255—Wm. and Margaret, 255.
Snell, Lewis George, 174, 254—Margaret Louise, 255.
Snowberger, Susan (Wagner), 170.
Snyder, Amanda, 69, 147—Catherine, 57, 119—Celesta, 57, 120—Charles Edward 148—Christena (Steffy), 236—Christina, 57, 120—Cora, 56, 119—George 55, 113—Henry, 33, 56, Pl. 18—Ida Luella, 147—Jacob Henry, 147—Jefferson Jay, 113, 207—John A., 56—John Ellsworth, 120—Joshua H., 57, 120—Lucinda, 56, 118—Mary Elizabeth, 56, 118—Mary Lena, 207—Matilda (Shoemaker), 92—Maudie Savilla, 148—Minerva, 113, 207—Priscilla, 56—Roscoe Franklin, 148—Sarah, 56, 118—Savilla, 56, 119.
Sommers, Anna Katherine, 232—Emma Ellen, 232—Florantine, 232—Georg Clavin, 232—John Henry, 232—John Wolfgang, 140, 232—Lillie Eva, 232—Lydia Lona, 232—Walter Henry, 232.
Sons of American Revolution, 25.
Sorrick, 29—Adam, 9, 26, 27—Catharine, 61, 64, Pl. 21—Elizabeth, 37, 61, Pl. 20—Eve, 37, 66—Frederick Wm., 160, 242, 243—George, 62—Josephine Lenora, 243—Margaret, 37, 62—Peter, 61, 65—Peter and Catharine, 61—Rachel (Garner), 159.
Southern, Minnie B., 123, 218.
Speck, Felix and Ann, 260—Harry Clayton, 179, 260—Mary (Lininger), 174-181—Mildred Almeda, 260.
Spink, Adolph, 131, 227—Frederick Bernard, 227—Meta Deloris, 227.
Sprague, Edna, 154, 239.
Sprankle, Ernest Bryan (Byron?), 160, 242.
Sprigle, Emanuel P., 71, 150—Harold H., 150—Martin R. 150.
Springer, Esther (Girton), 210.
Springfield Furnace, 13.
Stambaugh, Emma, 56, 117—Nelson, 148.
Stands, Sarah Ann, 206.
Star and Record, Bradford, Pa., 222.
Starr, Fannie Luella, 62, 132—Wm. and Mary, 132.
Steese, Mary Ella, 106, 199.
Steffe, Erra Glen, 204—John Ellsworth, 113, 204—Peter and Mary Ann, 204—Ruth Iola, 204.
Steffy, Clarence Donald, 237—David and Christena, 236—Israel, 147, 236—Leon Wilford, 237—Melvin Edward, 237.
Stephens, Delilah, 165, 247.
Stevenson, Mary, 20.
Stiber, Mary E., 110.
Stiffler, Catherine (Brumbaugh), 147.
Stokes, Homer, 114.
Stone, Elizabeth A., 173, 252—Elva Catherine, 252—Ethel Viola, 253—Harvey Glen, 252—Helen Elizabeth, 254—Ira, 173, 252—James, 79, 173—James Orville, 252—Laura Catharine, 173, 253—M. Ella, 173, 253—Margaret F., 173, 253—Mary Catharine, 254—Mary Elizabeth, 252—Thomas J., 174, 254—Wm., 173, 253.
Storms, Bertha (Kohlenburg), 132.
Stouffer, Daniel, etc., 36—LeRoy Otis, 245—Lester, 245—Maria, 50, 89—O., 163, 244.
Stover, Emma R., 82, 184.
Strickler, Hannah M., 118, 214.
Strosacker, Harry, 150, 238—John, 71, 150—John Nervin, 238—Sadie, 150, 238.
Suffecool, Martha Ellen, 119, 215—Wm. Harrison and Catherine, 215.
Summers family, 78—Barbara, 78-79—Blair S., 82, 183—Bruce, 89—Catharine, 37, 63, 79—Clara May, 183, 262—Daniel, 79—David, 79—Florence, 69, 144—Henry, 183-78, 262-79—Henry and Elizabeth, 79—Henry and Sarah (Boyer), 63, 78, 136, 183—Henry H., 63, 183—Jacob and Elizabeth, 79, 180-80, 90—Margaret, 79, 81, 180—Margaret Ann, 53, 80, 90, Pl. 39—Mary E., 82, 182—Rebecca 49, 80, 90—Sarah (Harris), 79, Susan, 79.
Swartz, Amelia E., 146, 236—George F., 124, 219.
Sweeney, Mary, 129, 224.
Sweetman, Eliz. Jane, 188.
Swope, Arthur, Archibald Charles, Ford, Jennie, John 152.

T

Telkamp, Alida, 264—August Frederick, 190, 263—Edna Martha, 264—Emmet Wm., 264—Frederick Basil, 264—Harold Isaac, 264—Irene Augusta, 264—Lizzie Mary, 264—Roy Bertin, 264—Vida Loretta, 264.
Thursby, Jessie, 117, 211.
Tobias, Clara, 177, 250.
Tool, Catherine Elizabeth, 184.
Tudor, Benjamin, 6.

U

Ulrich, Emil Charles, 268—Myron Wilbur, 268—Otto, M.D., 234, 268.

V

Valiant, George, 17.
Vanallman, Lola, 126, 221.
VanHassen, Kitty Myrtle, 191, 266.
Vanorman, Lemuel Lawrence, 77, 171—Margaret Grace, 171.
Vincent, Alvan Stuart, 224—Elizabeth Helen, 128, 224.
Vinson, Mary Amanda, 91, 192.
Vogel, Rosine (Hoeffner), 133.

W

Waddle, Arthur, 131, 228—Edward Dewalt, 131, 229—Fae Margaret, 229—Frederick, 131, 229—Garner, J., 228—Hattie, 131—Kenneth Lorraine, 228—Laura E., 131, 230—Lula Evelyn, 229—Nellie Mae, 131, 229—Raymond Arthur, 229—Reuben, 131, 229—Sterling Wm., 228—Thomas Warren, 131, 228—Wesley Warren, 229—Wm. Garner, 131, 228—Wm. Warren, 62, 108, 131.
Waggomon, Laura (Bowman), 205.
Wagner, Carl, 170—Caroline, (Werstler), 215—Irwin, 170—Jacob, 170—John and Susan, 170—Levi, 170—Lona, 170—Otis Warren, 170—Ruth Ella, 170—Wm. S., ;6, 170.
Wakeman, Catherine (Schuman) 17.
Walker, Charles, 167, 248—Clara (Bliss), 207—Closter Harold, 262—David and Leah, 261—Della Dart, 91, 192—Fred Russell, 262—Henry Esco, 179, 261—Mary Elizabeth, 248—Misanier (McCoy), 205—Susan (Vincent), 224.
Walt, Myrtle, L., 91, 192.
Walters, Ellen, 57, 122.
War, Civil, 46, 106—Record of Fouses in, 106—Revolutionary, 2, 11, 25, 34—Seven Years', 2, 25.
Washington Co., Md., 3, 25.
Waters, Violet, 168, 249.
Weaver, 29—Caleb and Anna, 259—Elizabeth May, 258—Ferne E., 208—Flora May, 178, 259—George and Charlotte (Ginther), 115—George and Lydia, 258—Hazel, 156—Lynn Albert, 258—Magdalena, 29—Melvina Amelia 56, 115, Pl. 54—Monroe C., 113, 207—Paul Ray, 208—Ruth Irene, 208—Samuel Albert, 177, 258—Stanford Dewig, 208—Valentine, 29—Viola May, 208.
Weber, Eleanore, 169—Emma Grace, 241—Godfey and Rachel, 169—J. Edwin, 159, 241, Pl. 63—Mary Luella, 241.
Weidner, Christina (Greaser), 167.
Weimer, Ida May (Pease), 215.
Weisbroett, Ethel, 135, 231.
Weisgerber, Magdalene Lavina, 73, 162.
Welker, Mordicai McKinney, 204, 268—Shipley and Mary (Ryan), 268.
Weller, David and Catharine, 257—Florence Lynn, 257—Frances Rhoda, 257—James Allen, 257—John Howard, 257—Laura Dorothy, 257—Minnie Catharine, 257—Nancy Margaret, 257.
Wells, Arthur Elois, 263—Beulah Loretta, 263—Blanche Irene, 263—Frank E., 190, 263—Gilbert Daniel, 263—Harlan Newton, 263—Neva Gladys, 263—Pearl Elizabeth, 263—Ralph Emerson, 263—Wayne Ellie, 263.
Weller, Samuel Calvin, 177, 257.
Weltner, Lt. Col., 25.
Wengert, Doris Mae, 234—Earl Ambrose, 234—Edwin Ambrose, 146, 233—George Edward, 234—Geraldine Blandie, 234—Grace Catherine, 234—Lucinda Edna, 234—Mary Adaline, 234—Ruth Edna, 234.
Werstler, Ira Jacob, 119, 215—Louis and Carolina, 215.
Wertenberger, Daniel, 70, 148—Hannah (Machamer), 117—Jacob and Susanna, 148—Linnie May, 148—Maggie Bell, 148.
Westphal, Charles O., 162, 243.
Wetzel, Fanny, 114, 208—Hubert Leroy, 116—Lizzie, 56, 117—Lizzie Irene, 116—Nathan and Elizabeth, 116—Owen E., 116—Solomon, 116.
Weyrick, Norman, 150, 238—Russell, 238.
Whitmore, Benjamin and Annie, 112—Curtis Cleveland, Edna Elinore, Fyanna Elizabeth, 112—Lydia May, Octavia Dell, Olive Goldie, 112, 203—Sampson Sollers, 112.
Whitner, Robert, 35.
Wicke, Casper and Elizabeth, Mary Louise, 171.
Wilaman, Edward, 115, 209.
Will of Abraham Miller, 30-32.
Williams, Laura May, 111, 201—Wm. Henry, 201.
Wilson, Elizabeth (Enyeart), 74—Jennie Elizabeth, 174, 254—Mary (Enyeart), 74.

Winebrenner, Christian, 42.
Winson, Converse, 129, 226.
Winters, Margaret (Leibert), 130.
Wise, Arthur E., 117, 211—Byron P., 117, 211—Clark J., 211—Emma J., 72, 155—Flossie May, 211—Glen Machamer, 211—Nancy (Cassler), 54, 55—Royale C., 211—Ruth Mozella, 211—Walter A., 117, 211—Wm. 56, 117—Williard Eugene, 211—Zella Grace, 211.
Wolf, Ratenra L., 118, 213.
Woodcock Valley, Pa., 23, 78.
Worstler, Elizabeth (Wetzel), 116.

Y

Yarrick, Beulah M., 151—Frank A., 71, 151—Warren, 151.
Yates, Charles W., 163, 245—Laverna Melvin, 245.
Yazel, Henry and Sarah A., 206—Nancy Jane, 113, 206.
Yockey, Leanna Catharine, 138.
York, Elizabeth, 29.
Youtzy, Ada Irene, 113, 206—Jacob J. and Sarah A., 206.

Z

Zentz, Mary A., 72, 153—Mollie, 71, 149.
Ziegler, Jacob, 42.
Zollars, Annie (Whitmore), 112.
Zweibrücken, 1, 2, 4.
Zysset, Christian Henry, 111, 202—Clifford Christian, 202—Esther May, 202—Faye Luella, 202—Fern Stella, 202—Opal Lee, 202.

www.ingramcontent.com/pod-product-compliance
Lightning Source LLC
Chambersburg PA
CBHW020945310726
48980CB00001B/64

* 9 7 8 1 5 9 6 4 1 3 3 1 3 *